AF711355

HIGH COURT CASE SUMMARIES

CORPORATIONS

Keyed to Eisenberg's Casebook on Corporations, 9th Edition

THOMSON
WEST

Mat #40448422

Thomson/West have created this publication to provide you with accurate and authoritative information concerning the subject matter covered. However, this publication was not necessarily prepared by persons licensed to practice law in a particular jurisdiction. Thomson/West are not engaged in rendering legal or other professional advice, and this publication is not a substitute for the advice of an attorney. If you require legal or other expert advice, you should seek the services of a competent attorney or other professional.

High Court Case Summaries and West Group are registered trademarks used under license.
All rights reserved. Do not duplicate.

© 2006 Thomson/West
610 Opperman Drive
P.O. Box 64526
St. Paul, MN 55164–0526
1–800–328–9352

Printed in the United States of America

ISBN–13: 978–0–314–16745–3
ISBN–10: 0–314–16745–5

TEXT IS PRINTED ON 10% POST CONSUMER RECYCLED PAPER

Table of Contents

*

Alphabetical Table of Cases

CHAPTER ONE

Agency

Morris Oil Co. v. Rainbow Oilfield Trucking, Inc.

Instant Facts: When a completely-controlled corporation goes bankrupt, an unpaid creditor sues its controlling corporation as principal.

Black Letter Rule: Principals are liable for their agents' contracts, even unauthorized ones, unless the third parties contracting with them knew they were unauthorized.

Tarnowski v. Resop

Instant Facts: When an investor purchases a business on his agent's recommendation and is defrauded, he sues the agent after learning the agent accepted a bribe.

Black Letter Rule: An agent who violates his duty of loyalty is liable to the principal for any secret profit earned, as well as his principal's consequential damages, including attorney fees.

Morris Oil Co. v. Rainbow Oilfield Trucking, Inc.

(*Creditor*) v. (*Independent Contractor*)

106 N.M. 237, 741 P.2d 840 (Ct.App.1987)

UNDISCLOSED PRINCIPALS ARE LIABLE FOR AN AGENTS' CONTRACTS

■ **INSTANT FACTS** When a completely-controlled corporation goes bankrupt, an unpaid creditor sues its controlling corporation as principal.

■ **BLACK LETTER RULE** Principals are liable for their agents' contracts, even unauthorized ones, unless the third parties contracting with them knew they were unauthorized.

■ PROCEDURAL BASIS

Appeal from judgment for plaintiff in contract action for damages.

■ FACTS

Dawn (D), a trucking corporation, was granted a "certificate of public convenience and necessity" [apparently granting it and its affiliates special rights to deliver oil]. Rainbow Oil field Trucking (D) contracted to use Dawn's (D) certificate while delivering oil in Hobbs, New Mexico. Under the contract, Dawn (D) assumed complete control over Rainbow's (D) operations in New Mexico. Dawn (D) was to collect all of Rainbow's (D) receivables in Dawn's (D) name, deduct fees and commissions, and pay Rainbow (D) the remainder. Rainbow (D) was to pay fuel and operating expenses. Dawn (D) was to supervise and control Rainbow's (D) fuel usage. A side terminal management agreement granted Dawn (D) complete control over Rainbow's (D) Hobbs terminal operation, but specified Rainbow (D) was *not* Dawn's (D) agent and not authorized to incur liability for Dawn (D) except in the ordinary course of business relating to terminal management. The agreement classified Rainbow (D) as an independent contractor rather than Dawn's (D) employee. Under it, any claims against Rainbow (D) were to be defended, paid or reimbursed by Rainbow (D). While operating, Rainbow (D) hired Morris Oil (P) to install a bulk dispenser and supply diesel fuel. Rainbow (D) later went bankrupt, still owing Morris (P) $25,000, and suggested Morris (P) demand payment from Dawn (D), which still held $73,000 in receipts from Rainbow (D). Dawn (D) established an escrow account to pay Rainbow's (D) debts, and convinced Morris (P) to suspend collection efforts, but when the account was depleted, Morris (P) was never paid from it. Morris (P) sued both Rainbow (D) and Dawn (D), contending Dawn (D) was in fact Rainbow's (D) employer and responsible for its debts. Rainbow (D) defaulted, but Dawn (D) defended, contending the contract explicitly made Rainbow (D) an independent contractor solely responsible for its own debts. At trial, the court held Rainbow (D) was Dawn's (D) agent because its operations were controlled by Dawn (D), which was liable for its debts.

■ ISSUE

Are principals liable for their agents' contracts?

■ DECISION AND RATIONALE

(Garcia) Yes. Principals are liable for their agents contracts, even unauthorized ones, unless the third parties contracting with them knew they were unauthorized. Here, Rainbow (D) was found by the trial court to be Dawn's (D) agent, and their contract does not negate that. The contract authorized Rainbow

(D) to bind Dawn (D) to pay debts incurred "in the ordinary course of business relative to terminal management," which it did in contracting with Merris (D) to supply its trucking business. Further, case law holds that, when a person contracts with an agent unaware of its contractual limitations, that person may demand performance from the principal. This is a case of undisclosed agency rather than apparent authority, because Rainbow (D) contracted in its own name, without disclosing its principal, rather than appearing to be authorized to contract in Dawn's (D) name. Under Restatement (Second) of Agency § 194 and § 195, an agent for an undisclosed principal subjects the principal to liability for acts done on his account if they are usual or necessary in such transactions, even if the principal previously forbade the agent to incur such debts. Case law holds that principals may limit agent's authority, and these limits bind third parties who are aware of them, but this is inapplicable here, where Morris (P) was unaware at execution that Rainbow (D) was another's agent, let alone the limitations of its agency. Thus, Dawn (D) as principal was bound to pay the debts incurred by its agent Rainbow (D) without disclosing its agency, including the debt to Morris (P). Further, case law holds that, even where an agent improperly purports to bind its principal without authorization, the principal becomes bound if it learns the material facts and ratifies the contract. Ratification of a contract is deemed to occur where the principal knows the contract's material facts and accepts contractual proceeds from the agent. Here, even assuming arguendo that Dawn (D) was not liable for the Morris (D) contract at formation, it still assumed liability by ratification when it was told the material terms of the contract, failed to dispute the debt, used Rainbow's (D) proceeds to pay its own fee, Rainbow's (D) debts and legal fees, and even assured Morris (P) it would pay from the revenues. Dawn (D) cannot be allowed to retain the benefits of its agency relationship but disclaim the responsibilities. Judgment affirmed.

Analysis:

Note that the courts rejected Dawn's contention that Rainbow should be deemed an independent contractor because it was so identified in their agreement, showing courts' willingness to impose liability on *de facto* principals. Public policy may justify this outcome, since it is easy for principals to force "independent contractor" status on their employees, which gives them the benefits of agency but may let them escape the responsibility. However, it may be harder to justify liability for *undisclosed* principals. If the third party made the contract with the agent, unaware a principal existed, the third party cannot claim it was deceived into believing the agent possessed other assets it could pursue.

■ CASE VOCABULARY

AGENT: a.k.a. "servant." One hired to work on behalf of, or represent, a principal or master.

APPARENT AUTHORITY: a.k.a. "ostensible authority." Constructive authority granted to agents when their *principals* suggest the agents have authority

ARGUENDO: For argument's sake.

EMPLOYEE: Agent whose employer-principal may dictate the manner of the agent's performance, but is liable for the employee's debts and torts.

INDEPENDENT CONTRACTOR: Agent whose principal cannot dictate the manner of the agent's work, and is not liable for the contractor's liabilities.

UNDISCLOSED AGENCY: Situation where an agent contracts with a third party without revealing the existence of the agent's principal.

Tarnowski v. Resop

(*Defrauded Investor*) v. (*Agent*)

236 Minn. 33, 51 N.W.2d 801 (Sup.Ct.1952)

DISLOYAL AGENT LIABLE FOR SECRET PROFIT AND CONSEQUENTIAL COSTS

■ **INSTANT FACTS** When an investor purchases a business on his agent's recommendation and is defrauded, he sues the agent after learning the agent accepted a bribe.

■ **BLACK LETTER RULE** An agent who violates his duty of loyalty is liable to the principal for any secret profit earned, as well as his principal's consequential damages, including attorney fees.

■ PROCEDURAL BASIS

Appeal from judgment for plaintiff in contract and tort action seeking damages.

■ FACTS

Tarnowski (P), wanting to invest his money, hired Resop (D) as his agent to investigate and negotiate the purchase of a string of coin-operated music machines. Resop (D) represented he had inspected all 75 business locations, and found each had new working machines and monthly income over $3,000. Relying on Resop's (D) advice, Tarnowski (P) bought the business from the owners, Loechler (D) and Mayer (D) for $30,620, with a down payment of $11,000. He soon discovered Loechler (D) and Mayer (D) had lied; there were only 47 locations, some with missing or obsolete machines, and each had much lower revenues. He also discovered Resop (D) had exaggerated his diligence, having inspected only 5 locations and simply passed on the sellers' (D) representations as true, in exchange for a $2,000 bribe. Tarnowski (P) sued Loechler (D) and Mayer (D), recovering most of his down payment. Tarnowski (P) then sued his agent, contending Resop (D) breached his duty of loyalty by accepting a bribe to recommend the purchase, and should repay the amount of the bribe, plus Tarnowski's (P) loss in operating the business and litigating, including attorney fees.

■ ISSUE

Is a disloyal agent liable for secret profits and consequential damages?

■ DECISION AND RATIONALE

(Knutson) Yes. An agent who violates his duty of loyalty is liable to the principal for any secret profit earned, as well as the principal's consequential damages, including attorney fees. Case law universally holds that any profit made by agents during their agency belongs to their principals, even if earned in violation of that agency, and even if the principal is unharmed. The policy basis for this rule is to ensure fidelity in the agent by removing the temptation of private profit, because the agent should be the principal's fiduciary. Under the Restatement of Agency § 407(2) Comment e, the principal has a cause of action against a disloyal agent who defrauds him, and may recover the secret profit, even if the principal has rescinded the fraudulent contract and recovered his payment. Here, Tarnowski (P) has an absolute right to recover from Resop (D) the $2,000 secret commission he received. Restatement of Agency § 407(1) states that, when an agent violates his duty of loyalty, the principal may recover not only his secret profit, but also any damages caused by the violation. Comment (a) explains that recoverable damages includes all improper payments plus compensation for all business losses. Tort law generally holds that tort damages include all reasonably foreseeable consequences. Under Minnesota case law, in *Bergquist v. Kreidler*, litigation costs and attorney fees were held to be "plainly traceable" consequences of an agent's misrepresentation. This rule is confirmed by American Jurisprudence on Damages, § 144, which says that, where a defendant's wrongful acts involve the plaintiff in necessary litigation, the defendant is liable for plaintiff's legal fees, because those fees are legal consequences of the wrongful act. Here, Tarnowski (P) was forced to litigate against the sellers to undo Resop's (D) wrongful act, and may recover from Resop (D) his expenses and attorney fees for that litigation, as well as compensation for time and money lost operating the business, investigating the fraud, and rescinding the sale. The amount of damages was quantified in Tamowski's (P) bill of particulars, which we assume is correct, since we have no other testimony. Judgment affirmed.

Analysis:

It is sound policy to require an agent's duty of loyalty and to confiscate profits he made in violation of that duty. This rule applies throughout the U.S. and was the rule in England as well. It is also sound to rule that agents should not be able to keep profits from crimes committed while in the principal's employ, to discourage otherwise illegal crimes. Perhaps less sound is the rule that agents cannot keep secret profits, even if earned without harming the principal. Economically, if the agent can earn gains for himself, without causing losses to his principal or others, it is more efficient to let him keep them than it is for no one to make the profit at all. Consequently, there is some case law suggesting that an agent may pursue a private profit if it first offers the profitable opportunity to its principal, but the principal declines to pursue it. The opinion in *Tarnowski* suggests this is improper, since it create incentives for disloyalty.

■ CASE VOCABULARY

BILL OF EXCEPTIONS: Pleading in equity court, equivalent to plaintiff's affidavit (sworn statement) of facts; usually lists damages.

DUTY OF LOYALTY: In agency law, an agent's fiduciary duty to act in his principal's best interests, including the obligation not to make a secret private profit or divert profits to himself.

FIDUCIARY: Relationship under which one party is required to act loyally in the best interests of another.

CHAPTER TWO

Partnership

Martin v. Peyton

Instant Facts: Lenders investing in a near-bankrupt partnership were granted profit sharing and some management rights until they were repaid. When the partnership defaulted on debts, a creditor sued the lenders, contending their rights made them partners and personally liable for partnership debts.

Black Letter Rule: Even partnership creditors who are granted a share of profits and some management control are not necessarily deemed partners if other factors indicate contrary intent.

Lupien v. Malsbenden

Instant Facts: When a business defaults on a customer's order, the customer sues its financier, contending the financier managed the business himself and thus became a partner.

Black Letter Rule: A creditor who actively manages its borrower's business may be liable as the borrower's partner.

Summers v. Dooley

Instant Facts: After one partner hires an employee over the other partner's objection, he demands the partnership reimburse him for paying the employee's wages.

Black Letter Rule: If a partner incurs expenses for the partnership, the partnership need not reimburse them unless those expenses were authorized by a majority of partners, absent contrary agreement or later ratification.

RNR Investments Limited Partnership v. Peoples First Community Bank

Instant Facts: Peoples First Community Bank (P) sought foreclosure of a construction project after RNR Investments (D) defaulted on its construction loan.

Black Letter Rule: A general partner's authority to act on behalf of the partnership in the ordinary course of partnership business is established, notwithstanding any limitation on the general partner's actual authority, if a third party did not know or have reason to know that the general partner in fact lacked authority to bind the partnership.

Northmon Investment Co. v. Milford Plaza Assoc.

Instant Facts: Milford Plaza Associates (P) challenged a long-term lease entered into by partners in its partnership.

Black Letter Rule: Partners may object to unauthorized transactions in assertion of their equal rights in the management and conduct of partnership business.

Rapoport v. 55 Perry Co.

Instant Facts: When 2 partners tried to name their children as partners, the others objected, prompting a suit to interpret their partnership contract.

Black Letter Rule: Partners may assign their partnership interests, but not their management rights, unless the other partners consent or have agreed otherwise.

Meinhard v. Salmon

Instant Facts: When a partnership is offered a profitable lease, one partner accepts it for himself, prompting the other to demand participation.

Black Letter Rule: Partners' fiduciary duties of loyalty forbid appropriating opportunities offered to the partnership.

Creel v. Lilly

Instant Facts: After the death of a partner, his personal representative sued the surviving partners for liquidation of the partnership assets.

Black Letter Rule: When the remaining partners wind up the partnership in good faith and provide an accurate accounting of the partnership's value, the departing partner has no right to compel liquidation.

Page v. Page

Instant Facts: When his partner demands dissolution, his copartner resists, arguing (i) the partnership was implicitly "for term," and (ii) the dissolution wrongfully diverts business to the other partner.

Black Letter Rule: Partners may dissolve "at will" partnerships anytime, unless the dissolution is done in bad faith.

Drashner v. Sorenson

Instant Facts: When an irresponsible partner wrongfully dissolved the partnership, he demanded a share of the partnership's goodwill.

Black Letter Rule: When a partner causes the partnership's dissolution wrongfully by making it impracticable to remain in partnership, the other partners may continue the partnership, and the dissolving partner is not entitled to share in the partnership's goodwill.

Martin v. Peyton

(*Partnership's Creditor*) v. (*Alleged Partner*)

246 N.Y. 213, 158 N.E. 77 (1927)

PARTNERSHIP CREDITORS MAY RECEIVE PROFIT-SHARING AND MANAGEMENT RIGHTS WITHOUT BECOMING PARTNERS

■ **INSTANT FACTS** Lenders investing in a near-bankrupt partnership were granted profit sharing and some management rights until they were repaid. When the partnership defaulted on debts, a creditor sued the lenders, contending their rights made them partners and personally liable for partnership debts.

■ **BLACK LETTER RULE** Even partnership creditors who are granted a share of profits and some management control are not necessarily deemed partners if other factors indicate contrary intent.

■ PROCEDURAL BASIS

Appeal from appellate court judgment, based on referee's report, for defendants in contract action seeking damages [and possibly declaratory judgment].

■ FACTS

Knauth, Nachod & Kuhne ("K.N. & K.") (D), a banking and brokerage partnership, made speculative investments which nearly bankrupted it. Needing money to keep the firm operating, Hall (D), a partner, arranged for it to borrow from his friend Peyton (D) $500,000 in bonds to use as collateral for needed bank loans. Needing more, Hall (D) then arranged for it to borrow another $2,500,000 from Peyton (D), and Freeman (D) [and possibly Perkins (D) and his wife (D)] in exchange for (i) 40% of K.N. & K.'s (D) profits until repayment, with a minimum of $100,000 and a maximum of $500,000, (ii) an option to join the firm as partners within 3 months of repayment, and (iii) collateral consisting of K.N. & K.'s (D) own junk securities. This exchange was memorialized by 3 contemporaneous contracts—an "agreement," "indenture" and "option." The "agreement" labels Peyton (D) and Freeman (D) "trustees" and (i) protects their collateral from commingling, (ii) requires they be informed of all transactions affecting their collateral, (iii) allows them to inspect the firm's business records, (iv) grants them all revenues from the collateral or its sale, (v) allows them to veto any business they deem risky, (vi) requires they be "consulted" on important matters, (vii) assigns to them each existing partner's partnership interest, (viii) restricts the firm's loans and distributions to partners, (ix) allows Peyton (D), Freeman (D), and Hall (D) to assess the firm's value, (x) specifies Hall (D) is to run the firm until repayment, and (xi) requires Hall's (D) life be insured for $1,000,000, with the lenders named beneficiaries. The "indenture" mortgages the collateral. The "option" permits the lenders to (i) become partners within 3 months of repayment by buying a minority share from any partners at a set price, (ii) propose the partnership be reincorporated into a corporation, and (iii) force the resignation of any partner. Amazingly, this opinion fails to mention who the plaintiff is or why he sued, which would have been helpful. Presumably, the partnership failed to pay its creditor Martin (P), who sued Peyton (D) and Freeman (D) as personally liable for the partnership's debts, contending they were made *de facto* partners by the agreements, which gave them sufficient management powers and a share of profits sufficient to constitute a partnership interest. Peyton (D) contended the agreements merely constituted a loan, without making him a partner liable for the partnership's debts. The trial court found Peyton (D) and the other lenders (D) were not partners, and the appellate court affirmed.

■ ISSUE

Is a partnership creditor who is granted a share of profits and some management control deemed a partner?

■ DECISION AND RATIONALE

(Andrews) No. Even partnership creditors who are granted a share of profits and some management control are not necessarily deemed partners if other factors indicate contrary intent. Under modem partnership law, only partners are liable for partnership debts, with few exceptions. Partnership may be inferred from an express or implied contract, written or verbal, which suggests a partnership. However, a contract denying a partnership is not necessarily dispositive, and may be voided as a sham if it disclaims a de facto partnership. An agreement to share profits should be given weight in determining whether a partnership was intended, but profit sharing alone is not decisive. The true test of whether a business association is a partnership comes from examining all facts and circumstances to determine whether there was an intent to do business as co-owners for profit. Here, the contractual rights granted to the lenders (D) were insufficient to make them partners. The "agreement's" provisions maintaining the value of the collateral do not indicate an intended partnership, since they are typical of loan agreements and intended to ensure repayment of the loan. Hall's (D) empowerment and insurance is not necessarily an indication to associate, since the lenders trusted Hall (D) and were justified in requiring his leadership to ensure the firm would return to profitability and repay their loan. The lenders' contractual veto power was not equivalent to a partner's stake, because they could not initiate transactions or bind the firm as partners could, and because veto power is deemed a proper precaution to their loan, since it allowed them to reduce speculative risks to their loan. For this precaution, it was also necessary they receive financial information about the firm. The "indenture" is basically a mortgage, and does not suggest the lenders were partners. The "option's" provision that the lenders may demand partners' resignations is somewhat unusual, but it was arguably justified to protect the lenders' loan against further speculation, and is not enough to prove an intent to make the lenders into partners. Judgment affirmed.

Analysis:

As this case shows, the determination of whether a business organization constitutes a partnership is made on a case-by-case basis considering all factors to determine whether they reveal the intent to do business as co-owners; no single factor is dispositive. Thus, an explicit partnership agreement may be deemed *not* to create a partnership, and an agreement specifically denying a partnership exists may be found void. The absence of clear standards creates risk for partnership creditors who insist on having some management control, since they risk being held liable for *all* partnership debts. However, *Martin* shows that, in practice, some courts will allow creditors to escape liability even when their "loan" grants them considerable control over the partnership's business.

■ CASE VOCABULARY

INDENTURE: A contract between multiple parties (possibly containing the terms and conditions concerning indebtedness).

OPTION: The right, but not obligation, to buy or sell a specified item at a specified price on/by a specified date.

REFEREE: A court-appointed official, usually a fact-finder or value assessor, authorized to prepare a report for the court.

Lupien v. Malsbenden

(*Customer*) v. (*Alleged Partner*)
477 A.2d 746 (Me.Sup.Jud.Ct.1984)

LENDER ACTIVELY MANAGING BUSINESS FOR YEARS IS DEEMED A PARTNER

■ **INSTANT FACTS** When a business defaults on a customer's order, the customer sues its financier, contending the financier managed the business himself and thus became a partner.

■ **BLACK LETTER RULE** A creditor who actively manages its borrower's business may be liable as the borrower's partner.

■ FACTS

Cragin (D) operated York Motor Mart ("Mart"), an unincorporated car repair shop which also constructed semi-custom "Bradley" cars. Malsbenden (D) apparently managed Mart, and had supplied Cragin money to buy inventory. Cragin (D), acting on behalf of Mart, contracted to build Lupien (P) a Bradley car for $8,020. Lupien (P) paid $4,450 down. When Lupien (P) periodically returned to Mart to oversee progress, he dealt with Malsbenden (D), who contracted to buy his pickup truck and supplied him a rental car. Mart never completed the Bradley. Since Cragin (D) had disappeared and couldn't be sued, Lupien (P) sued Malsbenden (D), contending he was Cragin's (D) partner in Mart. Malsbenden (D) denied liability, contending he was not a partner but merely a lender, who had loaned Cragin (D) $85,000 to run the Bradley-building portion of Motor's business, was waiting for repayment from the proceeds of each car sold, and was forced to protect his investment by selling off inventory after Cragin (D) disappeared. The trial court held Malsbenden (D) was liable because his "total involvement" in Mart's Bradley-building operation was sufficient to deem him a partner.

■ ISSUE

Is a business creditor involved in managing the business liable as a partner?

■ DECISION AND RATIONALE

(McKusick) Yes. A creditor who actively manages its borrower's business may be liable as the borrower's partner. The governing law—the Uniform Partnership Act § 281–323, as enacted in Maine—defines partnership as "an association of 2 or more persons . . . to carry on as co-owners a business for profit." Under our prior decisions, co-owners are characterized by the joint right to control the business, but not necessarily by joint title to assets. Whether a partnership exists is inferred from the facts. If the arrangement otherwise qualifies as a partnership, it is irrelevant that the parties never expressly agreed, or even intended, to form a partnership, because the law looks to the truth of their arrangement to assign legal consequences. Here, the trial court found Malsbenden (D) was not merely a "banker," but had "total involvement" in the Bradley operation sufficient to make him a partner. This holding was justified by testimony showing Malsbenden (D) (i) had "loaned" $85,000 without interest, (ii) had contributed this amount, not as a lump sum, but as periodic equipment purchases and wage payments, (iii) was entitled to repayment, not at fixed times, but upon the sale of Bradleys, (iv) was entitled to participate in management, (v) actually worked at Motor full-time daily, purchasing supplies, paying salaries and dealing with customers, and (vi) continued to operate the business for over 3 years, allegedly "just disposing of property." Even if Malsbenden (D) and Cragin (D) never viewed themselves as partners, the trial court made no clear error in holding their relationship a partnership, since their business involved a pooling of skill and capital, with joint control and an intent to share profits. Under our case law, the result might be different had a creditor advanced money for inventory purchases which was to be repaid from its resale, but been allowed no control over the business. Judgment affirmed.

Analysis:

This case confirms that the key elements for creating/construing a partnership are profit sharing and joint management. Still, both of these elements may be present legitimately as part of a loan arrangement, so courts are reluctant to establish a conclusive test based on these elements alone. Lenders often lend money for a business to purchase inventory, and are sometimes repaid from proceeds of the sale of that inventory, often as soon as each item is sold. Thus, the lender technically ends up "sharing" profits somewhat with the owner. Courts will not impose liability on lenders for such "profit-sharing" alone. More dispositive is the element of control. For example, if a lender such as a bank lends to a business and is not repaid, it must *foreclose* on (take over) the business's assets and eventually sell them off to generate cash to repay itself. However, if the bank decides it would obtain a low price from selling the business immediately, it may itself continue and manage the business temporarily, while awaiting a more favorable economic climate, or even make investments in the business that it hopes will raise its resale value.

Summers v. Dooley

(Partner) v. *(Partner)*
94 Idaho 87, 481 P.2d 318 (Sup.Ct.1971)

PARTNER'S EXPENSES NOT REIMBURSABLE UNLESS APPROVED BY MAJORITY

■ **INSTANT FACTS** After one partner hires an employee over the other partner's objection, he demands the partnership reimburse him for paying the employee's wages.

■ **BLACK LETTER RULE** If a partner incurs expenses for the partnership, the partnership need not reimburse them unless those expenses were authorized by a majority of partners, absent contrary agreement or later ratification.

■ PROCEDURAL BASIS

Appeal from district court judgment for defendant in contract action seeking damages.

■ FACTS

Summers (P) and Dooley (D) were partners in a trash collection business. When Summers (P) suggested the partnership hire an additional employee, Dooley (D) refused, saying it created unnecessary expense. Nevertheless, Summers (P) hired another employee and paid him from personal funds for over 1 year. Summers (P) then sued Dooley (D) for reimbursement of $11,000 of the employee's salary, contending Dooley (D) had ratified the hiring by accepting profits from the employee's labor for over a year, and thus should be estopped from denying acceptance and forced to reimburse Summers (P) for the wages as a partnership expense. Dooley (D) contended the wages were not a partnership expense, since he, as co-manager, had vetoed the hiring. The district court held Summers (P) was not entitled to reimbursement, though it awarded him $483 for unspecified partnership expenses.

■ ISSUE

If a partner incurs expenses for the partnership, over the other partners' objection, must the partnership reimburse him for those expenses?

■ DECISION AND RATIONALE

(Donaldson) No. If a partner incurs expenses for the partnership, the partnership need not reimburse them unless those expenses were authorized by a majority of partners, absent contrary agreement or later ratification. In Idaho, the law governing partnerships is the Uniform Partnership law, as codified in the Idaho Code. This code provides that "any difference arising as to ordinary matters connected with the partnership business may be decided by a majority of the partners." *Idaho Code § 53–318(8).* The legislative intent is inferable from the language or reasonable public policy. A careful reading of the whole provision shows an intent to give all partners equal rights to manage partnership business. The only reasonable interpretation is that business disagreements must be decided by a majority of partners, absent some other agreement. [Thus, in a 2-partner partnership, decisions must be unanimous to constitute a majority.] Here, Dooley (D) never ratified the hiring, because he objected continuously, so it is unjust to require him/the partnership to repay expenses incurred individually by Summers (P) for his own benefit. Judgment affirmed.

Analysis:

This case reinforces the statutory requirement that partnership expenditures must be approved by a majority of partners. In a 2-partner partnership, a majority is only possible if both agree. Although the statutes and holding reflect a policy choice to require consensus among partners, this policy can cause partnerships to be paralyzed if the 2 partners disagree, or if larger partnerships form equal opposing coalitions. Such paralysis can destroy a partnership's business, and thus create economic losses to society. Some other cases resolve this by holding that, when there is a deadlock among partners, each may incur expenses "necessary" or "customary" for keeping the partnership operating, and collect reimbursement from the partnership. Deadlock can also be prevented by contractual provisions.

RNR Investments Limited Partnership v. Peoples First Community Bank

(*Limited Partnership*) v. (*Bank*)

812 So. 2d 561 (Fla.Dist.Ct.App.2002)

PARTNERSHIPS BEAR THE RISK OF LOSS FOR THEIR PARTNERS' UNAUTHORIZED ACTIONS

■ **INSTANT FACTS** Peoples First Community Bank (P) sought foreclosure of a construction project after RNR Investments (D) defaulted on its construction loan.

■ **BLACK LETTER RULE** A general partner's authority to act on behalf of the partnership in the ordinary course of partnership business is established, notwithstanding any limitation on the general partner's actual authority, if a third party did not know or have reason to know that the general partner in fact lacked authority to bind the partnership.

■ PROCEDURAL BASIS

On appeal to review a trial court decision granting summary judgment to the plaintiff.

■ FACTS

RNR Investments (D) was a limited partnership formed to acquire and develop vacant land in Florida. Roeger was the general partner. Under the partnership agreement, Roeger was required to prepare a budget for the acquisition and reconstruction project and obtain the signatures of all partners approving the budget. The agreement further forbade the general partner from borrowing funds, spending partnership funds, or encumbering partnership assets unless approved in the budget. Roeger, on RNR's (D) behalf, entered into a construction loan agreement and mortgage with Peoples First Community Bank (P), which deposited the funds into RNR's (D) bank account without objection from the partners. When RNR (D) defaulted on the loan, Peoples First Community Bank (P) sought foreclosure of the house constructed on the property. RNR (D) claimed that the bank failed to review the limitations on Roeger's authority to act on the partnership's behalf and that Roeger had no authority to enter into the loan agreement. The bank moved for summary judgment. In opposition to summary judgment, RNR (D) submitted the affidavit of Waltz, the president of one of RNR's (D) limited partners, acknowledging that although financing was anticipated for the project, Roeger's actions were never approved in writing as required under the partnership agreement. The court granted summary judgment, but stayed foreclosure pending the appeal.

■ ISSUE

Is a partnership bound by the unauthorized acts of a partner when the third party neither knew nor should have known of restrictions on the partner's authority?

■ DECISION AND RATIONALE

(Van Nortwick, J.) Yes. Under the Revised Uniform Partnership Act, a general partner's authority to act on behalf of the partnership in the ordinary course of partnership business is established, notwithstanding any limitation on the general partner's actual authority, if a third party did not know or have reason to know that the general partner in fact lacked authority to bind the partnership. Although a third party has no duty to inspect the partnership agreement to detect any limitations on a general partner's authority, the partnership may file a statement of partnership authority to restrict a partner's authority.

To hold a partnership responsible for the acts of a partner, it must first be established that the act occurred while carrying on the partnership business in the usual or ordinary manner. If so, and absent actual knowledge by the third party, the partnership is bound by the partner's actions. Here, it is undisputed that the securing of financing for the construction project was in the ordinary course of RNR's (D) business. There is no evidence that the bank was aware of the partnership's limitations on Roeger's authority, and RNR (D) did not file a statement of partnership authority from which constructive notice may be established. Affirmed.

Analysis:

The court's decision reflects the fairness of apportioning risk of loss arising out of a partner's actions upon the partnership rather than upon one transacting business with the partner. Although both the partnership and the third party are innocent, the partnership is ordinarily in a better position to control the partner's actions and bear the financial loss. Indeed, the partnership could have placed the bank on notice of Roeger's limited authority by recording a statement to that effect. Regardless of who bears the initial burden of the loss, the unauthorized partner may be held liable for indemnification.

■ CASE VOCABULARY

ACTUAL AUTHORITY: Authority that a principal intentionally confers on an agent, including the authority that the agent reasonably believes he or she has as a result of the agent's dealings with the principal.

APPARENT AUTHORITY: Authority that a third party reasonably believes an agent has, based on the third party's dealings with the principal. Apparent authority can be created by law even when no actual authority has been conferred.

GENERAL PARTNER: A partner who ordinarily takes part in the daily operations of the business, shares in the profits and losses, and is personally responsible for the partnership's debts and obligations.

LIMITED PARTNER: A partner who receives profits from the business but does not take part in managing the business and is not liable for any amount greater than his or her original investment.

LIMITED PARTNERSHIP: A partnership composed of one or more persons who control the business and are personally liable for the partnership's debts (called general partners), and one or more persons who contribute capital and share profits but who cannot manage the business and are liable only for the amount of their contribution (called limited partners).

Northmon Investment Co. v. Milford Plaza Assoc.

(*Partnership*) v. (*Partner*)

284 A.D.2d 250, 727 N.Y.S.2d 419 (App.Div.2001)

A LONG–TERM LEASE EXCEEDING THE LENGTH OF THE PARTNERSHIP IS NOT WITHIN ORDINARY PARTNERSHIP BUSINESS

■ **INSTANT FACTS** Milford Plaza Associates (P) challenged a long-term lease entered into by partners in its partnership.

■ **BLACK LETTER RULE** Partners may object to unauthorized transactions in assertion of their equal rights in the management and conduct of partnership business.

■ PROCEDURAL BASIS

On appeal to review a trial court judgment for the plaintiff.

■ FACTS

Milford Plaza Associates (P) and Northmon Investment Co. (D) were partners in a partnership in which the only asset was real property. When Northmon (D) proposed entering into a ninety-nine-year lease of the property to a third party, Milford (P) challenged the action as outside its authority. The trial court entered judgment for Milford (P).

■ ISSUE

May a partner challenge the actions of another partner as outside the scope of its authority?

■ DECISION AND RATIONALE

(Sullivan, P.J.) Yes. Although a partner may bind a partnership by transactions made in the ordinary course of partnership business, the partners may object to transactions entered into with third parties by asserting their equal rights in the management and conduct of partnership business. Because the partnership agreement itself terminates the partnership before the expiration of the long-term lease, the lease is not within the ordinary course of partnership business.

Analysis:

Unlike most challenges to a partner's authority, this case involves a dispute among partners. While generally any partner may bind the partnership in his dealings with third parties, dissenting partners' equal rights to manage the partnership affairs allow them to contest the actions of their partners. Had Northmon (D) entered into the lease with the third party without Milford's (P) knowledge, the court could not set aside the lease if it was deemed to be made in the usual and ordinary manner of conducting the partnership business.

■ Case Vocabulary:

PARTNERSHIP AGREEMENT: A contract defining the partners' rights and duties toward one another—not the partners' relationship with third parties.

Rapoport v. 55 Perry Co.

(*Partner*) v. (*Partnership*)

50 A.D.2d 54, 376 N.Y.S.2d 147 (Sup.Ct.App.Div.1975)

PARTNERSHIP INTERESTS ARE ASSIGNABLE WITHOUT CONSENT, BUT MANAGEMENT RIGHTS ARE NOT

■ **INSTANT FACTS** When 2 partners tried to name their children as partners, the others objected, prompting a suit to interpret their partnership contract.

■ **BLACK LETTER RULE** Partners may assign their partnership interests, but not their management rights, unless the other partners consent or have agreed otherwise.

■ FACTS

55 Perry Co. (D) was a partnership owned by Rapoport (P) and the Parnes family (D). Each family owned 50% of the partnership. Rapoport (P) wanted to assign 10% of their partnership to their adult children. The Pameses (D) refused to amend the partnership agreement to include the Rapoport's (P) children, contending the original agreement prohibited the introduction of new partners without consent by all existing partners. The Rapoports (P) sued for judicial declaration to (i) declare the Rapoports (P) had an absolute right to assign their partnership interest to their adult children without consent, and (ii) name the children partners. Both parties requested summary judgment. The trial court dismissed their requests because it found the partnership agreement was sufficiently ambiguous to require trial to determine the parties intent. Both parties appealed.

■ ISSUE

May partners freely assign their management rights to designees?

■ DECISION AND RATIONALE

(Tilzer) No. Partners may assign their partnership interests, but not their management rights, unless the other partners consent or have agreed otherwise. Here, the partnership agreement unambiguously reflects the partners' intent to permit assignment of partnership interests, but not of partnership management rights. Paragraph 12 provides that "no partner . . . shall have the authority . . . to sell, transfer, assign . . . his . . . share in this firm, nor enter into any agreement as a result of which any person shall become interested with him in this firm, unless . . . agreed to in writing by a majority of the partners as determined by the percentage of ownership . . . except for members of his immediate family who have attained majority, in which case no such consent shall be required." The Rapoports (P) contend this authorizes them to name their children as partners, but the Parneses (D) contend this assignability extends only to the right to assign partnership profits. We agree with the Parneses (D), because the partnership agreement as a whole indicates an intent to differentiate between new partners and mere assignees of partnership profits. Under the New York Partnership Law [equivalent to the UPA], "no person can become a member of a partnership without the consent of all the partners," and assignees of partnership interests are not authorized "to interfere in the management or administration of the partnership business," but merely to receive "the profits to which the assigning partner would otherwise be entitled." Further, the Law again differentiates between partners and assignees, stating "the property rights of a partner are (a) his rights in specific partnership property, (b) his interest in the partnership, and (c) his right to participate in the management,'' while assignees are excluded from management and access to partnership books, absent contrary agreement. The law's clear delineation suggests that, while it allows free transfer of partnership interests, it will require the partners' consent before a person can become a full partner, absent contrary agreement. Here, the partnership agreement was clearly cognizant of the difference. The agreement's disputed Paragraph 12 refers to assignments only, without mentioning admission of new partners, which is covered separately by other provisions. Thus, we conclude Paragraph 12 was intended to allow free transfer of partnership interests without consent, but not to allow naming of new partners without consent. The court should grant summary judgment in the form of a declaration that the partnership agreement permits the Rapoports (P) to assign their interests to their children, but not to name them partners. Order reversed as modified.

■ DISSENT

(Nunez) Summary judgment is improper, because the partnership agreement is ambiguous and presents a triable issue of intent for the court to determine by trial.

Analysis:

It is difficult to determine whether the result here is correct, since the holding is based on a holistic reading of the entire agreement, which is not provided in the text. More importantly, however, this case emphasizes the significance of the rule that full partnership is not freely transferrable. Partners assume heavy risks for each other's behavior, since the consequences could cost them not just the partnership's assets, but also their own. Partners should thus have control over who they are partnered with and not be forced to accept partners in whom they have no faith. The assignment of income alone should not hurt the partnership's operations, but the inclusion of relatives on the managing board might, if they are not otherwise qualified.

■ CASE VOCABULARY

ASSIGN: To grant to another the right to receive the proceeds of one's own contract rights.

CROSS APPEAL: An appeal by an appellee. Here, the appellees—the Parneses (D) also [cross-] appealed, since their motion for summary judgment had been denied together with the appellant Rapoports's (P) motion.

PARTNERSHIP INTEREST: The right of a partner or his designees to receive that partner's share of partnership income, which doesn't include the right to co-manage the partnership.

Meinhard v. Salmon

(*Partner*) v. (*Partner*)

249 N.Y. 458, 164 N.E. 545 (Ct.App.1928)

PARTNERS HAVE A FIDUCIARY DUTY TO SHARE BUSINESS OPPORTUNITIES

■ **INSTANT FACTS** When a partnership is offered a profitable lease, one partner accepts it for himself, prompting the other to demand participation.

■ **BLACK LETTER RULE** Partners' fiduciary duties of loyalty forbid appropriating opportunities offered to the partnership.

■ PROCEDURAL BASIS

Appeal from appellate court judgment modifying and affirming a judgment for plaintiff, founded on referee's report, in contract action seeking declaratory judgment and equitable relief.

■ FACTS

Salmon (D), a real estate broker, leased a hotel from Gerry for 20 years, planning to convert it into shops, and took on Meinhard (P), a wool merchant, as his silent partner. [Yet it was Salmon who pulled the wool over Meinhard.] Their agreement provided that (i) Meinhard (P) would provide half the cost of leasing, maintaining and converting the hotel, (ii) Meinhard (P) would be paid 40% of the net profits for the first 5 years and 50% each year thereafter, and (iii) Salmon (D) alone was to manage the building. After 20 years, during which both partners earned rich returns, Gerry offered Salmon (D) a long-term lease on the building at favorable terms. Salmon (D), without telling Meinhard (P) about the offer, accepted it for himself alone through his controlled company. Meinhard (P), upon learning of the deal, demanded to be allowed to participate in the offer. When Salmon (D) refused, Meinhard (P) sued, contending that Salmon (D), as his partner, had a duty to offer him participation in the lucrative opportunity. Salmon (D) apparently contended that (i) Gerry offered the lease to him individually, (ii) since the partnership's original 20-year term was near its end, he was again free to act in his own interests, and (iii) Meinhard (P) effectively waived rights to the new lease because he never mentioned his interest in renewing. At trial, the referee found for Meinhard (P), but gave him only a 25% share in the new lease, because the 25% in the new, more profitable lease was calculated to have the same monetary value as his original 50% share in the old lease. On cross-appeal, the appellate court affirmed the decision for Meinhard (P) and modified it to award him a 50% share. Salmon (D) appealed.

■ ISSUE

As a joint venture terminates, can partners individually accept opportunities offered that relate to the partnership?

■ DECISION AND RATIONALE

(Cardozo) No. Partners' fiduciary duties of loyalty forbid appropriating opportunities offered to the partnership. Their agreement made Salmon (D) and Meinhard (P) coadventurers (partners), since they had agreed to share profits and losses. Thus, as partners they owed each other duties of loyalty. Salmon (D) had an even greater duty, as both partner and manager. The duty of loyalty is fiduciary, so partners as fiduciaries owe each other the very highest standard of loyalty, honesty, and honor. Since partners are "held to something stricter than the morals of the marketplace," their fiduciary duty may prohibit them from performing business acts which are otherwise legal, and arguably moral. Thus, here, Salmon (D) had a duty to inform Meinhard (P) of the lease offer, to at least allow him a chance to compete for it. We will not rule on the issue of whether Salmon (D), had he won this competition, would then be required to continue the partnership by granting Meinhard (P)pose a lease extension is also irrelevant, since he had no obligation to monitor matters which Salmon (D) handled exclusively as manager. We do not find that Salmon (D) intended to defraud Meinhard (P). It is likely he assumed in good faith that, since the partnership was ending, he was free to take the new lease for himself. This act would be proper for a competitor, but not for a managing coadventurer, whose duty of loyalty must be supreme, and here included bringing related opportunities to his partner's attention. The rule may be different if one partner is offered an opportunity unrelated to his position as a partner/manager. Here, however, the new opportunity was an extension of the old one, so Salmon (D) should have expected reproach for appropriating it. As for the proper relief, the court previously held that the new lease should be held in trust by Salmon (D) and his company for Meinhard (P), but we find this inefficient, since it restricts Salmon (D) from selling his portion. Partitioning the building itself would be impractical. Instead, we order that the new lease be divided into shares, and that Salmon (D) be awarded 50% plus one share, with Meinhard (P) taking the rest. This slight majority allows Salmon (D) to continue exercising control during the new lease, as he exercised during the old one, and as he would reasonably expect if the partnership continued.

■ DISSENT

(Andrews) The opinion would be correct if applied to a general partnership, but not to the instant agreement, which was a joint venture with a limited objective and time.

Analysis:

Generally, partners' and agents' fiduciary duty of loyalty prohibits them from appropriating for themselves profitable opportunities offered to the partnership/principal. The policy reasons are obvious, but the extent of the rule is not. This case leaves open the issue of whether opportunities seemingly unrelated to the partnership/agency properly belong to it. The holding that partners owe to each other the utmost duty and honor makes it difficult to limit a partnership's term or scope, even by explicit agreement. This may create uncertainty about how partners can provide for their future as a partnership is dissolving. For instance, consider a law firm/partnership that is dissolving, intentionally or not. Once the partnership terminates, the former partners will revert to competitors. In the meantime, it is likely the partnership still has continuing clients, which each partner would like to appropriate for his own later practice. To forbid any partner from soliciting them seems a waste of goodwill, but under the default rules set by *Meinhard v. Salmon*, it is unclear whether any of the partners can solicit them without violating his or her broad duty to other partners.

■ CASE VOCABULARY

FIDUCIARY: Relationship by which one is required to act in another's best interest, esp. an agent, partner, or legal guardian.

JOINT VENTURE: a.k.a. "joint adventure." A partnership with a specified aim or project.

Creel v. Lilly

(*Estate of Deceased Partner*) v. (*Former Partner*)
354 Md. 77, 729 A.2d 385 (Ct.App.1999)

A PARTNERSHIP'S VALUE CAN BE DETERMINED WITHOUT LIQUIDATION

■ **INSTANT FACTS** After the death of a partner, his personal representative sued the surviving partners for liquidation of the partnership assets.

■ **BLACK LETTER RULE** When the remaining partners wind up the partnership in good faith and provide an accurate accounting of the partnership's value, the departing partner has no right to compel liquidation.

■ PROCEDURAL BASIS

Certiorari to review a decision of the Maryland Court of Special Appeals affirming a trial court judgment.

■ FACTS

After operating a business selling NASCAR racing memorabilia from his wife's florist shop, Joseph Creel entered into a partnership agreement with Lilly (D) and Altizer (D) to expand the business in a new space. When Joseph died shortly thereafter, his wife (P) was appointed personal representative of his estate. Pursuant to UPA § 9–602(a), the partnership was automatically dissolved based on the death of one of the partners. Creel (P) filed a complaint seeking an accounting and a declaratory judgment against Lilly (D) and Altizer (D), who had created "Good Ole Boys Racing" to succeed the prior partnership business, claiming that rather than winding up the original business, the defendants continued to carry on the business under a different name. After determining that Joseph had owned a fifty-two-percent share of the partnership, the trial court found that the defendants took all reasonable steps to wind up the business and did not breach any fiduciary duty to the estate. The court held that the defendants had properly accounted for the value of the partnership and afforded the estate an opportunity to review and object to its calculations, which it declined to do. Having found that the defendants acted reasonably, the court refused to order liquidation of the partnership as a means of winding up, instead awarding the estate damages proportionate to Joseph's share. The Maryland Court of Special Appeals affirmed.

■ ISSUE

Does the winding up of a partnership require its liquidation?

■ DECISION AND RATIONALE

(Chasnow, J.) No. When the terms of a partnership agreement fail to establish the time or circumstances upon which the partnership will terminate, a partnership at will is created. Absent specific terms in the partnership agreement, a partnership dissolves upon the death of one of the partners, but the partnership is not terminated until the winding-up is complete. The UPA provides, "When dissolution is caused in any way . . . each partner . . . unless otherwise agreed, may have the partnership property applied to discharge its liabilities, and the surplus applied to pay in cash the net amount owing to the respective partners." Historically, this process has afforded a partner the right to compel liquidation of the partnership to satisfy his surviving share, as liquidation was seen as the only true measure of the partnership's value. More recently, however, alternatives have arisen to save the partnership from the harsh and drastic consequences of liquidation. RUPA recognizes this change in judicial thinking. Adopting the "entity" theory of partnership rather than the "aggregate" theory espoused by the UPA, RUPA allows for the continuation of a partnership after the departure of a partner because the partnership is recognized as an entity distinct from the individual partners. This change of view underscores that the remaining partners may continue the partnership business without liquidation by electing to buy out the partnership share of the departing partner. The departing partner's consent is not necessary nor is the departing partner entitled to compel liquidation of the partnership.

While Maryland has not adopted RUPA, compelled liquidation undermines the policies underlying the UPA. "Liquidation can be a harmful and destructive measure . . . and is often unnecessary to determining the true value of the partnership." By compelling the sale of all partnership assets to determine the partnership's value, the partnership, whether it is a continuing or successor partnership, is unable to operate. As was done here, the value of the partnership can appropriately be determined by using skilled accountants to evaluate the partnership assets in order to make a proportionate distribution in kind to the departing partner. When the remaining partners wind up the partnership in good faith and provide an accurate accounting of the partnership's value, the departing partner has no right to compel liquidation. While the departing partner may be entitled to "continuation" damages arising from the remaining partners' continued use of the partnership assets after termination, the partnership at issue here is a successor partnership, not a continuing partnership. No continuation damages are at issue. Affirmed.

Analysis:

The key to the outcome of this case is the omission of a procedure for winding up the partnership upon termination. The provisions of the UPA and RUPA generally do not apply unless necessary as a default in the absence of specific language in a partnership agreement. Had the parties intended for liquidation to be compelled upon termination, the terms of the agreement should have clearly so indicated. Otherwise, liquidation will generally be disfavored unless necessary to determine the true value of partnership assets.

■ CASE VOCABULARY

DISSOLUTION: The termination of a previously existing partnership upon the occurrence of an event specified in the partnership agreement, such as a partner's withdrawal from the partnership.

LIQUIDATION: The act or process of converting assets into cash, especially to settle debts.

PARTNERSHIP AT WILL: A partnership that any partner may dissolve at any time without thereby incurring liability.

WINDING UP: The process of settling accounts and liquidating assets in anticipation of a partnership's or a corporation's dissolution.

Page v. Page

(*Partner*) v. (*Partner*)
55 Cal.2d 192, 10 Cal.Rptr. 643, 359 P.2d 41 (Sup.Ct.1961)

PARTNERS CANNOT DISSOLVE PARTNERSHIP IN BAD FAITH

■ **INSTANT FACTS** When his partner demands dissolution, his co-partner resists, arguing (i) the partnership was implicitly "for term," and (ii) the dissolution wrongfully diverts business to the other partner.

■ **BLACK LETTER RULE** Partners may dissolve "at will" partnerships any time, unless the dissolution is done in bad faith.

■ PROCEDURAL BASIS

Appeal from appellate court judgment for plaintiff declaring partnership was "for term" rather than "at will."

■ FACTS

Plaintiff and Defendant entered an oral partnership agreement to operate a linen supply business. Each contributed $43,000 to purchase assets. The partnership lost money for years, and Plaintiff asked that it be dissolved, contending he had the right to dissolve it at will. Defendant maintained the partnership was for term, contending that this partnership, like their prior partnerships, was intended to endure until it earned enough to repay their investment. Defendant also alleged Plaintiff acted in bad faith to appropriate the partnership's new business opportunity. An air force base had opened near the linen supplier, promising a captive clientele. Plaintiff, he contended, was now forcing Defendant out of the suddenly-profitable partnership, and could prevent Plaintiff from selling his share of the partnership by threatening to call in his $47,000 demand note from the partnership if Defendant sold. Thus, Plaintiff would be forced to sell his share to Defendant, at whatever price Defendant offered. The court found the partners' understanding sufficient to create a partnership for term, which presumably could not be dissolved until it earned $86,000 or more in profit. Defendant appealed.

■ ISSUE

May partners dissolve a partnership at will?

■ DECISION AND RATIONALE

(Traynor) Yes. Partners may dissolve "at will" partnerships anytime, unless the dissolution is done in bad faith. Under California statutes, to create a partnership for term, the partnership agreement must suggest a "definite term or particular undertaking," either expressly or implicitly. In *Owen v. Cohen*, it was held a term could be implicit where partners borrowed heavily to launch the partnership and expected it to continue long enough to allow it to earn profits. Here, Defendant contends the partnership's term was understood by the partners to be similar to their prior partnerships, in that profits were to be retained until the partners recouped their investment. Yet this alone does not create a binding expectation that the partnership must continue as long as needed to repay the investment; it merely shows that, if the partnership were successful, the partners expected to recoup their investment, which is no more than a common hope of profit. Holding otherwise would make most partnerships "for term," undissolveable until they became profitable. Plaintiff's allegations of bad faith are unproven. Still, we note for future proceedings that partners are protected from dissolution in bad faith by their copartners' fiduciary duties. Although the UPA provides that partners may dissolve "at will" partnerships anytime, they remain bound to do so in good faith. This includes not using dissolution to "freeze out" a copartner and appropriate partnership business opportunities for themselves without compensating their partners. If it is proven on remand that Defendant acted in bad faith to appropriate the partnership's business for himself, he would be liable for wrongful dissolution in violation of his fiduciary duties. Judgment reversed.

Analysis:

This case shows the effectiveness of "freeze outs," which are more common in corporations than in 2-person partnerships. In a freeze out, the majority shareholder (or partner) forces the minority shareholders to sell him or her their shares at unfairly low prices. *Page* demonstrates how the freeze out can work even without majority control. Here, neither partner has total control over the partnership, but either has full control over dissolution. Upon dissolution, the partnership's assets would be sold at auction. Defendant would buy back his own share, but few would want to purchase Plaintiff's share of the partnership, because the partnership owes Defendant a large debt payable on demand. If anyone bought into the partnership, Defendant could immediately demand they pay him half of $47,000. Few would want to buy Plaintiff's share for full value, plus $23,500, and gain a hostile partner in the bargain.

■ CASE VOCABULARY

DEMAND NOTE: A promissory note (debt) which must be repaid any time the lender demands repayment.

"FOR TERM": A partnership is "for term" if it is intended to last for a specified duration or until a specified project is completed. It cannot be dissolved "at will."

FREEZE OUT: Business tactic whereby controlling partners/shareholders force minority partners/shareholders to sell them their shares at unfairly low prices; often accomplished using the business to advance the controlling members' private interests.

Drashner v. Sorenson

(*Partner*) v. (*Partner*)
75 S.D. 247, 63 N.W.2d 255 (Sup.Ct.1954)

PARTNER WRONGFULLY DISSOLVING PARTNERSHIP LOSES RIGHT TO GOODWILL

■ **INSTANT FACTS** When an irresponsible partner wrongfully dissolved the partnership, he demanded a share of the partnership's goodwill.

■ **BLACK LETTER RULE** When a partner causes the partnership's dissolution wrongfully by making it impracticable to remain in partnership, the other partners may continue the partnership, and the dissolving partner is not entitled to share in the partnership's goodwill.

■ PROCEDURAL BASIS

Appeal from judgment for defendants in contract action seeking accounting (including division of goodwill).

■ FACTS

Drashner (P), Sorenson (D), and Deis (D) became partners in a real estate, loan, and insurance business. They pooled $7,500 to buy an existing real estate/insurance agency, and their partnership agreement said their partnership was to continue for a term at least until gross earnings were enough to repay this amount. Sorenson (D) and Deis (D) allege they could not work with Drashner (P) because he was often drunk, neglected his work, and demanded extra money for family living expenses. Finally, even though the partnership had not yet repaid the $7,500 investment, Drashner (P) sued (and the others countersued), and demanded dissolution, winding up, and accounting. The trial court held that Drashner (P) had wrongfully dissolved the partnership by demanding dissolution before its term and by acting in ways that made it impracticable to remain in partnership with him. The court concluded that Sorenson (D) and Deis (D) could continue the partnership if they released Drashner (P) from future partnership obligations and either paid him the value of his partnership interest (not including goodwill) or filed bond sufficient to guarantee its payment. At a judicial hearing to assess the partnership's value, the court found the partnership's physical assets were worth only $4500, with debts of $4500, and so awarded Drashner (P) nothing as his share. Drashner (P) appealed, contending the court improperly excluded goodwill value in valuing the partnership, and that he was entitled to one-third of the partnership's goodwill value as well.

■ ISSUE

Is a partner who dissolves a partnership entitled to share in the partnership's goodwill?

■ DECISION AND RATIONALE

(Smith) No. The UPA provides that, when a partner causes the partnership's dissolution wrongfully by making it impracticable to remain in partnership, the other partners may continue the partnership, and the dissolving partner is not entitled to share in the partnership's goodwill. *UPA § 38(2).* This partnership was "for term," since the partnership agreement provided it was to continue at least until it had grossed $7,500 sufficient to repay the partners' initial investment. Both partnership factions sought dissolution before that term, contending the other had breached the agreement by making it impracticable to continue working together. The trial court was not unreasonable in finding it was Drashner (D) who caused the impracticability through his drinking, neglect, and demands for cash, although there was also some evidence to the contrary. Thus, Sorenson (D) and Deis (D) were properly granted dissolution prior to term. The court, in valuing the partnership, used a low estimate, but its finding was not "against the clear weight of the evidence," so we cannot reverse it. The court also properly excluded goodwill, as is required by statute. While it is true that the goodwill would have been substantial, the statute requires it be excluded as a penalty for wrongfully causing dissolution. Drashner (D) also requests to share in the partnership profits from the date of dissolution until the final judgment, but he did not present to the trial court this claim or evidence of the profits, so we cannot consider this issue on appeal. Judgment affirmed.

Analysis:

This case illustrates that, under the UPA, a partner who wrongfully dissolves the partnership faces drastic penalties, including (i) damages for breach of partnership contract, (ii) loss of his share of goodwill, and (iii) the right of the other partners to continue the partnership and retain its goodwill. Goodwill can be a significant part of any profitable business's value, particularly for service businesses with few physical assets but high profits and steady clients, e.g., law firms, and the loss of it can be a heavy penalty. Note this adds some risk to dissolving a partnership at will, since it is possible the court can find a nominally at will partnership was actually implicitly for term, and its dissolution at will is thus wrongful.

■ CASE VOCABULARY

GOODWILL: In accounting, the value ascribed to a business's reputation, brand name, regular clientele, and other intangibles. It is often a residual value computed by subtracting from the actual purchase price the net asset value; for example, if a business whose tangible assets are worth $600,000 is actually bought for $1M, the remaining $400,000 is ascribed to "goodwill."

CHAPTER THREE

The Corporate Form

Goodman v. Ladd Estate Co.

Instant Facts: A corporation's ultra vires guaranty agreement was held enforceable.

Black Letter Rule: Shareholders, including any successors and assigns, who have participated in an ultra vires act cannot later attack it as ultra vires.

A.P. Smith Mfg. Co. v. Barlow

Instant Facts: Stockholders challenged a donation by the corporation to Princeton University.

Black Letter Rule: Corporations have common-law and statutory powers to make reasonable donations to private academic institutions even absent an express authorization in its articles of incorporation.

Goodman v. Ladd Estate Co.

(*Shareholder*) v. (*Endorser*)
246 Or. 621, 427 P.2d 102 (1967)

ONE WHO HAS PARTICIPATED IN AN ULTRA VIRES ACT OR AGREEMENT CANNOT LATER ATTACK IT AS ULTRA VIRES

■ **INSTANT FACTS** A corporation's ultra vires guaranty agreement was held enforceable.

■ **BLACK LETTER RULE** Shareholders, including any successors and assigns, who have participated in an ultra vires act cannot later attack it as ultra vires.

■ PROCEDURAL BASIS

Appeal from dismissal of Goodman's (P) suit to enjoin a guaranty agreement.

■ FACTS

Walter Liles was the president of Westover Tower, Inc. and owned all of its common shares and voting rights. Dr. Wheatley was also a director of Westover Tower, Inc. In 1961 Dr. Wheatley borrowed $10,000 from Citizens Bank of Oregon and gave a promissory note for the debt which was endorsed by Ladd Estate (D). The money was not used for any corporate purpose. Contemporaneously with this loan, Westover, Inc., through its president Liles, agreed in writing to unconditionally guarantee Ladd Estate (D) against loss from Ladd Estate's (D) endorsement of Dr. Wheatley's note to Citizens Bank. The agreement recited that it was made at the request of Liles and Westover, Inc. and that Ladd Estate (D) would not have endorsed the note without the guarantee of Westover, Inc. Dr. Wheatley defaulted on the note, and Ladd Estate (D) paid the balance of $9,583 to Citizens Bank. Ladd Estate (D) then sought reimbursement from Westover, Inc. pursuant to the guaranty agreement. When Westover, Inc. refused payment, Ladd Estate (D) brought suit against Liles and Westover, Inc. Mr. and Mrs. Goodman (P) became involved in the case when they purchased all of the common shares of Westover, Inc. At the time they made the purchase, the Goodmans (P) were fully aware of the guaranty agreement given by Westover, Inc. and Liles to Ladd Estate (D). The Goodmans (P) then brought suit to enjoin Ladd Estate (D) from enforcing the Westover, Inc. guaranty agreement.

■ ISSUE

May an ultra vires agreement be enforced where the sole voting shareholder participated in and requested the agreement?

■ DECISION AND RATIONALE

(Lusk, J.) Yes. It is conceded that the guaranty agreement was ultra vires the corporation. This court may set aside and enjoin the performance of the ultra vires contract if we find it equitable to do so. The Goodmans (P) argue it would be "shocking" to enforce the agreement because Westover, Inc. entered it to allow one of its directors to obtain a loan for non-corporate purposes. We find nothing shocking in enforcing the agreement. Thirty-thousand shares of common stock were authorized and all were issued to Liles. The voting rights of the shareholders were vested exclusively in the holders of the common stock. The guaranty agreement states that at the request of Liles and Westover, Inc., Ladd Estate (D) guaranteed payment of the Wheatley note. Wheatley defaulted, Ladd Estate (D) made good on its endorsement, and now asks Westover, Inc. to honor its agreement. The fact that the Goodmans (P) were led to believe by the agent that purchased the shares for them that the guaranty was not a valid obligation, does not enhance their claim. Neither does the fact that the agreement was ultra vires. It is ultra vires because it does not further any corporate purpose. The statute, however, says an agreement is enforceable even though ultra vires. To allow the Goodmans (P) to set it aside because it is ultra vires would destroy the statute. Finally, the Goodmans (P) are in no position to invoke equity. Liles, the former owner of their shares, induced Ladd Estate (D) to endorse the Wheatley note. If a shareholder himself has participated in the ultra vires act he cannot later attack it as ultra vires. The Goodmans (P) as purchasers of Liles shares are in no better position than he would have been to attack the agreement. The Goodmans (P) are not entitled to equitable relief. Affirmed.

Analysis:

While this case is quite complicated factually, the rule it illuminates is fairly straightforward. If the primary shareholder in a corporation, here Liles, participates in an ultra vires agreement, the shareholder or his successors cannot later attack the agreement as ultra vires. The court finds that the Goodmans (P) were in no position to invoke the help of a court of equity, because their successor in interest, Liles, exercised the entire voting power of the corporation and agreed to the ultra vires act. Because Liles was "dirty," so were the Goodmans. This case illustrates the clean hands doctrine whereby the courts will not grant someone relief in equity if that person has previously acted in bad faith, unfairly, or contrary to equitable principles.

■ CASE VOCABULARY

ENDORSER: There are different kinds of endorsers, but it is generally the person or entity that agrees to pay the instrument in the event of dishonor.

GUARANTY AGREEMENT: A collateral agreement whereby the guarantor agrees to pay a debt of another if the original person liable fails to pay.

ULTRA VIRES: An act beyond the authorized powers of a corporation, as they are defined by its charter or the laws of the state of incorporation.

A.P. Smith Mfg. Co. v. Barlow

(*Corporation*) v. (*Stockholder*)

13 N.J. 145, 98 A.2d 581 (1953), appeal dismissed, 346 U.S. 861 (1953)

REASONABLE CHARITABLE DONATIONS CAN BE MADE BY A CORPORATION EVEN IF NOT EXPRESSLY AUTHORIZED BY ITS ARTICLES OF INCORPORATION

■ **INSTANT FACTS** Stockholders challenged a donation by the corporation to Princeton University.

■ **BLACK LETTER RULE** Corporations have common-law and statutory powers to make reasonable donations to private academic institutions even absent an express authorization in its articles of incorporation.

■ PROCEDURAL BASIS

Appeal from a declaratory judgment in favor of the A.P. Smith Co. (P).

■ FACTS

The A.P. Smith Manufacturing Company (P) was incorporated in 1896 and is engaged in the manufacture of valves, fire hydrants, and other equipment. In 1951 the board of directors adopted a resolution which stated that it was in the corporation's best interest to participate in the 1951 Annual Giving to Princeton University, and appropriated $1,500 to the university as a contribution. When this action was questioned by the stockholders, the corporation brought a declaratory judgment action and a trial was held.

■ ISSUE

May a corporation properly make a charitable donation which is not expressly authorized by its certificate of incorporation?

■ DECISION AND RATIONALE

(Jacobs, J.) Yes. Mr. O'Brien, the president of A.P. Smith Co. (P) testified that he considered the contribution to be a sound investment that would create good will for the company and a favorable environment for their business operations. He also stated that in contributing to such private institutions, corporations further their self-interest by assuring properly trained individuals for corporate employment. Others testified that it is not good business for a corporation to benefit from the community without accepting the obligations of good citizenship. It was also expressed that capitalism owes its very survival to independent, private institutions of learning. If corporations were not able to make contributions, only governmental institutions could survive. The stockholders acknowledge this and our statutes express a strong public policy in favor of corporate contributions. The stockholders argue, however, that the corporation's certificate of incorporation does not specifically authorize the contribution, and under common-law the company does not have any power to make it. They also argue that New Jersey statutes which authorize the contribution do not constitutionally apply to A.P. Smith Co. (P) because it was created long before their enactment. Early corporations were originally established for a better government. Modern corporations are primarily established for private profit, and the common-law rule has developed that a corporation cannot disburse funds to any cause unless the expenditure would benefit the corporation. This rule is applied broadly to allow corporate donations with indirect benefits to the corporation. Control of economic wealth is now largely in the hands of dominant corporations. Charitable organizations now depend on these corporations to assume the obligations of good citizenship. Corporations have realized that their contributions can improve society and create an economic and social environment in which they can prosper. We have no difficulty sustaining, within reasonable limits, a corporation's power to support academic institutions. These contributions are also justified by statute. In 1950 the legislature expressly authorized charitable contributions by corporations as long as the donee institution does not own more than 10% of the voting stock of the donor, and the contribution does not exceed 1% of capital, unless otherwise authorized by the shareholders. The stockholders contend that these statutes cannot apply to A.P. Smith Co (P) because it was created before their passage. However, even before the incorporation of A.P. Smith Co. (P) the legislature provided that all charters granted were subject to alteration, suspension and repeal, at the discretion of the legislature. Thus, the gift here is authorized by both common-law and statute. There is no suggestion that the contribution was inappropriate or made to a pet charity of the directors for their own benefit. It was of a modest amount and was well within the implied and incidental powers of the corporation. Affirmed.

Analysis:

The real point of this case has little to do with charitable contributions. It is important to note that what a corporation is permitted to do in its charter can be changed by subsequent amendment of statutes. This well-written case also upholds corporate giving while demonstrating the self-serving nature of such donations. Corporations can make charitable donations, but their ultimate goal must be to benefit the corporation and make a profit. What is a reasonable amount to donate? Should it depend on the assets and income of the company, or on the expected benefit to the company from the donation, or both?

CHAPTER FOUR

The Corporate Structure

Charlestown Boot & Shoe Co. v. Dunsmore

Instant Facts: The shareholders of Charlestown Boot & Shoe Co. (P) brought suit against its directors claiming the directors should have done what the shareholders wanted them to do.

Black Letter Rule: Shareholders have no power over the management of a corporation and cannot order the directors to take particular actions in managing the business of the corporation.

Schnell v. Chris–Craft Industries, Inc.

Instant Facts: Directors advanced the date of the annual shareholders' meeting in an attempt to stifle a proxy fight.

Black Letter Rule: Even if authorized by statute, the directors of a corporation cannot advance the date of the shareholders' meeting when this action would effectively eliminate the chances of a successful proxy fight.

Blasius Industries, Inc. v. Atlas Corp.

Instant Facts: The incumbent board of Atlas (D) sought to prevent Blasius (P) from gaining control of the corporation by increasing the number of board members.

Black Letter Rule: The board of directors may not take action for the primary purpose of interfering with a stockholders' vote, even if taken in good faith.

International Brotherhood of Teamsters v. Fleming Companies, Inc.

Instant Facts: Teamsters (P) sought to amend the bylaws of the corporation to require shareholder approval of new poison pill plans.

Black Letter Rule: Shareholders may enact bylaws which require the board of directors to obtain shareholder approval before implementing new poison pill plans.

MM Companies, Inc. v. Liquid Audio, Inc.

Instant Facts: MM Companies, Inc. (P) sued Liquid Audio, Inc. (D), challenging the defendant's decision to expand its board of directors and appoint two new directors to impede MM's (P) takeover attempts.

Black Letter Rule: When a plaintiff establishes that the primary purpose for board action was to impede or interfere with the effectiveness of the shareholders' vote, the burden shifts to the board to prove a compelling justification for the board's actions.

Fletcher v. Atex, Inc.

Instant Facts: Fletcher (P) was allegedly injured by an Atex (D) keyboard and sought to pierce the corporate veil to hold Atex's (D) parent company, Kodak (D), liable.

Black Letter Rule: To prevail on an alter ego theory of liability, it must be established that the corporation and the shareholder acted as a single economic entity and that there is an element of injustice or unfairness present.

Walkovszky v. Carlton

Instant Facts: Walkovszky (P) was hit by a taxicab and sought to hold the stockholder personally liable for his injuries.

Black Letter Rule: For personal liability to attach to stockholders, it must be shown that the stockholders were actually carrying on the business in their individual capacity for personal rather than corporate ends.

Minton v. Cavaney

Instant Facts: The Mintons' (P) daughter drowned in a pool owned by Seminole Hot Springs Corporation. They sought to hold Seminole's director liable for her death.

Black Letter Rule: The corporate veil can be pierced where the shareholders undercapitalize the corporation and actively participate in the conduct of corporate affairs.

Sea–Land Services v. Pepper Source

Instant Facts: After losing on remand, Marchese (D) appealed the court's finding that injustice would result if the corporate form was respected.

Black Letter Rule: Manipulating corporate funds to avoid creditors and unjust enrichment are a sufficient showing of additional wrongs to justify piercing the corporate veil.

Charlestown Boot & Shoe Co. v. Dunsmore

(*Shareholders*) v. (*Director*)
60 N.H. 85 (1880)

THE SHAREHOLDERS OF A CORPORATION CANNOT ORDER THE DIRECTORS TO TAKE PARTICULAR ACTIONS IN MANAGING THE CORPORATION

■ **INSTANT FACTS** The shareholders of Charlestown Boot & Shoe Co. (P) brought suit against its directors claiming the directors should have done what the shareholders wanted them to do.

■ **BLACK LETTER RULE** Shareholders have no power over the management of a corporation and cannot order the directors to take particular actions in managing the business of the corporation.

■ PROCEDURAL BASIS

Appeal from demurrer in favor of Dunsmore (D).

■ FACTS

Dunsmore (D) was the director of Charlestown Boot & Shoe Company (P), a manufacturing corporation. The shareholders of the corporation chose a committee to act with Dunsmore (D) to close up the corporation's business affairs. The shareholders chose Mr. Osgood to head the committee. Mr. Osgood offered his services, but Dunsmore (D) and the other directors refused to act with him, and contracted new debts larger than those allowed by law. The shareholders alleged that by Dunsmore's (D) negligence, the corporation lost several thousand dollars in bad debts and in the disposal of the corporation's goods. The shareholders also alleged the value of the corporation's buildings and machinery depreciated by $20,000 because the directors did not sell the assets when they should have, and when they were directed to do so by Mr. Osgood. The corporation also lost another $20,000 because an uninsured shop was destroyed by fire. The shareholders argued it was the duty of the directors to insure this property.

■ ISSUE

May the shareholders of a corporation force the directors to take certain actions on behalf of the corporation?

■ DECISION AND RATIONALE

(Smith, J.) No. Our corporate statutes provide that the business of a corporation shall be managed by the directors subject only to the by-laws and votes of the corporation. The statute does not authorize the shareholders to join another officer with the directors, nor compel the directors to act with one who is not a director. The directors are bound to use ordinary care and diligence in the management of the corporation, and are responsible for ordinary negligence. It would be unfair to hold the directors responsible for the management of the corporation if they were forced to act with one who could control their acts. Our statutes also give directors control over officers and agents. The directors have the power to appoint agents, not the shareholders. If the shareholders attempt to exercise powers which by their charter are lodged elsewhere, its action is void. The vote appointing Mr. Osgood to a committee to close up the affairs with the directors is void. Furthermore, there was no duty on the part of the directors to keep the property of the corporation insured. There is no statute requiring the directors to keep the corporate property insured, and no facts are alleged from which we can find a duty on the part of Dunsmore (D) to insure the property. Demurrer sustained.

Analysis:

In this case, the court sets forth the boundary between the powers of shareholders and directors. The shareholders would have probably made better directors than the directors did, but the court was unmoved. Shareholders have no power to force directors to take certain actions when the actions are within the exclusive discretion of the directors. The court notes that directors are bound to use ordinary care and diligence in managing the corporation. It concludes that failing to insure the property of the corporation was not a breach of this duty. It could be argued that even in the absence of a statute requiring the directors to insure corporate property, there should be a common law duty to do so, and the failure to do so amounts to negligence. Nevertheless, the court found that the directors did not act negligently and should not be forced to follow the advice of the shareholders.

■ CASE VOCABULARY

DEMURRER: The modern equivalent of a demurrer is the motion to dismiss for failure to state a claim upon which relief can be granted; generally, a demurrer assumes, for the sake of the motion, that all of the facts alleged in the complaint are true, but asserts that the facts are insufficient to state a claim under the law.

Schnell v. Chris-Craft Industries, Inc.

(*Shareholder*) v. (*Management*)
285 A.2d 437 (Del.1971)

DIRECTORS MAY NOT TAKE ACTION WHICH FRUSTRATES THE EFFECTIVENESS OF THE SHAREHOLDERS' VOTING RIGHTS

■ **INSTANT FACTS** Directors advanced the date of the annual shareholders' meeting in an attempt to stifle a proxy fight.

■ **BLACK LETTER RULE** Even if authorized by statute, the directors of a corporation cannot advance the date of the shareholders' meeting when this action would effectively eliminate the chances of a successful proxy fight.

■ PROCEDURAL BASIS

Appeal from denial of stockholders' petition to prevent management from changing the date of the annual stockholders' meeting.

■ FACTS

The managing directors of Chris-Craft Industries, Inc. (D) attempted to advance the date of the annual stockholders' meeting from January 11, 1972, as previously set by the by-laws, to December 8, 1971. The trial court found that the directors seized on a new section of the Delaware Corporations Law to cut down the amount of time which would otherwise have been available to the stockholders to wage a proxy battle. Dissident stockholders wanted a change in management to hopefully improve the present poor state of the company. The directors changed the date of the stockholders' meeting by amending its by-laws only two days after the stockholders' committee had filed its intention to wage a proxy fight with the S.E.C.

■ ISSUE

May the directors of a corporation change the date of the annual meeting of shareholders if such a change frustrates the ability of dissident shareholders' to wage a proxy fight?

■ DECISION AND RATIONALE

(Herrmann, J.) No. We find that the tactics employed by management give Schnell (P) and the other dissident stockholders insufficient time to wage a successful proxy fight. Management has attempted to use the corporate machinery and Delaware Law to perpetuate itself in office. These are inequitable purposes, and are against the established principles of corporate democracy. The by-laws of a corporation set the date for the annual meeting, and those wishing to contest the current management will gear their campaign to that date. Management cannot advance that date to gain an advantage. Management argues that it complied with the provisions of the new Delaware Corporation Law in changing the date. An inequitable action does not become permissible simply because it is legally possible. The judgment below is reversed and remanded with instructions to reinstate January 11, 1972 as the date of the next annual meeting of the stockholders.

Analysis:

The main purpose of most shareholders' meetings is to elect directors. The dissident shareholders in this case wanted new directors and attempted to solicit proxies for this purpose. The incumbent directors stalled access to the list of shareholders and advanced the date of the annual meeting, almost eliminating the challengers' chances of success. It is important to note that even though the directors complied with the statute, the court nevertheless found their actions improper. This case became the foundation for a number of later cases that set aside directors' actions that interfered with the shareholders' voting rights.

■ CASE VOCABULARY

PROXY: A person given authority to vote for another shareholder at a corporate meeting.

Blasius Industries, Inc. v. Atlas Corp.

(*Shareholders*) v. (*Board of Directors*)
564 A.2d 651 (Del.Ct.Ch.1988)

ACTIONS BY DIRECTORS MADE FOR THE PRIMARY PURPOSE OF INTERFERING WITH A SHAREHOLDER VOTE ARE IMPROPER, EVEN IF MADE IN GOOD FAITH

■ **INSTANT FACTS** The incumbent board of Atlas (D) sought to prevent Blasius (P) from gaining control of the corporation by increasing the number of board members.

■ **BLACK LETTER RULE** The board of directors may not take action for the primary purpose of interfering with a stockholders' vote, even if taken in good faith.

■ PROCEDURAL BASIS

Blasius (P) sought to have certain actions of the board of directors of Atlas (D) set aside.

■ FACTS

Blasius Industries (P) was the largest single (9.1%) shareholder of the Atlas Corporation (D). On October 29, 1987 Blasius (P) filed a Schedule 13D with the Securities Exchange Commission stating that it intended to encourage the management of Atlas (D) to consider a restructuring of the company. Blasius (P) had recently come under the control of Michael Lubin and Warren Delano who had made several unsuccessful attempts to effect leveraged buyouts. The management of Atlas (D) was not pleased with the prospect of Lubin and Delano becoming involved with the company. Weaver, the CEO of Atlas (D) had recently overseen a business restructuring of Atlas (D), and was perhaps thinking that it should be given a chance to produce results before attempting another restructuring. After filing its 13D, Blasius (P) met with the management of Atlas (D) and proposed that Atlas (D) engage in a leveraged restructuring and distribute cash to shareholders. This would involve the corporation raising cash by selling assets, taking out loans, and making large cash and non-cash dividends. The management of Atlas (D) believed the proposal was not feasible. Blasius (P) then sent to Atlas (D) a written consent recommending that the board adopt the restructuring proposal, amend the bylaws to expand the size of the board from seven to fifteen members (the maximum allowed under Atlas' charter), and elect eight named persons to fill the new positions. This would allow Blasius (P) to gain a majority on the board and implement its plans. The management of Atlas (D) viewed the consent as an attempt to take over the company and called an emergency meeting on December 31, 1987. At this meeting, the board voted to increase the board from seven to nine members and appointed two new individuals to these positions. This would prevent Blasius (P) from placing a majority of new directors on the board.

■ ISSUE

May the board of directors, without sufficient justification, take an action with the primary purpose of interfering with a shareholders' vote, even if taken in good faith?

■ DECISION AND RATIONALE

(Allen, J.) No. In creating and filling two new board positions, the management of Atlas (D) was primarily concerned with preventing the shareholders from placing a majority of new directors on the board through Blasius' (P) consent solicitation. Under other circumstances, this action would be appropriate, but here it was taken to impede the shareholders' from adopting Blasius' (P) proposal. Blasius (P) attacks the directors' actions as an attempt to maintain control and argues that the directors have a duty to exercise their powers in good faith consistent with the corporation's best interest. Atlas (D) argues the business judgment rule justifies their actions. They contend they acted without a conflict of interest because their positions on the board were not challenged. They also argue they acted with due care and in good faith because they were protecting the shareholders from having an impractical restructuring program forced upon them. This court concludes they acted in good faith in order to thwart the implementation of a recapitalization that they reasonably feared would hurt the company. However, the real question here is, whether the board may validly act to prevent the shareholders from electing a majority of new directors, even if the board is acting in good faith. A board may take steps such as having the corporation purchase its own shares that have the effect of defeating a change in management. These steps must be taken in good faith and in pursuit of a corporate interest. However, this rule does not apply to this situation where the primary purpose of the action was to interfere with the effectiveness of a stockholder vote. The business judgment rule does not apply here because we are dealing with the allocation of power between the board and the shareholders. Shareholders have two protections against poor performance. They may sell their stock or vote to replace the board. The legitimacy of the board's power to control the shareholders' wealth rests upon the shareholders' ability to select the board. When the integrity of the voting process is involved, the board may not be left to its own business judgment. This court is not adopting a *per se* rule of invalidity once a plaintiff has established that a board has acted for the primary purpose of thwarting a shareholder vote. Such a rule is too broad. However, once a showing has been made that a board acted for the primary purpose of thwarting a shareholder vote, the board bears the heavy burden of demonstrating a compelling justification for its action. Here, the board has not shown a sufficient justification. It was not faced with a powerful majority shareholder, but only a consent solicitation from a 9% shareholder. The board had time to inform the shareholders about its views on the merits of the proposal. It may be that Blasius' (P) restructuring proposal was unrealistic and unsound. The board thought it was and was entitled to take certain steps to avoid it. For example, it could spend corporate funds to convince shareholders to defeat the proposal. However, if a majority of the shareholders view the matter differently than the board, they are entitled to use the mechanisms provided by statue and Atlas' (D) certificate of incorporation to advance their view. This court concludes that even though the action was taken in good faith, it was an unintended violation of the duty of loyalty that the board owed to the shareholders. The board's action was invalid and must be voided.

Analysis:

The court refers to the business judgment rule, under which a director will not be liable for a decision unless the decision was irrational. The court here found that conduct that interferes with shareholder voting will not be reviewed under this lenient standard. Rather, there must be a compelling justification for such actions. The court does not specify what would satisfy the "compelling justification" standard, but seems to imply that coercive action taken by powerful shareholders against the interests of minority shareholders may be such a situation.

International Brotherhood of Teamsters v. Fleming Companies, Inc.

(*Shareholders*) v. (*Board of Directors*)
975 P.2d 907 (Okla.1999)

SHAREHOLDERS MAY ENACT BYLAWS WHICH REQUIRE SHAREHOLDER APPROVAL OF POISON PILLS

■ **INSTANT FACTS** Teamsters (P) sought to amend the bylaws of the corporation to require shareholder approval of new poison pill plans.

■ **BLACK LETTER RULE** Shareholders may enact bylaws which require the board of directors to obtain shareholder approval before implementing new poison pill plans.

■ PROCEDURAL BASIS

Appeal from district court ruling in favor of the Teamsters (P).

■ FACTS

The International Brotherhood of Teamsters (P) owns sixty-five shares of Fleming Companies, Inc. (D). In 1986, Fleming (D) implemented a shareholder's rights plan as an anti-takeover mechanism. These plans give the directors authority to execute discriminatory shareholder rights when a triggering event occurs such as when a certain percentage of shares has been amassed by a single shareholder. The result is to severely dilute the shareholder power of one trying to gain control of the company. These plans make it far more expensive to effect a takeover, and are often called "poison pills." Rights plans can serve the company in that they buy time to implement a merger strategy or secure better offers from other suitors. However, some shareholder groups oppose them because they stifle mergers which can often be lucrative for shareholders of the target company. Teamsters (P) saw the Fleming (D) rights plan as a means of entrenching the current board. In 1997, Teamsters (P) prepared a proxy statement for inclusion in the proxy materials for the annual meeting. With this proxy, the Teamsters (P) proposed an amendment to the bylaws which would require any rights plan implemented by the board to be put to the shareholders for a majority vote. This would force the board to implement a rights plan acceptable to both the shareholders and the board or do away with such a plan altogether. Fleming (D) unsuccessfully sought to postpone a vote on the proxy issue through litigation, and the Teamsters' (P) resolution passed with 60% of the voted shares.

■ ISSUE

May shareholders of a corporation propose resolutions requiring that shareholder rights plans be submitted to the shareholders for a vote at the next annual meeting?

■ DECISION AND RATIONALE

(Simms, J.) Yes. Under Oklahoma law there is no exclusive authority granted to boards to create and implement shareholder rights plans. Shareholders may propose bylaws which restrict board implementation of such plans as long as the certificate of incorporation does not provide otherwise. Fleming (D) argues that 18 O.S.1991 § 1038 gives the board exclusive authority to issue shareholder rights plans, subject only to the certificate of incorporation. Section 1038 states that "every corporation may create and issue . . . rights or options entitling the holders thereof to purchase from the corporation any shares of its capital stock . . ." Fleming (D) asserts that the word "corporation" is synonymous with "board of directors." However, both terms are used distinctly throughout the Corporation Act. Our legislature has an understanding of the different definitions assigned to these terms, and we find it unlikely that they would interchange them. Furthermore, a shareholder rights plan is essentially a variety of a stock option plan. Shareholder ratification of poison pill plans has not been tested by the courts, but shareholder ratification of stock option plans has. The case of *Michelson v. Duncan* reveals that stock option plans can be subject to shareholder approval. The Internal Revenue Code also provides for shareholder approval of stock option plans. We find no authority to suggest that shareholder rights plans are somehow exempt from shareholder adopted by-laws. A number of states have taken affirmative steps to ensure their corporations are able to implement shareholder rights plans to protect the company from takeover. These statutes are called shareholders rights plan endorsement statutes. However, Oklahoma has not passed such legislation. These statutes generally give the board of directors relative autonomy to enact shareholder rights plans. Without such a statute, the board is subject to the general procedures of corporate governance, including the enactment of by-laws which limit the board's authority to implement shareholder rights plans. We are not suggesting that all shareholder rights plans are required to submit to shareholder approval. Rather, we find that shareholders may, through proper channels of corporate governance, restrict the board of directors authority to implement these plans.

Analysis:

This decision is potentially very important because it upholds shareholders aggressively exercising their power over the bylaws. Another important issue raised by this case is the increasing importance of shareholders in general. Historically, shareholders were widely dispersed and quite passive. With the rise of institutional investors such as pension funds and investment companies, shareholders have taken a more active role in the activities of the corporation and demanded increased accountability from the board of directors.

■ CASE VOCABULARY

POISON PILL: A tactic used by a corporation to make its shares or financial condition less attractive to avoid an unwanted takeover.

MM Companies, Inc. v. Liquid Audio, Inc.

(Minority Shareholder) v. *(Corporation)*
813 A.2d 1118 (Del.2003)

A CORPORATION MUST PROVIDE A COMPELLING JUSTIFICATION FOR A DEFENSIVE MEASURE

■ **INSTANT FACTS** MM Companies, Inc. (P) sued Liquid Audio, Inc. (D), challenging the defendant's decision to expand its board of directors and appoint two new directors to impede MM's (P) takeover attempts.

■ **BLACK LETTER RULE** When a plaintiff establishes that the primary purpose for board action was to impede or interfere with the effectiveness of the shareholders' vote, the burden shifts to the board to prove a compelling justification for the board's actions.

■ PROCEDURAL BASIS

On appeal to review a chancery court judgment for the defendant.

■ FACTS

Liquid Audio, Inc. (D) is a Delaware corporation that provides software and services for the digital transmission of music over the Internet. MM Companies, Inc. (P) is part of a group that owns approximately seven percent of Liquid Audio's (D) common stock. For about a year, MM (P) sought control of Liquid Audio (D) and offered to purchase the company for three dollars per share. Liquid Audio (D) rejected the proposal. At the time of the proposal, Liquid Audio's (D) board of directors consisted of five members. Three of those directors were not elected by the shareholders, but rather were appointed by the board. MM (P) had earlier requested that Liquid Audio (D) convene a special meeting of the stockholders to hold an election, but Liquid Audio (D) denied the request. Under Liquid Audio's (D) bylaws, two directors were up for reelection the next year, and MM (P) announced its intention to nominate two directors to fill those seats when their terms expired. MM (P) thereafter notified Liquid Audio (D) that it intended to propose amendments to the bylaws at the annual meeting, expanding the board of directors from five members to nine.

After another offer to acquire Liquid Audio (D) was rejected, MM (P) submitted a written demand for a list of all shareholders. When Liquid Audio (D) failed to respond, MM (P) sued to enforce its right of inspection of the corporate books and records. While that action was pending, MM (P) filed a proxy statement with the Securities and Exchange Commission indicating its intent to take over the corporation by expanding the board of directors from five to nine members. Three days later, Liquid Audio (D) announced a stock-for-stock merger transaction with Alliance Entertainment Corp., postponing its annual meeting and announcing a special meeting to vote on the merger. MM (P) amended its complaint to direct Liquid Audio (D) to hold an annual meeting. After trial, the chancery court ordered Liquid Audio (D) to hold the annual meeting. Before the annual meeting, however, Liquid Audio (D) amended its bylaws to expand the size of the board of directors from five to seven members, appointing two hand-selected directors whose term would not expire for several years. MM (P) sued, challenging the amendment. MM (P) claimed that it interfered with its nomination of the two directors to fill vacancies on the board, because some shareholders may believe that their election would not change control of the board, so voting would be fruitless. At the annual meeting, MM's (P) two nominees were indeed elected, but the board disapproved MM's (P) takeover proposal to expand the board by four members and appoint its four additional nominees to the board. MM (P) then filed an amended lawsuit challenging Liquid Audio's (D) appointment of the two directors after the board was expanded to seven members, claiming its timing frustrated MM's (P) efforts to gain a "substantial presence" on the board of directors. After discovery, the chancery court concluded that the primary purpose of Liquid Audio's (D) amendment of its bylaws and the appointment of two new directors was to impede an effective vote on MM's (P) nominees and diminish their influence on the board. Nonetheless, the court denied MM's (P) relief, finding that the board's action was not illegal under *Blasius Industries, Inc. v. Atlas Corp.*, 564 A.2d 651 (Del.Ch.Ct.1988), or *Unocal Corp. v. Mesa Petroleum Co.*, 493 A.2d 946 (Del.1985).

■ ISSUE

When the primary purpose for board action is to impede or interfere with the effectiveness of the shareholders' vote, must the corporation provide a compelling justification for its actions?

■ DECISION AND RATIONALE

(Holland, J.) Yes. The shareholders' right to vote for the election of directors, who engage in the management of the corporation, is fundamental to the allocation of power within corporate governance. If shareholders are unhappy with the performance of the corporation's directors, their primary remedy is to replace them through a proper vote. Accordingly, corporate democracy may not be subverted by manipulating the corporate machinery to effectively frustrate the shareholders' rights to elect directors.

When reviewing claims of corporate manipulation, courts must give due deference to the business judgments of the directors and presume that corporate action is made "on an informed basis, in good faith and in the honest belief that the action taken was in the best interests of the company." The burden is on the challenging shareholders to overcome this presumption. If the presumption is not rebutted, the court may not substitute its judgment for that of the corporation if the action is reasonable.

Under *Blasius*, however, when a plaintiff establishes that the primary purpose for the board action was to impede or interfere with the effectiveness of the shareholders' vote, the burden shifts to the board to prove a compelling justification for the board's actions. While this review is rarely applied, the board here engaged in a defensive measure bearing on control of the board. Under such circumstances, the board has the burden of justifying its actions using the *Unocal* standards. *Unocal* requires that any defensive measure be "proportionate and reasonable in relation to the threat posed." The chancery court held that the board's actions were not preclusive or coercive, placing the focus of the inquiry on the reasonableness of the actions rather than their proportionality to the threat. However, because of the court's conclusion that the board's purpose was to interfere with the shareholders' voting rights, the burden shifts to the corporation to establish a compelling justification for its defensive measures. Applying *Blasius* within the *Unocal* standard of review, the board's burden must be met before proportionality and reasonableness can be considered. Here, the defendants failed to meet this threshold burden, and the court should not have reached the *Unocal* review. Reversed and remanded.

Analysis:

While courts have traditionally afforded considerable latitude to directors in matters relating to the operation of the corporation, judicial attitudes have become more scrutinizing in the wake of well-publicized corporate scandals, such as Enron and Worldcom. No longer do directors enjoy the benefit of unbridled discretion, but rather they must generally establish disinterest in their actions.

CASE VOCABULARY:

MERGER: The absorption of one company (especially a corporation) that ceases to exist into another that retains its own name and identity and acquires the assets and liabilities of the former.

Fletcher v. Atex, Inc.

(*Injured Consumer*) v. (*Manufacturer*)
68 F.3d 1451 (2d Cir.1995)

THE CORPORATE VEIL CAN BE PIERCED IF THE CORPORATION AND THE SHAREHOLDER OPERATED AS A SINGLE ECONOMIC ENTITY AND THERE WAS AN OVERALL ELEMENT OF UNFAIRNESS PRESENT

■ **INSTANT FACTS** Fletcher (P) was allegedly injured by an Atex (D) keyboard and sought to pierce the corporate veil to hold Atex's (D) parent company, Kodak (D), liable.

■ **BLACK LETTER RULE** To prevail on an alter ego theory of liability, it must be established that the corporation and the shareholder acted as a single economic entity and that there is an element of injustice or unfairness present.

■ PROCEDURAL BASIS

Appeal from summary judgment in favor of defendant Kodak (D) on Fletcher's (P) attempt to pierce the corporate veil.

■ FACTS

On December 4, 1992, Fletcher (P) filed suit against Atex, Inc. (D) and its parent, Eastman Kodak Company (D), for repetitive stress injuries allegedly caused by the use of Atex (D) computer keyboards. [Doc, it hurts when I use the keyboard. R—Don't use the keyboard.] From 1981 until December 1992, Atex (D) was a wholly-owned subsidiary of Kodak (D). In December 1992, Atex (D) sold all its assets to a third party and changed its name to 805 Middlesex Corp. Kodak (D) continues to be the sole shareholder of 805 Middlesex Corp. Kodak (D) made a motion for summary judgment which was opposed by Fletcher (D) who argued a genuine issue of material fact existed as to whether Atex (D) was merely an alter ego of Kodak (D). The district court granted Kodak's motion.

■ ISSUE

Is summary judgment appropriate on an alter ego theory of liability when the plaintiff failed to show that the corporation and shareholder operated as a single economic entity and that an element of injustice was present?

■ DECISION AND RATIONALE

(Cabranes, C.J.) Yes. Fletcher (P) claims the district court erred in granting Kodak (D) summary judgment on the alter ego theory of liability. Under New York choice of law principles, the law of the state of incorporation determines when the corporate form will be ignored and shareholders will be held liable. Atex (D) was a Delaware corporation so Delaware law determines whether the corporate veil can be pierced. Under the alter ego theory, Fletcher (P) must show that the parent and the subsidiary "operated as a single economic entity" and that an element of injustice or unfairness is present. The alter ego theory of liability does not require a showing of fraud as the lower court suggests. In determining whether a parent and subsidiary operate as a single economic entity, a number of factors should be considered. These include whether the corporation was adequately capitalized, whether the corporation was solvent, whether corporate records were kept, and other formalities were observed, whether a dominant shareholder siphoned corporate funds, and whether, in general, the corporation simply functioned as a facade for the dominant shareholder. Fletcher (P) faces a difficult task in seeking to persuade a Delaware court to disregard the corporate structure. Kodak (D) has shown that Atex (D) followed corporate formalities, and Fletcher (P) has offered no evidence to the contrary. Fletcher (P) argues that Kodak (D) exercised domination over Atex (D) because Kodak (D) used a cash management system. All of Kodak's (D) subsidiaries participated in such a system which involves each subsidiary maintaining a zero-balance bank account. Funds transferred from the subsidiary accounts are recorded as credits to the subsidiary, and when the subsidiary needs funds, they are transferred back. Courts generally refuse to find alter ego liability where a cash management system is used. Accounting records in such a system always reflect indebtedness of one entity to another and this is not the equivalent of intermingling funds. Fletcher (P) also argues that Kodak (D) dominated Atex (D) because Atex (D) required Kodak's (D) approval before major business decisions were made. This is typical of a parent corporation and does not mean the two corporations are "a single economic entity." Fletcher's (P) argument that Kodak (D) dominated the Atex (D) board of directors also fails. Between 1981 and 1988, there was only one director common to both Atex (D) and Kodak (D). This is entirely insufficient to raise a question of fact on the issue of domination. Fletcher (D) also argues that descriptions about the relationship between Atex (D) and Kodak (D) in Kodak's (D) promotional literature justify piercing the corporate veil. Various Kodak (D) documents describe a merger between Kodak (D) and Atex (D) and suggested that Atex (D) is a division of Kodak (D). Atex (D) paperwork and packaging materials also frequently displayed the Kodak (D) logo. Atex (D) never actually merged with Kodak (D), nor was it actually a division of Kodak (D). These statements in Kodak (D) documents and the use of the Kodak (D) logo are not alone evidence that the two companies operated as a "single economic entity." Other cases have held that boastful advertising does not prove that corporate identities were ignored. Finally, even if Fletcher (P) did raise a factual question about Kodak's (D) domination of Atex (D) summary judgment would still be appropriate because Fletcher (P) offered no evidence on the second prong of the alter ego analysis. This requires evidence of an overall element of injustice or unfairness that would result from respecting the two companies corporate separateness. Fletcher's (D) assertions, without more, are not evidence. Affirmed.

Analysis:

Presumably Fletcher (P) sought to pierce the "corporate veil" because he anticipated that he would have difficulty recovering a judgment against Atex (D). This is the usual reason for attempting to pierce the veil, to get at a deeper pocket. Fletcher's (P) main argument here was that Atex (D) was merely an alter ego of Kodak (D) because it was dominated and controlled by Kodak (D). The court concluded, however, that there was no evidence of injustice or unfairness. Basically, in order to pierce the corporate veil on an alter-ego theory, the courts will need to find that the alleged alter ego virtually completely ignored the corporate form, that it operated the subsidiary corporation as if it were the parent, and that it would be unfair not to pierce the veil.

Walkovszky v. Carlton

(Injured Party) v. *(Stockholder)*
18 N.Y.2d 414, 223 N.E.2d 6 (App.1966)

THE CORPORATE VEIL WILL BE PIERCED WHERE THE CORPORATION IS A DUMMY FOR ITS STOCKHOLDERS

■ INSTANT FACTS Walkovszky (P) was hit by a taxicab and sought to hold the stockholder personally liable for his injuries.

■ BLACK LETTER RULE For personal liability to attach to stockholders, it must be shown that the stockholders were actually carrying on the business in their individual capacity for personal rather than corporate ends.

■ PROCEDURAL BASIS

Appeal from reversal of dismissal of complaint for failure to state a claim.

■ FACTS

Walkovszky (P) was severely injured when he was hit by a taxicab owned by Seon Cab Corporation (D). The individual defendant, Carlton (D), is the stockholder of 10 corporations, including Seon, each of which has two cabs registered in its name and each cab has only the minimum liability insurance ($10,000) required by law. Basically, each corporation has little additional capital other than the two cabs. Walkovszky (P) brought suit and sought to hold Carlton (D) and the other shareholders personally liable for his injury, alleging that the various corporations were operated as a single entity, unit and enterprise, and that the entire structure was a sham to avoid liability.

■ ISSUE

To pierce the corporate veil, must it be shown that the corporation was a dummy for its stockholders who were actually carrying on the business in their personal capacity for personal rather than corporate ends?

■ DECISION AND RATIONALE

(Fuld, J.) Yes. The law allows the incorporation of businesses to enable its owners to escape personal liability. However, this is not without limits, and the courts will pierce the corporate veil whenever necessary to prevent fraud or achieve equity. In making this determination, courts are guided by the rules of agency. When someone uses the corporation to further his own rather than the corporation's business, he will be responsible for the corporation's acts under the principle of *respondeat superior.* In this case, Walkovszky (P) alleged that none of the corporations had a separate existence, and they have all been named as defendants. It is one thing to assert that a corporation is a fragment of a larger combination of corporations, and another to claim that the corporation is a "dummy" for its stockholders who are carrying on the business in their personal capacities for personal ends. In the first case, only the larger corporate entity would be liable, in the second, the stockholder would be personally liable. It is possible for a plaintiff to allege both theories. Here, however, the allegations in the complaint are inadequate to state a cause of action against Carlton (P) individually. There was no allegation that Carlton (D) was conducting business in his individual capacity. The corporate form cannot be disregarded merely because the assets of the corporation and its insurance are insufficient to assure

Walkovszky (P) the recovery sought. If the minimum insurance required by law is inadequate to protect the public, the remedy is with the legislature and not with the courts. It may be wise to require cabs to carry more insurance, but this is the legislature's decision to make, not the courts. We are not saying that it would be impossible for Walkovszky (P) to state a valid claim against Carlton (D). We are merely saying that he has not done so here. The complaint is lacking sufficiently particularized statements that Carlton (D) was actually doing business in his individual capacity, shuttling personal funds in and out of the corporations, without regard to formality. In fact, the principle relied upon in the complaint is not agency but fraud. This action cannot stand because it is not fraudulent for an owner of a cab company to maintain several different corporations with the minimum insurance required by law. Reversed.

■ DISSENT

(Keating, J.) Carlton (D) is the principal shareholder of the defendant corporations. From their inception, these corporations were intentionally undercapitalized for the purpose of avoiding liability for accidents which were bound to happen in the operation of a large fleet of taxis. During the course of the business, all income was drained from the corporation to avoid liability. The policy of this State is to afford those engaged in business the privilege of limited liability through the use of the corporate form. This policy, however, is not so strong that it will permit the privilege to continue if it is abused, and the corporation is operated irresponsibly at a cost to the public. The shareholders here should be held personally liable. If the capital of the corporation is illusory or trifling compared with the risks of loss, the corporation should be denied separate entity privilege.

Analysis:

Walkovszky's (P) case was dismissed for failure to state a claim. But, if the statute of limitations had not yet run, could he amend his complaint and allege facts to show that Carlton (D) and others effectively conducted the business in their individual capacities? In fact, that is exactly what happened. The amended complaint was held to state a valid cause of action. Recall the case of *Fletcher v. Atex, Inc.* where the court considered the alter ego theory. One of the factors considered in *Fletcher* was whether the corporation was adequately capitalized for the corporate undertaking. The dissent here seizes on this factor to find that the corporate veil should be pierced. Not only were the corporations undercapitalized, they were intentionally undercapitalized by Carlton (D) in the way they were organized and insured, and by taking the profits out of the companies. In the later case, the position taken by the dissent prevailed.

■ CASE VOCABULARY

RESPONDEAT SUPERIOR: The doctrine that the principal or master is responsible for certain acts of the agent or servant. The master is responsible for the agent's wrongs toward those to whom the master owes a duty of care.

Minton v. Cavaney

(*Parents of Child*) v. (*Director*)
56 Cal.2d 576, 364 P.2d 473 (1961)

SHAREHOLDERS MAY BE HELD LIABLE FOR THE DEBTS OF THE CORPORATION IF THEY PROVIDE INADEQUATE CAPITALIZATION AND THEY ACTIVELY PARTICIPATE IN CORPORATE AFFAIRS

■ **INSTANT FACTS** The Mintons' (P) daughter drowned in a pool owned by Seminole Hot Springs Corporation. They sought to hold Seminole's director liable for her death.

■ **BLACK LETTER RULE** The corporate veil can be pierced where the shareholders undercapitalize the corporation and actively participate in the conduct of corporate affairs.

■ PROCEDURAL BASIS

Appeal from judgment in favor of the Mintons (P) holding Cavaney (D) personally liable for the Corporation's debts.

■ FACTS

The Seminole Hot Springs Corporation was incorporated in California in 1954 and operated a swimming pool that it leased from the pool's owner. The Mintons' (P) daughter drowned in the pool, and they recovered a judgment for $10,000 against Seminole which remains unsatisfied. The Mintons then sued to hold Cavaney (D) personally liable for the Seminole judgment. At the time of the suit, Cavaney (D) had died, so his widow was substituted as defendant. Cavaney (D) was a director, secretary, and treasurer of Seminole. Several months after the drowning, Cavaney (D) applied for permission to issue three shares of Seminole stock, one to Cavaney (D) and the remaining two shares to other individuals. The commissioner of corporations refused to issue these shares, and no shares were ever issued. Cavaney (D), an attorney, kept the records of Seminole at his office for a time. During litigation, Cavaney (D) stated that the corporation did not have any assets and was duly organized but never functioned as a corporation.

■ ISSUE

May a shareholder be held liable for the debts of a corporation where he actively participates in conduct of the corporation and the corporation is not adequately capitalized?

■ DECISION AND RATIONALE

(Traynor, J.) Yes. Cavaney (D) argues he should not be held liable under the alter ego doctrine because the Mintons (P) failed to show that there was (1) such a unity of interest and ownership that the separate personalities of the corporation and the individual no longer exist and (2) that if the acts were treated as those of the corporation alone, an inequitable result would follow. The shareholders of a corporation are personally liable when they treat the assets of the corporation as their own, when they hold themselves out as personally liable, or when they provide inadequate capitalization and actively participate in the conduct of corporate affairs. In this case, there was no attempt to provide adequate capitalization for the corporation. Seminole only leased the pool, and that lease was terminated for failure to pay rent. Its capital was trifling compared to the risk of loss. The evidence that Cavaney (D) was to receive one-third of the shares to be issued supports an inference that he was an equitable owner. The fact that he kept the corporate records at his office supports an inference that he participated in the conduct of the business. His statement that he was only a "temporary" director for "accommodation" was not required to be believed by the trial court. A person may not free himself of the responsibilities of that office in this manner. In this current action against Cavaney (D), the Mintons (P) presented no evidence on the issue of Seminole's negligence or the amount of damages. They relied solely on the judgment against Seminole. Cavaney (D) is correct in arguing that he or his estate cannot be held liable for the debts of Seminole without an opportunity to re-litigate these issues. Cavaney (D) was not a party to the original action against Seminole Corporation, and the judgment in that action is not binding against him unless he controlled the litigation leading to the judgment. Reversed.

Analysis:

If the Mintons (P) had joined Cavaney (D) in the original action, Cavaney (D) would have had an opportunity to defend. The corporation likely defaulted. Thus, Cavaney (D) cannot be held to be responsible for the original judgment unless he is given a full and fair opportunity to contest Minton's (P) case. The court here carefully explains the reasons why the veil should be pierced and Cavaney (D) should be held liable only to conclude that he cannot be held liable, because he was not a party to the original action against Seminole. The court found that several factors weighed in favor of piercing the veil. One important one was that the corporation was inadequately capitalized. At least one court has found that inadequate capitalization alone may be a basis for holding a parent corporation liable for acts of its subsidiary.

Sea–Land Services v. Pepper Source

(*Creditor*) v. (*Sham Corporation*)
993 F.2d 1309 (7th Cir.1993)

UNJUST ENRICHMENT AND MANIPULATING CORPORATE FUNDS ARE SUFFICIENT "WRONGS" TO PIERCE THE CORPORATE VEIL

■ **INSTANT FACTS** After losing on remand, Marchese (D) appealed the court's finding that injustice would result if the corporate form was respected.

■ **BLACK LETTER RULE** Manipulating corporate funds to avoid creditors and unjust enrichment are a sufficient showing of additional wrongs to justify piercing the corporate veil.

■ PROCEDURAL BASIS

Appeal after Marchese (D) was defeated on remand.

■ FACTS

Sea-Land (P) won a default judgment against Pepper Source (D). It was unable to collect on this judgment so it sought to pierce the corporate veil and hold Marchese (D), the sole shareholder of Pepper Source, personally liable. Sea-Land (P) also sought to hold Marchese's (D) other corporations liable on the judgment. Sea-Land (P) won, the case was appealed. On appeal, the court remanded it for further fact finding as to whether Sea-Land had established enough to pierce the corporate veil. On remand from the first Sea–Land case, the court awarded Sea-Land (P) $118,132.61 in damages. The court found it had satisfied the second prong of the veil-piercing test by establishing wrongs beyond its inability to collect on its judgment.

■ ISSUE

Is a showing of unjust enrichment and manipulating corporate funds to avoid creditors sufficient to satisfy the requirement of a showing of additional wrongs beyond the inability to collect a judgment?

■ DECISION AND RATIONALE

(Timbers, J.) We agree with the trial court that Sea-Land (P) established additional wrongs to justify piercing the corporate veil. Sea-Land (P) demonstrated that Marchese (D) and his corporations were unjustly enriched in that they have received money which in equity belongs to someone else. Marchese (D) obtained many benefits at the expense of Sea-Land (P), the IRS, and other creditors. Marchese (D) used Pepper Source (D) funds to pay personal expenses and expenses of his other corporations. This left Pepper Source (D) with insufficient funds to satisfy creditors. Marchese (D) was thus unjustly enriched by his manipulation of corporate funds. Sea-Land also demonstrated that Marchese (D) used his corporations as playthings to avoid paying creditors. Accountants testified that Marchese (D) used corporate funds to pay personal expenses and took "shareholder loans" from the corporations to pay these expenses. His practices were replete with violations of the tax code. Marchese (D) was the dominant force behind all of his corporations and was responsible for manipulating funds to avoid creditors. The veil was properly pierced. Marchese (D) asserts that Sea-Land (P) failed to satisfy the requirement that a nexus exists between its injuries and the fraud or injustice committed by Marchese

(D). This argument fails because Marchese's (D) intentional financial maneuvering caused Sea-Lands's (P) inability to collect on its default judgment.

Analysis:

Sea-Land (P) had already established the first prong of the piercing-the-corporate-veil test by showing that there was such a unity of ownership and interest that the separate personalities of the corporation and the individual no longer existed. Sea-Land still needed to show that adherence to the fiction of separate corporate existence would sanction a fraud or promote injustice. This prong required a showing of some wrong in addition to the inability to collect on a judgment. Sea-Land (P) established this additional wrong by showing that Marchese (D) was unjustly enriched and manipulated the corporations to avoid creditors.

CHAPTER FIVE

Shareholder Informational Rights and Proxy Voting

Saito v. McKesson HBOC, Inc.

Instant Facts: Saito (P), a stockholder, sought inspection of McKesson HBOC (D) books and records to determine whether the corporation engaged in any wrongdoing.

Black Letter Rule: A stockholder has the right to make a written demand to inspect corporate books and records for a purpose reasonably related to such person's interest as a stockholder.

Mills v. Electric Auto–Lite Co.

Instant Facts: A corporation's minority shareholders brought a derivative action to set aside a merger between the corporation and the corporation that was its majority shareholder by charging that the proxy solicitation for the merger was materially incorrect in that it failed to mention the corporation's board of directors was controlled by majority shareholder corporation.

Black Letter Rule: Where there has been a finding of materiality, a shareholder has made a sufficient showing of causal relationship between the violation and the injury if he proves the proxy solicitation was an essential link in the accomplishment of the transaction.

Virginia Bankshares, Inc. v. Sandberg

Instant Facts: A shareholder, who withheld her proxy in a merger vote, sought damages from the bank holding company that acquired her shares, claiming that proxies were solicited by means of materially false or misleading statements because the board of directors did not believe their own assertion that the tender price was "high."

Black Letter Rule: (1) Knowingly false statements of reasons, opinion, or belief, even though conclusory in form, may be actionable under § 14(a) as misstatements of material fact; and (2) Minority shareholders whose vote is unnecessary to complete the transaction at issue must prove causation of damages in a § 14(a) suit.

Roosevelt v. E.I. Du Pont de Nemours & Co.

Instant Facts: A shareholder brought suit against a corporation under 14(a) claiming that the company improperly excluded her proposal from the annual proxy materials.

Black Letter Rule: A company may exclude a shareholder's proposal from the annual meeting proxy materials under the "ordinary business" exception if the proposal relates to the timetable for implementing corporate policy.

Rosenfeld v. Fairchild Engine and Airplane Corp.

Instant Facts: A stockholder brought a derivative action seeking to compel the return of monies paid out of the corporate treasury to reimburse both sides in a proxy contest for their expenses.

Black Letter Rule: In a contest over policy, as compared to a personal power contest, corporate directors acting in good faith have the right to make reasonable and proper expenditures from the corporate treasury for the purpose of persuading the stockholders and soliciting their support; and shareholders have the right to ratify reimbursement for such expenses incurred by non-directors.

Saito v. McKesson HBOC, Inc.

(*Stockholder*) v. (*Corporation*)
806 A.2d 113 (Del.2002)

A STOCKHOLDER'S RIGHT TO INSPECT CORPORATE BOOKS AND RECORDS IS BROAD

■ **INSTANT FACTS** Saito (P), a stockholder, sought inspection of McKesson HBOC (D) books and records to determine whether the corporation engaged in any wrongdoing.

■ **BLACK LETTER RULE** A stockholder has the right to make a written demand to inspect corporate books and records for a purpose reasonably related to such person's interest as a stockholder.

■ PROCEDURAL BASIS

On appeal to review a chancery court decision limiting the scope of the plaintiff's right to inspect corporate records.

■ FACTS

Saito (P) purchased McKesson stock three days after McKesson Corporation entered into a stock merger with HBO & Company (HBOC), becoming McKesson HBOC, Inc. (D). HBOC continued to operate as a separate, wholly owned subsidiary of McKesson HBOC (D). In the months that followed, McKesson HBOC (D) made several financial restatements that reduced its revenues by $327 million for the three prior fiscal years due to accounting irregularities in HBOC. Saito (P) joined three other shareholders in a derivative suit charging the McKesson directors with breach of fiduciary duty for failure to discover and remedy the irregularities before the merger. The chancery court dismissed the complaint without prejudice and suggested that the plaintiffs invoke 8 Del. C. § 220 to inspect the company's books and records to obtain the information to maintain a derivative suit.

Saito (P) did so, demanding access to accounting documents relating to HBOC's financial condition before the merger; communications among McKesson, HBOC and their advisors concerning HBOC's accounting practices; and discussions between the companies' boards of directors pertaining to reports representing HBOC's accounting practices and financial condition. Saito (P) justified these demands as necessary to uncover potential wrongdoing. After trial, the chancery court acknowledged the proper purpose for Saito's (P) demand, but held that his demand must be limited to any wrongdoing that occurred after his purchase of McKesson stock. The demand further excluded records demonstrating wrongdoing by the companies' third-party advisors and HBOC, since he was not an HBOC shareholder.

■ ISSUE

Is a stockholder's right to inspect corporate books and records limited by the date of the records or their sources?

■ DECISION AND RATIONALE

(Berger, J.) No. Under 8 Del. C. § 220, a stockholder has the right to make a written demand to inspect corporate books and records for "a purpose reasonably related to such person's interest as a stockholder." The right of inspection is limited, however, to review of those records necessary and essential to accomplish the stated purpose. The chancery court recognized the detection of potential wrongdoing as a proper purpose, but limited the right of inspection to those records relating to wrongdoing after the date of the stock purchase; those records pertaining only to the corporation's wrongdoing rather than a third party; and those records regarding McKesson's wrongdoing, since he was not an HBOC stockholder.

Although a plaintiff in a derivative suit must be a stockholder at the time the transaction complained of occurs, there is no temporal limitation on the right of inspection. If books and records predating the alleged wrongdoing are reasonably related to the person's interest as a stockholder, they fall within the right of inspection. Even when the wrongdoing predates the stock purchase, the stockholder may have a right of inspection, for the wrongdoing may constitute a continuing wrong that both predates and postdates the stock purchase. "If activities that occurred before the purchase date are 'reasonably related' to the stockholder's interest as a stockholder, then the stockholder should be given access to records necessary to an understanding of those activities."

Just as the date of the stock purchase does not affect the right of inspection, neither does the source of the documents. However, third-party documents must be reasonably related to the stockholder's interest and necessary to establish the stockholder's proper purpose justifying the inspection. It is not clear whether the chancery court improperly limited the right of inspection of third-party documents because of their sources or properly restricted access because they were unnecessary. On remand, the court must make this clarification.

Finally, Saito (D) is not a stockholder in HBOC, which operates after the merger as a wholly owned subsidiary of the defendant. A stockholder of a parent corporation ordinarily does not have a right of inspection of the books and records of a subsidiary of which he is not a stockholder. To the extent that HBOC books and records have not been disclosed to McKesson or McKesson HBOC (D), Saito (P) has no right of inspection.

Affirmed in part, reversed in part, and remanded.

Analysis:

The right to inspect corporate books and records is an acknowledgement of the shareholder's ownership interest in the corporation. At common law, shareholders maintained a right to review corporate records for a variety of proper purposes, such as to investigate mismanagement and determine the economic value of the corporation. Today, most states have adopted legislation codifying the common law right of inspection.

■ CASE VOCABULARY

DERIVATIVE ACTION: A suit by a beneficiary of a fiduciary to enforce a right belonging to the fiduciary; especially, a suit asserted by a shareholder on the corporation's behalf against a third party (usually a corporate officer) because of the corporation's failure to take some action against the third party.

PARENT CORPORATION: A corporation that has a controlling interest in another corporation (called a subsidiary corporation), usually through ownership of more than one-half the voting stock.

SUBSIDIARY CORPORATION: A corporation in which a parent corporation has a controlling share.

Mills v. Electric Auto–Lite Co.

(*Shareholder*) v. (*Corporation*)

396 U.S. 375 (1970)

A PRIVATE ACTION UNDER SECTION 14(a) OF THE 1934 SECURITIES EXCHANGE ACT HAS ONLY TWO ELEMENTS: 1) MATERIALITY; AND 2) A NEXUS BETWEEN THE PROXY AND THE TRANSACTION

■ **INSTANT FACTS** A corporation's minority shareholders brought a derivative action to set aside a merger between the corporation and the corporation that was its majority shareholder by charging that the proxy solicitation for the merger was materially incorrect in that it failed to mention the corporation's board of directors was controlled by majority shareholder corporation.

■ **BLACK LETTER RULE** Where there has been a finding of materiality, a shareholder has made a sufficient showing of causal relationship between the violation and the injury if he proves the proxy solicitation was an essential link in the accomplishment of the transaction.

■ PROCEDURAL BASIS

Appeal to the United State Supreme Court challenging the holding of the Court of Appeals requiring a hearing on the issue of the fairness of the transaction.

■ FACTS

Mills (P), a shareholder in Electric Auto–Lite Co. (Auto-Lite) (D), brought a derivative action and one on behalf of minority shareholders as a class to set aside a merger between Auto–Lite (D) and Mergenthaler Linotype Co. (Mergenthaler), the majority owner of Auto-Lite's common stock. Mills (P) charged that the proxy solicitation for the merger by Auto-Lite's (D) management was materially misleading and violated § 14 (a) of the Securities Exchange Act of 1934 and Rule 14a-9. Mills (P) claimed that Auto-Lite's (D) board of directors recommended the merger to the company's shareholders without disclosing that the directors were controlled by Mergenthaler. The District Court ruled that the omission from the proxy statement was material, and that the omission led to the completion of the merger because the votes of the minority shareholders were necessary to complete the transactions. According to the District Court, this established the causal link between the misstatement and the § 14(a) violation. The Court of Appeals affirmed, but held it was necessary to resolve at trial whether there was a causal relationship between the deficiency in the proxy statement and the merger. The Court of Appeals held that the issue was to be determined by proof of fairness of the merger; if Auto-Lite could prove the fairness of the merger, there was no deficiency in the proxy statement.

■ ISSUE

Must a plaintiff in a private cause of action under Section 14(a) of the 1934 Securities Exchange Act prove that the material defect in the proxy caused the injury?

■ DECISION AND RATIONALE

(Harlan, J.) No. Where there has been a finding of materiality, a shareholder has made a sufficient showing of causal relationship between the violation and the injury if he proves the proxy solicitation was an essential link in the accomplishment of the transaction. The decision below permits all liability to be foreclosed on the basis of a finding that the merger was fair. The import of this holding would have many consequences that frustrate the policies behind the implied private cause of action. First, it allows the judicial appraisal of a merger's merits to be substituted for the actual and informed vote of the stockholders. Second, it insulates from private redress violations relating to matters other than the merger. Further, it places an extra burden on small shareholders wishing to bring an action under § 14(a), thus discouraging the private enforcement meant to supplement SEC action. Nothing in the statute or the rules promulgated by the SEC require such a frustration of congressional policy. Use of a solicitation that is materially misleading is itself a violation of law. Where the misstatement or omission in a proxy statement has been shown to be "material," as it was here, that determination embodies a conclusion that the defect was of such a character that it might have been considered important by a reasonable investor who was deciding how to vote. There is no need to supplement this requirement with a requirement of proof of whether the defect actually had a decisive effect on the wrong. Our holding that Mills (D) has established his case by showing that proxies necessary to approval of the merger were obtained by a material defect in the proxy statement implies nothing about the form of relief that should be granted. In devising retrospective relief, a court should consider the same factors that it would in a case of fraud. The fairness of the merger is one such factor. Setting aside the merger is one possible form of relief, but such a determination should hinge whether setting aside the merger would be in the best interests of the shareholders as a whole. Monetary relief may be possible, but damages are recoverable only to the extent they are proved. Vacated and remanded.

Analysis:

The thrust of the Court's holding is, essentially, that a plaintiff in a § 14(a) private cause of action need not prove causation as a separate element. After this case, if a plaintiff proves a material defect in the proxy statement, and that the proxy was necessary to complete the proposed transaction, the only issue left to be determined is what remedy to apply. The defendant cannot rebut in any fashion. In divorcing the § 14(a) analysis from that of common law fraud, the Court collapses the issue of causation into the finding of materiality. The Court has good reason for its holding. Simply put, causation is too difficult to prove when thousands of investors are involved. Requiring causation would place a plaintiff in the position of having to call countless witnesses at great expense. The Court advances the objectives of the statute by deciding the issue in favor of those it was intended to protect, the investors.

Virginia Bankshares, Inc. v. Sandberg

(*Corporation*) v. (*Shareholder*)

501 U.S. 1083 (1991)

STATEMENTS OF REASONS, OPINIONS, OR BELIEFS MAY BE ACTIONABLE UNDER § 14(a) OF THE SECURITIES AND EXCHANGE ACT

■ **INSTANT FACTS** A shareholder, who withheld her proxy in a merger vote, sought damages from the bank holding company that acquired her shares, claiming that proxies were solicited by means of materially false or misleading statements because the board of directors did not believe their own assertion that the tender price was "high."

■ **BLACK LETTER RULE** (1) Knowingly false statements of reasons, opinion, or belief, even though conclusory in form, may be actionable under § 14(a) as misstatements of material fact; and (2) Minority shareholders whose vote is unnecessary to complete the transaction at issue must prove causation of damages in a § 14(a) suit.

■ PROCEDURAL BASIS

Appeal to the United States Supreme Court challenging the decision of the Fourth Circuit to affirm the jury's verdict.

■ FACTS

First American Bankshares, Inc. (FABI) (D), a bank holding company, proposed a "freeze-out" merger, in which First American Bank of Virginia (First American) would be merged into Virginia Bankshares, Inc. (VBI) (D), a wholly owned subsidiary of FABI (D) and an 85% shareholder in First American. First American's directors approved a price of $42 a share for the minority stockholders, who would lose their interests in the Bank after the merger. Because VBI held such a stake in First American, Virginia law did not require the minority shareholders to approve of the merger. First American's directors nevertheless solicited proxies for voting on the proposal. Their proxy statement, which recommended the merger, stated that the plan had been approved because it presented an opportunity for the minority shareholders to receive a "high" value for their stock. The directors also stated the merger was "fair." Sandberg (P) did not give the corporation her proxy, and after the merger, she filed suit in District Court, seeking damages from FABI (D) and VBI (D) for soliciting proxies in violation of § 14 (a) of the Securities Exchange Act of 1934 and SEC Rule 14a-9. Sandberg (P) claimed that the directors did not believe the price offer was "high" or merger "fair," despite their statements to the contrary in the proxy solicitation. A jury awarded her an amount equal to the difference between the offered price and her stock's true value. The Court of Appeals affirmed, holding that Sandberg (P) could maintain her cause of action even though her votes were not necessary to effectuate the merger.

■ ISSUE

May a conclusory statement explaining directors' reasons for recommending certain corporate actions be materially misleading within the meaning of Rule 14a-9; and can damages compensable under § 14(a) be shown by a member of a class of minority shareholders whose votes are not required by law to authorize the transaction?

DECISION AND RATIONALE

(Souter, J.) Yes; and no. First, knowingly false statements of reasons, opinion, or belief, even though conclusory in form, may be actionable under § 14(a) as misstatements of material fact. The fact that such statements may be materially significant raises no serious issue. A share owner faced with a proxy request will think it important to know the directors' beliefs about the course they recommend. We believe that statements of reasons, opinions, or beliefs are statements "with respect to material facts" under Rule 14a-9. Such statements are factual in two senses: as statements that the directors actually act for the reasons given or hold the belief given; and as statements about the subject matter of the reason or belief expressed. VBI and FABI (D) argue that the statements in this case expressed a reason in indefinite terms, "high" and "fair." However this ignores the fact that these conclusory statements rest on a factual basis that justifies them as accurate. These statements can be made with knowledge of their truth or falsity, just like more definite statements. Whether $42 was "high," and the merger "fair" depended on provable facts about First American's assets, market value, etc. In proving both, that the statements were misleading about its subject matter and the false expression of the director's reasons, Sandberg (P) provided evidence that First American's appreciated real estate holdings eliminated any premium offered by a $42 price. Sandberg (P) also showed that the market valuation was based on FABI's (P) domination of the market. These facts, along with other evidence, are enough to conclude that it was misleading to call $42 "high." We additionally hold, however, that proof of mere disbelief or belief undisclosed does not suffice for liability under § 14(a). There must also be proof, by objective evidence, that the statements assert something false or misleading about the subject matter. Our discussion above established that the statements themselves were false, for Sandberg (P) offered evidence that the company was worth more than $42 per share. VBI (D) and FABI (D) argue that liability should not be imposed where proxy statements disclose the facts upon which the statements were based. It is true that publishing accurate facts in a proxy statement can render a misleading proposition immaterial. The jury, however, was unconvinced that the factual statements contained in the proxy sufficiently neutralized the misleading statement. Moreover, the proxy withheld vital facts about First American's market price. Turning our attention to the second issue raised, we hold that damages cannot be shown by a member of a class of minority shareholders whose votes are not required by law or corporate bylaw to authorize the transaction. We reject Sandberg's (P) theories that purport to establish the proxy statement was an essential link between the proposal and the merger. As to the first, we cannot accept the theory that VBI (D) and FABI (D) would have been unwilling to proceed with the merger unless it obtained minority approval. Acceptance of this concept would give rise to speculative claims. As to the theory that VBI (D) and FABI (D) sought minority approval in order to save the merger from voidability on state law grounds, we find nothing in the record indicating that the proxy solicitation resulted in a loss of a cause of action.

CONCURRENCE

(Scalia, J.) I recognize that the Court's disallowance of an action based solely on misrepresentation of belief is a departure from the modem law of torts. I have no problem departing from modern tort law in this regard, because I think the federal cause of action at issue here was never enacted by Congress.

CONCURRENCE AND DISSENT

(Stevens, J.) I disagree with the court's conclusion that a member of a minority whose votes are not necessary to effectuate the transactions may not prove causation of damages. The merger at issue was found to be unfair. The interest in providing a remedy to the injured minority shareholders is stronger, not weaker. Once corporate officers decide to solicit proxies - whether required to or not—they must be subject to the constraints of the statute.

CONCURRENCE AND DISSENT

(Kennedy, J.) I agree with Justice Stevens. Both FABI and VBI retained the right to back out of the merger if the minority shareholders did not approve, or if there was concern as to a violation of duties owed to the minority shareholders. The Court's distinction between cases where the minority shareholder could have voted down the transaction and those where nonvoting causation must be proved is suspect. The real question should be whether an injury was shown by the effect the nondisclosure had on the entire merger process, including the period before votes are cast. The court presumes that a majority shareholder will vote in favor of management's proposal even if it is unfair to minority shareholders or opens the board or majority shareholder to liability under state law. That, of course, is not always the case. Moreover, those who lack the strength to vote down a proposal have all the more need for disclosure. Minority groups often have the right to bloc a transaction through court action, and disclosure may facilitate this. All the evidence supports a conclusion that FABI (D) would not have gone forth with the merger had all the facts been disclosed. FABI (D) wanted a friendly transaction with a price that any reasonable investor would take. Had the minority shareholders been informed of the possible inadequacy of the share price, they would not have voted for the transaction. FABI (D) would not have forced the issue.

Analysis:

The Court in this case addresses two major issues. First, the Court holds that directors' statements of reasons, opinions, or beliefs are facts that may be actionable under § 14(a). The second issue decided by the Court addresses causation. Under the rule stated in *Mills v. Electric Auto–Lite Co.*, 396 U.S. 375 (1970), a plaintiff who proves materiality in a § 14(a) suit need only show an essential nexus between the proxy and the transaction in order to recover. The Court here refuses to extend *Mills* to a situation where the minority votes are not necessary to complete the transaction. It holds that damages cannot be proved by Sandberg (P), because her vote was not necessary to complete the transaction. Sandberg (P) argued that the minority votes were necessary to ensure that the transaction could not be voided under state law. In other words, the minority shareholders did suffer a non-pecuniary damage—they lost the right to sue in state court. In the Court's view, however, the facts did not suggest that any state cause of action was lost. It is this second part of the opinion that is subject to the most criticism. The Court's holding seems to run counter to the purposes of the implied right of action.

Roosevelt v. E.I. Du Pont de Nemours & Co.

(*Shareholder*) v. (*Company*)
958 F.2d 416 (D.C.Cir.1992)

AS A GENERAL MATTER, SHAREHOLDERS HAVE NO RIGHT UNDER FEDERAL LAW TO PROPOSE THAT THE CORPORATION IMPLEMENT POLICIES IN A SPECIFIC MANNER

■ **INSTANT FACTS** A shareholder brought suit against a corporation under § 14(a) claiming that the company improperly excluded her proposal from the annual proxy materials.

■ **BLACK LETTER RULE** A company may exclude a shareholder's proposal from the annual meeting proxy materials under the "ordinary business" exception if the proposal relates to the timetable for implementing corporate policy.

■ PROCEDURAL BASIS

Appeal to the United States Court of Appeals for the District of Colombia from the District Court's judgment permitting the exclusion of a shareholder proposal from annual proxy materials.

■ FACTS

Prior to E.I. Du Pont de Nemours & Co.'s (Du Pont) (D) annual meeting, Amelia Roosevelt (P) submitted two proposals to the company regarding the timing of Du Pont's (D) phase-out of chlorofluorocarbons (CFCs) and halons, and regarding the presentation to shareholders of a report dealing with the phase-out. Du Pont (D) opposed the inclusion of the proposals, and notified the SEC of its intent to omit the proposal from the company's proxy materials. The SEC staff issued a "no-action letter;" citing the "ordinary business" exception it stated that it would not oppose the omission of the proposal. Roosevelt subsequently filed suit in District Court. The court ruled that Du Pont (D) could rely on the "ordinary business operations" exception to exclude Roosevelt's proposal.

■ ISSUE

May a company omit a shareholder's proposal from its annual proxy materials if the proposal relates to the timetable for implementing a corporate policy?

■ DECISION AND RATIONALE

(Ginsburg, Cir. J.) Yes. A company may exclude a shareholder's proposal from the annual meeting proxy materials under the "ordinary business" exception if the proposal relates to the timetable for implementing corporate policy. We first note that a shareholder does have an implied right of action under § 14(a) and Rule 14a-8 when a company refuses to included the shareholder's proposal in the proxy materials. The District Court ruled that Roosevelt's (P) proposal dealt with the ordinary business operations of Du Pont (D). The disagreement between Roosevelt (P) and Du Pont (D) is not about whether to eliminate CFCs; rather, the two parties differ on the rapidity with which the phase out should occur. Stated simply, Roosevelt (P) seeks a target date no later than 1995, while Du Pont has announced that the phase out will occur "as soon as possible," and sometime before 1996. In contrast to the SEC staff's view that the phase out is an "ordinary business matter," the view of the Commission is that the phase out proposal may not be excludable, but the shareholder report proposal may be omitted. We disagree. Both matters are excludable under the exception. Timing questions may reflect a significant policy when large differences are at stake. For example, if Du Pont (D) projected a phase out of 10 years, such a decision would not be "ordinary." But Roosevelt (P) seeks to move up the phase out by only one year. This is an "ordinary" business judgment. We conclude that what is at stake is the "implementation of a policy," "the timing for an agreed-upon action," and we therefore hold the target date for phase out is an excludable matter under Rule 14a-8(c)(7). As to the requirement that Du Pont (D) furnish a report to shareholders, we hold that it too falls within the exception. The SEC staff's "no action letter" with regard to this matter is in keeping with current practice. We do not, however, hold that requests for reports are always excludable. If it can be shown that the reports implicate significant policy issues, and not merely implementation issues, then they may not be excluded. But Roosevelt (P) has not made this showing. Affirmed.

Analysis:

This case illustrates that shareholders often attempt—usually unsuccessfully—to affect a company's social policy by demanding that their proposals be submitted for a shareholder vote. SEC Rule 14a-8 furnishes shareholders with a method for accomplishing their social policy goals. Nevertheless, corporations do not have to include every proposal in the proxy materials. In fact, Rule 14(a)-8(c) gives a corporation thirteen possible reasons it may rely on to omit shareholders' proposals. Here, Du Pont (D) sought to exclude Roosevelt's (P) phase out proposal because it was an "ordinary business matter" under Rule 14(a)-8(c). Justice Ginsburg, a circuit judge at the time of this opinion, does an excellent job of skirting a very fine line between the proposals a company is required to include and those it may omit from its proxy materials. The thrust of the opinion is the distinction between a proposal that Du Pont (D) eliminate CFCs and a proposal that Du Pont (D) eliminate CFCs within a certain time. In essence the court holds that proposals dealing with the implementation of corporate policy—as opposed to its adoption—are excludable as ordinary business matters, though this is not a per se rule.

Rosenfeld v. Fairchild Engine and Airplane Corp.

(*Shareholder*) v. (*Corporation*)

309 N.Y. 168, 128 N.E.2d 291 (1955)

A CORPORATION'S MANAGEMENT HAS THE RIGHT TO REASONABLY USE CORPORATE FUNDS TO SOLICIT PROXIES FROM SHAREHOLDERS

■ **INSTANT FACTS** A stockholder brought a derivative action seeking to compel the return of monies paid out of the corporate treasury to reimburse both sides in a proxy contest for their expenses.

■ **BLACK LETTER RULE** In a contest over policy, as compared to a personal power contest, corporate directors acting in good faith have the right to make reasonable and proper expenditures from the corporate treasury for the purpose of persuading the stockholders and soliciting their support; and shareholders have the right to ratify reimbursement for such expenses incurred by non-directors.

■ PROCEDURAL BASIS

Appeal to the Court of Appeals of New York challenging the decision of the Appellate Division affirming a dismissal on the merits.

■ FACTS

Mr. Rosenfeld (P) brought a shareholder's derivative action against Fairchild Engine and Airplane Corp. (Fairchild) (D) seeking the return of $261,522 paid out of the corporate treasury to reimburse both the old and new managing boards for their expenses in waging a proxy contest. Of this total, $134,000 was paid to the old board of directors, while the remaining $127,000 was paid to the new board. The payment to the new board was ratified by a majority of the shareholders.

■ ISSUE

1) May corporate officers seek reimbursement from the corporation for expenses incurred in a proxy contest; and 2) is it lawful for a corporation, on consent of a majority of its stockholders, to pay the expenses of a proxy contest, incurred by competing candidates for election as directors?

■ DECISION AND RATIONALE

(Frossel, J.) Yes; and yes. In a contest over policy, as compared to a purely personal power contest, corporate directors have the right to make reasonable and proper expenditures, subject to the scrutiny of the courts when duly challenged, from the corporate treasury for the purpose of persuading the stockholders of the correctness of their position and soliciting their support for policies which the directors believe, in all good faith, are in the best interests of the corporation. The stockholders, moreover, have the right to reimburse successful contestants for the reasonable and bona fide expenses incurred by them in any such policy contest, subject to like court scrutiny. But where such monies are spent for personal power, and individual gain, and not in the belief that such expenditures are in the best interests of the corporation, or where the amounts are unfair and unreasonable, courts will not hesitate to disallow them. If directors of a corporation cannot incur reasonable and proper expenses the corporate business might come to a standstill for failure to procure a quorum where there is no contest. Where there is a contest, a rule disallowing such expenditures would permit those with ample funds to wrest control of the corporation for their own purposes. We also see no reason to disturb the shareholders' decision to reimburse the successful contestants for achieving exactly what they, the owners of the corporation, wanted. The corporate body should have the power to determine how its own money will be spent. Affirmed.

■ CONCURRENCE

(Desmond, J.) I now believe that leave for this appeal was imprudently granted. The plaintiff failed to allege liability for specific expenditures. The cost of giving the shareholders routine notice is, of course, chargeable to the corporation. It is just as clear the payment by the corporation of the expense of proceedings by one faction in its contest with another for the control of the corporation *is ultra vires.* Approval by a majority of shareholders could not validate such expenditures. Some of these expenses were per se reasonable. As to others, however, the plaintiff has failed to particularize or prove which were inappropriate. He has failed to make a prima facie case.

■ DISSENT

(Van Voorhis, J.) It is not contested that some of the expenditures were not designed merely for the information of stockholders. Some of these expenditures went to pay for entertainment, airplanes and limousines, public relations counsel, and proxy solicitors. These were not necessary to inform the stockholders. This alone should require the incumbent directors to explain their expenditures under the "business judgment rule." Once the plaintiff has proved facts raising an inference of impropriety, the directors must explain and justify their conduct. The case should be remitted to the trail court for a determination of which payments were allowable and which were not. The plaintiff need not allege this. The majority's distinction between expenditures for policy and those for maintaining control is simply impracticable. A new board may be the symbol of the shift in policy as well as the means of obtaining it. In this case the question involved both policy and personnel, and the distinction is arbitrary. Management may charge the corporation for reasonable expenditures incurred in notifying stockholders of questions affecting the corporation, but unreasonable and excessive expenditures are *ultra vires.* The corporation lacks the power to defray these costs. The corporation also lacks the power to defray any of the expenses of the insurgent group. Proxy contest expenses incurred by shareholders may be reimbursed only by a unanimous vote. The court's rule has the potential to carry with it dire consequences. Taken to its logical end, a group seeking to wrest control of the company for some "policy" issue, could spend infinite amounts of money with the knowledge that they would be recompensed by the corporation.

Analysis:

The court here was presented with two questions: (1) Whether corporate management could seek reimbursement for expenses incurred during a proxy contest from the corporation, and (2) whether shareholders could ratify the reimbursement of expenses incurred by other shareholders in a proxy contest. The majority framed the first question in terms of the difference between reasonable expenses incurred by management for the purpose of informing the shareholders as to policy issues and those expenses incurred for the purpose of maintaining control of the board. It held that the former, if made in good faith, are compensable, while the latter are not. The majority saw the second part of the question as one of the corporate autonomy. The majority found there was no reason to deny the effect of the shareholder's ratification or to hold that the corporation is powerless to determine how its own money should be spent. The dissent, by contrast, applies the "business judgment rule." It found that the plaintiff had provided evidence that monies were spent on several items not necessary to inform the shareholders, thus piercing the presumption that directors act in the best interests of the company.

CHAPTER SIX

The Special Problems of Close Corporations

Donahue v. Rodd Electrotype Co.

Instant Facts: A minority shareholder of a closely-held corporation seeks to rescind the corporation's purchase of the controlling shareholder's stock.

Black Letter Rule: Stockholders in a close corporation owe each other a fiduciary duty of the utmost good faith and loyalty, similar to the duty that partners in a partnership owe to each other.

Ringling Bros.–Barnum & Bailey Combined Shows v. Ringling

Instant Facts: A shareholder of a closely-held corporation operating a circus sued to enforce the terms of a vote-pooling agreement entered into with another shareholder who had refused to vote according to the terms of the agreement.

Black Letter Rule: In general, shareholders may enter into an agreement to vote their shares jointly.

McQuade v. Stoneham

Instant Facts: After being voted off the board of directors and removed as an officer of a closely-held corporation, a minority shareholder sued to enforce an agreement requiring the controlling shareholders to use their best efforts to keep him in office.

Black Letter Rule: An agreement among shareholders of a corporation to restrict their discretion as directors of the corporation is invalid and unenforceable as against public policy.

Galler v. Galler

Instant Facts: The widow of one of two principal shareholders of a closely-held corporation sued the other principal shareholder seeking to enforce an agreement prescribing how the shareholders would vote for corporate offices and requiring the declaration of annual dividends and the payment of a widow's pension.

Black Letter Rule: A shareholder agreement limiting the discretion of the board of directors of a close corporation will be upheld where no minority shareholder is prejudiced, neither the corporate creditors nor the public are injured, and no clearly prohibitory statutory language is violated by its enforcement.

Sutton v. Sutton

Instant Facts: The controlling shareholders of a closely-held corporation sued to compel a minority shareholder/director of the corporation to sign an amendment to the corporation's certificate of incorporation striking a provision requiring unanimous shareholder approval, including for any amendment of the certificate.

Black Letter Rule: A unanimity provision of a corporation's certificate of incorporation may not be amended by a less than unanimous vote of the shareholders of the corporation.

Wilkes v. Springside Nursing Home, Inc.

Instant Facts: After being removed as an officer and director of a close corporation and having his weekly salary discontinued, a founding investor in the corporation sued the controlling shareholders for breach of their fiduciary duty to him as a minority shareholder.

Black Letter Rule: In deciding if the controlling shareholders of a close corporation have breached their fiduciary duty to a minority shareholder, a court must weigh any legitimate business purpose the controlling shareholders can demonstrate for their action against the feasibility of an alternative course of action that is less harmful to the minority shareholder.

Smith v. Atlantic Properties, Inc.

Instant Facts: Three of four equal shareholders in a close corporation sued to remove the fourth shareholder from the board of directors, after the fourth shareholder used a supermajority veto power contained in the corporation's articles of organization to prevent the company from declaring any dividends.

Black Letter Rule: A minority shareholder in a close corporation, whose conduct is controlling on a particular corporate issue, is held to the same fiduciary duty to which a majority shareholder would be held.

Merola v. Exergen Corp.

Instant Facts: An at-will employee and minority shareholder of a closely-held corporation sued the corporation and its majority shareholder, alleging a breach of fiduciary duty for terminating the minority shareholder's employment without cause.

Black Letter Rule: The mere fact that a close corporation, without cause, terminates the employment of a minority shareholder who is an employee in the corporation will not automatically constitute a breach of fiduciary duty to the minority shareholder.

Piemonte v. New Boston Garden Corp.

Instant Facts: Some minority shareholders of a close corporation acquired in a merger sought a judicial determination of the value of their shares and payment for those shares under a state statute permitting them to opt out of the merger.

Black Letter Rule: The "Delaware Block Approach" is an acceptable procedure for valuing corporate stock under an appraisal statute allowing shareholders to opt out of a merger approved by the majority of the shareholders of the corporation.

F.B.I. Farms, Inc. v. Moore

Instant Facts: Moore (P) sought a declaratory judgment to establish that F.B.I. Farms, Inc.'s restrictions on the transfer of stock were unreasonable and inapplicable to an involuntary transfer.

Black Letter Rule: A stock-transfer restriction is reasonable if it is designed to serve a legitimate purpose of the party imposing the restraint and the restraint is not an absolute restriction on the recipient's right of alienability.

Gallagher v. Lambert

Instant Facts: After his employment with a close corporation was terminated, an employee/minority shareholder sued to void a mandatory buy-back provision of a stockholders' agreement giving the corporation a right to repurchase his shares at book value.

Black Letter Rule: A mandatory buy-back provision of a shareholders' agreement, permitting a corporation to repurchase an employee/shareholder's stock in the event his employment is terminated, is generally enforceable.

Wollman v. Littman

Instant Facts: One of two groups of fifty percent shareholders of a closely-held corporation sued for dissolution of the corporation, asserting that another lawsuit between the shareholder groups made it impossible to effectively conduct corporate business.

Black Letter Rule: Dissolution is inappropriate, even if shareholders are deadlocked, if the result would be to permit one shareholder group to divert the corporation's business to itself.

Matter of Kemp & Beatley, Inc.

Instant Facts: Two shareholders who were formerly employees of a close corporation sued for dissolution of the corporation after the corporation changed its policy regarding corporate distributions in a way that ensured the shareholders would not get a return on their investment.

Black Letter Rule: Conduct by majority shareholders that substantially defeats the "reasonable expectations" held by minority shareholders in committing their capital to a close corporation is appropriate grounds for dissolution of the corporation, provided that the majority shareholders are first given an opportunity to buy out the complaining minority at a fair price.

McCallum v. Rosen's Diversified, Inc.

Instant Facts: A minority shareholder who was the former chief executive officer of a closely-held corporation sued to require the corporation to buy back his shares for fair value after the corporation terminated his employment.

Black Letter Rule: Conduct by a majority shareholder of a close corporation towards a minority shareholder can be grounds for a court to order the majority to buy out the interest of the minority when the minority's reasonably expectations are defeated.

Charland v. Country View Golf Club, Inc.

Instant Facts: A minority shareholder appealed a judicial appraisal of his shares that had discounted their value due to their lack of marketability and the fact that they were not enough shares to control corporate decisions.

Black Letter Rule: In appraising the fair market value of the stock of a minority shareholder in a close corporation who has filed for dissolution, a court should not apply either a minority discount or a lack of marketability discount to determine the value of the stock.

Donahue v. Rodd Electrotype Co.

(*Minority Stockholder*) v. (*Closely-held Corporation*)
367 Mass. 578, 328 N.E.2d 505 (1975)

A SPECIAL DUTY OF THE UTMOST GOOD FAITH AND LOYALTY EXISTS AMONG SHAREHOLDERS OF A CLOSELY-HELD CORPORATION

■ **INSTANT FACTS** A minority shareholder of a closely-held corporation seeks to rescind the corporation's purchase of the controlling shareholder's stock.

■ **BLACK LETTER RULE** Stockholders in a close corporation owe each other a fiduciary duty of the utmost good faith and loyalty, similar to the duty that partners in a partnership owe to each other.

■ PROCEDURAL BASIS

Appeal from the Massachusetts Superior Court's dismissal of a suit in equity for recision of a stock purchase agreement.

■ FACTS

Euphemia Donahue ("Donahue") (P) was a minority shareholder in Rodd Electrotype Co. of New England, Inc. ("Rodd Co.") (D1), a small corporation. Donahue had inherited her shares from her husband, a former employee of the company. Harry Rodd ("Harry") (D2), the former president and general manager of the company was the controlling shareholder in Rodd Co. (D1). The Rodd Co. (D1) board of directors consisted of Harry's two sons and a lawyer. At a special meeting, the Board of Directors voted to purchase most of Harry's (D2) shares at $800 a share. On hearing these terms, Donahue (P) offered her shares to Rodd Co. (D1) for the same share price. Rodd Co. (D1) refused to buy at $800 a share and offered Donahue (P) a much lower price. Donahue (P) then sued Rodd Co. (D1) and Harry (D2), seeking to rescind the purchase of Harry's (D2) shares as a violation of the fiduciary duty owed to her as a minority shareholder. The trial court dismissed Donahue's (P) suit, finding that the stock purchase had been carried out in good faith. The appeals court affirmed the trial court and Donahue (P) appealed to the Supreme Judicial Court of Massachusetts.

■ ISSUE

Do stockholders in a close corporation owe each other a fiduciary duty of the utmost good faith and loyalty, similar to the duty that partners in a partnership owe to each other?

■ DECISION AND RATIONALE

(Tauro, C.J.) Yes. A close corporation is typified by: (1) a small number of shareholders; (2) no ready market for the corporate stock; and (3) substantial majority stockholder participation in the management, direction, and operations of the corporation. These features make a close corporation resemble a partnership, where, in order for the entity to succeed, the relationship among the owners must be one of trust and absolute loyalty. In general, minority shareholders are vulnerable to oppressive actions by the majority known as "freeze-outs," which can include the refusal to declare dividends, a draining of corporate earnings through exorbitant salaries and bonuses to majority shareholders, and the exclusion of the minority from corporate offices and employment. While the minority can file suit against the majority and the corporate directors under such circumstances, such suits are often difficult to win because corporate directors generally have wide latitude on matters such as dividends and employment. The minority is then left trapped in a disadvantageous situation or is forced to sell out to the majority at less than fair market value. Because of the resemblance of a close corporation to a partnership, we hold that the stockholders of a close corporation owe each other a duty of the utmost good faith and loyalty, similar to the duty that partners in a partnership owe to each other. Under this standard, if a controlling stockholder causes the corporation to purchase his shares, the controlling stockholder must also cause the corporation to offer every other stockholder the chance to sell a ratable number of shares to the corporation at an identical price. Otherwise, the controlling stockholder unfairly benefits from the creation of a market for company shares and from the preferential distribution of company assets. Here, Rodd Co. (D1) is a close corporation and Harry's (D2) family constituted a "controlling group." Since Donahue (P) was not given an equal opportunity to sell her shares, the controlling group breached its fiduciary duty to her. On remand, the trial court is to enter an order to either rescind the purchase of Harry's (D2) shares or compel Rodd Co. (D1) to buy all of Donahue's (P) shares at the same price paid for Harry's (D2) shares. Reversed and remanded.

■ CONCURRENCE

(Wilkins, J.) The rule concerning the purchase of a controlling stockholder's shares does not necessarily apply to all operations of the corporation as they affect minority shareholders. The majority's comments regarding dividend and salary policy involve matters not directly in issue in this case and the partnership analogy might not hold in a future case concerning such items.

Analysis:

As their very name suggests, close corporations can involve small, intimate, and personal relationships. The same people will often be both the shareholders, management, and employees of the company. Having the same people own and manage a business can create difficulties for the business when those people disagree over management policies. These difficulties can be magnified when, as with most close corporations, there is no readily available market in which the shareholders can sell their shares. The court here imposes a very strict duty of good faith and loyalty on the shareholders of a closely held corporation, analogous to the duty held by partners in a partnership and much more demanding than the duty required of shareholders and management of publicly held companies. By imposing this stricter duty, this court offers a potential solution, short of dissolution of the corporation, when the close corporation shareholders cannot agree and the minority shareholders might otherwise be unfairly frozen out of the company.

■ CASE VOCABULARY

CLOSE CORPORATION: A corporation with a small number of stockholders who lack a ready market for their stock and in which there is substantial majority stockholder participation in the management, direction, and operations of the company.

FIDUCIARY DUTY: A special duty imposed by law on various business relationships, requiring a high standard of loyalty and trust, even at some personal cost.

FREEZE-OUT: An attempt by the majority shareholder of a corporation to exclude the minority shareholders from the economic benefits of corporate ownership or participation in corporate policy decisions.

Ringling Bros.–Barnum & Bailey Combined Shows v. Ringling

(*Circus Corporation*) v. (*Shareholder*)
29 Del.Ch. 610, 53 A.2d 441 (1947)

SHAREHOLDER VOTE-POOLING AGREEMENTS ARE NOT AUTOMATICALLY UNLAWFUL

■ **INSTANT FACTS** A shareholder of a closely-held corporation operating a circus sued to enforce the terms of a vote-pooling agreement entered into with another shareholder who had refused to vote according to the terms of the agreement.

■ **BLACK LETTER RULE** In general, shareholders may enter into an agreement to vote their shares jointly.

■ PROCEDURAL BASIS

Appeal from an order of the Delaware Chancery Court enforcing the terms of a shareholder voting agreement.

■ FACTS

The outstanding shares of the stock of Ringling Bros.-Barnum & Bailey Combined Shows, Inc. ("Circus Co.") (D1) were divided among three shareholders as follows: Edith Conway Ringling ("Mrs. Ringling") (P) held 315 shares; Aubrey B. Ringling Haley ("Mrs. Haley") (D2) held 315 shares; and John Ringling North ("Mr. North") (D3) held 370 shares. Mrs. Ringling (P) and Mrs. Haley (D2) had entered into a contract under which each agreed, among other things, to consult and confer with the other and act jointly in exercising corporate voting rights. If the two women could not agree about a matter, they agreed to submit the issue to an arbitrator. For three years, the women voted their shares in accordance with their mutual agreement, each year jointly voting in a way that would let them name five of the seven directors of Circus Co. (D1). Just before the 1946 annual stockholders' meeting, Mrs. Ringling (P) and Mrs. Haley (D2) could not agree on who should be named the fifth director for that year. Mrs. Haley (D2) refused a sixty-day delay of the stockholders' meeting to try to work out an agreement on the issue. Mrs. Ringling (P) then took the matter to the arbitrator. The arbitrator directed that the stock of both women be voted to delay the meeting for sixty days. Mrs. Ringling (P) voted to delay the meeting. Mrs. Haley (D2) and Mr. North (D3) voted against a delay. Although the corporate chairman ruled that Mrs. Haley's stock could not be voted other than in accordance with the arbitrator's ruling, the meeting nevertheless proceeded to the election of directors. Mrs. Ringling voted for one set of directors and the arbitrator directed Mrs. Haley (D2) to vote in a way that would elect those directors. Instead, Mrs. Haley (D2) attempted to vote in a way that would benefit Mr. North's (D3) slate of directors. Even though the corporate chairman ruled that Mrs. Ringling's (P) slate should be seated as the directors of the corporation, the other set of directors tried to participate in voting for corporate officers. Mrs. Ringling (P) then filed a complaint in equity with the Delaware Chancery Court to determine the validity of the election and which set of directors could sit on the Circus Co. (D1) board. The Chancery Court ruled that the "stock pooling agreement" between Mrs. Ringling (P) and Mrs. Haley (D2) gave their arbitrator an implied and irrevocable proxy to vote their shares as he determined. It ordered a new election where Mrs. Haley (D2) would be required to vote according to the direction of the arbitrator. Contending that the vote-pooling agreement was invalid, Mrs. Haley (D2) appealed.

■ ISSUE

Is a vote-pooling agreement among shareholders automatically unlawful?

■ DECISION AND RATIONALE

(Pearson, J.) No. Mrs. Haley (D2) contends that the voting agreement in this case is really a disguised voting trust which must meet certain Delaware statutory requirements in order to be enforced, such as the actual conveyance of legal title to the shares to the voting trustee. Mrs. Haley argues that the agreement she signed does not meet those statutory requirements and therefore cannot be enforced. We think that the voting trust statute does not apply and that, in general, a vote-pooling agreement among shareholders is not unlawful. Traditionally, shareholders have been permitted to exercise wide discretion in corporate voting. It is not legally objectionable if the shareholder's motives in casting a vote are for personal profit or based purely on whim, so long as the shareholder is not violating any duty owed to the other shareholders of the company. In fact, there is no requirement that a shareholder vote at all. A group of shareholders, then, can properly vote their shares so as to obtain the advantage of joint action. They can lawfully contract with each other to vote in the future in such a way as they or a majority of their group determine is appropriate. Moreover, the group can provide for deadlock-breaking measures like the arbitrator used in this case. Legal consideration for such an agreement is found in the mutual promises of the shareholders in the group. Here, the agreement to act according to the decision of the arbitrator is valid. The arbitrator's good faith has not been challenged and the record indicates he acted in good faith. Mrs. Haley (D2) breached the contract by not voting in accordance with the arbitrator's direction. We do not, however, agree with the Chancery Court that the election should be held again. The agreement here did not create an implied and irrevocable proxy permitting the arbitrator to cast any votes. Mr. North (D3) was not a party to the vote-pooling agreement and did not do anything wrong at the shareholders' meeting. Instead of a new election, we hold that Mrs. Haley's (D2) votes should not be counted. Reversed.

Analysis:

As this case shows, under modern law, vote-pooling agreements among shareholders requiring them to vote their shares together as a unit are generally considered valid contracts. Courts around the country, however, have split over whether such vote-pooling agreements will be specifically enforced when breached. Here, the Delaware Supreme Court refused to grant specific performance of the vote-pooling agreement at issue. The result was that only six out of seven directors would actually be seated, and three of the six would be chosen by Mrs. Ringling (P), and the other three would be chosen by Mr. North (D3). This corporate deadlock was exactly what Mrs. Ringling (P) had tried to avoid by entering into the vote-pooling agreement in the first place. Recognizing this irony, most courts today would specifically enforce such an agreement. In response to the result in this case, the Delaware legislature and the legislatures of many other states have passed laws making vote-pooling agreements specifically enforceable.

■ CASE VOCABULARY

ARBITRATOR: A neutral person chosen by parties disputing an issue to hear and decide the dispute.

PROXY: A power to vote a shareholder's stock given by the shareholder to an agent. A proxy is generally revocable, but may be made irrevocable when "coupled with an interest" (i.e., when the proxy holder has an independent interest in the shares being voted; as where the shares have been pledged to the proxy).

VOTE-POOLING AGREEMENT: A contract in which two or more shareholders of a corporation agree to vote their stock together as a unit on one or more corporate issues.

VOTING TRUST: A legal device in which corporate shareholders transfer legal title and voting rights to a voting trustee who is authorized to vote on their behalf, but still retain the beneficial right to corporate distributions and stock appreciation.

McQuade v. Stoneham

(*Minority Stockholder*) v. (*Majority Stockholder*)
263 N.Y. 323, 189 N.E. 234 (1934)

NEW YORK COURT OF APPEALS HOLDS THAT A SHAREHOLDER AGREEMENT PURPORTING TO RESTRICT THE SHAREHOLDERS' POWERS AS DIRECTORS IS UNENFORCEABLE, EVEN IN A CLOSE CORPORATION

■ **INSTANT FACTS** After being voted off the board of directors and removed as an officer of a closely-held corporation, a minority shareholder sued to enforce an agreement requiring the controlling shareholders to use their best efforts to keep him in office.

■ **BLACK LETTER RULE** An agreement among shareholders of a corporation to restrict their discretion as directors of the corporation is invalid and unenforceable as against public policy.

■ PROCEDURAL BASIS

Appeal from a judgment of an appellate court affirming a trial court judgment awarding damages for wrongful discharge.

■ FACTS

Charles A. Stoneham ("Stoneham") (D1) was the majority shareholder of the close corporation operating the New York Giants baseball franchise. Stoneham sold a minority stake in the franchise to John J. McGraw ("McGraw") (D2), the team manager, and Francis X. McQuade ("McQuade") (P), a New York City magistrate. As part of the stock sale, the three men entered into an agreement that they would each use their best efforts to maintain each other as directors and officers of the corporation. For six years, all three men served on the board of directors and as paid corporate officers. After a disagreement between McQuade (P) and Stoneham (D1), Stoneham (D1) and McGraw (D2) refused to vote for McQuade's (P) re-election as a corporate officer and McQuade (P) was not elected. He was later dropped from the board of directors, as well. McQuade (P) sued for breach of contract, seeking reinstatement as an officer and a director. The trial court and the appellate court both refused the reinstatement remedy, but gave McQuade (P) damages for wrongful discharge. Stoneham (D1) and McGraw (D2) appealed.

■ ISSUE

Is an agreement among shareholders of a corporation to restrict their discretion as directors of the corporation valid and enforceable?

■ DECISION AND RATIONALE

(Pound, C.J.) No. Directors are the exclusive executive representatives of a corporation and are charged with the management and administration of its assets. Directors have a legal duty to act for the corporation. Past cases have held that an agreement among shareholders that attempts to prevent a board of directors from firing an unfaithful employee is illegal as against public policy. We now find that shareholders may not, by agreement, among themselves, control the power of a board of directors to elect officers or fix salaries. The directors must be free to exercise their independent business judgment. While shareholders can unite to elect directors, they cannot unite to limit the power of elected directors to manage the business according to their best judgment. Here, Stoneham (D1) and McGraw (D2) were not trustees for McQuade (P) as an individual. Their duty as directors was to exercise their lawful judgment for the benefit of the corporation and all of its stockholders. To the extent it attempts to restrict a board of directors from changing officers, salaries, or other corporate policies, a contract violates public policy and is illegal. This result is preferable to a judicial inquiry into the motives of directors in the exercise of their business judgment. Reversed.

Analysis:

This court finds that the traditional notion that a corporate director owes a fiduciary duty of undivided loyalty to the corporation should apply in all circumstances, even in the special context of a closely held corporation, to prevent any shareholder agreement attempting to limit a shareholder's discretion *as a director.* The rationale for this result appears to have been a concern that such agreements could do harm to other shareholders who were not parties to the agreement. More recent decisions, however, have been willing to enforce voluntary agreements among investors in closely held corporations under certain circumstances. The modern trend recognizes that in the context of a closely held corporation, these contracts limiting the discretion of the board can play an important role in helping to protect minority shareholders from the tyranny of the majority. Several states also now have laws making such agreements enforceable.

■ CASE VOCABULARY

BOARD OF DIRECTORS: The governing body of a corporation, elected by the corporation's shareholders and charged with the power to elect or appoint corporate officers and set corporate policy.

Galler v. Galler

(*Widow*) v. (*Controlling Shareholder*)
32 Ill.2d 16, 203 N.E.2d 577 (1964)

ILLINOIS SUPREME COURT ADOPTS MODERN VIEW AND UPHOLDS SHAREHOLDER AGREEMENT LIMITING DIRECTOR DISCRETION

■ **INSTANT FACTS** The widow of one of two principal shareholders of a closely-held corporation sued the other principal shareholder seeking to enforce an agreement prescribing how the shareholders would vote for corporate offices and requiring the declaration of annual dividends and the payment of a widow's pension.

■ **BLACK LETTER RULE** A shareholder agreement limiting the discretion of the board of directors of a close corporation will be upheld where no minority shareholder is prejudiced, neither the corporate creditors nor the public are injured, and no clearly prohibitory statutory language is violated by its enforcement.

■ PROCEDURAL BASIS

Appeal from an order of the First District Appellate Court reversing a Superior Court decree in equity for specific performance of a shareholder agreement.

■ FACTS

Emma Galler ("Emma") (P) was the widow of Benjamin Galler, one of two founding shareholders of Galler Drug Co., a wholesale drug business. The other founding shareholder of the company was Benjamin's brother, Isadore Galler ("Isadore") (D). Benjamin and Isadore (D) each owned approximately one half of the shares of the company. In order to assure their families equal control of the business in the event either brother died, the brothers signed a shareholders' agreement which, among other things, prescribed how the parties would vote for corporate directors and officers, required certain dividends to be paid by the corporation each year and, in the event of the death of either brother, established a pension to be paid to his widow. After Benjamin's death, Isadore (D) refused to honor the agreement and Emma (P) brought a suit in equity for specific performance and an accounting. The trial court ruled in favor of Emma (P), but on appeal, the First District Appellate Court of Illinois reversed that ruling. Emma (P) appealed to the Illinois Supreme Court.

■ ISSUE

Are there circumstances where a shareholder agreement limiting the discretion of the board of directors of a close corporation will be upheld?

■ DECISION AND RATIONALE

(Underwood, J.) Yes. We think that special rules, not applicable to a publicly-held corporations, should apply to shareholder agreements in a close corporation context. A shareholder of a publicly-held corporation generally has a ready market for his shares and can sell them if he disagrees with the way management is operating the business. A minority shareholder in a close corporation, however, has no ready market for his shares, and may find himself at the mercy of an oppressive or unknowledgeable majority, if he cannot rely on a shareholder agreement to protect his interest. As in this case, the shareholders of a close corporation are often also the directors and officers of the company. Thus, unlike a publicly-held corporation, in a close corporation, with the directors and officers often having a major financial interest in the company, it is often impossible to obtain a truly neutral, independent judgment of the board of directors. In our view, these conceptual differences between a close corporation and a publicly-held corporation justify permitting the shareholders of a close corporation to reach agreements concerning its management. We will uphold such agreements where no minority shareholder is prejudiced, there is no fraud or injury to a corporate creditor or the public, and no clearly prohibitory statutory language is violated by their enforcement. Here, those conditions are met. No shareholder who was not a party to the agreement has claimed injury as a result of the proposed enforcement of the agreement. We disagree with the Appellate Court that the public policy of this state demands a voiding of this shareholder agreement and will uphold the agreement under these circumstances. Reversed.

Analysis:

Understanding that close corporations usually involve "close," personal relationships and that the shareholders of such companies often have their blood, sweat, and tears wrapped up in the business, this court goes out of its way to offer some protection to such shareholders from a potentially oppressive majority. A stockholders' agreement in a close corporation is usually the result of careful deliberation and negotiation by all of the initial investors. In the absence of a state statutory scheme protecting such shareholders, this court gives the minority shareholder in a close corporation a chance to protect himself, by developing judicial rules that will uphold certain protective agreements where they can be negotiated by the shareholders and no other minority shareholder is prejudiced by their enforcement. Most courts today would agree with this view. More significantly, most states have adopted comprehensive statutory schemes that specifically govern close corporations and approve the kinds of protective agreements at issue in this case.

■ CASE VOCABULARY

ACCOUNTING: An equitable remedy to determine the earnings and profits of a company and recover any profits taken by a party in breach of a fiduciary duty to another party.

PUBLICLY-HELD CORPORATION: A corporation with stock held by and available for sale to the public at large, usually through a government-regulated stock exchange.

Sutton v. Sutton

(Minority Shareholder) v. *(Member of Controlling Shareholder Group)*

84 N.Y.2d 37, 637 N.E.2d 260, 614 N.Y.S.2d 369 (1994)

NEW YORK COURT OF APPEALS FINDS IT TAKES SHAREHOLDER UNANIMITY TO STRIKE A UNANIMITY PROVISION FROM A CORPORATION'S CERTIFICATE OF INCORPORATION

■ **INSTANT FACTS** The controlling shareholders of a closely-held corporation sued to compel a minority shareholder/director of the corporation to sign an amendment to the corporation's certificate of incorporation striking a provision requiring unanimous shareholder approval, including for any amendment of the certificate.

■ **BLACK LETTER RULE** A unanimity provision of a corporation's certificate of incorporation may not be amended by a less than unanimous vote of the shareholders of the corporation.

■ PROCEDURAL BASIS

Appeal from an Appellate Division order reversing a trial court's order declaring as valid a corporate resolution amending a certificate of incorporation and requiring respondent to sign and deliver the certificate for filing.

■ FACTS

Solomon A. Sutton ("Solomon") (P1) and his mother, Yvette Sutton ("Yvette) (P2) owned 70% of the outstanding stock of Bag Bazaar, Ltd., a close corporation which they inherited from Solomon's (P1) father, Abraham Sutton. The other 30% of the corporation was owned by David S. Sutton ("David") (R), Abraham's brother. The corporation's certificate of incorporation included a unanimity provision which provided that all of the shareholders of the corporation had to agree on any corporate business transactions, including the amendment of the certificate of incorporation. After Abraham's death, Solomon (P1) and David (R) [this is shaping up to be a case of Biblical proportions] could not agree on how to run the company. They were the only two directors of the company. At a 1992 shareholders' meeting, Solomon (P1) and Yvette (P2) voted their 70% of the company shares for a resolution to eliminate the unanimity provision from the certificate of incorporation. David (R) opposed the resolution with his 30% of the shares and would not sign a certificate of amendment as a director of the company. Solomon (P1) and Yvette (P2) then petitioned a New York trial court for an order declaring the resolution valid and compelling David (R) to sign the amendment certificate. David (R) argued that the purported amendment was invalid because the certificate of incorporation required unanimous approval for any amendment. Solomon (P1) and Yvette (P2) contended that New York's corporations statute permitted a change to the unanimity provision supported by a mere two-thirds shareholder vote because the certificate of incorporation did not provide "specifically" for a greater vote in order to amend the unanimity provision. The trial court ruled for Solomon (P1) and Yvette (P2). On appeal, the Appellate Division reversed that decision and Solomon (P1) and Yvette (P2) appealed to the New York Court of Appeals.

■ ISSUE

May the unanimity provision of a corporation's certificate of incorporation be amended by a less than unanimous vote of the shareholders of the corporation?

■ DECISION AND RATIONALE

(Simons, J.) No. New York's corporations statute provides that supermajority provisions in a certificate of incorporation may be amended by a two-thirds vote unless the certificate "specifically" provides otherwise. Solomon (P1) and Yvette (P2) contend that the legislature added the word "specifically" to the statute because it recognized that a unanimity provision gives minority shareholders the ability to deadlock any and all corporate action. They say that the legislature intended to minimize such deadlocks by permitting a two-thirds majority of the shareholders to alter or delete a unanimity requirement unless the certificate of incorporation explicitly stated otherwise. David (R) argues that the word "specifically" was added to the statute to clarify that, if more than a two-thirds vote was needed to amend a unanimity provision, the certificate should state the exact greater percentage that is needed. David (R) contends that the certificate here meets that requirement by providing that a unanimous vote is needed for *any* amendment. We look to the history of the corporations statute to decide the issue. The legislature passed the original version of the provision at issue here in 1948 in order to legislatively overrule a prior decision of this court which held a unanimity provision invalid because it interfered with the basic concept of corporate governance by majority rule. The original statutory provision required a unanimous vote in order to add or amend a unanimity provision. That provision was later amended to allow adoption or amendment of a supermajority provision by a two-thirds or greater vote. Unanimity was still required, however, where the certificate called for a unanimous vote. According to the legislative history, when the current version of the statute was subsequently adopted, the word "specifically" was added to simply clarify existing language. It was not intended to change existing law. Thus, the present statute should be construed the same way the old version of the statute was. Here, the certificate is unambiguous. It requires unanimity for the transaction of any business, *including amendment of the certificate of incorporation.* Thus, unanimity is required here and the certificate cannot be amended by a mere two-thirds vote. Affirmed.

Analysis:

As the court in this case notes in going through the history of the statutory provision at issue, traditionally, courts refused to enforce supermajority voting requirements, taking the view that they impeded the basic concept that the will of the majority should govern in a corporate setting. By statute, most states today permit supermajority voting requirements, including provisions of a certificate of incorporation requiring a unanimous vote of the shareholders in order to alter corporate policies. As this case shows, however, there is a legislative policy against supermajority provisions unless they are made explicit in the certificate of incorporation. Such a view is based on the belief that the more supermajority provisions there are, the more likely it is a corporation will become deadlocked. This court found the provision at issue here to be explicit and permitted the corporate deadlock between Solomon (P1) and David (R) to continue.

■ CASE VOCABULARY

CERTIFICATE OF INCORPORATION: A document filed with the appropriate state agency to incorporate a business under the state's corporations statute. It commonly contains the name of the corporation, the authorized classes of stock, the powers of the corporation, and the rights and liabilities of shareholders and directors.

DEADLOCK: A situation in which a corporation is unable to exercise its corporate powers because a shareholder faction has blocked or vetoed corporate action by its vote under the corporation's governing structure.

SUPERMAJORITY PROVISION: A provision in a corporation's certificate of incorporation requiring more than the usual fifty percent majority vote to constitute shareholder approval of a corporate resolution.

UNANIMITY PROVISION: A provision in a corporation's certificate of incorporation requiring the consent of all shareholders to approve a corporate resolution.

Wilkes v. Springside Nursing Home, Inc.

(*Minority Shareholder*) v. (*Close Corporation*)

370 Mass. 842, 353 N.E.2d 657 (1976)

MASSACHUSETTS SUPREME COURT CREATES BALANCING TEST FOR DETERMINING A BREACH OF FIDUCIARY DUTY IN A CLOSE CORPORATION

■ **INSTANT FACTS** After being removed as an officer and director of a close corporation and having his weekly salary discontinued, a founding investor in the corporation sued the controlling shareholders for breach of their fiduciary duty to him as a minority shareholder.

■ **BLACK LETTER RULE** In deciding if the controlling shareholders of a close corporation have breached their fiduciary duty to a minority shareholder, a court must weigh any legitimate business purpose the controlling shareholders can demonstrate for their action against the feasibility of an alternative course of action that is less harmful to the minority shareholder.

■ PROCEDURAL BASIS

Direct appeal to the Massachusetts Supreme Court from a Probate Court order dismissing a suit for declaratory relief and damages for a breach of fiduciary duty.

■ FACTS

Stanley Wilkes ("Wilkes") (P) and three other investors, T. Edward Quinn ("Quinn") (D1), Leon Riche ("Riche") (D2) and Dr. Hubert Pipkin formed Springside Nursing Home, Inc. ("Springside") (D3), a company organized to own and operate a nursing home. The four investors had a general understanding that each would share equally in the profits, salary and management of the business. Quinn (D1), Riche (D2), and Wilkes (P) each served as officers of the company and all four investors served as directors of the company. Each of the four investors also worked in some capacity to operate the nursing home, receiving a weekly cash salary payment from the corporation. The corporation never declared any dividends. Eventually, Pipkin sold his shares to Lawrence Connor ("Connor") (D4), a banker, who then became a director of the company. While not performing a formal service for the company, Connor (D4) was paid a weekly cash payment equal to the salary amount that each of the other investors received. After several years of operating the company, Wilkes (P) and Quinn (D1) had a dispute over the price that would be paid for the sale of certain corporate property to Quinn (D1). At a director's meeting that followed, the board of directors set a new, formal schedule of weekly payments to Springside's (D3) officers and employees. The new payment plan substantially increased Quinn's (D1) weekly payment, left Riche's (D2) and Connor's (D3) weekly payments the same as they had been, and halted all salary payments to Wilkes (P). Soon after, at the company's annual meeting, Wilkes (P) was not reelected as either a director or officer of Springside (D3). Upset at being frozen out of the company, Wilkes (P) filed suit against the other investors, seeking declaratory relief and damages. Among other things, Wilkes (P) argued that the controlling group had breached a fiduciary duty to him as a minority stockholder by denying him a salary and removing him from the board and management of Springside (D3). The trial court dismissed Wilkes' (P) case on the merits and the Massachusetts Supreme Court granted direct appellate review.

■ ISSUE

When a breach of fiduciary duty by a controlling shareholder is alleged by a minority shareholder of a close corporation, should a court consider whether any legitimate business purpose for the action taken by the controlling shareholder outweighs the feasibility of an alternative course of action that would be less harmful to the minority shareholder?

■ DECISION AND RATIONALE

(Hennessey, C.J.) Yes. Springside (D4) is a dose corporation. Thus, the shareholders of the corporation owe each other a duty of the utmost good faith and loyalty under the standard set forth in *Donahue v. Rodd Electrotype Co.* [holding that a close corporation is like a partnership with the shareholders having the same kind of fiduciary duty that partners have to each other]. We are concerned, however, that this strict standard might make it too difficult for a controlling group to effectively manage a close corporation. We think that the controlling group in a close corporation must have some room to maneuver in establishing the business policy of the company. Thus, we now hold that when a minority shareholder in a close corporation alleges a breach of fiduciary duty by the controlling shareholders, the controlling shareholders have the opportunity to demonstrate that a legitimate business purpose exists for their actions which affect the minority shareholder. If the controlling shareholders can assert a business purpose for their actions, however, we also hold that a court must weigh any legitimate business purpose that they can demonstrate for their action against the feasibility of an alternative course of action that would have been less harmful to the minority shareholder. Here, the controlling shareholders, Quinn (D1), Riche (D2), and Connor (D4) have not shown a legitimate business purpose for their "freeze-out" of Wilkes (P). By terminating his salary and refusing to reelect him an officer or director of Springside (D3), they disregarded the long-standing policy of the stockholders that each would share equally in the profits, salary and management of the business. Moreover, since the company never paid any dividends, the action of the majority ensured that Wilkes (P) would never get *any* return on his investment. We reverse the lower court's order dismissing Wilkes' (P) complaint and remand on the issue of damages. Reversed and remanded.

Analysis:

Expressing its concern that a majority shareholder not be completely hampered in its ability to manage a close corporation, the court in this case sets down a balancing test that weighs the majority's right of self-interest against the fiduciary duty it owes to the minority. Thus, if a minority shareholder asserts a breach of fiduciary duty, the majority is entitled to explain its conduct by offering a legitimate business purpose for its action. If the majority can offer such a purpose, the court permits the minority shareholder to show that an alternative course of action that would have been less harmful to his interests was possible. If such a showing is made, the court would then weigh the majority's purpose against the feasibility of the alternative action proposed by the minority. Under this case-by-case approach, the court sought to give controlling shareholders in a close corporation some flexibility in setting corporate policy, while also continuing to offer some protection to minority shareholders at risk from potential majority oppression.

■ CASE VOCABULARY

CONTROLLING GROUP: A set of shareholders who together own enough shares or hold enough voting power of a corporation to be able to outvote the other shareholders of the corporation on any issue.

DIVIDEND: A distribution of a corporation's earnings to its shareholders in the form of cash or other property.

Smith v. Atlantic Properties, Inc.

(*25% Shareholder*) v. (*Close Corporation*)

12 Mass.App.Ct. 201, 422 N.E.2d 798 (1981)

COURT FINDS UNREASONABLE USE OF VETO POWER BY MINORITY SHAREHOLDER TO CONSTITUTE A BREACH OF FIDUCIARY DUTY

■ **INSTANT FACTS** Three of four equal shareholders in a close corporation sued to remove the fourth shareholder from the board of directors, after the fourth shareholder used a supermajority veto power contained in the corporation's articles of organization to prevent the company from declaring any dividends.

■ **BLACK LETTER RULE** A minority shareholder in a close corporation, whose conduct is controlling on a particular corporate issue, is held to the same fiduciary duty to which a majority shareholder would be held.

■ PROCEDURAL BASIS

Appeal from a Superior Court judgment finding a breach of fiduciary duty.

■ FACTS

Dr. Louis E. Wolfson ("Wolfson") (D1) and three other investors, including Paul T. Smith ("Smith") (P), were equal shareholders in Atlantic Properties, Inc. ("Atlantic") (D2), a corporation organized to own and operate certain real estate. Atlantic's (D2) articles of organization and corporate bylaws contained a provision requiring *any* resolution or act by the corporation's board of directors or officers to be approved by a vote of at least 80% of the stock of the corporation. Thus, this supermajority provision gave each of the four equal shareholders a veto power over all corporate decisions. When the corporation grew profitable, Smith (P) and two of the other investors sought to have it declare dividends to the shareholders. Wolfson (D1) refused, exercising his veto power. He claimed that he wanted the corporate earnings to be used for repairs and improvements to the property owned by the company. Wolfson (D1) continued to veto the dividend proposals for several years, despite the fact that the Internal Revenue Service ("IRS") assessed a penalty tax each year that the corporation did not declare a dividend. Finally, Smith (P) and the other shareholders filed suit in equity seeking Wolfson's (D1) removal from the board of directors, a determination that Atlantic (D2) should pay a dividend, and reimbursement from Wolfson (D1) for the penalty taxes the corporation had been required to pay. The trial court found that Wolfson (D1) had breached his fiduciary duty to the other shareholders, ordered the reimbursement of the tax money, and ordered the board to declare an annual dividend.

■ ISSUE

Does a minority shareholder have the same fiduciary duty to the other shareholders in a close corporation that a majority shareholder would have to the minority?

■ DECISION AND RATIONALE

(Cutter, J.) Yes. Massachusetts law imposes a fiduciary duty of the utmost good faith and loyalty on the controlling shareholders of a closely-held corporation. There are instances where, because of devices like a supermajority voting provision of a corporation's articles of organization, a minority shareholder in a closely-held corporation can obtain an effective controlling interest in the company. The legislature authorized devices like a supermajority provision in order to try to protect minority shareholders in close corporations from oppression by their colleagues. Used *reasonably*, these devices can have that effect. Used *unreasonably*, however, such devices can lead to deadlock and corporate paralysis. A minority shareholder in a close corporation, whose conduct is controlling on a particular corporate issue, should be held to the same fiduciary duty to which a majority shareholder would be held. Our case law permits a controlling group of shareholders to defend a breach of fiduciary duty claim by asserting a legitimate corporate purpose for their action. Here, Wolfson's (D1) veto power under the articles of organization gave him effective control over the company's ability to declare a dividend. Wolfson (D1) has offered no legitimate business purpose for his refusal to allow a dividend to be declared. While he did seek to have the company earnings used for repairing and improving the company's property, he offered no improvement plan that would have satisfied the IRS and prevented the annual penalty tax assessments. By recklessly permitting the corporation to be repeatedly assessed a penalty tax, Wolfson (D1) violated his fiduciary duty to the other shareholders. Accordingly, we affirm the trial judge's order that Wolfson (D1) reimburse the corporation for the assessed tax. We modify the trial court's judgment with respect to the requirement that the board declare an annual dividend. We direct that the parties should attempt to confer and stipulate to an appropriate dividend and to a repair and improvement policy. If they cannot agree, the trial court can direct the adoption of a dividend policy that would minimize the risk of further penalty taxes. Affirmed and modified.

Analysis:

This case shows that fiduciary duty standards can be applied to more than just the nominal majority shareholders in a close corporation. When any shareholder in a close corporation has the ability to control the actions of the corporation, this court would require that shareholder to exercise his power in a manner consistent with the duty of utmost good faith and loyalty. Applying the reasoning of the court in *Wilkes v. Springside Nursing Home*, 353 N.E.2d 657 (Mass.1976), this court would have weighed any legitimate business purpose for the shareholder's actions against the practicality of achieving that purpose through means less harmful to the other shareholders. Here, Wolfson (D1) had no legitimate business purpose for his actions and so his action was unjustified. This case also shows the willingness of courts to involve themselves directly in the corporate business decisions (here, the timing and amount of a dividend) of closely held corporations. In general, courts are much less willing to take such an active role in the business decisions of publicly held corporations.

■ CASE VOCABULARY

ARTICLES OF ORGANIZATION: Another name often used for a corporation's articles of incorporation or certificate of incorporation. These are documents that are filed with the state in order to incorporate a business under the state's corporations statute.

BYLAWS: Rules adopted by a corporation establishing matters such as the rights and duties of corporate officers, voting methods, and the structure for corporate meetings.

Merola v. Exergen Corp.

(*Employee/Minority Shareholder*) v. (*Close Corporation*)

423 Mass. 461, 668 N.E.2d 351 (1996)

AT-WILL EMPLOYEE WHO WAS ALSO A SHAREHOLDER OF A CLOSE CORPORATION COULD NOT ASSERT A BREACH OF FIDUCIARY DUTY CLAIM FOR HIS TERMINATION

■ **INSTANT FACTS** An at-will employee and minority shareholder of a closely-held corporation sued the corporation and its majority shareholder, alleging a breach of fiduciary duty for terminating the minority shareholder's employment without cause.

■ **BLACK LETTER RULE** The mere fact that a close corporation, without cause, terminates the employment of a minority shareholder who is an employee in the corporation will not automatically constitute a breach of fiduciary duty to the minority shareholder.

■ PROCEDURAL BASIS

Appeal from a decision of the Court of Appeals affirming a Superior Court judgment finding a breach of fiduciary duty by the majority shareholder.

■ FACTS

The founder and controlling shareholder of Exergen Corp. ("Exergen") (D1), Francisco Pompei ("Pompei") (D2), persuaded Steven Merola ("Merola") (P) to leave his job at another corporation for full-time employment with Exergen (D1). Exergen (D1) was a close corporation. Pompei (D2) told Merola (P) that in joining the company, Merola (P) would have the chance to become a major shareholder of Exergen (D1). After joining the company, Merola (P) began purchasing shares in the corporation and became a significant minority shareholder. Subsequently, Merola's (P) employment was terminated. Merola (P) sued Exergen (D1) and Pompei (D2) in Superior Court, claiming that the termination of employment breached the fiduciary duty of good faith and loyalty to him as a minority shareholder. The Superior Court agreed. On appeal, the Court of Appeals affirmed the Superior Court's decision, but held only Pompei (D2) and not Exergen (D1) liable for the breach of fiduciary duty. Pompei (D2) appealed.

■ ISSUE

Will the fact that a close corporation terminates, without cause, the employment of a minority shareholder who is an employee in the corporation automatically constitute a breach of fiduciary duty to the minority shareholder?

■ DECISION AND RATIONALE

(Lynch, J.) No. In general, employment law principles allow the termination of employees at will, with or without cause. There are certain narrow public policy exceptions to this general rule. One such exception can include the termination of a minority shareholder of close corporation, where to terminate his employment would freeze out the shareholder from the company and would therefore constitute a breach of fiduciary duty by the majority shareholder to the minority shareholder. This is because, typically, a minority shareholder depends on his salary as the principal return on his investment, because in a close corporation, corporate earnings are generally distributed in the form of salaries, bonuses, and retirement benefits. That was the situation in a prior Massachusetts case, *Wilkes v. Springside Nursing Home, Inc.* [controlling shareholders of a close corporation did not show a legitimate business purpose for terminating minority shareholder's salary in disregard of longstanding corporate policy that each shareholder would be a director and employee of the company]. Here, however, although Merola (P) invested in Exergen (D1) with the reasonable expectation of continued employment, the company had no general policy that stock ownership and employment would go hand-in-hand. Also, Merola (P) actually got a return on his investment in the close corporation other than in the form of salary. The value of his stock appreciated greatly from the initial purchase to the time he sold it and he admits the price at which he sold the stock was fair. This is very different from the situation in *Wilkes.* We conclude that not every discharge of an at-will employee of a close corporation who owns stock in the corporation will give rise to a successful breach of fiduciary duty claim. Reversed.

Analysis:

This court draws a line indicating a limit on the ability of an employee who is a minority shareholder in a closely held corporation to bring a suit for breach of fiduciary duty by the controlling shareholders of the corporation. Here, Merola's (P) employment was terminated through the action of the controlling shareholder, Pompei (D2). While no legitimate business purpose existed for the termination, there was no breach of fiduciary duty because the termination was not for the financial gain of the controlling shareholder. The court correctly contrasted this case with the situation existing in *Wilkes v. Springside Nursing Home, Inc.*, 353 N.E.2d 657 (Mass.1976). There, the controlling shareholders froze out Wilkes for their own financial benefit, ensuring that he would get no fair return on his investment in the company. Here, Pompei (D2) had no direct financial gain from the termination of Merola (P) and Merola (P) was able to obtain a significant return on his stock when he sold it. Recognizing the legitimate business needs and rights of controlling shareholders, this court sets forth a rule allowing a controlling shareholder in a close corporation to tailor his treatment of the minority shareholders within a legally permissible range of action.

■ CASE VOCABULARY

AT-WILL EMPLOYEE: A person who is hired by an employer for no specific period of time and who may quit or have his employment terminated at any time and for any reason.

WITH CAUSE: Having a legitimate business reason justifying the termination of an employee.

Piemonte v. New Boston Garden Corp.

(*Minority Shareholder*) v. (*Acquiring Corporation*)

377 Mass. 719; 387 N.E.2d 1145 (1979)

MASSACHUSETTS HIGH COURT ACCEPTS TRIAL COURT'S USE OF THE "DELAWARE BLOCK METHOD" OF STOCK APPRAISAL

■ **INSTANT FACTS** Some minority shareholders of a close corporation acquired in a merger sought a judicial determination of the value of their shares and payment for those shares under a state statute permitting them to opt out of the merger.

■ **BLACK LETTER RULE** The "Delaware Block Approach" is an acceptable procedure for valuing corporate stock under an appraisal statute allowing shareholders to opt out of a merger approved by the majority of the shareholders of the corporation.

■ PROCEDURAL BASIS

Appeal from a Superior Court decision determining the fair market value of stock in a close corporation.

■ FACTS

After the majority of the stockholders of Boston Garden Arena Corporation ("Old Garden") decided to merge that corporation into New Boston Garden Corp. ("New Garden") (D), Gabriel F. Piemonte ("Piemonte") (P) and fourteen other minority shareholders in Old Garden sought an appraisal of and payment for their shares in Old Garden under the terms of the merger agreement and in accordance with a Massachusetts statute permitting a judicial appraisal of the fair value of their shares on the date prior to the merger. After reviewing the evidence presented by the parties, including the valuation opinions of experts for each side, the trial judge made a determination of the value of Piemonte's (P) stock and the value of the stock of the other minority shareholders using the "Delaware Block Approach" to valuation. Under that method, the court valued the corporation by determining the market value of the company's stock, the value of the company's net assets, and the company's "earnings value." The court then weighted each of the three values based on its opinion of which method provided the best valuation estimate and added the values, adjusted by their relative weights. Both parties appealed the trial court's determination of value. Piemonte (P) and the other minority shareholders challenged the judge's use of the market value method, asserting that the limited trading in Old Garden stock made market value unascertainable. They also challenged various decisions the judge made in applying the "net asset method" and "earnings value method." New Garden argued that the judge was required to reconstruct market value using comparable companies and also challenged various decisions made by the judge in applying the "net asset method" and "earnings value method."

■ ISSUE

Is the "Delaware Block Approach" an acceptable procedure for valuing corporate stock under an appraisal statute allowing shareholders to opt out of a merger approved by the majority of the shareholders of the corporation?

■ DECISION AND RATIONALE

(Wilkins, J.) Yes. Massachusetts law permits the appraisal of the stock of shareholders who opt out of a merger approved by the majority of the shareholders of the corporation. The Massachusetts provisions were based on similar Delaware statutory law. The Delaware courts have adopted the so-called "Delaware Block Approach" to stock valuation which calls for a determination of the market value, earnings value, and net asset value of the stock, followed by the assignment of a percentage weight to each of these valuation methods. We think that a Massachusetts judge appraising stock under state law, may appropriately follow the "Delaware Block Approach." Here, the judge was acting within the reasonable limits of his appraisal discretion when he determined a market value for the Old Garden stock based on the last prior sale of the stock on the Boston Stock Exchange. We reject Piemonte's (P) contention that the fact that the stock was rarely traded on the exchange meant that the market value should be disregarded. We also think that the judge did not have to "reconstruct" market value, as New Garden (D) claims, by using the stock of comparable companies. His conclusion that a reconstruction using comparisons of the stock of other companies would rely on too many factors that had nothing to do with Old Garden was also within his discretion. The parties' objections regarding the earnings value and net asset value determined by the judge are also rejected. The trial judge, however, did indicate in certain of his valuation decisions that he felt *constrained* to accept a value estimate presented by one or the other of the experts. While the judge would have been warranted in determining that those estimates were proper, he is not obliged to do so. Therefore, we will remand the case, directing the trial judge to exercise his own judgment concerning the bases for the conclusions arrived at by the experts. He need not change the result, but we believe that he should clarify that the result was determined by his own judgment. Remanded.

Analysis:

The court in this case recognizes that the fact finder in a valuation case has a range of discretion within which to operate in valuing a property. In general, most appellate courts will rarely overturn a valuation ruling in the absence of clear error by the fact finder. While the valuation approach used in this case is called the "Delaware Block Approach," a few years after this case, the Delaware courts actually abandoned this method in favor of an approach that would consider any approach that is generally accepted in financial and appraisal circles for ascertaining property value, such as the discounted cash flow method of valuation.

■ CASE VOCABULARY

APPRAISAL: The right of a shareholder of a corporation who objects to certain corporate actions to require the corporation to purchase the shareholder's stock at its value immediately prior to the approval of the corporate action.

DELAWARE BLOCK APPROACH: Valuation of a corporation through a determination of the market value of the company's stock, the value of the company's net assets, and the company's "earnings value." These values are weighted based on an opinion of which method provides the best valuation estimate and then added, adjusted by their relative weights.

EARNINGS VALUE: A method of valuing a corporation based on its earnings, in which an average of the earnings of the corporation for the past five years is computed, extraordinary gains and losses are excluded, and a multiplier is selected and applied, reflecting the perceived future financial condition of the corporation and the risks of investment.

F.B.I. Farms, Inc. v. Moore

(*Corporation*) v. (*Shareholder*)
798 N.E.2d 440 (Ind.2003)

A CORPORATION MAY ADOPT REASONABLE RESTRICTIONS ON THE TRANSFER OF STOCK TO PROTECT CORPORATE INTERESTS

■ **INSTANT FACTS** Moore (P) sought a declaratory judgment to establish that F.B.I. Farms, Inc.'s restrictions on the transfer of stock were unreasonable and inapplicable to an involuntary transfer.

■ **BLACK LETTER RULE** A stock-transfer restriction is reasonable if it is designed to serve a legitimate purpose of the party imposing the restraint and the restraint is not an absolute restriction on the recipient's right of alienability.

■ PROCEDURAL BASIS

On appeal to review a decision of the Indiana Court of Appeals affirming a trial court decision for the plaintiff.

■ FACTS

F.B.I. Farms, Inc. (D) was a family-owned corporation owned by three couples, including Moore (P) and his then-wife. In exchange for the transfer of farms and machinery, each couple received common stock in the corporation. At a 1977 meeting, the board of directors adopted restrictions on the transfer of shares, requiring director approval before any stock transfer, allowing the corporation a right of first refusal, and restricting any sale of stock to blood members of the family. Moore (P) and his wife, Linda, divorced and Linda was awarded all the couple's shares in the corporation. Moore (P) obtained a money judgment secured by a lien on Linda's stock. When the money judgment went unsatisfied, Moore (P) obtained a writ of execution and purchased Linda's shares at a sheriff's sale. Moore (P) thereafter filed suit against F.B.I. (D) for a declaratory judgment that the corporation's attempted cancellation of the shares was invalid, that he properly retained ownership of the shares, and that he owned the shares unencumbered by the transfer restrictions. The trial court granted partial summary judgment to Moore (P), holding that the cancellation was invalid, that Moore (P) was the lawful owner of the shares, that the transfer restriction requiring director approval was unreasonable, and that the restriction of transfer to "blood members" only was unreasonable. On appeal, the court of appeals affirmed, finding that the restrictions applied only to voluntary transfers and thus were inapplicable to a subsequent purchaser at a sheriff's sale. The court similarly reasoned that the restrictions were unreasonable.

■ ISSUE

Are restrictions on the transfer of shares requiring board approval and a right of first refusal reasonable in a family-owned corporation, and are they applicable to an involuntary transfer at a sheriff's sale?

■ DECISION AND RATIONALE

(Judge undisclosed.) Yes. By statute, a corporation may impose restrictions on the transfer of shares to serve a variety of legitimate purposes, including control of the corporation's ownership and management free from outsider interference. Such restrictions, however, are valid and enforceable against the transferee only if the restrictions comply with state law and are "noted conspicuously on the front or back of the certificate or [are] contained in the information statement required" by state statute. Transfer restrictions, as contractual obligations between multiple shareholders or between a shareholder and the corporation, are given their plain and ordinary meaning to manifest the intention of the parties. Whether the restrictions are noted conspicuously on the stock certificates, they bind a person with actual notice of the restrictions. Here, Moore (P) was a member of the board of directors that approved the restrictions in 1977. Because he had notice of the restrictions before his purchase at the sheriff's sale, he is bound by the restrictions.

The restrictions created a right of first refusal in the corporation and its shareholders to invalidate any stock transfer. While the restrictions do not apply to Moore (P) because he was not an owner of the stock until after the purchase, as the purchaser with notice of the restriction, he had a right to insist that Linda first offer the sale to the corporation or its shareholders. The corporation, however, also had notice of this right and failed to invoke it before the sale. The corporation cannot forgo a known right, await the future consequences, and thereafter seek to enforce the right against a subsequent purchaser. Thus, while Moore (P) is bound by the right of first refusal, F.B.I. (D) may not enforce the right because of its failure to do so at the time of the sale.

With respect to the requirement of board approval, the restriction is valid only if it is reasonable. "A restriction is reasonable if it is designed to serve a legitimate purpose of the party imposing the restraint and the restraint is not an absolute restriction on the recipient's right of alienability." Reasonableness is determined, in part, by considering the size of the corporation, the degree of restraint on alienation, the time the restriction was to continue in effect, the method to be used in determining the transfer price, the connection to corporate objectives, the possibility of a hostile takeover, and the best interests of the corporation. When the restrictions arise out of fraud or a breach of fiduciary duty, they will not be upheld. Here, the restrictions impose substantive limitations on transfer, but do not arise to fraud or breach of fiduciary duty. The reasonableness of the restrictions, like all contract terms, must be determined as of the time of their adoption without regard to later events. Therefore, because the requirement of board approval was reasonable at the time it was adopted, it cannot be invalidated because of the parties' later disputes. Corporations are allowed to insist upon board approval to protect the corporate interests and maintain ownership and management over corporate affairs.

Similarly, the restriction of transfer to "blood members" only is valid and enforceable. As a family-owned farming corporation, the shareholders had a legitimate interest in excluding outside ownership of the corporation. And finally, the restrictions make no distinction between a voluntary transfer and an involuntary transfer, such as a sheriff's sale. Because the restrictions expressly apply to "all transfers," the parties' intent is clearly to restrict ownership of all shares to a designated group. The rights of third parties, however, cannot be infringed by private agreement. Thus, a creditor's right of foreclosure cannot be defeated because the corporation places private restrictions that leave the creditor powerless to enforce its lien. Therefore, Moore (P), as a creditor, lawfully acquired the shares at the sheriff's sale. Because he had notice of the restrictions, however, he acquired no more property rights than Linda, the prior owner. By Moore's (P) purchase at the sheriff's sale he acquired the stock encumbered to the same extent as it was in Linda's hands. While these restrictions may render the stock unmarketable, Moore (P) succeeds to the shareholder's interest in the corporation. Affirmed in part, reversed in part, and remanded.

Analysis:

In general, a corporation may restrict the transfer of shares in any reasonable manner necessary to manage and control the corporation. This corporate interest is necessarily stronger in small, family-owned corporations than it is in large, publicly traded corporations. Small close corporations are often formed among family members or those who have utmost trust in one another for a precise business objective. In such corporations, stringent transfer restrictions are more likely to be considered reasonable, given the important interest in limiting the shareholders to a chosen few.

■ CASE VOCABULARY

ALIENATION: Conveyance or transfer of property to another.

CLOSE CORPORATION: A corporation whose stock is not freely traded and is held by only a few shareholders (often within the same family).

EXECUTION: A court order directing a sheriff or other officer to enforce a judgment, usually by seizing and selling the judgment debtor's property.

LIEN: A legal right or interest that a creditor has in another's property, lasting usually until a debt or duty that it secures is satisfied.

RIGHT OF FIRST REFUSAL: A potential buyer's contractual right to meet the terms of a third party's offer if the seller intends to accept that offer.

Gallagher v. Lambert

(*Employee/Minority Shareholder*) v. (*Majority Shareholder*)
74 N.Y.2d 562, 549 N.Y.S.2d 945, 549 N.E.2d 136 (1989)

NEW YORK COURT OF APPEALS UPHOLDS MANDATORY-BUYBACK PROVISION

■ **INSTANT FACTS** After his employment with a close corporation was terminated, an employee/minority shareholder sued to void a mandatory buy-back provision of a stockholders' agreement giving the corporation a right to repurchase his shares at book value.

■ **BLACK LETTER RULE** A mandatory buy-back provision of a shareholders' agreement, permitting a corporation to repurchase an employee/shareholder's stock in the event his employment is terminated, is generally enforceable.

■ PROCEDURAL BASIS

Appeal from an order of the Appellate Division dismissing a suit for breach of fiduciary duty and ordering a buyback of stock at its book value.

■ FACTS

James Gallagher ("Gallagher") (P) was an at-will employee of Eastdil Realty ("Eastdil") (D), a close corporation. In 1981, in response to an offer by the corporation to all of its executive employees, Gallagher (P) purchased a minority interest in Eastdil (D). The corporation had offered the stock subject to a mandatory buy-back provision, which allowed the corporation to repurchase the shares for book value if a purchaser's employment ended for any reason prior to January 31, 1985. After that date, the price would be based on a formula tied to the company's earnings. On January 10, 1985, Eastdil (D) fired Gallagher (P). Gallagher (P) did not contest the firing, but did demand payment for his shares according to their earnings value, rather than their lower book value as required by the buyback provision. Book value was $89,000, while the earnings value was close to $3,000,000. Eastdil (D) refused, and Gallagher (P) sued, alleging a breach of fiduciary duty. The trial court denied Eastdil's (D) motion for summary judgment. On appeal, the Appellate Division reversed and dismissed Gallagher's (P) claims, ordering payment for the shares at book value. Gallagher (P) appealed.

■ ISSUE

Is a mandatory buy-back provision in a shareholders' agreement, permitting a corporation to repurchase an employee/shareholder's stock in the event his employment is terminated, enforceable?

■ DECISION AND RATIONALE

(Bellacosa, J.) Yes. The parties negotiated a written contract containing a very common provision permitting a buy-back of the stock. A mandatory buy-back provision in a shareholders' agreement permitting a corporation to repurchase an employee/shareholder's stock in the event his employment is terminated is generally enforceable. Gallagher (P) freely negotiated and agreed to accept book value for his shares in the event his employment ended before the specified date. There is no basis for the court to interfere with that contract. Gallagher (P) got what he bargained for in the contract. Affirmed.

■ DISSENT

(Kaye, J.) Since we are reviewing a summary judgment motion, we must accept everything Gallagher (P) asserts as true for purposes of the motion. Gallagher (P) contends that the buy-out provision represented "golden handcuffs" designed to induce employees to remain on with the corporation until January 31, 1985. Gallagher (P) alleges that Eastdil (D) and its board had no legitimate business reason to fire him when they did. He says that they fired him solely to get his shares back at an unfairly low price and redistribute them among themselves. If Gallagher (P) were a minority shareholder and not an employee, Eastdil (D) and its board would not have been able to act so selfishly and opportunistically. In the absence of evidence that Gallagher (P) knowingly agreed to waive rights he might otherwise have possessed as a minority shareholder, I cannot agree that the general language in the clause he signed unambiguously expresses an understanding by both parties that the repurchase provision could be exploited for the sole personal gain of the controlling shareholders. The repurchase provision contains no reference to Gallagher's (P) at-will employment status and no reservation of a right to terminate Gallagher's (P) employment status for any reason at all. Although there is generally no implied covenant of good faith in an employment relationship, one should be found under these circumstances, because it is necessary to help the employee to receive the benefits of promised performance.

Analysis:

This court emphasizes freedom-of-contract principles, believing strongly in the efficiency of allowing parties to attempt to rationally maximize their outcomes in a transaction by freely bargaining with each other. The court reasoned that the parties had rationally and freely negotiated and understood the consequences of their bargaining when they signed the agreement in this case. One important factor driving the court here may have been that Gallagher (P) started as an employee and then later became a shareholder. Had he been a shareholder first or begun with the corporation as both a shareholder and an employee, the court might have viewed his reasonable expectations differently. Since he began as an at-will employee with no expectations beyond his salary, however, the court might have been justified in concluding that he was aware of what he was signing away when he accepted the terms of the shareholders' agreement.

■ CASE VOCABULARY

BOOK VALUE: The value of property as initially recorded on a corporation's accounting books. It is generally the transfer value or purchase price paid for the property, without additions or subtractions for later increases or decreases in value.

MANDATORY BUY-BACK PROVISION: A clause in a shareholders' agreement giving the corporation or other shareholders the absolute right to repurchase a shareholder's stock on the happening of a specified event.

Wollman v. Littman

(50% Shareholder Group) v. *(50% Shareholder Group)*
35 A.D.2d 935, 316 N.Y.S.2d 526 (1970)

NEW YORK COURT OF APPEALS REFUSES TO DISSOLVE A DEADLOCKED CLOSE CORPORATION

■ **INSTANT FACTS** One of two groups of fifty percent shareholders of a closely-held corporation sued for dissolution of the corporation, asserting that another lawsuit between the shareholder groups made it impossible to effectively conduct corporate business.

■ **BLACK LETTER RULE** Dissolution is inappropriate, even if shareholders are deadlocked, if the result would be to permit one shareholder group to divert the corporation's business to itself.

■ PROCEDURAL BASIS

Appeal from a trial court order appointing a receiver to dissolve a closely-held corporation.

■ FACTS

The stock of a closely-held corporation that made and sold artificial fur was owned 50% by the Nierenberg sisters ("Nierenbergs") (P) and 50% by the Littmans ("Littmans") (D), each group having equal representation on the board of directors. The Nierenbergs (P) were responsible for buying the fur fabric for the corporation, while the Littmans (D) would re-sell the fabric to customers they found, creating the corporation's profit. In a separate case, the Littmans (D) charged the Nierenbergs (P) with trying to lure away the customers the Littmans (D) had found, to sell fabric directly to them. After being sued, the Nierenbergs (P) then brought this case, seeking to dissolve the corporation under a New York statute, on the grounds that the management was so divided that no effective business could be done. The trial court agreed to dissolve the corporation and appointed a receiver to do so. The Nierenbergs (P) appealed.

■ ISSUE

Is dissolution of a corporation appropriate whenever the corporation's management is deadlocked?

■ DECISION AND RATIONALE

(Per Curiam) No. Irreconcilable differences even among an evenly divided board of directors do not always mean that a corporation should be dissolved. While New York law permits dissolution in the event of deadlock between the shareholders, here, we think a trial should be held which would consider two issues. First, since both groups of shareholders perform different functions for the corporation, (one group buys and the other sells), can each group still perform its function, supervised by a receiver, without the other's input? Second, since the Nierenbergs (P) are charged in a separate case with trying to lure away corporate business to their own separate company, would a grant of dissolution, actually enable the Nierenbergs (P) to succeed in achieving their allegedly wrongful plan? Dissolution is inappropriate, even if shareholders are deadlocked, if the result would be to permit one shareholder group to divert the corporation's business to itself. We affirm the appointment of a receiver. He should be limited to ensuring the business functions in an orderly way until after the trial on these two issues. Order modified.

Analysis:

In general, courts do not like to order a profitable corporation to break itself apart over the objections of some of the shareholders, especially when other remedies might exist to solve the difficulties between the shareholders. Sometimes a court will order a provisional director appointed to break the deadlock. A court might also require the objecting party to buy out the party seeking dissolution at a fair price. Here, although one half of the shareholders and board of directors directly opposed the other half, creating a deadlock scenario, the court, as a court of equity, rightly recognized that an order of dissolution would unfairly benefit the party accused of wrongdoing. Involuntary dissolution would have made it easier for the Nierenbergs (P) to sell directly to the customers found by the Littmans (D), making it easier for their alleged wrongdoings to succeed. The court was able to "see" that if the corporation were dissolved, it would effectively enable the Nierenbergs (P) to obtain the whole business.

■ CASE VOCABULARY

DISSOLUTION: A judicial or statutory remedy for shareholder deadlock in which a corporation's assets are sold, its debts paid, and any amount of money left after payment of the debts is distributed to the shareholders.

RECEIVER: An impartial person appointed by a court to oversee the running of a business for a specified period of time or to oversee its dissolution.

Matter of Kemp & Beatley, Inc.

(Closely-held Corporation)

64 N.Y.2d 63, 484 N.Y.S.2d 799, 473 N.E.2d 1173 (1984)

OPPRESSIVE CONDUCT BY A MAJORITY SHAREHOLDER IS GROUNDS FOR DISSOLUTION OF THE COMPANY, WHERE THE MAJORITY DOES NOT WANT TO BUY OUT THE MINORITY AT A FAIR PRICE

■ **INSTANT FACTS** Two shareholders who were formerly employees of a close corporation sued for dissolution of the corporation after the corporation changed its policy regarding corporate distributions in a way that ensured the shareholders would not get a return on their investment.

■ **BLACK LETTER RULE** Conduct by majority shareholders that substantially defeats the "reasonable expectations" held by minority shareholders in committing their capital to a close corporation is appropriate grounds for dissolution of the corporation, provided that the majority shareholders are first given an opportunity to buy out the complaining minority at a fair price.

■ FACTS

Gardstein (P1) was a longtime shareholder, director, and officer of Kemp & Beatley, Inc., a close corporation. Dissin (P2) was a longtime employee and shareholder of the corporation. Together they held 20.33% of the company stock. Gardstein (P1) resigned and Dissin (P2) was fired. During their employment with the corporation, both had received annual dividends or bonus compensation as a distribution of the corporation's earnings according to the amount of stock they owned in the company. After Gardstein (P1) and Dissin (P2) left the corporation's employment, the controlling shareholders changed the company's method of distributing corporate earnings, from payment based on stock ownership to payment allegedly based on services rendered to the corporation. Gardstein (P1) and Dissin (P2) petitioned for the dissolution of the corporation, alleging that they had been unfairly frozen out of the company and denied the opportunity to get a return on their stock. The trial court agreed, ordering dissolution, but only in the event that the controlling shareholders refused to buy the stock of Gardstein (P1) and Dissin (P2) for a fair price. The Appellate Division affirmed and the controlling shareholders appealed.

■ ISSUE

Is dissolution of a corporation appropriate where a majority shareholder engages in "oppressive conduct" toward a minority shareholder and the majority shareholder does not want to buy out the minority shareholder at a fair price?

■ DECISION AND RATIONALE

(Cooke, C.J.) Yes. Under New York statutes, dissolution can be ordered where at least 20% of the shareholders complain of illegal, fraudulent, or oppressive conduct against them by the other shareholders of the company. We know what illegal and fraudulent conduct is, but oppressive conduct is not defined in the statute and so must be defined by this court. Oppression is conduct that substantially defeats the "reasonable expectations" held by minority shareholders in committing their capital to a close corporation. A court considering a petition alleging oppressive conduct must investigate what the majority shareholders knew or should have known to be the minority's reasonable expectations in entering the company. Mere disappointment of the minority's subjective hopes and desires is not enough, however. The conduct must substantially defeat expectations that, objectively, were reasonable and central to the petitioner's desire to join the company. Only where dissolution is the sole means of protecting the complaining shareholder's reasonable expectations, however, will we order dissolution. If there is an alternative remedy that can satisfy the minority shareholder's desire to get his capital out of the company, without destroying an otherwise profitable company, we will insist on that remedy. Thus, we find that any dissolution order must be conditioned on first allowing any shareholder of the corporation to choose to purchase the complaining shareholder's stock at fair value. Here, Gardstein (P1) and Dissin (P2) had for years relied on the corporation's distribution method. This policy was changed immediately after they left the employment of the company. It was not unreasonable for the trial court to determine that this change in policy was an attempt to exclude Gardstein (P1) and Dissin (P2) from gaining any return on their investment. Given the deterioration in relations between different company factions, it was permissible to order dissolution, so long as it was conditioned on a right of the majority to avoid dissolution by buying out the complaining minority. Affirmed.

Analysis:

Historically, courts have not been willing to order dissolution of a profitable corporation, even in an instance of corporate deadlock. This case represents the more modern approach that recognizes that dissolution may be necessary when a majority shareholder has engaged in oppressive conduct that has prevented a shareholder from receiving a return on his investment or achieving the reasonable expectations from his investment that he had on entering the company. This court recognizes, however, that while some remedy is necessary in such an instance, dissolution of a profitable corporation is such a harsh remedy that it should only be granted when the majority has been given an opportunity to buy out the minority shareholder's stock and has refused. Many states have enacted statutes that specifically provide for the remedy announced in this case. Those statutes dictate that the majority shareholders may avoid corporate dissolution by purchasing the shares of the minority for fair value.

■ CASE VOCABULARY

OPPRESSION: Conduct that substantially defeats the "reasonable expectations" held by minority shareholders in committing their capital to a close corporation.

McCallum v. Rosen's Diversified, Inc.

(*Minority Shareholder*) v. (*Closely-Held Corporation*)

153 F.3d 701 (8th Cir.1998)

COURT ORDERS BUY-OUT OF MINORITY SHAREHOLDER AT FAIR MARKET VALUE AFTER MAJORITY SHAREHOLDERS ENGAGE IN UNFAIRLY PREJUDICIAL CONDUCT

■ **INSTANT FACTS** A minority shareholder who was the former chief executive officer of a closely-held corporation sued to require the corporation to buy back his shares for fair value after the corporation terminated his employment.

■ **BLACK LETTER RULE** Conduct by a majority shareholder of a close corporation towards a minority shareholder can be grounds for a court to order the majority to buy out the interest of the minority when the minority's reasonably expectations are defeated.

■ PROCEDURAL BASIS

Appeal by a minority shareholder of a close corporation from a grant of summary judgment by a federal district court dismissing his request to have his shares redeemed by the corporation for fair market value.

■ FACTS

William B. McCallum ("McCallum") (P) was the former chief executive officer of Rosen's Diversified, Inc. ("RDI") (D), a close corporation engaged in meat packing and livestock trading. When RDI (D) increased its profits under McCallum's (P) leadership, the board gave McCallum (P) a cash bonus and a sizeable bonus of the corporation's stock stating that it constituted a reward for the improvement and was also an effort to keep him on with the company. Subsequently, McCallum's (P) employment was terminated. McCallum (P) asked RDI (D) to buy back his shares solely because he was no longer working for the company. RDI (D) sought to pay a price well below the stock's fair market value. McCallum (P) sued, seeking an order compelling a buy-back of the shares at their fair market value. The trial court dismissed McCallum's request for a buy-out on a summary judgment motion. McCallum appealed.

■ ISSUE

Can unfairly prejudicial conduct by a majority shareholder of a close corporation towards a minority shareholder be grounds for a court to order the majority to buy out the interest of the minority for fair market value?

■ DECISION AND RATIONALE

(Beam, J.) Yes. By statute, the Minnesota legislature has provided the courts with broad equitable authority to protect the interests of minority shareholders in a close corporation, including giving the courts the authority to order a buy-out of a minority shareholder's interest in the event the controlling shareholders have acted in an unfairly prejudicial way toward the minority shareholder. In deciding if a buy-out should occur, courts should consider whether the "reasonable expectations" of the minority shareholder have been defeated by the majority. Here, we find that McCallum's (P) reasonable expectations were defeated by the conduct of the majority. His primary expectations as a shareholder were to play an active role in management and to have input as an employee. This expectation was reasonable, because he was chief executive officer of RDI (D) when he got the shares. We do not say that a majority shareholder that terminates a minority shareholder's employment must always buy out the shares of the terminated minority shareholder. We do hold that when a CEO is terminated, as opposed to an employee without a major role in management, the company that gave him stock to lure him to remain at the company must pay a fair value for his stock under the Minnesota statute at issue in this case. Reversed.

Analysis:

This court adopts the "reasonable expectations" approach. Recognizing that the shares were given to McCallum (P) at least in part to convince him to stay with the company, this court points out that to deny him a fair price for his shares would defeat his reasonable expectations with regard to the stock. He stayed with the company, at least in part, because he was given the stock and expected to play a major role in the corporation's management. Once McCallum (P) was forced out of the company's management, the Minnesota statute would permit him to leave entirely, escaping with the fair value of his shares and allowing the corporation to continue without him. Note that McCallum (P) does not claim any fraud or oppression. He merely claims that his reasonable expectations were not met.

■ CASE VOCABULARY

CHIEF EXECUTIVE OFFICER: The leader and highest ranking executive in a corporation.

Charland v. Country View Golf Club, Inc.

(*Minority Shareholder*) v. (*Closely-held Corporation*)

588 A.2d 609 (R.I.1991)

MINORITY DISCOUNT AND LACK OF MARKETABILITY DISCOUNT SHOULD NOT APPLY WHEN MAJORITY SHAREHOLDER PURCHASES MINORITY'S SHARES TO AVOID DISSOLUTION OF THE CORPORATION

■ **INSTANT FACTS** A minority shareholder appealed a judicial appraisal of his shares that had discounted their value due to their lack of marketability and the fact that they were not enough shares to control corporate decisions.

■ **BLACK LETTER RULE** In appraising the fair market value of the stock of a minority shareholder in a close corporation who has filed for dissolution, a court should not apply either a minority discount or a lack of marketability discount to determine the value of the stock.

■ PROCEDURAL BASIS

Appeal by a minority shareholder of a close corporation from a grant of summary judgment by a federal district court dismissing his request to have his shares redeemed by the corporation for fair market value.

■ FACTS

Gilbert Charland ("Charland") (P) was a minority shareholder in Country View Golf Club, Inc. ("Country View") (D), a close corporation that owned an 18-hole golf course. Alleging illegal activities by an officer of Country View (D), Garland (P) filed suit for dissolution of the corporation. Under a Rhode Island statute, Country View (D) elected to purchase Garland's (P) shares at a price equal to fair value on the day the dissolution petition was filed. The parties could not agree on the fair value, so the court ordered an appraiser to determine the value. The appraiser applied a "minority discount" in valuing the shares, discounting the value of the shares to account for the fact that Garland (P) did not have any decision-making power in the corporation. Garland appealed.

■ ISSUE

In appraising the fair market value of the stock of a minority shareholder in a close corporation who has filed for dissolution, should a court apply either a minority discount or a lack of marketability discount to determine the value of the stock?

■ DECISION AND RATIONALE

(Kelleher, J.) No. A minority discount is a discount applied to the value of a minority shareholder's stock because the shareholder lacks corporate decision-making power. Most courts that have considered the question agree that no minority discount should be applied when a corporation elects to buy out a shareholder who has petitioned for dissolution of the company. While it is true that if the shares were placed on the open market, their minority status would decrease their value, this devaluation does not really matter when the shares are being bought by the corporation, itself. In that instance, the fact that the shares are noncontrolling is irrelevant. We agree with that rationale and will not discount the shares here solely because of their minority status. As for the issue of whether the shares should be discounted because of lack of marketability, we apply similar reasoning. While normally, shares of a close corporation are not readily marketable and a discount should apply, when the shares are bought by the corporation, itself, the discount should not apply. Where the majority seeks an appraisal instead of dissolution of the corporation, complaining minority shareholders should never receive less than their pro rata share of the assets that they would have received if the corporation had been dissolved. Reversed and remanded.

Analysis:

Like most courts around the country, this court recognizes a difference between the value of a minority shareholder's stock in a close corporation to a third-party buyer and the value of the shares to the majority shareholders in that close corporation. A third-party buyer who purchases the shares of a minority shareholder will simply be in the same position as the minority shareholder was, lacking control over corporate decisions due to a lack of voting power and lacking a ready market in which to sell his shares. When the corporation, or really the majority shareholder of the corporation, buys the minority shareholder's stock, however, the majority shareholder will not have the same difficulties. Moreover, the majority shareholder will be ridding himself of the problems created by the minority shareholder, a clear benefit that has real value to the majority in many cases.

■ CASE VOCABULARY

LACK OF MARKETABILITY DISCOUNT: A discount applied to the value of stock in a closely-held corporation due to the fact that there is no ready market for the shares.

MINORITY DISCOUNT: A discount applied to the value of the stock of a minority shareholder of a corporation due to the fact that the shareholder does not have enough voting power to control decisions of the corporation.

CHAPTER SEVEN

Alternative Forms of Business Organization: Limited Partnerships, Limited Liability Companies, and Limited Liability Partnerships

Gateway Potato Sales v. G.B. Investment Co.

Instant Facts: When a limited partnership defaults, its unpaid supplier sues a limited partner, contending it actually controlled the partnership.

Black Letter Rule: Under RULPA (1976 version), limited partners are not personally liable for their limited partnerships' debts unless they either (i) exercised enough control to make them "substantially the same as" the general partner, or (ii) exercised lesser control and the creditor knew of the limited partners' control before extending credit.

In re USACafes, L.P. Litigation

Instant Facts: After an L.P. is sold, the limited partners sue their general partner, its owners, and its directors, contending they accepted secret payments from the buyer to sell at an unfairly low price.

Black Letter Rule: If a limited partnership has a corporate general partner, its officers (including directors) owe fiduciary duties to the limited partners.

Gotham Partners, L.P. v. Hallwood Realty Partners, L.P.

Instant Facts: Gotham Partners, L.P. (P) sued a limited partnership for breach of contractual fiduciary duties relating to a reverse split and odd lot tender offer approved by the board of directors.

Black Letter Rule: A limited partnership agreement may provide for contractually created fiduciary duties substantially mirroring traditional fiduciary duties that apply in corporate law.

Kaycee Land and Livestock v. Flahive

Instant Facts: Roger Flahive (D), through Flahive Oil & Gas (D), a limited liability company, leased undeveloped property from Kaycee Land and Livestock (P) and contaminated the property.

Black Letter Rule: The common law doctrine of piercing the corporate veil is not abrogated by the limited liability company act and may be used against limited liability company members in appropriate cases.

Solar Cells, Inc. v. True North Partners, LLC

Instant Facts: Solar Cells, Inc. (P) sought a preliminary injunction to enjoin the completion of a merger by True North Partners, LLC (D).

Black Letter Rule: To justify a preliminary injunction, the plaintiff must demonstrate a likelihood of success on the merits and irreparable harm for which there is no adequate remedy at law.

Gateway Potato Sales v. G.B. Investment Co.

(*Limited Partnership's Creditor*) v. (*Limited Partner*)
170 Ariz.137, 822 P.2d 490 (Ct.App.1991)

LIMITED PARTNERS WHO CONTROL PARTNERSHIP ARE PERSONALLY LIABLE FOR ITS DEBTS

■ **INSTANT FACTS** When a limited partnership defaults, its unpaid supplier sues a limited partner, contending it actually controlled the partnership.

■ **BLACK LETTER RULE** Under RULPA (1976 version), limited partners are not personally liable for their limited partnerships' debts unless they either (i) exercised enough control to make them "substantially the same as" the general partner, or (ii) exercised lesser control and the creditor knew of the limited partners' control before extending credit.

■ PROCEDURAL BASIS

Appeal from summary judgment for plaintiff in contract action seeking damages.

■ FACTS

The Sunworth Packing Limited Partnership ("Sunworth Packing") (D) was a potato farm formed by Sunworth Corporation (D) as general partner and G.B. Investment ("G.B.") (D) as limited partner. The limited partnership agreement, filed with the Arizona Secretary of State, specified that the limited partner (i) would not participate in control of the business, and (ii) would not be liable for the L.P.'s debts beyond its initial contribution. Sunworth Packing (D) ordered potato seeds from Gateway Potato Sales ("Gateway") (P), which (allegedly) sold to Sunworth (D) only because Sunworth's (D) president gave assurances G.B. (D), a large financier, was financing the venture, was actively managing it, and had approved the purchase, which (allegedly) led Gateway (D) to believe Sunworth Packing (D) was a *general* partnership. It is disputed whether G.B. (D) gave assurances of payment to Gateway (P). When Sunworth (D) defaulted on payment for the seeds, Gateway (P) sued to recover from Sunworth Packing (D) a limited partnership, its general partner Sunworth Corporation (D), and its limited partner G.B. (D). G.B. (D) moved for summary judgment, contending there was no evidence it had controlled Sunworth Packing (D). There was contradictory testimony on G.B.'s (D) degree of control, with Sunworth Packing's president's affidavit claiming G.B. (D) supervised daily operations, demanded to approve most decisions and expenditures, purchased machinery, obtained some financing independently, prepared financial statements, and spent some of the L.P.'s funds independently. G.B. (D) contradicted this evidence in its sworn affidavit. Sunworth Packing's (D) president also testified via affidavit that he had described G.B.'s (D) control over business operations to Gateway (P). The trial court granted G.B.'s (D) summary judgment motion. Gateway (P) appealed, contending there was conflicting evidence of G.B.'s (D) control of Sunworth Packing (D) sufficient to raise a triable issue of fact.

■ ISSUE

Are limited partners personally liable for their general partnerships' debts?

■ DECISION AND RATIONALE

(Taylor) Yes. Under RULPA (1976 version), limited partners are not personally liable for their limited partnerships' debts unless they either (i) exercised enough control to make them "substantially the same as" the general partner, or (ii) exercised lesser control and the creditor knew so before extending credit. Under Arizona statutory law [equivalent to RULPA (1976 version) § 303(a)], a limited partnership's limited partner may become liable for the limited partnership's obligations if either (i) it is also a general partner, or (ii) the limited partner whose participation in control of the business is "substantially the same as" that of a general partner, or (ii) the limited partner controlled the partnership to a lesser degree than the general partner, *and* the claimant creditor had actual knowledge of the limited partner's participation in control. Here, Gateway (P) contended in its pleadings that, alternately, either (ii) G.B. (D) exercised more control over Sunworth Packing (D) than the general partner, or (iii) it exercised some control, which imposes liability when coupled with Gateway's (P) knowledge of its control. The trial court gave summary judgment against Gateway (P), apparently concluding G.B. (D) was not liable as a matter of law by both (i) reasoning that under the statute, a claimant creditor must have had contact with the limited partner prior to the transaction to be liable, and finding the evidence showed Gateway (P) had no contact with G.B. (D) prior to the sale, and (ii) finding Gateway failed to allege specific facts necessary to conclude G.B. (P) exercised sufficient control over Sunworth Packing (D). "To the extent the trial court's ruling [was] based on a belief a limited partner [is] never . . . liable under the statute unless the creditor had contact with the limited partner and learned directly from him of his participation . . . [in] the business, . . . that ruling [is] in error." The statute's language and legislative history show the legislature intended *not* to require such direct contact, as is the rule under RULPA (1976 version) § 303(a). The new RULPA (1985 revision) would have changed the rule to hold that, when a limited partner exercises some degree of control (but less than that of a general partner), the limited partner is only liable to those creditors who (i) had actual knowledge of that control before the transaction and (ii) acquired that knowledge through direct dealings with the limited partner. But the Arizona legislature specifically rejected the new RULPA (1985), showing a legislative intent to retain the rule under the old RULPA (1976) that, while the creditor must have knowledge, it need not have acquired that knowledge through direct dealings with the limited partner. Here, Gateway (P) presented evidence sufficient to withstand summary judgment and raise the triable issue of what degree of control G.B. (D) exerted over Sunworth Packing (D), by alleging specific acts by G.B.'s (D) employees. Some of the acts alleged fell withing the Arizona statute's "safe harbor" provision, but others do not and may create liability. Reversed and remanded for trial.

Analysis:

This case is notable for expounding the rule of limited partners' liability under ULPA, old RULPA (1976) , and new RULPA (1985). Limited partners are generally not personally liable for the full extent of a limited partnership's debts, except to the extent of their investment. Thus, in this case, it may seem desperate for Gateway (P) to sue the limited partner for partnership debts on a control theory. Of course, it may also seem unfair that the limited partnership here tried to avoid normal liability for its *general* partner by making that general partner a limited-liability corporation. Apparently, courts are reluctant to pierce this additional "corporate veil."

■ CASE VOCABULARY

"SAFE HARBOR" PROVISION: In a statute, a provision listing certain persons/actions which are specifically not intended to be within the statute's scope, and are thus not liable/actionable.

In re USACafes, L.P. Litigation

(*Limited Partners*) v. (*Buyer of L.P.*)
600 A.2d 43 (Del.Ch.1991)

CORPORATE GENERAL PARTNER'S OFFICERS OWE FIDUCIARY DUTIES TO LIMITED PARTNERS

■ **INSTANT FACTS** After an L.P. is sold, the limited partners sue their general partner, its owners, and its directors, contending they accepted secret payments from the buyer to sell at an unfairly low price.

■ **BLACK LETTER RULE** If a limited partnership has a corporate general partner, its officers (including directors) owe fiduciary duties to the limited partners.

■ PROCEDURAL BASIS

Class action suit in contract action seeking equitable constructive trust and damages.

■ FACTS

USACafes Inc., a failing corporation was reorganized into a Limited Partnership (L.P.), USACafes, L.P. (D). USACafes General Partner, Inc. ("General Partner") (D) became the corporate general partner. General Partner (D) was owned by the [aptly-named] Wyly brothers (D), who also owned 47% of USACafes, L.P. (D). Later, USACafes, L.P. (D) was acquired by Metsa Acquisition Corp. (D) for a questionably low price, with no other bidders. The limited partners (P) sued USACafes, L.P. (D), the Wylys (D), General Partner (D), four of General Partner's (D) Directors (D), and Metsa (D), contending the Wylys (D) and Directors (D) breached their fiduciary duties to them by accepting side payments from Metsa (D) to sell the limited partnership at an unfairly low price. Specifically, they first alleged the breach occurred when (i) the Wylys (D) accepted $11 million from Metsa (D) disguised as payments for non-competition covenants, (ii) the General Partner (D) (wholly owned by the Wylys (D)) received $1.5 million disguised as releases for a bogus claim, and (iii) various Directors (D) received debt forgiveness and lucrative "change of control" bonuses. On these facts, the limited partners (P) claimed either (i) the defendants breached their fiduciary duties by failing to seek a better price from other buyers, or (ii) the defendants' "side payments" should have been shared with the limited partners (P). Second, the limited partners (P) alternately alleged the General Partner (D) and its Directors (D) breached their duty of care in selling the Partnership by failing to inform themselves of its value or shop for higher bids. Third, the shareholders (P) contended that shareholders in the predecessor, USACafes Inc., were misled by a prospectus into believing future acquisition would require majority shareholder approval, and were thus implicitly entitled to a retroactive vote/recision of the purchase. Fourth, the shareholders (P) contend that, since Metsa (D) induced the other defendants to breach their fiduciary duties, Metsa (D) should be jointly liable for resulting damages. The Wylys (D) and Directors (D) moved to dismiss for failure to state a claim, contending that, while General Partner (P) owed the limited partners (P) fiduciary duties of loyalty and care, they themselves owed no such duties to the limited partners (P) merely because they were General Partner's (D) owners/directors.

■ ISSUE

If a limited partnership has a corporate general partner, do its officers and directors owe fiduciary duties to the limited partners?

■ DECISION AND RATIONALE

(Allen) Yes. If a limited partnership has a corporate general partner, its officers (including directors) owe fiduciary duties to the limited partners. This rule is deduced from general principles and trust law. Fiduciary duty requires that one who controls another's property not intentionally use that property to benefit himself at the other's expense, absent contrary agreement. Trust case law extends this principle by making corporate directors and controlling shareholders fiduciaries for the other shareholders. Leading scholars suggest this principle should be extended to require that, in a trust with a corporation as trustee, the corporate trustee's officers and directors have fiduciary duties to prevent the corporate trustee's misappropriation of trust property, and are personally liable to the beneficiaries if they intentionally breach those duties. If the corporate trustee's officers improperly acquire an interest in trust property, they become personally liable for any losses and accountable to the beneficiary for any profits. Thus, under trust theory, the corporate trustee's officers owe fiduciary duties not only to the trustee corporation, but also to trust beneficiaries. We now extend this duty to corporate general partners and their officers, because this rule will prevent self-dealing transactions by general partners and their officers at the expense of limited partners. Further, our prior case law suggests this rule. We will not attempt to delineate here the exact scope of the fiduciary duties of general partners and their officers. "But it surely entails the duty not to use control over [partnership] property to advantage the corporate director at the expense of the partnership." Here, the complaint alleges the corporate Directors (D) and owners did just that, so that complaint states a valid cause of action. The Directors (D) also moved to dismiss on the grounds they owed a duty only to General Partner (D) as its agents, but their motion must also be dismissed, since if they did the acts alleged, they will have breached their duties to General Partner (D) as well. Motion denied.

Analysis:

In this case, a general partner's officers untenably claimed that, while the general partner *itself* (as an entity) admittedly owes a fiduciary duty to limited partners, the general partner's *officers* (who control the general partner) owe no such duty to limited partners. Thus, the defendants claim, if they (as officers) cause the general partner to cheat the limited partners, they are not personally responsible. This is as incongruous as a corporation's directors disclaiming responsibility for the corporation's action, even though they are in full control of the corporation and personally authorized those actions. The holding of *USACafes* makes a sound public policy decision in imposing on a corporate general partner's officers a fiduciary duty toward limited partners. As the court notes, holding otherwise would create unfair results; the general partners' directors, who in practice run the partnership for the limited partners, would be allowed to personally loot that same partnership, so long as they did so in their own names (rather than the general partner's) and avoided also looting the general partner, which would effectively leave limited partners at the complete mercy of unscrupulous directors.

■ CASE VOCABULARY

"CHANGE OF CONTROL" BONUS: Bonus payment, usually to a business's officer/director, paid if the business is acquired.

CLASS ACTION: Litigation procedure where one/several plaintiff(s) sue on behalf of all similarly-situated plaintiffs, with court permission. The "named" plaintiff conducts the lawsuit, but any recovery is divided among all plaintiffs. Here, some limited partners are suing Metsa (D) as representatives of the entire class of limited partners, contending Metsa (D) cheated all the limited partners.

CONSTRUCTIVE TRUST: Equitable doctrine where, if a fiduciary earns profits by breaching its fiduciary duties to a beneficiary, those profits can be seized as (constructively) belonging to the beneficiary. Here, plaintiffs argue that Metsa's (D) profits were made in violation of its duty to them, and thus should be awarded to them.

Gotham Partners, L.P. v. Hallwood Realty Partners, L.P.

(*Limited Partner*) v. (*Limited Partnership*)
817 A.2d 160 (Del.2002)

DAMAGES FOR BREACH OF FIDUCIARY DUTY MUST CONSIDER THE VALUE OF THE LOSS OF CONTROL OVER A PARTNERSHIP

■ **INSTANT FACTS** Gotham Partners, L.P. (P) sued a limited partnership for breach of contractual fiduciary duties relating to a reverse split and odd lot tender offer approved by the board of directors.

■ **BLACK LETTER RULE** A limited partnership agreement may provide for contractually created fiduciary duties substantially mirroring traditional fiduciary duties that apply in corporate law.

■ PROCEDURAL BASIS

On appeal to review a chancery court decision for the plaintiff.

■ FACTS

Gotham Partners, L.P. (P) was the largest independent limited partner in Hallwood Realty Partners, L.P. ("The Partnership") (D). Hallwood Realty Corporation ("General Partner") (D) was the only general partner of the Partnership (D) and was a wholly owned subsidiary of Hallwood Group Incorporated ("HGI"). When the Partnership's (D) units were trading at a low price, Guzzetti, a member of the General Partner's (D) board of directors, proposed a reverse split and odd lot tender offer subject to HGI's willingness to provide financing for the transactions. HGI agreed to finance the reverse split and purchased approximately 6.3% of the Partnership's (D) equity, doubling its interest in the Partnership (D). Thereafter, HGI agreed to finance the odd lot tender offer. Because the odd lot offer was then pitched to the public as a resale of existing, listed Partnership (D) units, the Partnership's (D) accounting books did not treat the resale to HGI as an issuance of units. The Partnership (D) thereafter resold all purchased units resulting from the odd lot offer to HGI at the same price it had paid for them. As a result, HGI held approximately 29.7% of the Partnership's (D) equity and solidified its control over the Partnership (D).

Gotham (P) owned 14.8% of the Partnership's (D) equity and, although it was aware of the reverse split and odd lot tender offer, did not object until several years later, at which time it requested access to the Partnership's (D) books and records. When the Partnership (D) denied the request, Gotham (P) brought a books and records action. Several months later, Gotham (P) filed a separate derivative action relating to the reverse split and odd lot offer, alleging that they were unfair to the Partnership's (D) unitholders because HGI was allowed to purchase controlling interest in the Partnership (D) at an unfairly low price. Gotham (P) alleged breaches by the General Partner (D) of traditional and contractual fiduciary duties. On a motion for summary judgment, the chancery court dismissed the traditional fiduciary duty claims as supplanted by contractual fiduciary duties. Under the partnership agreement, the court held that the defendants owed a duty of entire fairness towards the plaintiff. After trial, the court concluded that no breach occurred with respect to the reverse split. However, the court concluded that the odd lot resale did not involve the issuance of units and was thus subject to the contractual fiduciary duties. The court concluded that the defendants breached their fiduciary duties by failing to form a committee to review and approve the odd lot offer as required by the agreement and by failing to obtain a reliable financial analysis to confirm that the resale was fair. The court awarded Gotham (P) money damages, but denied rescission of the odd lot resale. Gotham (P) appealed the remedy, and the defendant appealed the court's determination that its actions were subject to contractual fiduciary duties.

■ ISSUE

May a limited partnership supplant the common law fiduciary duties of loyalty and care by contract?

■ DECISION AND RATIONALE

(Veasey, C.J.) Yes. A general partner owes the limited partnership and its limited partners the traditional fiduciary duties of care and loyalty. By statute, however, these duties may be modified or enhanced by the partnership agreement. In such circumstances, the unambiguous terms of the partnership agreement establish the duties owed by the general partner. The partnership agreement here unambiguously establishes the General Partner's (D) fiduciary duty of entire fairness to Gotham (P) and other limited partners by restricting the General Partner's (D) authority to undertake self-dealing transactions that are not substantially equivalent to the terms available from a third person and establishes financial procedures for ensuring fairness. Having established this duty by agreement, the common law duties of loyalty and care were supplanted. Because the odd lot resale to HGI was made from existing shares, it was not governed by the contractual provision affording the General Partner (D) absolute authority over the transaction. The contractual fiduciary duties apply and were breached by the failure to ensure entire fairness to Gotham (D) and other limited partners.

While the chancery court's decision not to order rescission of the sale was proper because the General Partner (D) did not intend to become entrenched or for HGI to become unjustly enriched, the money damages awarded are an insufficient remedy for the loss of control the limited partners experienced from the General Partner's (D) actions. Because the partnership agreement is silent as to damages for a breach of fiduciary duty, the court may properly award equitable relief when money damages are an insufficient remedy for the breach. Although the General Partner (D) did not intend to become entrenched or to unjustly enrich HGI, the odd lot resale had that result. The damages failed to account for the premium on control of the Partnership (D), awarding only the per unit value of each unit resold to HGI. The matter is remanded for recalculation of the damages, taking into account the value of control over the Partnership (D). Affirmed in part, reversed in part, and remanded.

Analysis:

In a limited partnership, partners generally owe only the duties of care and loyalty to one another. Because, unlike corporations, limited partnerships are especially governed by the terms of the partnership agreement, such agreements must be carefully and unambiguously drafted to clearly establish the duties owed. Absent such language, partners' duties will not be expanded beyond their traditional scope.

■ CASE VOCABULARY

ODD LOT TENDER OFFER: A tender offer by the issuer for blocks of fewer than one hundred outstanding units or shares.

TENDER OFFER: A public offer to buy a minimum number of shares directly from a corporation's shareholders at a fixed price, usually at a substantial premium over the market price, in an effort to take control of the corporation.

Kaycee Land and Livestock v. Flahive

(*Real Estate Lessor*) v. (*Judgment–Proof Lessee*)
46 P.3d 323 (Wyo.2002)

A COURT MAY PIERCE THE CORPORATE VEIL OF A LIMITED LIABILITY COMPANY

■ **INSTANT FACTS** Roger Flahive (D), through Flahive Oil & Gas (D), a limited liability company, leased undeveloped property from Kaycee Land and Livestock (P) and contaminated the property.

■ **BLACK LETTER RULE** The common law doctrine of piercing the corporate veil is not abrogated by the limited liability company act and may be used against limited liability company members in appropriate cases.

■ PROCEDURAL BASIS

On appeal from the district court's certification of a question of law to the Wyoming Supreme Court.

■ FACTS

Roger Flahive (D) was the managing member of Flahive Oil & Gas (D), a limited liability company (LLC), which negotiated a lease with Kaycee Land and Livestock (P) for certain real estate. Kaycee (P) contended that Flahive Oil (D) contaminated the property. Kaycee (P) did not allege that Flahive Oil (D) acted fraudulently, but wanted to pierce Flahive Oil's (D) corporate veil to reach Roger Flahive's (D) personal assets to satisfy the LLC's debt for cleaning up the property.

■ ISSUE

In the absence of fraud, may a court pierce the corporate veil of a limited liability company to reach its members' assets?

■ DECISION AND RATIONALE

(Kite, J.) Yes. Because Wyoming was one of the first states to adopt a limited liability company statute, the statute contains only minimal formation requirements and remains silent concerning the remedy of piercing the company veil. However, Wyoming has long recognized piercing of a corporate veil under particular circumstances. When determining whether to pierce the veil of a corporate entity, Wyoming courts consider, among other things, whether funds have been commingled, the treatment by an individual of corporate assets as his own, the failure to issue stock, the holding out by an individual as being responsible for corporate debts, and the use of the corporation as a shell to evade creditors. Piercing the corporate veil is permissible when necessary to prevent injustice.

Although the Wyoming Limited Liability Company statute does not address the circumstances under which the company's veil may be pierced, it is illogical to assume that the legislature did not consider whether such a remedy would be available. While the factors justifying the piercing of the corporate veil are not entirely applicable to an LLC, there is no reason to treat an LLC differently than a corporation when liability of its members is at issue. The factors to be considered to pierce the LLC veil need not be established at this time, and the district court is obligated to conduct an intensive review of the facts to determine whether piercing would be equitable.

Analysis:

Some state statutes, such as Colorado's and Minnesota's, specifically include provisions that allow courts to apply the common law principles of piercing the corporate veil to an LLC. Because tax or other financial considerations drive most choice-of-entity decisions, it makes sense to treat all entities alike and, if the entity is misused, to allow creditors to make claims directly against the LLC membership for moneys owed. The Internal Revenue Service, however, is not entitled to disregard the LLC for collection purposes, even though it ignores the LLC when LLC members file their individual returns. However, as noted in I.R.S. Chief Couns. Adv. 199930013, 1999 WL 554351 (July 30, 1999), and I.R.S. Chief Couns. Adv. 199922053, 1999 WL 358245 (June 4, 1999), in the case of a single-person LLC, the IRS will pursue a claim for unpaid employment taxes against the single member.

■ CASE VOCABULARY

CERTIFIED QUESTION: A point of law on which a federal appellate court seeks guidance from either the U.S. Supreme Court or the highest state court by the procedure of certification.

CORPORATE VEIL: The legal assumption that the acts of a corporation are not the actions of its stockholders, so that the stockholders are exempt from liability for the corporation's actions.

LIMITED LIABILITY COMPANY: A company—statutorily authorized in certain states—that is characterized by limited liability, management by members or managers, and limitation on ownership transfer.

PIERCING THE CORPORATE VEIL: The judicial act of imposing personal liability on otherwise immune corporate officers, directors, and stockholders for the corporation's wrongful acts.

Solar Cells, Inc. v. True North Partners, LLC

(*Business Partner*) v. (*Business Partner*)

2002 WL 749163 (Del.Ch.Ct.2002)

DIRECTORS OWE A FIDUCIARY DUTY TO OTHER DIRECTORS TO ACT WITH ENTIRE FAIRNESS

■ **INSTANT FACTS** Solar Cells, Inc. (P) sought a preliminary injunction to enjoin the completion of a merger by True North Partners, LLC (D).

■ **BLACK LETTER RULE** To justify a preliminary injunction, the plaintiff must demonstrate a likelihood of success on the merits and irreparable harm for which there is no adequate remedy at law.

■ PROCEDURAL BASIS

Chancery court consideration of the plaintiff's motion for a preliminary injunction.

■ FACTS

Solar Cells, Inc. (P) and True North Partners, LLC (D) formed First Solar, a Delaware limited liability company. Under the Operating Agreement, Solar Cells (P) contributed certain patented and proprietary technology needed to produce solar power and True North (D) contributed the operating capital. The company was run by two managers elected by Solar Cells (P) and three elected by True North (D). When the initial funding was depleted, First Solar sought an additional investor. In the meantime, however, True North (D) provided a $15–million loan to the company to keep it operating. After failing to bring in other investors, the three True North (D) managers approved the merger of First Solar into First Solar Operating, LLC (FSO), a Delaware limited liability company wholly owned by True North (D). The merger would be based on a total valuation of $32 million with ownership units of First Solar being exchanged for equal units in FSO. As a result, Solar Cell's (P) interest would be decreased from fifty percent of First Solar to five percent of the merged company. Solar Cell (P) filed a complaint for breach of fiduciary duty and requested a preliminary injunction to enjoin the merger.

■ ISSUE

Is Solar Cells (P) entitled to a preliminary injunction enjoining the proposed merger that would result in a significant decrease in its ownership interest?

■ DECISION AND RATIONALE

(Chandler, J.) Yes. To justify a preliminary injunction, Solar Cells (P) must demonstrate a likelihood of success on the merits and irreparable harm for which there is no adequate remedy at law. The defendants claim the plaintiff is not likely to succeed on the merits of its breach of fiduciary duty claim because Solar Cells (P) waived liability for a conflict of interest in the Operating Agreement so long as True North (D) managers act in good faith. Solar Cells (P) does not, however, seek to impose liability on the defendants for their actions, but rather seeks to prevent the merger as inequitable. Furthermore, the agreement does not waive all fiduciary duties, for True North (D) must still act in good faith. The True North (D) merger approval came one day after a meeting of all managers, where there was no mention of the proposed merger. Solar Cells (P) was given no prior notice of the proposed merger and was notified of the True North (D) managers' approval only a week before the merger was expected to be completed. Given the appearance of bad faith, the burden at trial will be on True North (D) to establish entire fairness by showing that the "transaction was the result of fair dealing and offered a fair price" considering all economic and financial circumstances surrounding the merger. Given the lack of notice to Solar Cells (P) and the significant dilution in Solar Cells' (P) voting strength in the merged company, there is a reasonable likelihood that the defendant will not be able to establish that the merger resulted from fair dealing.

As to the fairness of the price, there is a reasonable likelihood that True North (D) will not be able to demonstrate that its merger valuation was fair. True North (D) retained an investment consultant to value First Solar before the merger. The $32–million valuation was approximately one-third that calculated by the consultant just five months earlier. The valuation was "quick and dirty" to facilitate a timely merger and discounted a cash-flow analysis that was likely to increase the valuation. Solar Cells (P) has demonstrated a likelihood of success on its entire fairness claim.

Likewise, Solar Cells (P) has shown irreparable harm for which no adequate remedy at law exists. The dilution in voting strength and the power to appoint managers that comes with it is a significant injury to Solar Cells (P). Whether the right to appoint managers includes the right to control the group, the right is integral to Solar Cells' (P) participation in the management of the company. If the merger is permitted, Solar Cells (P) will be irreparably harmed. The preliminary injunction is granted.

Analysis:

The limited liability company is a statutory enterprise including both partnership and corporate characteristics. Like corporations, a limited liability company is an entity distinct from its owners. It may hold property and enter into transactions on its own behalf. It also enjoys significant tax advantages and insulates its owners from personal liability for business liabilities. Like partnerships, however, the LLC is highly subject to internal governance provisions established by its formation agreement. LLCs are growing in number across the country and are becoming a more favorable choice of entity than general partnerships.

■ CASE VOCABULARY

CAPITAL: Money or assets invested, or available for investment, in a business.

PRELIMINARY INJUNCTION: A temporary injunction issued before or during trial to prevent an irreparable injury from occurring before the court has a chance to decide the case.

CHAPTER EIGHT

Duty of Care and the Duty to Act in Good Faith

Francis v. United Jersey Bank (N.J. 1981)

Instant Facts: When a corporate director's sons, also directors, embezzled client funds, the director was sued for breaching her duty of care by not preventing the theft.

Black Letter Rule: Corporate directors are personally liable for violating their duty of care by failing to prevent wrongful acts by other corporate officers, if (i) they owed a duty to the victim, (ii) they were negligent in monitoring the other officers, and (iii) their negligence was the proximate cause of the injury.

Kamin v. American Express Co.

Instant Facts: When a corporation's directors ordered in-kind dividends which did not utilize available tax deductions, some shareholders sued, contending the directors carelessly wasted corporate assets.

Black Letter Rule: Corporate directors' decisions on dividends are not actionable as breaches of care, absent fraud, self-dealing, bad faith, or oppression.

Smith v. Van Gorkom (Del. 1985)

Instant Facts: When a corporate CEO convinces the Directors to sell the corporation without calculating its value, shareholders allege they breached their duty of care.

Black Letter Rule: Corporate directors who sell the corporation without determining its true value have breached their duty of care.

In re Caremark International Inc. Derivative Litigation

Instant Facts: When a corporation charged with health care bribery is forced to pay $250 million and promise better management in a settlement with government agencies, angry shareholders request the court reject the settlement and permit them to sue the directors for negligently permitting bribery.

Black Letter Rule: Corporate directors have a duty to make good faith efforts to institute a corporate monitoring system they believe will alert them of material events, but are not liable if the system fails to detect wrongdoing.

Malpiede v. Townson

Instant Facts: Shareholders sued corporate directors for breach of the duties of loyalty and care for failing to accept the highest bid on an announced merger.

Black Letter Rule: The plaintiff bears the burden of properly pleading claims of breach of the duties of loyalty and care against a director.

In re the Walt Disney Co. Derivative Litigation

Instant Facts: Shareholders brought a derivative action against Walt Disney Co. (D) for blindly approving the hiring of a new president and his subsequent non-fault termination.

Black Letter Rule: The business judgment rule does not save directors from liability for the conscious disregard of the consequences of corporate action upon the corporation or its shareholders.

Miller v. American Telephone & Telegraph Co.

Instant Facts: When a phone company fails to collect payment from the Democratic Party, the shareholders contend the failure is an illegally-disguised campaign contribution.

Black Letter Rule: The failure to collect claims is entitled to the business judgement presumption, unless that failure is otherwise illegal.

Francis v. United Jersey Bank

(*Corporation's Bankruptcy Trustee*) v. (*Corporation's President's Estate*)

87 N.J. 15, 432 A.2d 814 (1981)

CORPORATE DIRECTORS LIABLE FOR NEGLIGENTLY IGNORING OTHER DIRECTORS' MISDEEDS

■ **INSTANT FACTS** When a corporate director's sons, also directors, embezzled client funds, the director was sued for breaching her duty of care by not preventing the theft.

■ **BLACK LETTER RULE** Corporate directors are personally liable for violating their duty of care by failing to prevent wrongful acts by other corporate officers, if (i) they owed a duty to the victim, (ii) they were negligent in monitoring the other officers, and (iii) their negligence was the proximate cause of the injury.

■ PROCEDURAL BASIS

Appeal from judgment for plaintiffs in business tort action seeking damages.

■ FACTS

Mrs. Pritchard (D) and her sons (D) were officers, directors, and shareholders of Pritchard & Baird Intermediaries Corp. (D), a reinsurance broker. The sons (D) embezzled $12 million from Pritchard & Baird (P), misappropriating accounts commingled with clients' funds as "loans" to themselves, and bankrupting Pritchard & Baird (P). The sons (D) disguised their pilfering somewhat, but Pritchard & Baird's (P) financial statements still showed huge and ever-increasing loans. Mrs. Pritchard (D) never participated in the embezzlement, but did not stop it, apparently because she was unaware of Pritchard & Baird's (P) finances. Finally, Pritchard & Baird's (P) creditors petitioned it into bankruptcy, and on their behalf Pritchard & Baird's (P) bankruptcy trustees sued, among others, Mrs. Pritchard (D), as director, for negligent violation of her directorial duty of care in not noticing or preventing the misappropriation. Evidence showed Mrs. Pritchard (D), while nominally a director of Pritchard & Baird (P), never participated in its management and knew nothing of its corporate affairs. The trial court found the Pritchards' (D) payments were fraudulent conveyances and found Mrs. Pritchard (D) liable for negligence in permitting the embezzlement, and found other defendants liable for accepting wrongful payments. The appellate court affirmed, but found the payments were a conversion of trust funds rather than fraudulent conveyance. The NJ Supreme Court granted certification limited to the issue of whether Mrs. Pritchard (D), as a director, is liable for other directors' embezzlement.

■ ISSUE

Are corporate directors personally liable for violating their duty of care by failing to prevent wrongful acts by other corporate officers?

■ DECISION AND RATIONALE

(Pollock, J.) Yes. Corporate directors are personally liable for violating their duty of care by failing to prevent wrongful acts by other corporate officers, if (i) they owed a duty to the victim, (ii) they were negligent in monitoring the other officers, and (iii) their negligence was the proximate cause of the injury. The governing law for this case is New Jersey's, since New Jersey is the state with the most significant relation to the defendants and transactions. Under the NJ Business Corporation Act [and all states' common law], directors must "discharge their duties in good faith and with the degree of diligence, care and skill which ordinarily prudent men would exercise under similar circumstances in like positions." Though the exact degree of care depends on circumstances, generally "a director should acquire at least a rudimentary understanding of" the corporation's business, because lack of knowledge is no defense to the duty of care. Also, "directors are under a continuing obligation to keep informed" about corporate activities, to enable them to act with care . . . The sentinel asleep at his post contributes nothing to the enterprise he is charged to protect . . . Directorial management does not require a detailed inspection of day-to-day activities, but rather a general monitoring of corporate affairs . . . ." Directors should attend board meetings regularly, especially since, under New Jersey law, absent directors are presumed to concur with the action taken, unless they subsequently file a dissent. "While directors are not required to audit corporate books, they should maintain familiarity with the [corporation's] financial status . . . by a regular review of financial statements . . . In some circumstances, directors may be charged with assuring that bookkeeping methods conform to industry custom," though the extent of review required depends on the corporation's size, ownership, and industry. Under the statute, generally, directors are immune from liability if, in good faith, they rely on the corporation's legal counsel, independent public accountants' reports, or internal reports approved by the chairman or CEO. Upon reviewing financial statements and finding improprieties, the director has a duty to object, and if that fails, to resign, seek legal advice about the actions, or even prevent improprieties by threatening suit. Greater action is required where the corporation is either large and publicly held, or engaged in business bearing on the public interest,e.g., banking. Directors' duty of care is directed towards specific obligees, especially the corporation and shareholders, to whom the director is a fiduciary. Generally, case law holds that directors do *not* owe similar fiduciary duties to corporate creditors, unless either (i) the corporation is insolvent, or (ii) the business and/or creditors are of a special class [involving an unusual degree of trust], e.g., banks' depositors, trust beneficiaries, etc. Here, Pritchard & Baird's (P) business was a reinsurance brokerage, which qualifies as a special class of business, because of its bank-like function and the "unqualified trust and confidence reposed by" client-insurers in entrusting brokers with payments meant for reinsurers, which created a reasonable expectation that Mrs. Pritchard (D), as director, would prevent conversion. Thus, Mrs. Pritchard (D) owed fiduciary duties of care to clients, which included a duty to read Pritchard & Baird's (P) financial statements, which would have disclosed the conversion disguised as loans. She breached that duty by ignoring those financial statements. Nevertheless, a director's negligence creates liability only if that negligence proximately caused the loss. When dealing with negligent omissions, the test of proximate causation is to determine what steps the director should reasonably have taken, and whether reasonable steps would have averted the loss. The act/failure must be a substantial factor in producing the harm. Usually, directors absolve themselves from liability if they alert the other directors of the impropriety, vote against it, and resign if outvoted. However, they may have to take greater steps when the corporation is insolvent or involved in an industry involving unusual trust. Here, Mrs. Pritchard (D) should have actually stopped the misappropriation, because the corporation was nearly insolvent and had a fiduciary duty to depositor-clients. Her inaction was a "substantial factor" in permitting the misappropriation, since the sons (D) stole freely knowing Mrs. Pritchard (D) ignored their conduct, and the court believes she could have prevented it by threatening suit. Judgment affirmed.

Analysis:

Generally, this case stands for the proposition that corporate directors have a duty to read corporate financial statements. But the law does not require that they report an impropriety. Instead, the law allows them to resign, while permitting the corporation to go forward with the impropriety and cause damages. Here, for instance, had Mrs. Pritchard (D) learned of her sons' (D) embezzlement and resigned, she would have enabled them to continue looting client funds with even greater abandon.

■ CASE VOCABULARY

CONVERSION: In tort, wrongful possession or use of another's property. Here, it means embezzlement of trust funds.

FRAUDULENT CONVEYANCE: In bankruptcy, a sham property transfer from a near-bankrupt debtor to another person, done to prevent creditors from seizing the property in bankruptcy. Under bankruptcy law, property thus conveyed must be returned to the debtor's bankruptcy estate.

REINSURER: Insurance company which sells insurance to other insurance companies, usually for very large risks. Here, Pritchard & Baird (D) was a broker/intermediary between the insurer and its reinsurer, and handled funds paid by one to the other.

Kamin v. American Express Co.

(*Shareholders, on Corporation's Behalf*) v. (*Corporation & Directors*)

86 Misc.2d 809, 383 N.Y.S.2d 807, aff'd 54 A.D.2d 654, 387 N.Y.S.2d 993 (1st Dept.1976)

CORPORATE DIRECTORS ENTITLED TO BUSINESS JUDGMENT PRESUMPTION ON DIVIDEND DECISIONS

■ **INSTANT FACTS** When a corporation's directors ordered in-kind dividends which did not utilize available tax deductions, some shareholders sued, contending the directors carelessly wasted corporate assets.

■ **BLACK LETTER RULE** Corporate directors' decisions on dividends are not actionable as breaches of care, absent fraud, self-dealing, bad faith, or oppression.

■ PROCEDURAL BASIS

Defendants' motion for summary judgment and dismissal for failure to state cause of action in corporate derivative action seeking damages or declaratory judgment.

■ FACTS

American Express (D) acquired for investment shares of Donald, Lufken and Jenrette, Inc. ("DLJ") for \$29.9 million. Later, those shares' value plummeted to \$4 million. American Express's Directors (D) decided to give those shares to shareholders as in-kind dividends, rather than selling them and recognizing a \$25 million loss. [The effects of the distribution are that (i) the Directors (D) avoid having to admit on financial statements that the company lost \$25 million through bad investments during their tenure, and (ii) some Directors receive more in performance-based compensation, but (iii) American Express (D) and its shareholders lose an \$8 million tax deduction for capital losses.] Kamin and other minority shareholders (P) sued to require the Directors (D) to rescind the dividend, contending they were breaching their fiduciary duties of care in wasting corporate assets by denying American Express (D) tax deductions. Kamin (D) did not allege the Directors (D) acted in bad faith. The dividend was paid, so Kamin (D) requested damages.

■ ISSUE

Have corporate directors violated their duty of care by ordering dividends which do not maximize tax savings?

■ DECISION AND RATIONALE

(Greenfield, J.) No. Corporate directors' decisions on dividends are not actionable as breaches of care, absent fraud, self-dealing, bad faith, or oppression. Under Delaware case law's "business judgment" presumption, corporate directors are not liable to shareholders for their business decisions absent fraud, self-dealing, bad faith, or oppression. Specifically, the manner and amount of distributions is exclusively a matter of business judgment for the directors. This rule is justified by the statutory powers conferred on directors by the Delaware corporate statutes, and by the fact that courts are unqualified to second-guess directors' business decisions. Delaware Business Corporation Law § 720 seemingly permits actions against a director for "the neglect of, or failure to perform, ... his duties in the management ... of corporate assets," but the "neglect" referred to is neglect of duties (i.e., malfeasance or nonfeasance), not negligent misjudgment. Here, even if the Directors' (D) decision imprudently lost tax advantages, this imprudence is not actionable absent bad faith, which was not alleged here. There is also evidence the Directors (D) properly considered Kamin's (P) request, made a valid and legal decision to forego the tax savings to avoid lowering American Express's (D) stock's market value by recognizing a $25 million loss. The only hint of self-interest, which was raised late by Kamin (P), is that 4 of the 20 Directors stood to receive greater compensation by not recognizing the loss, but this is speculative, since there is no showing the interested directors dominated the others. Also, directors' actions inevitably benefit some shareholders more than others, so we are reluctant to make their every decision actionable by disadvantaged shareholders. Here, Kamin (D) failed to make an actionable claim by not alleging wrongdoing. Complaint dismissed and summary judgment granted.

Analysis:

This case illustrates the broad discretion generally given to corporate directors in making business decisions. Under Delaware's common law "business judgment rule," (more accurately, "business judgment presumption"), directors' business decisions are conclusively presumed to be non-negligent if they were made without bad faith. Thus, directors of Delaware-incorporated businesses are rarely found liable for the consequences of their mistaken judgments, if those judgments were taken in good faith and upon reasonable deliberation. Here, the court dismisses the possibility that some directors might have wanted to inflate earnings to bolster their earnings-based bonuses, because it claims most of the directors had no such incentive. But it ignores the possibility that all the directors would naturally want to report having lost $25 million on their watch, and thus ordered in-kind distribution to save face at shareholders' expense However, procedurally, it is hard for the court to consider this claim when Kamin (D) unwisely failed to allege it in his complaint.

■ CASE VOCABULARY

BUSINESS JUDGMENT [RULE/PRESUMPTION]: In Delaware corporate case law, the presumption that directors' business decisions are deemed non-negligent if done without bad faith, self-interest, fraud, or oppression of shareholders.

CAPITAL LOSSES: In tax, losses from property held as investments, which can be used to reduce taxes by offsetting capital gains (profits on same). Here, it was alleged that $25 million in capital losses could have been used to reduce taxable income from other investments by $25 million, thus saving (assuming the corporation would otherwise have to pay 33% corporate income tax on the $25 million) about $8 million.

IN–KIND DIVIDEND: Corporate distribution paid out in non-cash assets, such as shares of stock.

MALFEASANCE: Wrongful or unlawful act by officer.

MISFEASANCE: Legal act by officer performed in a wrongful way.

Smith v. Van Gorkom

(*Shareholders, as class*) v. (*Chairman-CEO & Directors*)
488 A.2d 858 (Del.1985)

BEFORE SELLING CORPORATION, DIRECTORS MUST ASSESS ITS VALUE

■ **INSTANT FACTS** When a corporate CEO convinces the Directors to sell the corporation without calculating its value, shareholders allege they breached their duty of care.

■ **BLACK LETTER RULE** Corporate directors who sell the corporation without determining its true value have breached their duty of care.

■ PROCEDURAL BASIS

Appeal from judgment for defendants in shareholder class action seeking rescission or damages.

■ FACTS

Trans Union Corporation stood to lose tax benefits if it could not raise its taxable income. CEO Van Gorkom (D) and other Directors (D) considered a leveraged buy-out (LBO) [which would merge Trans Union into another higher-income corporation, allowing its tax credits to offset the combined corporation's taxable income]. The CFO (D) made [extremely] preliminary calculations showing an LBO would be profitable if the company were valued at $50 per share, but unprofitable at $60. There was no agreement Trans Union was actually worth $50 or $60 per share. Van Gorkom (D) secretly approached LBO financier Pritzker (D) and offered to permit an LBO for $55 per share. Van Gorkom (D) may have wanted to cash out his shares at $55 immediately, since he was approaching mandatory retirement and the market share price was only $38. Pritzker (D) agreed, but gave Trans Union only 3 days to accept. Trans Union's senior managers felt $55 was too low. Nevertheless, Van Gorkom (D) called an immediate Board meeting to present the LBO's general terms, without reading the LBO agreement. The Directors (D) received no prior notice an LBO was contemplated, never saw the merger agreement, and were never told how the $55 price was computed. The CFO (D) suggested he had done a study valuing the company at $55 to $65 per share, though he never showed this study to the Directors (D), and it is unclear whether the study was done. Under the LBO's terms, Trans Union would "auction" itself; it could accept, but not solicit, competing bids, and could disclose only limited information to other bidders. If another bidder prevailed, Trans Union would sell Pritzker (D) 1 million shares at $38. [This "poison pill" discouraged other bidders, who, if they won, would immediately have to sell 1 million shares, bought at $55+, for $38 to a large hostile shareholder.] Trans Union's attorney (D) told the Directors (D) they may be sued for failing to accept. The Directors (D) accepted the agreement after 2 hours of deliberation, though it is unclear if they demanded the right to accept higher bids and share information with bidders. Trans Union immediately issued a press release announcing Trans Union had entered into a "definitive" merger agreement with Pritzker (D). Facing protest, Trans Union recanted, retaining investment bankers to solicit bids and noting that in a press release, but also announcing Pritzker (D) had already arranged financing [thus arguably binding Trans Union to accept] and purchased 1 million shares. Van Gorkom (D) then asked the Directors (D) to approve changes to the LBO agreement purportedly allowing a freer auction, and the Directors (D) agreed, without seeing the changes. Van Gorkom (D) signed the revised agreement Pritzker (D) presented, apparently unaware it actually *impaired* Trans Union's ability to accept other bids or reject Pritzker, and was more onerous than he had represented to the Directors (D). Van Gorkom (D) and Pritzker (D) also discouraged the bidders, who withdrew. Eventually, the Directors (D) approved Pritzker's (D) offer. The shareholders also voted to approve by a 69.9% majority. Smith, (P) a shareholder, filed a class action to rescind the LBO or recover damages, contending (i) the Directors breached their duty of care by selling the company without proper valuation, and (ii) the shareholder vote was invalid because shareholders were misinformed. The Directors (D) contended their decision was reasonable because (i) the $55 offer was above the $38 market value, (ii) it still allowed them to accept higher offers, (iii) the Directors (D) were experienced and knowledgeable about the company's value, and (iv) they relied on Trans Union's attorney's (D) recommendation they accept. The trial court found that (i) the Directors (D) acted upon information sufficient to invoke the business judgment rule, and (ii) the shareholder vote should not be set aside because the shareholders (P) were "fairly informed." The shareholders (P) appealed.

■ ISSUE

Have corporate directors who sell the corporation without determining its true value breached their duty of care?

■ DECISION AND RATIONALE

(Horsey) Yes. Corporate directors who sell the corporation without determining its true value have breached their duty of care. The trial court was clearly erroneous in concluding the Director's (D) decision was eligible for the business judgment presumption, because the Directors (D) were grossly negligent in informing themselves before deciding. Under case law, a properly informed decision is one where directors inform themselves of "all material information reasonably available to them," and directors are liable only if grossly negligent. Here, the Directors (D), were grossly negligent in approving the initial LBO agreement, because they (i) did not examine Van Gorkom's (D) role in negotiating and pricing the sale, (ii) never calculated Trans Union's intrinsic value, (iii) adopted their decision after only 2 hours' consideration, without prior notice and without any need for rush, (iv) relied solely on Van Gorkom's (D) presentation without examining the documents. Delaware statutory corporate law permits directors to rely on officers' "reports" in good faith, and case law construes "reports" to include summaries of informal personal investigations. Here, however, Van Gorkom's (D) presentation was not a reliable "report," because Van Gorkom (D) himself never knew the LBO agreement's terms, never supported his valuation with any study, and never presented documentation, which should have put the Directors (D) were on inquiry notice. That a buyout offer pays a premium over current market value is not legally sufficient to make it fair. Here, Trans Union's stock was depressed at the time, so its then-market value did not reflect its true value, and the Directors (D) were required to assess the true value. We do not hold that a proper company valuation necessarily requires external valuations or an investment banker's fairness opinion, but it does require *some* study. The Directors' (D) contention the ensuing "auction" period presented a "market test," which proved no other buyer would offer more, proves nothing, because it is unclear the LBO agreement actually permitted an auction. That the defendants inexplicably refuse to produce the agreement permits inference that it does not. "The directors' unfounded reliance on both the premium and the market test as the basis for accepting the Pritzker [(D)] proposal undermines [their] remaining contention that . . . [their] collective experience and sophistication was a sufficient basis for" finding their decision reasonable. We conclude that Trans Union's Board (D) was grossly negligent in initially approving the LBO agreement, and again in approving the LBO revisions without reading them, as was Van Gorkom (D). The documents he actually signed effectively foreclosed any auction, so the alleged "market test" does not indicate the price or procedure was reasonable. Legally, careless directorial decisions may be "cured" of liability if approved through informed shareholder vote. Here, however, the shareholders (P) were improperly informed, [reasons omitted] so their vote does not absolve the Directors (D) of liability. Reversed and remanded to determine damages.

■ DISSENT

(McNeilly) In this case, the business judgment rule should apply, since the evidence sufficiently shows the Directors (D) deliberated carefully by discussing Trans Union's value and tax problems months before the LBO, listening to Trans Union's attorney (D), and insisting the final agreement allow them to accept higher bids.

Analysis:

Van Gorkom is usually cited as a landmark decision on directors' duty of care, but its holding does not clearly delineate what constitutes "due care." *Van Gorkom* explicitly holds that when directors are about to sell a corporation, they cannot assume that any price above the current market price is necessarily "fair." Thus, the case unambiguously obligates directors, prior to selling a corporation, to attempt *some* sort of valuation of their company. Though the case says that the valuation need not be done by an independent auditor/appraiser, in practice, *Van Gorkom* has driven almost all directors to commission an independent investment banker's valuation and "fairness opinion" prior to selling the corporation as a shield against liability for damages from faulty valuations. The main lesson of *Van Gorkom* is that directorial "due diligence" cases will continue to be highly fact-specific; future Delaware cases show that the burden of proof for shareholder suits alleging directorial negligence is extremely high.

■ CASE VOCABULARY

LEVERAGED BUY-OUT (LBO): Purchase of controlling interest in a corporation using money borrowed (leveraged) from investors or bankers, and usually secured by the corporation's assets.

POISON PILL: In a merger/acquisition, a contractual provision which favors a preferred partner/buyer buy requiring all other buyers, should they prevail, to pay a penalty, usually to the preferred partner.

In re Caremark International Inc. Derivative Litigation

(*Shareholders, for Corporation*) v. (*Directors*)

698 A.2d 959 (Del.Ch.1996)

CORPORATE DIRECTORS MUST IMPLEMENT CORPORATE MONITORING SYSTEM IN GOOD FAITH

■ **INSTANT FACTS** When a corporation charged with health care bribery is forced to pay $250 million and promise better management in a settlement with government agencies, angry shareholders request the court reject the settlement and permit them to sue the directors for negligently permitting bribery.

■ **BLACK LETTER RULE** Corporate directors have a duty to make good faith efforts to institute a corporate monitoring system they believe will alert them of material events, but are not liable if the system fails to detect wrongdoing.

■ PROCEDURAL BASIS

Motion to approve settlement of derivative action.

■ FACTS

Caremark Corporation (P) operated health care centers and prescription drug programs. Caremark (P) and its predecessor often awarded contracts and grants to physicians who prescribed Caremark's (P) services to patients, which may have violated the federal Anti-Referral Payments Law ("ARPL") prohibiting "kickbacks." Eventually, Caremark was investigated by federal and state agencies. Caremark's Directors (D) and managers attempted to curb these payments and improve supervision, though many Directors (D) remained unsure whether the payments were illegal. The Directors (D) (i) revised Caremark's (P) employee guides to be ARPL-compliant, (ii) required payments to be approved by managers, (iii) disclosed the investigations in financial statements, (iv) hired auditors to assess its control structure, (v) reviewed compliance policies, and (vi) trained employees in compliance. Nevertheless, after 4 years of investigations, it was discovered that at least some of the payments were outright bribes, and Caremark (P) was ordered to adopt further safeguards and fined $250 million for criminal and civil violations, most of which began in the predecessor corporation but continued throughout the Directors' cleanup attempt. Shareholders (P) filed several derivative suits, consolidated here, alleging that the Directors (D) breached their duty of care by (*un*intentionally) failing to supervise employees or institute effective controls, causing the fines. Caremark proposed in a settlement with state and federal agencies, which would bar Shareholders' (P) suits, that Caremark would further (i) have employees stop paying referral fees, (ii) discuss compliance regularly with physicians, (iii) disclose to patients any financial incentives paid to their doctors, (iv) establish a compliance committee with outside directors, (v) review its contracts—existing and future—to ensure compliance. This settlement was submitted for court approval, as required.

■ ISSUE

Should the court allow a settlement which dismisses charges against directors for negligently failing to institute corporate controls which could have prevented fines?

■ DECISION AND RATIONALE

(Allen) Yes. Corporate directors have a duty to make good faith efforts to institute a corporate monitoring system they believe will alert them of material events, but are not liable if the system fails to detect wrongdoing. Courts deciding whether to approve derivative litigation settlements must decide whether the settlement offered is fair compensation for the corporation and its absent shareholders. In doing so, courts should not determine contested facts, but should evaluate the parties' relative claims and defenses, to substitute for an adversarial process. The parties proposing the settlement bear the burden of persuading the court it is fair and reasonable. Directors may be liable in negligence for either (i) making ill advised decisions not protected by the business judgment rule, or (ii) failure to monitor reasonably, if monitoring would have prevented losses. In suits for failure to monitor, directors may be held liable for negligently but unintentionally failing to monitor other employees' actions/decisions. Despite an old case, *Graham v. Allis-Chalmers* (Del. 1963) [directors not liable for not discovering employees' antitrust violations, absent grounds for suspicion], suggesting otherwise, we now hold the law to require directors have a duty to make good faith efforts to institute an effective corporate monitoring system (which would alert them to material events and noncompliance), even if they have no reason to suspect wrongdoing. The level of detail necessary for this informational system is a question of business judgment, and directors are obviously not liable every time a reasonable system fails to detect wrongdoing. Our holding stems from (i) our belief the Delaware Supreme Court would today require this of directors, considering recent cases' imposition of greater duties on corporate boards, (ii) public policy choices, founded on recent events demonstrating the large damages, reputational and monetary, that unsupervised employees can cause, and (iii) the increasing risks of large Federal penalties for corporate criminal liability. Here, we find the settlement fair and reasonable. While the changes demanded by the settlement are small, since they were largely adopted in Caremark's ongoing cleanup effort, they are fully adequate consideration for dismissing the claims against the directors, since the evidence suggest the directors will have the claims against them dismissed. Here, Shareholders (P) would have to prove the Directors (D) (i) knew/should have known about the violations, (ii) took no good faith steps to prevent them, and (iii) proximately caused the losses. Claims of directorial liability for negligent failure to monitor must allege sustained or systematic failures to exercise oversight or create an information system, which would suggest bad faith. Here, the evidence suggests the Directors (D) made good faith efforts to inform themselves. Approving this settlement would dismiss an "extremely weak" claim in return for modest assurances of better management in the future. Settlement approved.

Analysis:

This case sets a sort of "business judgment rule" for corporate monitoring; directors are responsible for instituting a reasonable corporate monitoring system, but are not held personally liable each time the reasonable system fails to detect wrongdoing. Here, the decision to foreclose shareholder suits seems fair in light of evidence the directors made honest and reasonable efforts to avoid liability. Bear in mind many of the practices seem to have predated the Directors' (D) appointment, so that even if they could have immediately stopped all of the suspect payments, the company would still remain liable for past payments that had already occurred before the Directors' (D) tenure. Thus, it would have been truly unfair and contrary to good policy to hold the Directors (D) personally liable, because they would automatically face large personal liability for their predecessors' misdeeds/mistakes as soon as they became directors.

■ CASE VOCABULARY

DERIVATIVE LITIGATION: Lawsuit filed by corporate shareholders suing on behalf of the corporation for damages done to the corporation. Here, the shareholders are claiming the directors' (D) crimes harmed the corporation by imposing $250 million in fines.

Malpiede v. Townson

(*Shareholder*) v. (*Corporate Director*)
780 A.2d 1075 (Del.2001)

EXCULPATORY PROVISIONS ENABLE DIRECTORS TO TAKE BUSINESS RISKS WITHOUT FEAR OF LIABILITY

■ **INSTANT FACTS** Shareholders sued corporate directors for breach of the duties of loyalty and care for failing to accept the highest bid on an announced merger.

■ **BLACK LETTER RULE** The plaintiff bears the burden of properly pleading claims of breach of the duties of loyalty and care against a director.

■ PROCEDURAL BASIS

On appeal to review a chancery court dismissal of the plaintiff's complaint for money damages.

■ FACTS

Frederick's of Hollywood announced it had retained an investment bank to conduct a search for a suitable buyer of the corporation. From its search, Frederick's board of directors approved a merger transaction with Knightsbridge Capital Corporation to purchase all outstanding shares for $6.14 each. Frederick's was prohibited from soliciting any other bids unless required by its fiduciary duties to its shareholders. Before the merger closed, Frederick's received an unsolicited bid from Milton Partners to purchase the corporation for $7.00 per share. Several days later, Knightsbridge increased its offer to $6.90 per share and entered into an agreement with Frederick's in which Knightsbridge received a proxy to vote forty-one percent of the outstanding Class A shares, subject to Frederick's termination upon receipt of a higher bid. Within days, Frederick's received another unsolicited offer from Veritas Capital Fund to purchase the outstanding shares for $7.75 per share. The board postponed the Knightsbridge merger to meet with the new bidders. After Milton failed to comply with Frederick's bidding demands, Frederick's met with Veritas to discuss its bid. That same day, Knightsbridge and the holders of the forty-one-percent voting block amended their agreement to eliminate the termination rights. Knightsbridge subsequently purchased the voting block and informed the board of its intention to vote against any third-party bids.

The next day, the board informed Veritas that if it accepted its bid, it would offer an option to purchase all unissued stock necessary to defeat Knightbridge's voting block and demanded indemnification if Knightbridge sued Frederick's. On the following day, Knightsbridge increased its offer to match Veritas's $7.75 per share price, subject to restrictions on Frederick's right to consider better offers. Knightsbridge followed this offer by purchasing all outstanding stock, giving it a majority of all voting and nonvoting shares issued. Veritas responded by increasing its bid to $9.00 per share. The board rejected Veritas's bid and scheduled a date for the Knightsbridge merger. Before the merger closed, Frederick's shareholders filed a class action and moved for a preliminary injunction against the merger. After injunctive relief was denied, the plaintiffs amended their complaint to allege a breach of fiduciary duties and recovery of damages caused by the rejection of the higher bid. The chancery court granted the directors' motion to dismiss, holding that the complaint failed to state a claim for a breach of the duty of loyalty and that the corporate charter's exculpatory clause precluded damages against the directors for a breach of the duty of care.

■ ISSUE

Does the plaintiffs' complaint sufficiently state claims for breaches of the duty of loyalty and the duty of care to survive a motion to dismiss?

■ DECISION AND RATIONALE

(Veasey, C.J.) No. To establish a breach of the duty of loyalty by a director, the plaintiffs must adequately plead sufficient facts to support their claims that the director improperly failed to take prudent actions to maximize the sale price of the enterprise. Here, the plaintiffs alleged a conflict of interest only with respect to one director. The complaint does not allege, however, that the conflicted director dominated the other directors who approved the merger. Absent such domination, the plaintiffs have not sufficiently alleged that the merger was not approved by a majority of disinterested directors.

To establish a breach of the duty of care in this case, the plaintiffs must allege that the directors were grossly negligent in failing to implement a routine strategy that could enable the board to negotiate for a higher bid or otherwise enhance stockholder value. Here, the complaint alleges gross negligence by hastily accepting the Knightsbridge offer and restricting further negotiation with higher bidders. Although the business judgment rule presumes the directors' actions were reasonable, the plaintiffs are entitled to the reasonable inferences drawn from their complaint. Based on these inferences, the plaintiffs have adequately alleged a claim for a breach of the duty of care.

However, the corporate charter exculpates the directors for any breach of the duty of care. Exculpatory clauses are beneficial to a corporation and its stockholders because they free up directors to take good faith business risks without the fear of liability for negligence. While public policy approves of such provisions with respect to the duty of care, they are inapplicable to claims for the breach of the duty of loyalty, bad faith, and other intentional wrongs by directors. Although the plaintiffs' complaint includes allegations beyond the breach of the duty of care, the plaintiffs failed to meet their burden to properly plead those claims, leaving only claims for the breach of the duty of care. The court properly dismissed these claims on the basis of the exculpatory provision. Had the plaintiffs met their burden to properly plead their claims for breach of loyalty and bad faith, their claims would have survived. Affirmed.

Analysis:

Exculpatory provisions adopted pursuant to a state director protection statute protect directors from good faith business decisions that may result in damage to the shareholders or the corporation. Successful corporations require that directors take some measure of risk to grow the corporate business and maximize the stock value. These risks are as valuable to shareholders' interests as they are to the corporation. Accordingly, shareholders who adopt such provisions may not reap the rewards of successful risks while holding directors liable for transactions that go awry.

■ CASE VOCABULARY

CARE: Under the law of negligence, the conduct demanded of a person in a given situation.

EXCULPATORY CLAUSE: A contractual provision relieving a party from any liability resulting from a negligent or wrongful act.

In re The Walt Disney Co. Derivative Litigation

(*Shareholders*) v. (*Corporation*)
825 A.2d 275 (Del.Ch.Ct.2003)

DIRECTORS OWE THE CORPORATION AND ITS SHAREHOLDERS A DUTY OF GOOD FAITH

■ **INSTANT FACTS** Shareholders brought a derivative action against Walt Disney Co. (D) for blindly approving the hiring of a new president and his subsequent non-fault termination.

■ **BLACK LETTER RULE** The business judgment rule does not save directors from liability for the conscious disregard of the consequences of corporate action upon the corporation or its shareholders.

■ PROCEDURAL BASIS

Chancery court consideration of the defendants' motion to dismiss.

■ FACTS

Michael Eisner (D) was the Chief Executive Officer of Walt Disney Co. (D). Due to vacancies on the board of directors, Eisner (D) explored candidates to serve as president. Although he had never served as an executive of an entertainment company, Eisner (D) unilaterally chose his longtime friend, Ovitz, to serve as president, despite internal documents warning of adverse publicity. The compensation committee met to consider Ovitz's hiring, but received no advance draft employment agreement. The committee met for about an hour and primarily discussed two unrelated matters. The proposed employment agreement was not questioned, nor were any documents reviewed prior to the approval of the Ovitz hiring. Eisner (D) was authorized to negotiate and finalize the hiring. The board of directors immediately convened and approved the Ovitz hiring without substantial discussion or finalization of the terms of his employment agreement. Ovitz eventually reached an agreement with Eisner (D) that substantially differed from the original draft, but neither the committee nor the board reviewed it before execution.

Ovitz served as Disney (D) president for approximately a year when Eisner (D) realized that the hiring was a mistake due to Ovitz's management style. Mutually agreeing that Ovitz should seek alternative employment, Eisner (D) and Ovitz negotiated a non-fault termination that would preserve Ovtiz's benefits and reputation. After a new board of directors was elected, Ovitz's non-fault termination was announced, granting Ovitz $38 million and three million shares of Disney stock. Neither the new board nor the compensation committee had been consulted or approved the termination. Disney (D) bylaws required board approval for the non-fault termination. Nonetheless, the board failed to question the termination, explore alternatives, or consider the terms of Ovitz's severance package. Disney shareholders (P) brought a derivative action, alleging that the directors breached fiduciary duties by blindly approving the Ovitz hiring and non-fault termination. After the complaint was dismissed and later remanded by the Delaware Supreme Court with leave to amend, the plaintiffs served a second amended complaint alleging the directors breached their fiduciary duties. Disney (D) moved to dismiss the complaint, arguing that the plaintiffs had alleged only a breach of the duty of care, which was defeated by the corporate charter waiving or limiting director liability.

■ ISSUE

Must the plaintiffs' complaint for breach of fiduciary duties be dismissed based on the corporate limitation of director liability or the business judgment rule?

■ DECISION AND RATIONALE

(Chandler, J.) No. Under Disney's (D) corporate charter, director liability is eliminated or limited for, among others, any breach of the duty of loyalty and "acts or omissions not in good faith or which involve intentional misconduct or a knowing violation of the law." A fair reading of the plaintiff's complaint raises doubt as to whether the directors' actions were taken in good faith or were unintentional. The allegations in the complaint, therefore, do not fall within the liability limitation provisions.

Likewise, the plaintiff's complaint cannot be defeated by the business judgment rule. The complaint does not, however, allege negligence in the exercise of the directors' business judgment. Instead, the plaintiffs allege that the directors failed to exercise any business judgment in good faith. On such facts, the business judgment rule does not relieve the directors of liability for their actions. Taken as true, the allegations of the plaintiffs' complaint portray the directors' conscious indifference to the consequences of the Ovitz hiring and termination without regard to the best interests of the corporation or its shareholders. The motion to dismiss is denied.

Analysis:

Note the distinction between holding directors liable for poor business judgment and the total failure to exercise *any* business judgment. While the business judgment rule protects directors when making a well-informed, reasoned decision, it does not exempt them from the duty to investigate corporate activity and act in the corporation's best interests.

■ CASE VOCABULARY

BUSINESS–JUDGMENT RULE: The presumption that in making business decisions not involving direct self-interest or self-dealing, corporate directors act on an informed basis, in good faith, and in the honest belief that their actions are in the corporation's best interest.

GOOD FAITH: A state of mind consisting in (1) honesty in belief or purpose, (2) faithfulness to one's duty or obligation, (3) observance of reasonable commercial standards of fair dealing in a given trade or business, or (4) absence of intent to defraud or seek unconscionable advantage.

Miller v. American Telephone & Telegraph Co.

(*Shareholders*) v. (*Corporation & Directors*)
507 F.2d 759 (3d Cir.1974)

CORPORATE DIRECTORS MAY NOT CAUSE CORPORATION TO VIOLATE LAW

■ **INSTANT FACTS** When a phone company fails to collect payment from the Democratic Party, the shareholders contend the failure is an illegally-disguised campaign contribution.

■ **BLACK LETTER RULE** The failure to collect claims is entitled to the business judgment presumption, unless that failure is otherwise illegal.

■ PROCEDURAL BASIS

Appeal from judgment for defendants in shareholder derivative action seeking injunction and damages.

■ FACTS

AT&T (D), a long-distance phone company, failed to collect a debt of $1.5 million from the Democratic National Committee ("DNC") for phone service during the 1968 Democratic National Convention. Shareholders (P) sued, contending the failure to collect was a breach of the Directors' (D) duty of care, and furthermore violated federal law as (i) a preference in collection procedures and (ii) effectively an illegal campaign "contribution." The Shareholders sought (i) an injunction for AT&T (D) to collect the debt. (ii) an injunction against providing further service to the DNC until paid, and (iii) interest on the debt. The case was brought in federal court on diversity jurisdiction. The Directors (D) moved to dismiss for failure to state a claim. The trial court dismissed the case, holding that collection procedures were within directorial discretion and could not be overturned absent allegations they were "illegal, unreasonable, or in breach of a fiduciary duty." The Shareholders (D) appealed.

■ ISSUE

Does a corporation's choice to forbear collecting a valid debt constitute a breach of the directors' duty of care?

■ DECISION AND RATIONALE

(Seitz) No. The failure to collect claims is entitled to the business judgment presumption, unless that failure is otherwise illegal. Here, the controlling law is New York's, since AT&T (D) is incorporated there. The business judgment rule prevents judicial intervention in corporate affairs absent self-interest or bad faith. Generally, the failure to collect claims is entitled to the business judgment presumption, unless that failure is otherwise illegal. New York case law holds that performing illegal acts may be a breach of fiduciary duty, even if done to benefit the corporation. *Roth v. Robertson* (N.Y. 1909) [corporate director individually liable for "wasting" corporate funds to bribe corporation's blackmailers]. This is predicated on public policy, since holding otherwise tacitly encourages corporations to act illegally. Here, the Directors' (D) alleged acts are illegal campaign contributions, and contravene Congressional policy by allowing corporations to influence elections with shareholder funds. That the Shareholders (D) were the intended class to be protected by these laws suggests they should have a cause of action for return of their corporate funds. Further, the Shareholders (D) have alleged damages of $1.5 million. Reversed and remanded for trial.

Analysis:

Generally, businesses may have valid reasons for not pursuing collection of money owed to them. For example, the debtor may be insolvent and judgement-proof; the collection may involve hassle and legal fees that make it unprofitable to pursue; the company may wish to preserve a profitable customer and be willing to avoid disputing even a valid debt; etc. In this case, however, it is suspicious that AT&T (D) would forbear collecting on a $1.5 million debt, since the debt is huge and apparently undisputed and the DNC is hardly insolvent. Even more suspicious is that the phone company would continue to provide the DNC with phone service in spite of $1.5 million in overdue bills.

CHAPTER NINE

The Duty of Loyalty

Lewis v. S.L. & E., Inc.

Instant Facts: A shareholder brought a derivative action against his family's closely-held corporation and its directors, claiming that the directors' failure to charge their own corporation the fair market rental value constituted corporate waste.

Black Letter Rule: When a derivative action challenges a corporate transaction in which members of the board have a personal interest, the burden is upon the directors to show that the transaction is fair and reasonable on its merits.

Talbot v. James

Instant Facts: A shareholder sued the officer and director of a corporation for violating his fiduciary duty when the director failed to disclose his interest in a contract entered into by the corporation.

Black Letter Rule: The officers and directors of a corporation stand in a fiduciary relationship to the individual stockholders and in every instance must make a full disclosure of all relevant facts when entering into a contract with said corporation.

Cookies Food Products v. Lakes Warehouse

Instant Facts: The minority shareholders in a closely held corporation sued the corporation's dominant shareholder arising out of the corporation's contracts with the dominant director's family-owned companies.

Black Letter Rule: Corporate profitability may be relevant factor in testing the fairness and reasonableness of a self-dealing transaction.

Hawaiian International Finances, Inc. v. Pablo

Instant Facts: A corporation sued its president for the broker commissions he received while negotiating for the purchase of real estate on behalf of the corporation.

Black Letter Rule: A corporate officer or director, acting for the corporation in the purchase of real estate, may not retain commissions received from the real estate brokers representing sellers, absent disclosure and consent by the corporation.

Northeast Harbor Golf Club, Inc. v. Harris

Instant Facts: A country club sued one of its former directors claiming that the director's efforts to purchase and develop land adjacent to the club amounted to a breach of her fiduciary duty to refrain from taking a corporate opportunity for herself.

Black Letter Rule: A director must make a full disclosure prior to taking advantage of any corporate opportunity, and failure to do so is a per se breach of the director's fiduciary duty.

Zahn v. Transamerica Corporation

Instant Facts: A minority shareholder in a tobacco company alleged that the board of directors exercised the corporation's option to redeem a class of stock in order to benefit the majority shareholder, which held another class of stock.

Black Letter Rule: Directors may not take any corporate action for the purpose of benefiting a dominant shareholder.

Sinclair Oil Corporation v. Levien

Instant Facts: A minority shareholder in a wholly owned subsidiary sued the parent corporation for causing the subsidiary to pay out excessive dividends and for breach of contract.

Black Letter Rule: When the transaction involves a parent and a subsidiary, with the parent controlling the transaction and fixing the terms, the test of intrinsic fairness, with its resulting shift of the burden of proof, is applied.

Kahn v. Lynch Communications Systems, Inc.

Instant Facts: Kahn (P) sued Lynch Communications Systems, Inc. (D) and Alcatel U.S.A. Corporation (D) for breach of fiduciary duties concerning a cash-out merger.

Black Letter Rule: "[A] shareholder owes a fiduciary duty only if it owns a majority interest in or *exercises control* over the business affairs of the corporation."

Jones v. H.F. Ahmanson & Co.

Instant Facts: A minority shareholder in a savings and loan association sued the majority shareholders, alleging that the latter breached their fiduciary duty by creating a market for the association's shares to the exclusion of the minority.

Black Letter Rule: The majority shareholders have a duty of good faith and inherent fairness to the minority in any transaction where control of the corporation is material.

Zetlin v. Hanson Holdings, Inc.

Instant Facts: A minority shareholder claimed that he and the other minority shareholders were entitled to the premium received by the controlling shareholders when they sold their controlling interest.

Black Letter Rule: Absent looting of corporate assets, conversion of a corporate opportunity, fraud, or other acts of bad faith, a controlling shareholder is free to sell, and a purchaser if free to buy, that controlling interest at a premium price.

Gerdes v. Reynolds

Instant Facts: The trustees for a bankrupt corporation sued the corporation's former board of directors for resigning from their positions and electing individuals that intentionally wasted corporate assets, driving the company to bankruptcy.

Black Letter Rule: Directors and officers cannot accept pay in any form for their own resignation or for the election of others in their place.

Perlman v. Feldman

Instant Facts: A steel company's minority stockholders brought a derivative action against the corporation's former controlling stockholder for selling his controlling bloc at a premium to a group of buyers who were solely interested in using the corporation's supply of steel during a tight market.

Black Letter Rule: Where a call on a corporation's product commands an unusually large premium, a fiduciary may not appropriate to himself the value of this premium.

Brecher v. Gregg

Instant Facts: A minority shareholder brought a derivative action against a former officer/director of a corporation after the latter sold his 4% stake in the company at a premium, paid in exchange for a promise of control over the board of directors.

Black Letter Rule: An agreement that provides for a premium in exchange for a promise of control, with only four percent of the outstanding shares being transferred, is contrary to public policy and illegal.

Essex Universal Corp. v. Yates

Instant Facts: A corporation sued a controlling shareholder from whom it had agreed to purchase a 28% share and immediate control of the board.

Black Letter Rule: An agreement to sell 28.3% of the stock of a corporation is not illegal and unenforceable merely because the agreement provides for the immediate resignation of members of the board followed by the election of the purchaser's nominees.

Lewis v. S.L. & E., Inc.

(*Shareholder*) v. (*Corporation*)
629 F.2d 764 (2d. Cir.1980)

WHEN ANY SELF-INTERESTED TRANSACTION IS CHALLENGED, THE DIRECTORS MUST SHOW THAT THE MERITS OF THE TRANSACTION WERE FAIR TO THE CORPORATION

■ **INSTANT FACTS** A shareholder brought a derivative action against his family's closely-held corporation and its directors, claiming that the directors' failure to charge their own corporation the fair market rental value constituted corporate waste.

■ **BLACK LETTER RULE** When a derivative action challenges a corporate transaction in which members of the board have a personal interest, the burden is upon the directors to show that the transaction is fair and reasonable on its merits.

■ PROCEDURAL BASIS

Appeal to the Second Circuit Court of Appeals, which reversed the decision of the District Court granting judgment for the defendants in a diversity suit.

■ FACTS

Donald E. Lewis (P), a shareholder of S.L. & E., Inc. (SLE) (D), brought a derivative action against the corporation and its directors, all of whom were brothers of Lewis (P). Lewis (P) claimed that the directors had wasted corporate assets by causing SLE (D) to charge its tenant, Lewis General Tires, Inc. (LGT), unreasonably low rental from 1966 to 1972. LGT was owned by SLE's directors. Under a ten-year lease signed in 1956, SLE (D) charged LGT rent at a rate of $14,400 per year. In 1966 the lease between LGT and SLE (D) had expired. No new lease was singed. At trial, the directors testified that they never thought of raising LGT's rent. They further testified that they never treated the two corporations as separate entities, but merely believed that SLE (D) existed as a shell for LGT. The District Court entered a judgment for SLE (D) and its directors because Lewis (P) had failed to prove that the rent charged was unreasonably low.

■ ISSUE

Must a plaintiff prove the unreasonableness of a transaction between a corporation and its directors?

■ DECISION AND RATIONALE

(Kearse, Cir., J.) No. When a shareholder attacks a transaction in which the directors have a personal interest other than as directors of the corporation, the directors must prove that the transaction is fair and reasonable to the corporation. The district court erred in placing upon the plaintiff the burden of proving waste. Under normal circumstances the business judgment rule dictates that the decisions of a corporation's directors to enter into a transaction will not be reviewed by courts. The business judgment rule, however, presupposes that the directors have no conflict of interest. Thus when a transaction is challenged in a derivative action against interested directors, it is the directors that have the burden of proving that the transaction was fair and reasonable. In the present case, the directors of SLE (D) have failed to do so. The directors never made an effort to determine the fair rental value of SLE's (D) property. Rather, they merely assumed that SLE existed for the benefit of LGT, their own corporation. The directors (D) offered evidence as to the rent paid by similarly situated tenants in other buildings. But those leases were under different circumstances and for different periods than the one at issue. Although such evidence is not irrelevant, it does not establish what the rental property could have fetched from 1966 to 1972, or that the rent actually charged LGT was fair and reasonable. The directors (D) also offered evidence as to the general downturn of the neighborhood. This evidence merely proves that the fair rental value of the property in 1972 should have been less than the value in 1966, but it does not prove what the amount of rent should have been at either time. In fact, some of the directors' (D) own evidence tended to prove that the fair rental value in 1966 neared $38,000 per year. Also, we find unacceptable the argument that LGT could not afford to pay any rent over $14,400. First, there is a serious question as to whether LGT was in fact unable to afford higher rental payments. Assuming that LGT could not "afford" rental payments, the argument ignores the fact that LGT may have over compensated the directors of both corporations. More importantly, however, even if LGT's financial status was a proper basis for evaluating the lease terms, their was no evidence that showed SLE was unable to find another tenant. We concluded that SLE's (D) directors failed to prove that the rent paid by LGE to SLE for the years 1966–1972 was fair and reasonable. Reversed.

Analysis:

This case provides an excellent overview of the requirements of the "merit based" fairness test. The court first notes that directors who have an interest in both sides of a corporate transaction are not entitled to the protection of the business judgment rule. Although fairness under the business judgment rule entails a judicial examination of the process by which a transaction was effected, the issue of fairness in a conflict of interest transaction requires an examination of the *merits of the transaction.* Moreover, the court here holds that, in contrast to the heavy burden a plaintiff faces under the business judgment rule, the burden of proving fairness in a conflict of interest transaction befalls the interested directors.

■ CASE VOCABULARY

WASTE: Under corporate law, waste constitutes the transfer of a corporate asset for either no consideration, or consideration so low as to be beyond any reasonable business judgment.

Talbot v. James

(Shareholder/Director) v. *(Shareholder/Director)*
259 S.C. 73 (1972)

DIRECTORS HAVE A DUTY TO DISCLOSE ANY PERSONAL INTEREST THEY HAVE IN A TRANSACTION EFFECTED BY THE CORPORATION

■ **INSTANT FACTS** A shareholder sued the officer and director of a corporation for violating his fiduciary duty when the director failed to disclose his interest in a contract entered into by the corporation.

■ **BLACK LETTER RULE** The officers and directors of a corporation stand in a fiduciary relationship to the individual stockholders and in every instance must make a full disclosure of all relevant facts when entering into a contract with said corporation.

■ PROCEDURAL BASIS

Appeal to the South Carolina Supreme Court, challenging the decision of the Circuit Court to reverse the judgment rendered by Master in Equity in favor of the plaintiffs.

■ FACTS

Mr. and Mrs. Talbot (P) and W.A. James (D) formed a corporation, Chicora Apartments, Inc. (Chicora), in order to develop the Talbots' (P) land into apartment rental property. James (D) agreed to obtain financing and construction contracts and the Talbots (P) agreed to transfer their property, each promise made in exchange for an equal share in the corporation. At an organizational meeting, James (D) and Mr. Talbot (P) were elected directors of the corporation; James (D) was also elected President. The board then passed a resolution empowering James (P) to execute and deliver all contracts necessary to complete the project. Acting on behalf of the Chicora, James (D) subsequently entered into a construction contract with his own construction company. The contract sum was to be the actual sum of the cost of construction plus a fee equal to $20,000. The contract also allowed for overhead expenses nearing $32,000. Although James (D) had testified that he explained to Mr. Talbot (P) that the project's viability depended on James (D) being the contractor, Talbot (P) denied that he knew James (D) was to be the contractor. After completion of the project, Chicora fell into financial straits. After the Talbots (P) fought to obtain the right to inspect the corporation's financial records, they sued James (D) claiming a breach of his fiduciary duty to the corporation.

■ ISSUE

Do directors and officers of a corporation have a fiduciary duty that prevents them from contracting with the corporation for their profit without first disclosing the terms of the contract to the disinterested officers and directors of the corporation?

■ DECISION AND RATIONALE

(Moss, C.J.) Yes. The officers and directors of a corporation stand in a fiduciary relationship to the individual stockholders and in every instance must make a full disclosure of all relevant facts when entering into a contract with said corporation. The purpose of this rule is to prevent directors from secretly using their fiduciary positions to their own advantage and to the detriment of the corporation and of the stockholders. We first note that because this is an equity case where the Circuit Court and the Master made contrary findings of fact, we may consider the evidence and make findings in accordance with our view. First, assuming that James (D) revealed to Mr. Talbot (P) that he was to be the contractor, James testimony fails to show that he disclosed the terms of the contract. It was James' (D) duty to make a full disclosure and the burden of proof was upon him to show that such disclosure had been made. Moreover, if James had actually disclosed that he was to be the contractor, the corporation's minutes should reflect this. The minutes, however, are devoid of any such facts. We may also assume from James' (D) refusal to permit the Talbots (P) access to Chicora's books and records that he did not want the appellants to discover how the funds of the corporation had been disbursed and that he received a benefit from the disbursement. We agree with James (D) that he was authorized to sign a construction contract on behalf of the company, but that did not authorize him to sign one on behalf of the corporation for his own benefit. We therefore conclude that James (D) entered into a contract with himself without making full disclosure of his interest to the other officers and stockholders of the corporation. Chicora is thus entitled to judgment against James (D) for the amount of corporate funds received by James (D). The Master found that under the language of the pre-incorporation agreement James (D) received his share of stock in exchange for his agreement to oversee all aspects of the construction project. As general contractor, James' (D) role was simply that, supervisory. He was not entitled to any compensation beyond the ten shares in Chicora that he received. Reversed and remanded.

■ DISSENT

(Bussey, J.) I believe that the evidence favors a finding for James (D). First, the evidence indicates that Mr. Talbot (P) initiated this suit as a result of his being ousted from Chicora's management. Although made aware in 1965 that Chicora had drawn $15,000 check in favor of James (D), Talbot (P) made no issue thereabout until four years later, after being ousted from active management operation. Moreover, the terms of the pre-incorporation agreement only required James (D) to supervise construction as a corporate officer, not a general contractor. The supervisory obligations of a general contractor run much deeper. There is uncontradicted evidence that James' (D) construction company performed services above and beyond that contemplated by the pre-incorporation agreement. Furthermore, even Mr. Talbot (P) admits that any other general contractor would have cost at least $25,000 more. James' overhead for the construction project was $22,817, or $2,208 less than the total dispersed by Chicora. If the corporation is to recover at all, it should only be for the profit actually received.

Analysis:

The court here states the proposition that a director must fully disclose details in those contracts he enters into with the corporation on his own behalf. The court finds that the evidence in this case tends to support the view that James (D) failed to fully disclose the terms of the contract he signed on behalf of the corporation in favor of himself. Technically, that would amount to a breach of James' (D) fiduciary duty, and the court finds as much. The court also notes, however, that the reason directors and officers are required to make full disclosure is to prevent them from secretly using their positions to profit to their, own advantage and to the detriment of the corporation. But here, James (D) did not profit to the detriment of the corporation or shareholders. In fact, his breach may have saved the corporation thousands of dollars. According to the majority's own findings of fact, James (D) should only be liable for his profit. Requiring James (D) to repay his expenses, it could be argued, unjustly enriches the corporation and its shareholders.

Cookies Food Products v. Lakes Warehouse

(*Corporation's Shareholders*) v. (*Corporation's Director*)
430 N.W.2d 447 (Iowa 1988)

APPROVAL OF A SELF-INTERESTED TRANSACTION BY DISINTERESTED DIRECTORS OR BY SHAREHOLDERS DOES NOT MAKE THE TRANSACTION IMMUNE FROM JUDICIAL REVIEW FOR FAIRNESS

■ **INSTANT FACTS** The minority shareholders in a closely held corporation sued the corporation's dominant shareholder arising out of the corporation's contracts with the dominant director's family-owned companies.

■ **BLACK LETTER RULE** Corporate profitability may be a relevant factor in testing the fairness and reasonableness of a self-dealing transaction.

■ PROCEDURAL BASIS

Appeal to the Supreme Court of Iowa affirming the judgment of the district court, which found no breach of a fiduciary duty.

■ FACTS

Duane Herrig (D) was a minority shareholder in Cookies Food Products (Cookies) (P) when the company began to produce and distribute barbecue sauce in Iowa. In order to improve Cookies' (P) dismal financial performance, the corporation's board of directors approached Herrig (D) with the idea that he distribute the company's products through his auto parts distribution company, Lakes Warehouse Distributing (D). The agreement proved profitable to Cookies. Herrig (D) eventually purchased a majority of Cookies' stock and acquired control of the board of directors, selecting four of its five members. Under Herrig's (D) leadership, the Cookies' board extended the term of the exclusive dealership agreement with Lakes (D) and expanded the scope of services to be rendered thereunder, thus increasing the compensation paid to Lakes (D) and Herrig (D). The Cookies (P) board then approved a royalty fee to be paid to Herrig (D) for a taco sauce recipe that he developed and Cookies (P) began to produce. The board twice approved additional compensation for Herrig (D) for services he rendered to the corporation as a "consultant." The shareholders (P) claimed that all these transactions were entered into in breach of Herrig's (D) fiduciary duty to the corporation because Herrig (D) did not fully disclose the benefit he was to receive.

■ ISSUE

May a court appropriately focus on the corporate profitability in determining the fairness of a self-dealing transaction?

■ DECISION AND RATIONALE

(Neuman, J.) Yes. Although it should not be the sole criteria, corporate profitability may be a relevant factor in testing the fairness and reasonableness of a self-dealing transaction. The Iowa legislature has established three circumstances under which a director may engage in self-dealing without violating the duty of loyalty: 1) If the interest is disclosed to the directors or a committee which authorizes, approves or ratifies the transaction; 2) if the interest is disclosed to the shareholders and a majority authorize the transaction; and 3) the contract is fair and reasonable to the corporation. Compliance with these alternatives, however, does not establish that the director has fully met the duty of loyalty. Rather, such compliance merely precludes us from voiding the transaction solely on the basis of the self-dealing. The duty of loyalty also requires that the director act in good faith honesty, and fairness. Cookies' (P) shareholders correctly assert that self-dealing transactions must have the earmarks of arms-length transactions before a court can find them fair or reasonable. We also agree that the burden of establishing fairness requires a showing of "fair price" and a showing of the fairness of the bargain to the interests of the corporation. Applying this standard we believe that Herrig's services were fairly priced and consistent with Cookies corporate interest. All of the agreements benefitted Cookies. Herrig (D) was the driving force behind the corporation's success, a fact that the board noted before Herrig (D) took over. Cookies' (P) evidence admits that Herrig (D) has done the work of at least five people. The record demonstrates that all of the members of the board were aware of Herrig's (D) interest. Herrig (D) was under no obligation to disclose the extent of his profits. Therefore, the disclosure made was sufficient to enable the board to make an informed decision concerning the contracts. Affirmed.

■ DISSENT

(Schultz, J.) I believe that the trial court and the majority opinion have substituted evidence of Cookies' (P) success for an examination of whether the self-dealing transactions were fair to the stockholders. Herrig (D) failed to produce evidence of the fair market value of the services he rendered. Herrig (D) also failed to show that his taco sauce royalty was fair. Cookies' (P) shareholders, in contrast, produced evidence that the company could have accomplished just as much by paying others to perform those services provided by Herrig. Herrig is not entitled to skim off the majority of profits through self-dealing transactions unless they are fair to the corporation and its shareholders.

Analysis:

This case provides a good illustration of the difficulty courts face in examining a self-dealing transaction to determine its fairness. Some courts have held that the value of what a corporation gives up versus what it receives in a self-dealing transaction should be determined at the time the contract is entered into. This holding stems from the fact that a corporation's directors can value a contract only at the time they enter into it. But the majority here seems to eschew this approach be focusing on the impact the transactions had on Cookies' success. Of broader importance is the court's interpretation of the statutory safe harbors created for self-interested transactions. Most states have passed statutes that, in essence, provide that a transaction is not void or voidable if there is either disinterested director approval or an informed shareholder ratification. Consistent with the interpretation these statutes have been given by most courts, the decision of the Iowa Court provides that the safe harbor merely protects a self-interested transaction from being voided simply due to the conflict of interest.

Hawaiian International Finances, Inc. v. Pablo

(*Corporation*) v. (*Corporate President*)

53 Haw. 149 (1971)

WHEN AN OPPORTUNITY TO MAKE A PROFIT ARISES FROM THE POSITION OCCUPIED BY A CORPORATE FIDUCIARY, THAT PROFIT BELONGS TO THE CORPORATION

■ **INSTANT FACTS** A corporation sued its president for the broker commissions he received while negotiating for the purchase of real estate on behalf of the corporation.

■ **BLACK LETTER RULE** A corporate officer or director, acting for the corporation in the purchase of real estate, may not retain commissions received from the real estate brokers representing sellers, absent disclosure and consent by the corporation.

■ PROCEDURAL BASIS

Appeal to the Supreme Court of Hawaii, from a judgment of the circuit court providing that a corporation's president was not liable for real estate commissions received for his participation in real estate investments on behalf of the corporation.

■ FACTS

Pastor Pablo (D) was president of Hawaii International Finances, Inc. (D) (HIF). Pablo (P) and his wife, Rufina (D), also operated a realty company. While in California on personal business, Pablo (D) became aware of real estate investments that might interest HIF (P). HIF's board of directors then sent Pablo (D) and three others to California to investigate the investments. While there, Pablo (D) signed a contract on behalf of the corporation to purchase two parcels of land. The real estate brokers representing the sellers split their commission with Pablo (D). The commissions totaled over $22,000. HIF was completely unaware of such payments. A year later Pablo (D) disclosed the commissions to HIF, and this case ensued. The trial court concluded that Pablo committed no wrong and HIF was not entitled to the commissions.

■ ISSUE

May a corporate officer or director, acting for the corporation in the purchase of investment real estate, retain a commission received from the real estate brokers representing the sellers, absent disclosure and an agreement with the corporation?

■ DECISION AND RATIONALE

(Kobayashi, J.) No. A corporate officer or director, acting for the corporation in the purchase of real estate, may not retain commissions received from the real estate brokers representing sellers, absent disclosure and consent by the corporation. It is widely held that a director while engaged in a transaction for his corporation cannot retain an undisclosed profit. Pablo's (D) attempt to escape this rule by arguing that HIF (P) was not entitled to commissions because the corporation was not a licensed broker. We have held that an corporate officer that claims the profits of a transaction for himself may not contend *ultra vires*. Even if Pablo (D) were able to make this argument, it ignores the fact that HIF could have acquired the property for the purchase price minus the commission he received. Had Pablo (D) disclosed the fact that he anticipated a commission, HIF (P) would have then had the opportunity to attempt to purchase the property at a lower price or acquiesce in letting him retain the commission. The judgment in favor of Pablo (D) is reversed, but the judgment in favor of Mrs. Pablo is affirmed.

Analysis:

Corporate officers and directors are prohibited from using their position, or corporate assets, for personal profit. Pablo (D) also argued that HFI (P) was not entitled to the commission because the corporation had no legal right to the commission. The court appropriately rejects this argument. The court reasons that HFI (P) could have negotiated for a lower purchase price equal to the amount of the commission. However, the court need not have addressed this issue. Under traditional corporate law, any profit arising out of the use of corporate assets—the position of president in this case—rightfully belongs to the corporation, even if the corporation suffered no harm. As the court notes the only defense to profiting from the use of corporate assets is approval by disinterested directors or ratification by shareholders, both after full disclosure. If no such approval or ratification occurs, the profit must be paid to the corporation.

■ CASE VOCABULARY

ULTRA VIRES: Beyond the scope of legal authority.

Northeast Harbor Golf Club, Inc. v. Harris

(Corporation) v. *(Former Director)*

661 A.2d 1146 (Me.1995)

DIRECTORS AND OFFICERS ARE PROHIBITED FROM USURPING FOR THEMSELVES A BUSINESS OPPORTUNITY THAT RIGHTFULLY BELONGS TO THE CORPORATION

■ **INSTANT FACTS** A country club sued one of its former directors claiming that the director's efforts to purchase and develop land adjacent to the club amounted to a breach of her fiduciary duty to refrain from taking a corporate opportunity for herself.

■ **BLACK LETTER RULE** A director must make a full disclosure prior to taking advantage of any corporate opportunity, and failure to do so is a per se breach of the director's fiduciary duty.

■ PROCEDURAL BASIS

Appeal to the Supreme Judicial Court of Maine challenging the trial court's finding that no breach of a fiduciary duty had occurred.

■ FACTS

Nancy Harris (D) was president of the Northeast Harbor Golf Club (Club) (P) from 1971 to 1990, when she was asked to resign. In 1979, Harris (D) was informed by a listing agent that property adjacent to the Club (P) was up for sale. The agent testified that he contacted Harris (D) because he thought the club might be interested in buying the property to prevent development. Harris (D) did not disclose this to members of the Club's (P) board. Instead, Harris (D) purchased the property on her own behalf. Harris (D) later disclosed her purchase to the board, but told the board members that she did not plan to develop the property. In 1984, while playing golf with the postmaster, Harris (D) learned that another parcel adjacent to the Club (P) might be available for purchase. After making the necessary inquiries, Harris (D) also purchased this parcel. Harris (D) formally disclosed this purchase at a 1985 board meeting. Once again, Harris (D) stated she had no plans for development. But in 1988, Harris began the process of development. Harris then resigned as president. After an unsuccessful challenge to the subdivision, the Club (P) instituted this law suit claiming Harris breached her fiduciary duty by purchasing the lots without providing notice and an opportunity for the Club (P) to purchase the property. The trial court found Harris (D) did not usurp a corporate opportunity because real estate was not in the Club's (P) line of business, and the Club (P) lacked the financial ability to purchase the real estate.

■ ISSUE

Does the corporate opportunity doctrine require a director or officer to disclose only those business opportunities that are in the corporation's line of business and that the corporation is financial able to undertake?

■ DECISION AND RATIONALE

(Roberts, J.) No. This case requires us to define the scope of the corporate opportunity doctrine in Maine. Various courts have embraced different versions of the corporate opportunity doctrine. The trial court adopted the "line of business" test, which defines a corporate opportunity as any business opportunity which the corporation is financially able to undertake and is in the line of the corporation's business, such that the self-interest of the director or officer is will be brought into conflict with the corporation. The problem with this formulation is that is suffers from two major weaknesses. First, as this case points out, the question of what is the corporation's line of business may prove difficult to answer. Here, the Golf Club (P) was in the business of running a golf course, but there is no doubt that the club had a significant interest in preventing development around the golf course. A second weakness inherent in the "line of business" test is its focus on the corporation's financial ability to undertake the opportunity. Reliance on this factor will cause officers and directors to refrain from solving financial difficulties in favor of the corporation. Other courts have developed a "fairness test" which requires an application of ethical standards to the facts of the case. The uncertainty involved with this type of inquiry is patent, for it provides no guidance to directors and officers who are seeking to measure their obligations. A third test has sought to combine these two tests. Under that approach the court first determines whether the opportunity was within the corporation's line of business, and then scrutinizes the equitable considerations surrounding the case. This third approach merely piles the uncertainty of the fairness test on top of the weaknesses of the line of business test. We choose instead to adopt the version adopted by the American Law Institute (ALI). The ALI approach first requires the corporation to prove that the opportunity is a corporate opportunity by showing: 1) That the opportunity was offered to the director or officer in his official capacity under circumstances which should reasonably lead him to believe that the offeror expects the opportunity to be offered to the corporation; 2) the director became aware of the opportunity through the use of corporate information or property, if the opportunity is one that the director should believe is of interest to the corporation; or 3) that the senior executive knows the opportunity is closely related to a business in which the corporation is engaged or expects to engage. After showing that the opportunity is a corporate opportunity, the corporation must show that it was either not offered the opportunity by the director, or the corporation did not properly reject the offer. If the offer was not properly rejected, the director may defend on the basis that the taking of the opportunity was fair to the corporation. If the director did not disclose the opportunity, the director has violated her fiduciary duty and may not defend in any case. This disclosure oriented approach provides a clear procedure whereby a corporate officer may insulate herself from a legal challenge by making a full disclosure. Since we have adopted a new legal standard, fairness demands that we remand for a new trial so the parties may have an opportunity to adequately develop the record.

Analysis:

The Supreme Court of Maine clearly favors the certainty that the ALI disclosure-oriented approach provides. The ALI version of the corporate opportunity doctrine differs in several respects from those approaches adopted by other courts, all of which the Maine court rejects. The first major difference lies in the efforts to define "corporate opportunity." The line of business test, the fairness test, and the hybrid approach take a subjective approach by scrutinizing the substance of the opportunity. The ALI approach, on the other hand, focuses on an objective evaluation of the director or officer's conduct, knowledge, and state of mind; if the director or officer becomes aware of the opportunity in his capacity or through the use of corporate property and he should reasonably know that the corporation has an interest in the opportunity, then it is a "corporate opportunity." The ALI approach also differs with respect to what is required of a director or officer who is confronted with a corporate opportunity. Basically, he is under an absolute duty to disclose it. Any failure to do so constitutes a breach of his duty of loyalty under the ALI approach. Under the other approaches disclosure is merely a factor in determining whether the director or officer breached his duty.

Zahn v. Transamerica Corporation

(*Minority Shareholder*) v. (*Controlling Shareholder*)
162 F.2d 36 (3d Cir.1947)

A SHAREHOLDER WHO CONTROLS OR DOMINATES THE BOARD OF DIRECTORS OWES THE CORPORATION AND THE MINORITY SHAREHOLDERS A DUTY OF COMPLETE DISCLOSURE WHEN TRANSACTING WITH THE CORPORATION

■ **INSTANT FACTS** A minority shareholder in a tobacco company alleged that the board of directors exercised the corporation's option to redeem a class of stock in order to benefit the majority shareholder, which held another class of stock.

■ **BLACK LETTER RULE** Directors may not take any corporate action for the purpose of benefitting a dominant shareholder.

■ PROCEDURAL BASIS

Appeal to the Third Circuit, challenging the decision of the District Court, which dismissed the complaint for failure to state a cause of action.

■ FACTS

Mr. Zahn (P), a holder of Class A stock of Axton-Fisher Tobacco Company (Axton-Fisher), a Kentucky corporation, sued Transamerica Corporation (Transamerica) (D) on behalf of himself and all other stockholders similarly situated. Axton-Fisher had authorized and outstanding three classes of stock, designated as preferred stock, Class A stock, and Class B stock. Axton-Fisher's charter provided that each share of Class A stock was convertible into one share of Class B Stock. The charter also provided that all or any of the shares of Class A stock were callable by the corporation upon sixty days notice, and at $60 per share plus accrued dividends. Upon liquidation, holders of Class A stock were entitled to receive twice as much per share as holders of Class B stock. Through several purchases of both classes of stock, and after conversion of its Class A stock to Class B stock, Transamerica (D) came to own virtually all of the outstanding Class B stock. As a result, Transamerica (D) had control of and dominated the management and directorate of Axton-Fisher. Zahn (P) alleged that Transamerica (D) caused Axton-Fisher's board of directors to redeem the Class A stock at the price of $60 per share so that Transamerica (D) could liquidate Axton-Fisher's assets and appropriate the entire value of the company's tobacco surplus, having a market value of $20,000,000.

■ ISSUE

May a board of directors take any action it is empowered to in order to favor one shareholder over the others?

■ DECISION AND RATIONALE

(Biggs, Cir., J.) No. Directors may not take any corporate action for the purpose of benefitting a dominant shareholder. The majority has the right to control; but when it does so, it occupies a fiduciary relationship toward the minority, as much so as the corporation itself or its officers and directors. When a stockholder votes as a director he represents all the stockholders in the capacity of a trustee for them and cannot use his office as a director for his personal benefit at the expense of the stockholders.

Transamerica (D) argues that the Kentucky courts have held that when the Class A stock received its allocation of $60 per share plus accrued dividends it received its full due and that the directors had the right at any time to eliminate Class A stock for the benefit of Class B stock. We believe, however, that the Kentucky courts were faced with a different issue. The settled law of Kentucky is that directors may not declare or withhold dividends for the purpose of personal profit or, by analogy, take any corporate action for such a purpose. The problem with accepting Transamerica's (D) view is that the directors of Axton-Fisher were instruments of Transamerica (D) who voted in favor of their special interests, failing to exercise an independent judgment in calling the Class A stock. A disinterested board could have legally consummated this transaction, but in this case the action was effected at the direction of the principal holder in Class B stock, Transamerica (D). The framers of the charter intended that the board of directors were to act in a disinterested manner when deciding to make the call for Class A stock. If Zahn's (P) allegations are true, it follows that The directors of Axton Fisher have violated their fiduciary obligations. Liability must be imposed upon Transamerica (D) which, under the allegations, constituted the board of Axton-Fisher. Zahn (P)may recover the value of the Class A stock retained by him, and the difference between the $60 and the amount he would have received upon the liquidation of Axton-Fisher. Remanded.

Analysis:

The import of the court's decision in this case is that a dominant shareholder owes a fiduciary duty to the corporation and the minority shareholders. But unlike that of a director or officer, the fiduciary obligations do not apply to every action taken by the dominant shareholder. A controlling shareholder always retains the right to vote his shares in any manner he pleases. Think of the controlling shareholder's fiduciary duties as vicarious rather than direct. In cases dealing with the duties of a controlling shareholder there is usually some sort of action taken by the board of directors, not just a shareholder vote. These cases really focus on the independence of the board of directors. A board that is dominated by a controlling shareholder is more like an instrument of the controlling shareholder, and it is through the board's actions that a controlling shareholder must observe his fiduciary duty. For example, in this case the court holds that Axton-Fisher's board members violated their fiduciary duty because they favored one class of stock over another. As a consequence of the board's breach, Transamerica, the controlling shareholder, is liable because the board was acting at the direction and as an instrument of Transamerica.

Sinclair Oil Corporation v. Levien

(*Parent Company*) v. (*Subsidiary's Shareholder*)
280 A.2d 717 (Del.1971)

WHEN A PARENT COMPANY ENGAGES IN SELF-DEALING WITH ITS SUBSIDIARY, THE PARENT HAS THE BURDEN OF PROVING THE INTRINSIC FAIRNESS OF THE CHALLENGED TRANSACTION

■ **INSTANT FACTS** A minority shareholder in a wholly owned subsidiary sued the parent corporation for causing the subsidiary to pay out excessive dividends and for breach of contract.

■ **BLACK LETTER RULE** When the transaction involves a parent and a subsidiary, with the parent controlling the transaction and fixing the terms, the test of intrinsic fairness, with its resulting shift of the burden of proof, is applied.

■ PROCEDURAL BASIS

Appeal from an order of the Court of Chancery, requiring a parent company to account for damages sustained by its subsidiary as a result of excessive dividends paid by the subsidiary, and a breach of contract between the parent and the subsidiary.

■ FACTS

Levien (P), a shareholder of Sinclair Venezuelan Oil Company (Sinven), brought a derivative action against Sinclair Oil Corporation (Sinclair) (D), owner of 97% of Sinven's stock. Levien (P) alleging that Sinclair (D) caused Sinven to pay excessive dividends, denied Sinven opportunities to develop and expand, and breached a requirements contract with Sinven. As a parent company, Sinclair (D) nominated the members of Sinven's board of directors, all of whom were directors or employees of Sinclair (D). For a period of six years Sinven paid out dividends that exceeded earnings in the amount of $38,000,000. Levien (P) claimed that the dividends were paid in order to infuse Sinclair (D) with cash. Levien (P) also claimed that Sinclair (D)'s policy of pursuing development through other subsidiaries denied Sinven any opportunity to expand its operations. Levien's (P) final claim stemmed from a requirements contract between Sinven and International, one of the Sinclair (D) subsidiaries. Levien (P) alleged that International breached the contract by consistently being late on payments and by purchasing less oil than the contract's minimum.

■ ISSUE

Should challenged transactions between a parent company and its subsidiary be tested by the business judgment rule?

■ DECISION AND RATIONALE

(Wolcott, C.J.) No. When the transaction involves a parent and a subsidiary, with the parent controlling the transaction and fixing the terms, the test of intrinsic fairness, with its resulting shift of the burden of proof, is applied. A parent does owe a fiduciary duty to its subsidiary when there are parent-subsidiary dealings. However, this alone will not invoke the intrinsic fairness standard. This standard will be applied only when the fiduciary duty is accompanied by self-dealing—the situation where a parent is on both sides of the transaction. Self-dealing occurs when the parent, by virtue of its domination of the subsidiary causes the subsidiary to act in such a way that the parent receives something from the subsidiary to the exclusion and detriment of the minority stockholders of the subsidiary. Applying this rule to the facts we find that the excessive payment of dividends did not involve self-dealing because both, Sinclair (D) and the minority shareholders received a proportionate share. Thus, the business judgment rule should have applied, and Sinclair's (D) motives are immaterial, unless the payments amounted to waste. As to the claim of denied expansion, Levien (P) has not pointed to any particular opportunities that were presented to Sinven, and usurped by Sinclair (D). Sinclair (D) was under no duty to actively seek expansion opportunities for Sinven. We do find, however, the contract between International and Sinven was self-dealing. Sinclair (D), through its subsidiary, received the products but failed to comply with the terms of the contract, all to the detriment of Sinven's minority shareholders. As a result, Sinclair (D) was required to prove that the contract was intrinsically fair. This, it failed to do. Affirmed in part and reversed in part.

Analysis:

The court's holding in this case that Sinclair (D) was under no duty to expand Sinven's operations serves as an indication of the limit of the parent company's duty to its subsidiary. This limited duty is breached when self-dealing occurs, i.e., when the parent stands on both sides of the transaction and there is a disproportionate transfer of assets in favor of the parent. Without self-dealing, any parent-subsidiary transaction is subject to business-judgment protection. According to the court, the major consequence of self-dealing is not that the transaction is voided, rather the parent or subsidiary's board of directors must prove that the transaction was intrinsically fair to the minority shareholders. In applying this analysis to the facts, the court finds that the dividend payment was protected by the business-judgment rule because there was no self-dealing. In other words, both the parent and the minority shareholders received a similar benefit.

Kahn v. Lynch Communications Systems, Inc.

(*Shareholder*) v. (*Corporation*)
638 A.2d 1110 (Del.1994)

THE BURDEN OF PROVING THE FAIRNESS OF A MERGER SHIFTS TO MAJORITY OR CONTROLLING SHAREHOLDERS

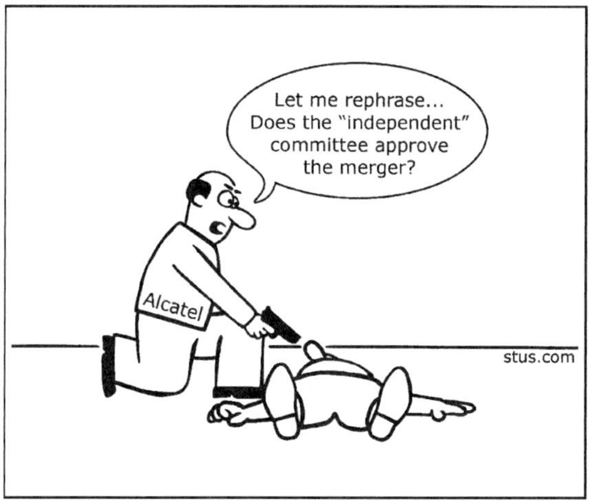

■ **INSTANT FACTS** Kahn (P) sued Lynch Communications Systems, Inc. (D) and Alcatel U.S.A. Corporation (D) for breach of fiduciary duties concerning a cash-out merger.

■ **BLACK LETTER RULE** "[A] shareholder owes a fiduciary duty only if it owns a majority interest in or *exercises control* over the business affairs of the corporation."

■ PROCEDURAL BASIS

On appeal to review a chancery court judgment for the defendants.

■ FACTS

In 1981, Alcatel U.S.A. Corporation ("Alcatel") (D) acquired 30.6% of Lynch Communications Systems, Inc. ("Lynch") (D) as part of a stock agreement in which Lynch (D) amended its certificate of incorporation to require 80% approval of any merger. Alcatel (D) also obtained representation on Lynch's (D) board of directors and the right to purchase 40% of any securities offered to third-party purchasers. In 1986, Lynch (D) determined that to remain competitive it would have to obtain fiber optics technology. Lynch (D) targeted Telco Systems, Inc., but Alcatel (D), whose approval was needed to reach 80% approval, disapproved. Instead, Alcatel (D) suggested a merger with Celwave Systems, Inc., a subsidiary owned by its parent corporation. Alcatel (D) presented the Celwave merger to the Lynch (D) board of directors, which unanimously established an independent committee to negotiate with Celwave and recommend terms for the merger.

When the independent committee's financial advisors considered Alcatel's assessment of Celwave overvalued, the committee unanimously opposed the merger. Alcatel (D) therefore withdrew the Celwave proposal and offered to acquire Lynch (D) itself. The board of directors authorized the Independent Committee to negotiate the terms of the Alcatel (D) merger, but later determined that the offering price was inadequate. After some continuing negotiations, Alcatel (D) increased its offer and declared it final. Alcatel (D) also informed the committee that if the final offer was not accepted, it would proceed with an "unfriendly tender" at a lower price to take control of the corporation. After concluding that no better alternatives existed, the Independent Committee unanimously approved Alcatel's (D) final offer. The Lynch (D) board of directors approved the merger. Kahn (P) brought an action to enjoin the merger, alleging breaches of fiduciary duties by Alcatel (D). After the court denied Kahn's (P) motion for a preliminary injunction, he amended his complaint to seek money damages. The action was converted to a class action on behalf of all Lynch (D) shareholders and the case went to trial. The chancery court concluded that Alcatel (D) was a controlling shareholder of Lynch (D), therefore owing fiduciary duties to Lynch (D) and its shareholders, but it determined that Alcatel (D) did not in fact breach any fiduciary duties. In so holding, the chancery court determined that the merger was negotiated by an independent committee, shifting the burden of persuasion on the issue of entire fairness to Kahn (D). Judgment was entered for the defendants.

■ ISSUE

When an independent committee has no real bargaining power that it can exercise with the majority shareholder on an arms length basis during a proposed merger, does the burden of proving the merger is unfair shift to the shareholders?

■ DECISION AND RATIONALE

(Holland, J.) No. "[A] shareholder owes a fiduciary duty only if it owns a majority interest in or *exercises control* over the business affairs of the corporation." To show that a shareholder controls business affairs absent a majority interest, the plaintiff must establish "domination by a minority shareholder through actual control of corporation conduct." Here, Alcatel (D) owned less than a fifty-percent share of Lynch (D) stock. However, the facts indicate that Alcatel (D) did exercise control over the corporation. With respect to the renewal of compensation contracts of Lynch's (D) top managers, the record indicates that Alcatel (D) utilized its 43%-voting power to exert pressure without regard to the board's opinion. Alcatel (D) also vetoed Lynch's (D) merger with Telco despite the board's perception that the Telco merger was important to Lynch's (D) business. Because of Alcatel's (D) voting strength, the board deferred to Alcatel (D) on all matters of importance rather than exercise its own business judgment.

As a controlling shareholder, Alcatel (D) owed Lynch (D) and its shareholders (P) the fiduciary duty of entire fairness, including fair dealing and a fair price. Fair dealing involves the manner in which a transaction is conducted, including its timing, structure, negotiations, disclosure, and approval. Fair price focuses on the financial considerations of the proposed merger. Both components must be viewed as a whole to determine entire fairness. Ordinarily, the party standing on both sides of an interested merger bears the burden of establishing entire fairness. When the merger is considered and approved by an independent committee of disinterested directors, however, the burden of proof has been shifted to the shareholders to demonstrate that the merger was unfair. To shift the burden, the majority shareholder must not dictate the terms of the merger and the independent committee "must have real bargaining power that it can exercise with the majority shareholder on an arms length basis." Here, the Independent Committee's ability to bargain at arms length was questionable given Alcatel's (D) demonstrated pattern of domination. Upon the committee's rejection of the Celwave merger proposal, the committee learned that Alcatel (D) was unwilling to negotiate on the terms of its proposals. The testimony of one of the committee members revealed that he voted to approve the Alcatel (D) merger, though he felt it was unfair, because he believed there was no other alternative in the face of Alcatel's (D) threats to take over the corporation through an unfriendly tender offer at a lower price. Furthermore, Lynch (D) was not in a position to find alternative suitors because Alcatel (D) had veto power over any merger by virtue of its voting strength. Under the threat of an unfriendly tender offer, the committee was likewise powerless to refuse the proposal in the best interests of the corporation. Because the committee had no bargaining power with which it could operate on an arms length basis, the burden of proving entire fairness does not shift to Kahn (P). Reversed and remanded.

Analysis:

Special committees are important to corporate governance because they protect the interests of minority shareholders and ensure that corporate action is unaffected by interested directors or shareholders. When acting with complete independence, special committees offer objectivity and assist the corporation in meeting its duty of entire fairness to the shareholders.

■ CASE VOCABULARY

ARMS LENGTH: Of or relating to dealings between two parties who are not related or not on close terms and who are presumed to have roughly equal bargaining power; not involving a confidential relationship.

Jones v. H.F. Ahmanson & Co.

(*Minority Shareholder*) v. (*Majority Shareholder*)
1 Cal.3d 93 (1969)

A CONTROLLING SHAREHOLDER OWES MINORITY SHAREHOLDERS A GENERAL FIDUCIARY DUTY WHENEVER HE USES THE POWER TO CONTROL THE CORPORATION

■ **INSTANT FACTS** A minority shareholder in a savings and loan association sued the majority shareholders, alleging that the latter breached their fiduciary duty by creating a market for the association's shares to the exclusion of the minority.

■ **BLACK LETTER RULE** The majority shareholders have a duty of good faith and inherent fairness to the minority in any transaction where control of the corporation is material.

■ PROCEDURAL BASIS

Appeal from the trial court's order dismissing a complaint without leave to amend for failure to state a cause of action.

■ FACTS

June Jones (P), the owner of 25 shares of United Savings and Loan Association (Association), brought an action on behalf of herself and all similarly situated minority stockholders of the Association. Jones (P) alleged that a group of former and present Association shareholders and officers breached their fiduciary duty by creating and operating United Financial, a holding company that owned 87% of the outstanding Association stock. Although the shares of the Association were not widely traded due to their high value - over $1,000 per share, H.F. Ahmanson & Co. (D) and several other shareholders came to possess a majority of the Association's stock. In order to take advantage of the growing demand in the stocks of savings and loan associations by increasing the marketability of Association stock, the majority shareholders incorporated United Financial in 1959. In essence, United Financial's value was its ownership of Association stock, which it acquired by trading 250 of its own shares for each share held by H.F. Ahmanson & Co. (D) and the others. United Financial made several public offerings, from which the company saw returns in excess of $22,000,000. The public trading of United Financial's stock eliminated any market for Association stock. United Financial offered to purchase the minority's stock at a price well below value, but the shareholders resisted due to perceived unfairness. This suit ensued.

■ ISSUE

Do controlling shareholders owe any fiduciary duty to other shareholders absent reliance on inside information, use of corporate assets, or fraud?

■ DECISION AND RATIONALE

(Traynor, C.J.) Yes. The majority shareholder has a duty of good faith and inherent fairness to the minority in any transaction where control of the corporation is material. Our courts have often recognized that majority shareholders, either singly or acting in concert to accomplish a joint purpose, have a fiduciary responsibility to the minority and to the corporation to use their ability to control the corporation in a fair, just, and equitable manner. The controlling shareholders in this case had available to them two courses for marketing their shares. First, they could have made the stock price more attractive to investors by effectuating a stock split or they could have created a holding company and permitted all the stockholders to participate. The second course entailed doing exactly what the controlling shareholders did—create a holding company to market the Association's shares to the exclusion of the minority shareholders. By taking this route the majority ensured that no equivalent market would be created for Association stock, leaving the minority with the option of either selling their shares to United Financial at whatever price was offered or keeping their shares. This action is inconsistent with the duty of good faith and inherent fairness. We therefore hold that controlling shareholders may not use their power to control the corporation for the purpose of promoting a marketing scheme that benefits themselves alone to the detriment of the minority. If Jones (P) wins at trial she is entitled to receive at her election, the appraised value of her shares on the date of exchange, with interest or a sum equivalent to the fair market value of a 250 share bloc of United Financial on the date of the exchange, plus a return on investment equal to that paid by United Financial after its first public offering, with interest.

Analysis:

The general rule, subscribed to by most courts, regarding the fiduciary duty of controlling shareholders is that the controlling shareholder does not owe the minority a general fiduciary duty. But in this case, the California Supreme Court imposes a general fiduciary duty upon controlling shareholders whenever they use their control for a personal benefit. The duty applies not only to individual controlling shareholders, but also to shareholders who, in concert, constitute a controlling bloc. It is important to note the factual difference between this case and the Delaware cases dealing with controlling shareholder duties. This case involves no self-dealing—there was no transfer of corporate assets. In fact, there was a complete absence of any transaction between the corporation and the controlling shareholders. Rather, the controlling shareholder used its majority ownership to market its shares and in doing so rendered unmarketable those of the minority.

Zetlin v. Hanson Holdings, Inc.

(*Minority Shareholder*) v. (*Controlling Shareholders*)

48 N.Y.2d 684 (1979)

A CONTROLLING SHAREHOLDER IS FREE TO SELL HIS CONTROLLING INTEREST AT A PREMIUM PRICE

■ **INSTANT FACTS** A minority shareholder claimed that he and the other minority shareholders were entitled to the premium received by the controlling shareholders when they sold their controlling interest.

■ **BLACK LETTER RULE** Absent looting of corporate assets, conversion of a corporate opportunity, fraud, or other acts of bad faith, a controlling shareholder is free to sell, and a purchaser if free to buy, that controlling interest at a premium price.

■ PROCEDURAL BASIS

Appeal to the New York Court of Appeals from an order issued by the Appellate Division of the Supreme Court of New York.

■ FACTS

Hanson Holdings, Inc. (D) and Sylvestri (D), owners of over 44% of the outstanding shares in Gable Industries, Inc. (Gable), sold their entire controlling share to Flintoke Co. for a premium price of $15 per share, at a time when the stock was trading at $7.38 per share. The stock acquired represented effective control of Gable.

■ ISSUE

Are minority shareholders entitled to an opportunity to share equally in any premium paid for a controlling interest in the corporation?

■ DECISION AND RATIONALE

(Memorandum) No. Absent looting of corporate assets, conversion of a corporate opportunity, fraud, or other acts of bad faith, a controlling shareholder is free to sell, and a purchaser is free to buy, that controlling interest at a premium price. Minority shareholders are entitled to protection against abuse. They are not, however, entitled to inhibit the legitimate interests of the other stockholders. Any other rule would affect the manner in which controlling stock interests are now transferred by requiring such transfers to be conducted only through tender offers.

Analysis:

The court's opinion here is straightforward. The court refuses to extend a controlling shareholder's fiduciary duty by recognizing the general rule that absent bad faith, a controlling shareholder may sell his controlling interest to any willing purchaser and receive a premium price. In other words, a controlling shareholder "owns" the ability to control the corporation, and like any asset, that control may be sold for a profit.

Gerdes v. Reynolds

(*Trustee in Bankruptcy*) v. (*Former Board of Directors*)
28 N.Y.S.2d 622 (Sup.Ct.1941)

A CONTROLLING SHAREHOLDER MAY NOT SELL HIS CONTROL BLOCK TO A BUYER IF HE KNOWS OR SHOULD KNOW THE BUYER INTENDS TO LOOT CORPORATE ASSETS

■ **INSTANT FACTS** The trustees for a bankrupt corporation sued the corporation's former board of directors for resigning from their positions and electing individuals that intentionally wasted corporate assets, driving the company to bankruptcy.

■ **BLACK LETTER RULE** Directors and officers cannot accept pay in any form for their own resignation or for the election of others in their place.

■ PROCEDURAL BASIS

Cause of action for negligence brought in state court by the Federal Bankruptcy Trustee.

■ FACTS

Clarence Reynolds (D), William Woodard (D), Richard Reynolds (D) and Richard Reynolds, Jr. (D) were the officers, directors and majority shareholders in Reynolds Investing Company, an investment trust. Reynolds invested assets consisted of its stock portfolio, which totaled just over $5,000,000, which, when combined with the corporation's liabilities, gave the company's common stock a net asset value of 6 cents per share. Prentice & Brady, a small stock exchange firm, approached Reynolds (D) and the other directors with an offer to purchase control of Reynolds Investing for $2 per share, an amount representing a total purchase price of over $2,000,000. After performing only a cursory investigation into Prentice & Brady, the directors agreed to sell their control in the company. Upon sale, the directors resigned positions, and elected new officers and directors at the direction of Prentice & Brady. The new board proceeded to waste corporate assets and use them for the sole benefit of Prentice & Brady. The company went bankrupt, and the trustee filed this action to recover from the old board of directors for their negligence in transferring control of the corporation.

■ ISSUE

May corporate officers and directors accept pay for their resignations or the election of others?

■ DECISION AND RATIONALE

(Walter, J.) No. Officers and directors are prohibited from terminating their agency or accepting the resignation of others if the immediate consequence would be to leave the interests of the company without proper care and protection. Nor may they accept pay for their own resignations or for the election of others. The questions here are: (1) Whether, under the circumstances, Reynolds (D) and the rest of the board were put on notice as to the unlawful plans of Prentice & Brady; and (2) whether any part of the price paid for the stock represented payment for the resignations of the directors and the election of Prentice & Brady's nominees. As to the first, considering that Reynolds Investment's assets were highly liquid and negotiable, there existed a greater risk that corporate assets would be misapplied. This risk placed upon the directors the duty to further investigate to whom they were entrusting with corporate assets. A person dealing on his own account may be as trustful as he wishes, but those acting as fiduciaries have a duty to be reasonably vigilant. Notwithstanding, there is an additional element upon which liability here is based. Gross excessiveness of price may be sufficient to charge a seller with notice of a fraudulent intent on the part of the buyer. In this case, Prentice & Brady's purchase price exceeded the fair market value of the company by well over $1,000,000. Thus, I find that the price paid by it for the shares totaled only $791,250, while the remaining $1,318,750 represented payment for the resignation of the officers and directors and their election of the buyer's nominees as their successors. The directors and officers of the corporation must account to the corporation for the amount of $1,318,750.

Analysis:

This case applies the "looting" exception to the rule found in *Zetlin v. Hanson Holdings, Inc.*, 48 N.Y.2d 684 (1979), in which the court held that a controlling shareholder, absent fraud, may sell his control block for a premium. Under this exception, a shareholder may not sell his control block if he knows or suspects that the buyer intends to loot the corporation by diverting its assets. The court takes a two step approach in analyzing the case. First the court deals with the mental state required. Although it finds that Reynolds (D) was unaware of the buyer's intent, the court holds that the circumstances indicated that looting was a distinct possibility. But the court refuses to predicate liability solely on a failure to recognize the risk of looting. Instead, the court combines the directors' negligence with their receipt of a grossly excessive premium price. The premium price is enough to charge the directors with bad faith.

Perlman v. Feldmann

(*Minority Shareholder*) v. (*Controlling Shareholder*)
219 F.2d 173 (2d Cir.1955)

A DOMINANT SHAREHOLDER MAY NOT RECEIVE A PREMIUM FOR THE CONTROL OVER CORPORATE ASSETS OR BUSINESS OPPORTUNITIES

■ **INSTANT FACTS** A steel company's minority stockholders brought a derivative action against the corporation's former controlling stockholder for selling his controlling bloc at a premium to a group of buyers who were solely interested in using the corporation's supply of steel during a tight market.

■ **BLACK LETTER RULE** Where a call on a corporation's product commands an unusually large premium, a fiduciary may not appropriate to himself the value of this premium.

■ PROCEDURAL BASIS

Appeal in a diversity action to the Second Circuit Court of Appeals, challenging the district court's holding for the defendants.

■ FACTS

C. Russell Feldman (D) was a director and the controlling shareholder in the Newport Steel Corporation. In order to combat the short supply of steel caused by the Korean War, the Wilport Company, a syndicate of end-users of steel, offered to purchase Feldman's (D) controlling bloc at $20 per share. At the time of the purchase the market price for Newport's shares was under $12. Following the purchase minority shareholders filed suit, claiming that the premium paid was not for control of the corporation. Rather, they argued that a portion of the consideration was for the sale of a corporate asset, specifically the power to control the allocation of the steel in a time of short supply. The district court found that the sale involved only control rights, thus Feldman (D) was entitled to act in his own interests. The court also held that Perlman (P) failed to prove that the sales price was not a fair price for the stock per se.

■ ISSUE

May a stockholder sell his controlling share at a premium in any manner he wishes, absent fraud or foreseeable looting?

■ DECISION AND RATIONALE

(Clark, C.J.) No. Where a call on a corporation's product commands an unusually large premium, a fiduciary may not appropriate to himself the value of this premium. It is well established that as a dominant stockholder. Feldman (D) owed a duty to the minority shareholders. Feldman's (D) siphoned off for personal gain corporate advantages deriving from a favorable market situation. This diversion of corporate opportunities represented a breach of his fiduciary duty. The corporate opportunities that were misappropriated need not have been certain for Feldman (D) to be held liable. Since fiduciaries always have the burden of proof in establishing the fairness of their dealings with trust property, the burden was on Feldman (D) to completely negate the possibility that Newport would benefit from its supply of steel in a tight market. This, he failed to do. We do not mean to suggest that a majority stockholder cannot dispose of his controlling bloc of stock to outsiders without having to account to his corporation for profits or even never do this with impunity when the buyer is an interested customer for the corporation's product. But when the sale necessarily results in a sacrifice of this element of corporate good will and consequent unusual profit to the fiduciary who has caused the sacrifice, he should account for his gains. Therefore, to the extent the price paid to Feldman (D) represented a bonus, he is accountable to the corporation. The case is remanded for a determination as to the exact premium paid.

Analysis:

The exception applied in this case prevents a controlling shareholder from selling control in a manner that deprives the corporation of a business opportunity. This exception implies a fine distinction between the ability to control corporate affairs and the ability to control corporate assets. It is the former that may be sold at a premium. The ability to control corporate assets, however, belongs to the corporation. The corporation is entitled to any profit derived from the use, sale, or diversion of corporate assets. The court here believed that a portion of Feldman's (D) sale price represented a premium for the corporation's ability to take advantage of a short market in other words, Feldman (D) was given money for his shares, a premium for control, and another premium for the right to purchase Newport's steel. It is the latter that Feldman (D), as a controlling shareholder, director, and officer could not sell for his own profit. Such a transaction is viewed as self-dealing.

Brecher v. Gregg

(*Minority Shareholder*) v. (*Corporate President*)

392 N.Y.S.2d 776 (Sup.Ct.1975)

EVEN A MAJORITY SHAREHOLDER MAY NOT ACCEPT A PREMIUM FOR CONTROL IN A SALE OF HIS SHARES

■ **INSTANT FACTS** A minority shareholder brought a derivative action against a former officer/director of a corporation after the latter sold his 4% stake in the company at a premium, paid in exchange for a promise of control over the board of directors.

■ **BLACK LETTER RULE** An agreement that provides for a premium in exchange for a promise of control, with only four percent of the outstanding shares being transferred, is contrary to public policy and illegal.

■ PROCEDURAL BASIS

Shareholder derivative action.

■ FACTS

Frederic Gregg (D), the principal founder and former president of LIN (but also a majority shareholder of LIN), and the Saturday Evening Post Corporation (SEPCO) entered into an agreement in which SEPCO agreed to purchase Gregg's (D) 82,000 shares (4%) for $3.5 million, more that $1,260,000 over the market price. Shortly thereafter, Gregg (D) resigned as president, another director's previously submitted resignation was accepted, and the board voted to expand its size. As a result, three SEPCO-nominated directors were elected to the board, with one of them taking Gregg's (D) position as president. Within a few weeks the LIN board fired the new president, and all three SEPCO nominated directors subsequently resigned. SEPCO sued for a refund of the premium, but the trial court dismissed the action because of the illegality of the agreement. Louis Brecher (P), a shareholder in Lin Broadcasting Corporation (LIN), brought this derivative suit against Gregg (D) and LIN's board of directors. Brecher (P) claimed, and the court found, that SEPCO paid Gregg (D) a premium for Gregg's (D) promise to resign as president of LIN; bring about the election of SEPCO's nominee as president; bringing about the immediate election of three SEPCO nominees as directors; and bringing about an absolute majority of SEPCO nominees to the board.

■ ISSUE

Is a corporation entitled to receive the premium paid to a director or officer in a sale of his minority shares in exchange for a promise of control?

■ DECISION AND RATIONALE

(Harvey, J.) Yes. This court concludes as a matter of law that an agreement which provides for a premium in exchange for a promise of control, with only 4% of the outstanding shares actually being transferred, is contrary to public policy and illegal. Here, the purchase price of $3,500,00 exceeded the market value of the stock by over $1,200,000. I therefore find that this amount represented a premium paid for the corporate presidency and board representation. Consequently, Gregg (D) must forfeit to the corporation any illegal profit derived from his sale of stock. He must account to the corporation for any profits made in his sale to SEPCO over and above that which he would have realized, had the sale been consummated in an arm's length transaction. But since it has not been shown that the actions of any other directors led to any pecuniary loss by the corporation or to the realization of any profit to themselves, they cannot be held liable.

Analysis:

The court here provides an example of the rule that corporate offices or control of management may not be sold by themselves. This rule also applies when the sale is accompanied by a transfer of stock insufficient to carry voting control. The rationale behind the rule is that, much like any asset, a corporate office and management belong to the corporation, and not to officers and directors. Thus, the court appropriately requires the premium paid for those positions to be returned to the corporation. Note that, once again, the New York court relies heavily on the portion of the purchase price that exceeds the market value of the stock to determine whether the premium was for an illegal purpose. Here the court found that a premium of over $1,200,000 was for the sole purpose of corporate control.

Essex Universal Corp. v. Yates

(*Stock Purchaser*) v. (*Controlling Shareholder*)
305 F.2d 572 (2d Cir.1962)

ALTHOUGH A SALE OF A MAJORITY OF CORPORATE STOCK MAY BE ACCOMPANIED BY AN AGREEMENT FOR CONTROL OF THE BOARD, A SALE OF A CONTROLLING SHARE THAT IS LESS THAN 50% MAY OR MAY NOT BE ACCOMPANIED BY A PROMISE OF CONTROL

■ **INSTANT FACTS** A corporation sued a controlling shareholder from whom it had agreed to purchase a 28% share and immediate control of the board.

■ **BLACK LETTER RULE** An agreement to sell 28.3% of the stock of a corporation is not illegal and unenforceable merely because the agreement provides for the immediate resignation of members of the board followed by the election of the purchaser's nominees.

■ PROCEDURAL BASIS

Appeal to the Second Circuit, challenging the district court's grant of summary judgment after the case had been removed from New York state court of the basis of diversity of citizenship.

■ FACTS

Essex Corporation (P) entered into a contract with Herbert Yates (D), the president and chairman of Republic Pictures Corporation, for the purchase of 28.3% of Republic's outstanding stock. The agreement provided that, prior to the closing date, Yates (D) would deliver the resignation of the majority of the board of directors and cause the election of Essex's (P) nominees to the board. On the date of closing, Yates (D) backed out of the agreement. Essex (P) then sued for breach of contract in the New York Supreme Court; Yates (D) subsequently removed the case to federal court. The District Court then granted Yates' (D) motion for summary judgment on the grounds that the provision for immediate transfer of control of the board rendered the agreement unenforceable.

■ ISSUE

Is a contract for the sale of a controlling share of a corporation invalid as against public policy solely because it provides for the resignation of a majority of the board of directors and the immediate election of the purchaser's nominees?

■ DECISION AND RATIONALE

(Lumbard, C.J.) No. An agreement to sell 28.3% of the stock of a corporation is not illegal and unenforceable merely because the agreement provides for the immediate resignation of members of the board followed by the election of the purchaser's nominees. It is well established that it is illegal to sell a corporate office or control of management by itself, i.e., accompanied by no sale of stock or a sale of stock insufficient to carry voting control. The rationale behind the rule is that persons who hold these positions do so on behalf of the corporation, and may not regard it as their own property. Here, however, Essex (P) was contracting for the purchase of a substantial percentage of stock. If this percentage gave Essex (P) the power to elect a majority of the board of directors, then the contract was not a simple agreement for the sale of office to one having no ownership interest in the corporation. But under Republic's bylaws Essex (P) would have to wait over 18 months to achieve control over the board of directors. The question then becomes whether it is legal to give and receive payment for the immediate transfer of management control to one who has achieved majority share control, but would not otherwise be able to convert that share into operating control for some time. Under some circumstances controlling shareholders transferring immediate control may be compelled to account to the corporation for the part of the consideration received which exceeds the fair market value. Moreover, a controlling shareholder is not permitted to profit from the facilitation of actions on the part of the purchaser which are detrimental to the corporation. There is, however, no such threat in this case. The general rule is that a bargain for the sale of a majority of stock is not made illegal by a plan for immediate transfer of management control. In this case, Essex (P) contracted for only 28.3% of Republic's shares, an amount well short of a majority. Since it is commonly known that such a share often gives the holder de facto control, it must be determined whether such a share gave Essex (P) the equivalent of majority stock control. Because 28.3% is usually tantamount to majority control, Yates (D) has the burden of proving circumstances which would have prevented Essex (P) from electing a majority of the board in due course. To do this, Yates (D) must show there was at the time some concretely foreseeable reason why Essex' (P) wishes would not have prevailed in shareholder voting.

■ CONCURRENCE

(Friendly, Cir., J.) I believe that this type of agreement violates public policy. Stockholders recognize that death, incapacity, or other hazard may prevent a director from serving a full term, but they are entitled to expect that the remaining directors will fill the vacancy in the exercise of their fiduciary responsibility. A mass resignation followed by an election of nominees without any consideration as to there character interferes with stockholders' reasonable expectations. However, my task is not to determine what I believe the law ought to be. Rather, I must predict how the New York Court of Appeals would decided the matter. Consequently, I am unable to find any indication that counters the general rule that a bargain for the sale of a majority of stock is not made illegal by a plan for immediate transfer of management control. I find that the New York courts would also apply this rule to a situation where the agreement called for a purchase of a controlling—but minority—share of the corporation. I must, nevertheless, disagree with Chief Judge Lombard's formulation that such a contract may be struck down if a party challenging the provision can prove that the buyer would not be able to elect his nominees. First, there are no New York Cases which intimate such a distinction. Second, the test is difficult to apply because it depends on factors such as the dispersion of ownership, the success of the corporation, the general satisfaction of the shareholders, the presence of cumulative voting, and many others. One who believes he owns a "controlling share" may often be surprised at his inability to elect a majority of the board. Thus, we should leave the development of this area of the law to the New York courts.

Analysis:

The question presented by this case is, to what extent may a sale of a controlling minority share include an agreement to transfer control of the board? Chief Judge Lombard's opinion creates a presumption in favor of agreements to transfer corporate control where there is a sale for a controlling share. In his view, any challenge to such an agreement must be accompanied by proof that the controlling shareholder would not have eventually gained such control. In contrast, Judge Friendly held that an agreement to transfer control of the board upon sale of a controlling share interferes with the expectations of the shareholders. Nevertheless, Judge Friendly upholds the validity of the agreement on the ground that the New York courts would so the same. Judge Friendly's opinion differs from Chief Judge Lombard's opinion in that the former creates no distinction between sales of a majority share and those of a controlling share. In Judge Friendly's view, discerning when the holder of a large stake in the company has the ability to control the election of officers and directors is simply too difficult a task for courts to undertake.

CHAPTER TEN

Insider Trading

The Wharf (Holdings) Limited v. United International Holdings, Inc.

Instant Facts: The Wharf (Holdings) Limited (D) reneged on an oral agreement to sell to United International Holdings, Inc. (D) an option to purchase an interest in a foreign cable television system.

Black Letter Rule: Section 10(b) of the Securities Exchange Act forbids the use of any manipulative or deceptive device or contrivance relating to the sale of a security that is misleading or operates as a fraud or deceit.

Securities and Exchange Commission v. Texas Gulf Sulphur Co.

Instant Facts: The federal government sued several officers and employees of a mining corporation to rescind their trades in the corporation's stock or the issuance of stock options to them by the corporation because they had bought the stock or accepted the options without disclosing information they knew about a major mineral strike which was not known by the market or the corporation's stock options committee.

Black Letter Rule: A person may not trade in the stock of a corporation without disclosing confidential information about the corporation which the person knows is not known to the public and, if known, would affect the price of the corporation's stock.

SEC v. Zandford

Instant Facts: The SEC (P) brought a civil complaint against Zandford (D) for violating federal securities laws.

Black Letter Rule: When fraudulent activity coincides with the sale or purchase of securities, violations of § 10(b) and Rule 10b–5 have occurred.

Basic Inc. v. Levinson

Instant Facts: Following the announcement of a merger by a corporation which had previously denied it was negotiating a merger, a group of shareholders who had sold their stock following the denial filed a class action lawsuit against the corporation for violation of SEC Rule 10b–5.

Black Letter Rule: A court may adopt a rebuttable presumption of shareholder reliance on a corporation's material misstatements of fact under a "fraud-on-the-market" theory for purposes of establishing the reliance requirement for bringing an action against the corporation under SEC Rule 10–b5.

Chiarella v. United states

Instant Facts: An employee of a financial printing company appealed a criminal conviction for having violated § 10(b) of the Securities Exchange Act of 1934 by trading in the stock of several companies that were to be acquired, on the basis of information about the impending acquisitions he had learned from merger announcement documents.

Black Letter Rule: Under § 10(b) of the Securities Exchange Act of 1934, a duty to disclose material nonpublic corporate information or abstain from trading in the stock of the corporation which is the subject of that information requires a fiduciary relationship with the corporation that is the subject of the stock trade.

Dirks v. Securities and Exchange Commission

Instant Facts: An investment analyst appealed his administrative censure for allegedly violating SEC Rule 10b–5 by disclosing material nonpublic information about fraudulent activity at an insurance company which he learned from corporate insiders at the insurance company to his investor clients, who sold their stock in the insurance company before the information became public.

Black Letter Rule: A person receiving a stock tip from a corporate insider violates SEC Rule 10b–5 when the corporate insider has breached his fiduciary duty to the corporation's shareholders by tipping information for his own personal benefit and the person receiving the tip knows or should know that the tip was a breach of the corporate insider's fiduciary duty.

United States v. O'Hagan

Instant Facts: An attorney who worked for a law firm that represented the potential acquirer in a takeover bid of a target corporation was convicted of criminal charges for violating SEC Rule 10b–5 by trading in the stock of the target corporation on the basis of information he had learned from his firm's representation of the acquirer.

Black Letter Rule: A person can commit fraud in connection with a securities transaction and thereby violate Rule 10b–5, by misappropriating material nonpublic information for trading purposes in breach of a duty owed to the source of that information.

Santa Fe Industries, Inc. v. Green

Instant Facts: The minority shareholders of a corporate subsidiary brought an action in federal court claiming that an alleged breach of fiduciary duty by the majority shareholder of the corporate subsidiary regarding the price paid to cash out the minority shareholders in a short-form merger constituted a violation of SEC Rule 10b–5.

Black Letter Rule: A mere breach of fiduciary duty by a majority stockholder, without any deception, misrepresentation, or nondisclosure, does not violate SEC Rule 10b–5.

Gratz v. Claughton

Instant Facts: A corporate insider, owning more than ten percent of the stock of a corporation, was sued by a shareholder of the corporation under § 16(b) of the Securities Exchange Act of 1934 to recover on behalf of the corporation alleged short-swing profits made by the insider by trading in the stock of the corporation.

Black Letter Rule: A lowest purchase price, highest sale price method of matching stock sales and purchases is the appropriate way to compute short-swing profits under § 16(b) of the Securities Exchange Act of 1934 when there is more than one purchase and sale transaction within a six-month period.

Kern County Land Co. v. Occidental Petroleum Corp.

Instant Facts: A corporation that had made an unsuccessful takeover bid for a target corporation was sued by a successor to the target corporation under 16(b) to recover short-swing profits allegedly made from the exchange of its shares in the target corporation for shares in the corporation which successfully took over the target corporation.

Black Letter Rule: Where there is no reason to believe that there has been a speculative abuse of inside information, there has not been a "sale" within the meaning of § 16(b) of the Securities Exchange Act of 1934 when a statutory insider becomes irrevocably bound to exchange its shares in a corporation for new shares pursuant to a merger agreement over which the insider had no control.

Diamond v. Oreamuno

Instant Facts: A shareholder of a corporation brought a derivative action on behalf of the corporation under state law against two corporate insiders, alleging that they had breached their fiduciary duty to the corporation by trading in the corporation's stock on the basis of material inside information.

Black Letter Rule: An insider can be liable to his corporation for breach of fiduciary duty as a result of trading corporate stock on the basis of material inside information, even in the absence of actual tangible harm to the corporation.

Malone v. Brincat

Instant Facts: Several shareholders of a corporation brought a state law claim of breach of fiduciary duty against the corporation's board of directors, asserting that the directors had breached their fiduciary duties by overstating the corporation's earnings in their periodic reports to the shareholders.

Black Letter Rule: A director who knowingly disseminates false information that results in corporate injury or damage to an individual stockholder violates his fiduciary duty to the corporation or shareholder and may be held accountable under state law.

The Wharf (Holdings) Limited v. United International Holdings, Inc.

(*Government Contractor*) v. (*Investor*)
532 U.S. 588 (2001)

AN ORAL SALE OF SECURITIES FALLS UNDER § 10(B) OF THE SECURITIES AND EXCHANGE ACT

■ **INSTANT FACTS** The Wharf (Holdings) Limited (D) reneged on an oral agreement to sell to United International Holdings, Inc. (D) an option to purchase an interest in a foreign cable television system.

■ **BLACK LETTER RULE** Section 10(b) of the Securities Exchange Act forbids the use of any manipulative or deceptive device or contrivance relating to the sale of a security that is misleading or operates as a fraud or deceit.

■ PROCEDURAL BASIS

Certiorari to review a decision of a federal appeals court affirming a judgment for the plaintiff.

■ FACTS

In preparation of a bid for an exclusive license from the Hong Kong government to operate a cable television system, The Wharf (Holdings) Limited (D) approached United International Holdings (P) to be a business partner. As compensation for its assistance with the preparation of the bid, The Wharf (D) provided United (D) an option to purchase ten percent of the stock in the cable system if The Wharf (D) received the license. When The Wharf (D) submitted its bid, it represented that it would be the sole owner of the cable system, but would consider allowing United (D) to invest. United (P) and The Wharf (D) engaged in substantial negotiation concerning United's (P) option, but never reduced the agreement to writing. After The Wharf (D) was granted the license, United (D) attempted to exercise the option, which The Wharf (D) refused. United (P) filed suit in federal court for violations of § 10(b) of the Securities Exchange Act of 1934. In its complaint, United (P) alleged that The Wharf (D) secretly intended not to allow United (D) to exercise the option. Evidence of The Wharf's (D) secret intention not to recognize the option was offered at trial, and a jury awarded United (P) compensatory and punitive damages. The judgment was affirmed on appeal.

■ ISSUE

Does the oral sale of an option to buy stock with the intention never to honor the option constitute a manipulative or deceptive device or contrivance in connection with the purchase or sale of a security in violation of § 10(b) of the Securities Exchange Act of 1934?

■ DECISION AND RATIONALE

(Breyer, J.) Yes. Section 10(b) of the Securities Exchange Act forbids the use of "any manipulative or deceptive device or contrivance in contravention of" SEC rules and regulations. Under SEC Rule 10b–5, a manipulative or deceptive device or contrivance includes "any device, scheme, or artifice to defraud," "any untrue statement of a material fact," the omission of "a material fact necessary in order to make the statements made ... not misleading," or an "act, practice, or course of business ... [that]

operates . . . as a fraud or deceit." If the plaintiff establishes the existence of one of these practices in connection with the sale of a security, the plaintiff may succeed in its suit.

Here, the security at issue is not the cable system stock, but rather the option to purchase the stock. Although the sale of the option was oral, there is nothing in the language of the statute or rule to exclude oral contracts. Oral contracts are common and enforceable under federal securities law. Furthermore, The Wharf's (P) secret intention not to honor the option was misleading, for its refusal to honor the option rendered it worthless, affecting the value of the security. Finally, United's (D) claim is not merely that The Wharf (P) breached its oral contract to sell securities, but encompasses a fraudulent scheme to deprive United (D) of the purchase from the beginning. Affirmed.

Analysis:

For many years, the Supreme Court had cautiously approached Rule 10b–5 cases. From its language, Rule 10b–5 can be construed to apply to a broad array of conduct depending on the sitting court's view of the relationship between a defendant's conduct and the sale or purchase of securities. Recognizing this, courts tended to apply the rule narrowly so as to limit its reach to the typical securities transaction. *Wharf*, however, marked a departure from this approach, applying the rule to arguably a mere state-law breach of contract claim.

■ CASE VOCABULARY

SECURITIES EXCHANGE ACT OF 1934: The federal law regulating the public trading of securities.

SECURITY: An instrument that evidences the holder's ownership rights in a firm (e.g., a stock), the holder's creditor relationship with a firm or government (e.g., a bond), or the holder's other rights (e.g., an option).

SEC v. Texas Gulf Sulphur Co.

(*Government Agency*) v. (*Mining Company*)

401 F.2d 833 (2d Cir.1968)

SECOND CIRCUIT IMPOSES A "DISCLOSE OR ABSTAIN" TEST FOR THOSE TRADING WITH KNOWLEDGE OF "MATERIAL" CONFIDENTIAL CORPORATE INFORMATION

■ **INSTANT FACTS** The federal government sued several officers and employees of a mining corporation to rescind their trades in the corporation's stock or the issuance of stock options to them by the corporation because they had bought the stock or accepted the options without disclosing information they knew about a major mineral strike which was not known by the market or the corporation's stock options committee.

■ **BLACK LETTER RULE** A person may not trade in the stock of a corporation without disclosing confidential information about the corporation which the person knows is not known to the public and, if known, would affect the price of the corporation's stock.

■ PROCEDURAL BASIS

Appeal of a federal district court decision holding that certain stock trading by corporate insiders had not violated SEC Rule 10b-5.

■ FACTS

Texas Gulf Sulphur Co. ("TGS") (D1) explored an area in eastern Canada, looking for mineral deposits. Four TGS (D1) employees, Mollison (D2), Holyk (D3), Clayton (D4), and Darke (D5), discovered a potential mineral strike on rock located on a segment of land known as Kidd 55. The group conducted a survey and did initial drilling on the land. The results of the initial drilling convinced them that TGS (D1) should buy the portions of the Kidd 55 land it did not already own. To facilitate the purchase of the surrounding land, Stephens (D6), the president of TGS (D1), instructed the exploratory group to keep all results of the initial drilling confidential, even from TGS (D1) officers, directors, and employees. TGS also shut down all drilling on the site, attempting to conceal its exploration on the land. Subsequently, lab tests done by the company showed that the Kidd 55 land would produce a major mineral strike. After buying up the surrounding land over a period of four months, TGS (D1) resumed drilling on the Kidd 55 site and a major ore deposit was actually found. During the drilling shutdown, Mollison (D2), Holyk (D3), Clayton (D4), Darke (D5), Stephens (D6) had bought TGS (D1) stock or calls to purchase such stock. In addition, Mollison (D2), Holyk, (D3), Stephens (D6), Fogarty (D7), and Kline (D8) had accepted incentive stock options granted to them by a committee of the board of directors without disclosing to the committee the results of the Kidd 55 drilling. Eventually, the Securities and Exchange Commission ("SEC") (P) brought an action in federal district court under Rule 10b-5 [SEC regulation making it unlawful to defraud or deceive a person in connection with the purchase or sale of securities] which, among other things, sought to compel the employees who had traded on the basis of inside information about the results of the Kidd 55 drilling to rescind their stock transactions and give up their profits. The SEC (P) also sought to rescind the incentive stock options granted to Mollison (D2), Holyk (D3), Stephens (D6), and two TGS (D1) vice-presidents, Fogarty (D7), and Kline (D8). The district court dismissed the complaint against those employees who had traded prior to the date the ore deposit had actually been discovered. The district court judge concluded that, prior to that date, the insider trading activity was not illegal because the drilling results were not yet "material." The judge also found that Mollison (D2) and Holyk (D3), as minor officers of the company, had no obligation to report the drilling to the stock options committee before accepting their options. The judge determined that, while Stephens (D6), Fogarty (D7), and Kline (D8) had a duty as directors and major officers of the company to report material information before accepting the options, since the drilling information was not material, they had not acted improperly. The SEC (P) appealed as to all the defendants on the issue of their stock trades and appealed as to Stephens (D6), Fogarty (D7), and Kline (D8) on the issue of the acceptance of the options.

■ ISSUE

Can a person trade in the stock of a corporation without disclosing confidential information about the corporation which the person knows is not known to the public and, if known, would affect the price of the corporation's stock?

■ DECISION AND RATIONALE

(Waterman, J.) No. The SEC's (P) Rule 10b-5 is based on the justifiable expectation of the securities marketplace that all investors trading on impersonal exchanges have relatively equal access to material information. The essence of the rule is that anyone trading in the securities of a corporation who has access to information intended to be available only for a corporate purpose and not for the personal benefit of anyone may not take advantage of such information knowing it to be unavailable to the investing public. Someone with such information has a duty to either disclose the information or abstain from trading in the company's stock. Such a duty arises, however, only in the event that such information is "material." Information is "material" if a reasonable person would attach importance to it in determining his choice of action in the transaction in question. Whether facts are material within Rule 10b-5 will depend on a balancing of the indicated probability the event will occur and the anticipated magnitude of the event in light of the overall business activity of the company. Here, the trial court found that the results of the initial drilling were too remote to be deemed material. We disagree. Knowledge of the more than marginal possibility of the existence of a mine of the quality and magnitude indicated by the initial drilling would certainly have been important to a reasonable, if speculative, investor in deciding if he should buy, sell, or hold his TGS (D1) stock. The insiders here were not trading on an equal footing with the outside investors. They alone were in a position to evaluate the probability and magnitude of the ore strike and could invest safely, secure that the stock price would rise if a major strike should materialize, but would decline little, in the event of a failed mine because the public would be unaware of the exploration and the costs were too little to affect the stock price. We therefore hold that all transactions by individuals who knew of the Kidd 55 drilling results were made in violation of Rule 10b-5. As for the acceptance of the incentive stock options without disclosure to the options committee of the results of the preliminary drilling on Kidd 55, we hold that Stephens (D6), Fogarty (D7), and Kline (D8), as high-level TGS (D1) officers and directors, violated Rule 10b-5 by accepting the options without disclosure of the material information they possessed regarding the drilling. Reversed.

■ CONCURRENCE

(Friendly, J.) A rule requiring a minor officer to reject an incentive stock option given to him, on its own initiative, by a directors' committee administering an option plan at a time when the minor officer knows the option price is unfair to the corporation, would not comport with the realities of human nature or of corporate life. If the SEC (P) had appealed the ruling dismissing this complaint issue as to Mollison (D2) and Holyk (D3), two minor officers, I would have upheld the dismissal. They were entitled to believe that their superiors had reported the drilling facts to the options committee unless they had information to the contrary. Stephens (D6), Fogarty (D7), and Kline (D8), however, as senior officers had a duty to inform the options committee that this was not the right time to grant options at 95% of the current price. I am unimpressed with their argument that the corporate need for secrecy during the execution of the plan to acquire the surrounding land required them to remain silent when they received the options. It should be possible for officers to communicate with directors, of all people, without fearing a breach of confidence.

Analysis:

This was the first case in which a court, rather than merely the SEC, found that trading on the basis of material confidential corporate information without disclosing such information to the public violated Rule 10b-5. Rule 10b-5, itself, while prohibiting "fraud and deceit," does not specifically indicate that a person who trades silently on the basis of material confidential information, without making any affirmative statements at all, has engaged in conduct prohibited by the rule. While the facts in this case are quite complicated, the rule established by the Second Circuit is quite simple. A person in possession of material confidential corporate information can either disclose the information to the public and gain the ability to trade in the corporation's stock or abstain from trading and not be required to disclose the information to the public. Significantly, the court here defined the scope of materiality to include any information to which a reasonable person would attach importance in determining whether to buy, sell, or hold his stock in the corporation. In a series of later decisions, the U.S. Supreme Court narrowed the scope of persons to whom the "disclose or abstain" rule applies to those with some kind of fiduciary relationship to the corporation or those who misappropriated confidential corporate information in breach of a duty owed to the source of the information.

■ CASE VOCABULARY

CALL: A negotiable option contract under which the bearer has the right to buy from the other party to the contract a certain number of shares of stock at a fixed price, on or before a certain date.

INCENTIVE STOCK OPTION: A contract right granted by a corporate board of directors to management and employees of the corporation as part of their annual compensation, permitting them to buy stock at a future date for a price fixed in advance by the contract.

INSIDER: In general, insiders are directors, officers, or employees of a corporation, but can include anyone with a fiduciary duty to the corporation who holds knowledge regarding the corporation that is not available to the public.

SEC v. Zandford

(Federal Agency) v. *(Securities Broker)*
535 U.S. 813 (2002)

COMMON LAW FRAUD MAY BE COVERED BY FEDERAL SECURITIES LAWS

■ **INSTANT FACTS** The SEC (P) brought a civil complaint against Zandford (D) for violating federal securities laws.

■ **BLACK LETTER RULE** When fraudulent activity coincides with the sale or purchase of securities, violations of § 10(b) and Rule 10b–5 have occurred.

■ PROCEDURAL BASIS

Certiorari to review a decision of the Fourth Circuit Court of Appeals reversing a trial court grant of summary judgment to the plaintiff.

■ FACTS

Zandford (D), a securities broker, persuaded Wood, an elderly man, to open a joint investment account for himself and his mentally retarded daughter. The Woods granted Zandford (D) a power of attorney to effect transactions without prior approval, with the understanding that transactions would be conservative to maintain the safety of the investment principal and interest. Over the next four years, the Woods had lost over $400,000. The National Association of Securities Dealers (NASD) conducted a routine examination of Zandford's (D) firm and found that, on numerous occasions, Zandford (D) had transferred money from the Woods' account to his own. Zandford (D) was later convicted of wire fraud. Before the conviction, the Securities and Exchange Commission (SEC) (P) filed a civil complaint against Zandford (D) for violating § 10(b) of the Securities Exchange Act and SEC Rule 10b–5 by engaging in a scheme to defraud the Woods and misappropriate their funds. After Zandford's (D) conviction, the SEC (P) moved for partial summary judgment, arguing that the conviction estopped Zandford (D) from contesting the facts establishing the § 10(b) violation. Zandford (D) moved for further discovery to determine whether the fraud had the requisite "connection to" the purchase or sale of securities under § 10(b). The court denied Zandford's (D) motion and entered summary judgment against him. On appeal, the Fourth Circuit Court of Appeals reversed and remanded for dismissal of the complaint. The Fourth Circuit reasoned that the complaint failed to establish a connection to the purchase or sale of securities and instead alleged merely a scheme to steal the Woods' investment assets.

■ ISSUE

Does the theft of an investment client's assets "in connection with the purchase or sale of any security" fall within the meaning of § 10(b) and Rule 10b–5?

■ DECISION AND RATIONALE

(Stevens, J.) Yes. Section 10(b) of the Securities Exchange Act forbids the use of "any manipulative or deceptive device or contrivance in contravention of" SEC rules and regulations. Rule 10b–5 implements § 10(b), forbidding the use, "in connection with the purchase or sale of any security," of "any device, scheme, or artifice to defraud," or any other "act, practice, or course of business . . . [that] operates . . . as a fraud or deceit." The Act was established to promote investor confidence and maintain high ethics in the securities industry. In light of this purpose, the Act is to be construed flexibly to accomplish its goals. While not every common law fraud rises to a violation of securities laws, a misrepresentation as to the value of a security is not required to establish a § 10(b) violation.

Because the Court of Appeals remanded for dismissal of the complaint, the Court need only determine whether the SEC (P) has stated a claim for relief on the face of the complaint, without determining whether an actual violation occurred. Here, the complaint clearly alleges that Zandford (D) engaged in a scheme to defraud the Woods by making a series of securities transactions that enabled him to convert the proceeds to his own use. As alleged, the securities sales are not independent from Zandford's (D) subsequent fraudulent actions. Instead, the sales were a "course of business" within the meaning of Rule 10b–5 through which the fraud operated. Without the sales, Zandford's (D) fraud could not have occurred. Because the sales and Zandford's (D) breach of fiduciary duties coincide, the complaint adequately alleges § 10(b) and Rule 10b–5 violations "in connection with" the sale of securities. Reversed and remanded.

Analysis:

As demonstrated by this case, the meaning of "in connection with" is crucial to the application of federal securities laws. It is the nexus between one's act and the sale or purchase of securities that converts a state-law violation into a federal securities law violation. Unfortunately, there is little guidance to determine when such a nexus exists. Clearly, when the state-law fraud coincides with the sale of securities, federal law is implicated. Yet, federal law may nonetheless apply on much less of a connection.

■ CASE VOCABULARY

SECURITIES ACT OF 1933: The federal law regulating the registration and initial public offering of securities, with an emphasis on full public disclosure of financial and other information.

FRAUD: A knowing misrepresentation of the truth or concealment of a material fact to induce another to act to his or her detriment; a misrepresentation made recklessly without belief in its truth to induce another person to act; unconscionable dealing, especially in contract law; the unfair use of the power arising out of one of the parties' relative positions and resulting in an unconscionable bargain.

Basic Inc. v. Levinson

(*Corporation*) v. (*Shareholder*)

485 U.S. 224 (1988)

U.S. SUPREME COURT ACCEPTS "FRAUD-ON-THE-MARKET" THEORY OF RELIANCE FOR ASSERTION OF A RULE 10b-5 CAUSE OF ACTION

■ **INSTANT FACTS** Following the announcement of a merger by a corporation which had previously denied it was negotiating a merger, a group of shareholders who had sold their stock following the denial filed a class action lawsuit against the corporation for violation of SEC Rule 10b-5.

■ **BLACK LETTER RULE** A court may adopt a rebuttable presumption of shareholder reliance on a corporation's material misstatements of fact under a "fraud-on-the-market" theory for purposes of establishing the reliance requirement for bringing an action against the corporation under SEC Rule 10-b5.

■ PROCEDURAL BASIS

Appeal following a grant of certiorari by the U.S. Supreme Court of a federal appeals court's affirmance of a district court's certification of a class action lawsuit alleging a violation of SEC Rule 10b-5.

■ FACTS

Beginning in September 1976, representatives of Combustion Engineering Inc. ("Combustion") and Basic Inc. ("Basic") (D) had discussions about the possibility of merging the two companies. While these discussions were continuing, Basic (D) made public statements denying that it was engaged in merger negotiations and denying knowledge of any reason why the company's stock was trading heavily and climbing in price. Subsequently, Basic (D) asked the New York Stock Exchange to suspend trading in its shares and issued a press release stating that it had been "approached" by another company concerning a merger. The next day, Basic's (D) board of directors voted to accept Combustion's offer to merge. Levinson (P) and two other former Basic (D) shareholders had sold their Basic (D) stock following Basic's (D) first public statement denying merger negotiations and prior to the suspension of trading on the stock exchange and Basic's (D) announcement of merger discussions. After the announcement of the merger, these shareholders brought a class action lawsuit in federal district court against Basic (D) and its board of directors, asserting that the company had issued false and misleading public statements in violation of SEC Rule 10b-5 [regulation making it unlawful to defraud or deceive a person in connection with the purchase or sale of securities]. Levinson (P) and the other shareholders contended that they had been injured by selling their Basic (D) stock at prices that were artificially low because the market had been affected by the company's misleading statements about the merger. The district court adopted a presumption of reliance by the selling shareholders on the company's public statements and certified the class action as involving common questions of fact or law which predominated over particular questions relating to individual shareholders as required for class certification under the Federal Rules of Civil Procedure. The court, however, granted summary judgment in favor of Basic (D), holding as a matter of law that any misstatements by the company were "immaterial." On appeal, the Sixth Circuit Court of Appeals reversed the district court's grant of summary judgment, finding that, while the company was under no general duty to disclose discussions with Combustion, if it did voluntarily release a statement, that statement could not be so incomplete as to mislead the public. The Sixth Circuit did affirm the district court's certification of the shareholder class, finding a rebuttable presumption that the class had relied on Basic's (D) material misrepresentations. Accepting the shareholders' fraud-on-the-market theory of reliance, as opposed to requiring each shareholder in the class to demonstrate direct reliance on Basic's (D) misstatements, the appeals court explained that without such a rebuttable presumption, it would be impractical to certify a class in such circumstances under the Federal Rules of Civil Procedure. Basic (D) then appealed to the U.S. Supreme Court which granted certiorari to consider the standard of materiality to be applied and whether a rebuttable presumption of reliance could be adopted by the court.

■ ISSUE

May a court adopt a rebuttable presumption of shareholder reliance on a corporation's material misstatements of fact under a "fraud-on-the-market" theory for purposes of establishing the reliance requirement for bringing an action against the corporation under SEC Rule 10-b5?

■ DECISION AND RATIONALE

(Blackmun, J.) Yes. Levinson (P) and the other named plaintiffs in this class action lawsuit alleged that, in reliance on Basic's (D) statements, they sold their shares of Basic (D) stock in an artificially depressed market. Requiring proof of individualized reliance from each member of the proposed class of plaintiff shareholders effectively would have prevented the shareholders from proceeding with a class action lawsuit under the Federal Rules of Civil Procedure, since individual issues would have overwhelmed the common issues. Basic (D) argues that reliance is a required element of a Rule 10b-5 cause of action, just as it is a required element of the common-law tort of fraud. We agree that reliance is an element of a Rule 10b-5 cause of action. It provides the necessary causal connection between a defendant's misrepresentation and a plaintiff's injury. There is more than one way to demonstrate that causal connection, however. The modern securities markets, involving the exchange of millions of shares every day, differ from the face-to-face transactions involved in the common-law fraud cases. Our understanding of the Rule 10b-5 reliance requirement should take into account those differences. The market is interposed between the buyer and seller and transmits information to the investor in the form of a market price. Thus, the market performs a substantial part of the valuation process performed by the buyer or seller in a face-to-face transaction. The courts below accepted a presumption, created by the "fraud-on-the-market theory" and subject to rebuttal, that those who traded Basic (D) shares did so in reliance on the integrity of the price set by the market. That presumption is consistent with the legislative purpose behind the federal securities laws to facilitate investor reliance on the integrity of the markets. Those laws were drafted by Congress, expressly relying on the premise that securities markets are affected by information. Common sense and probability also support this notion. It is hard to imagine that there is ever a buyer or seller who does not rely on market integrity. Who would knowingly roll the dice in a crooked crap game? Because most publicly available information is reflected in market price, an investor's reliance on any public material misrepresentations may therefore be presumed for purposes of a Rule 10b-5 action. This presumption may be rebutted. Thus here, if Basic (D) could show that an individual shareholder would have sold his shares for unrelated reasons, without relying on the integrity of the market, that shareholder could not assert a cause of action under Rule 10b-5. While the courts below agreed about the presumption of reliance, they disagreed on the standard of materiality to be applied in this case. We find that materiality depends on the significance a reasonable investor would place on the withheld or misrepresented information and will differ from case to case. An omitted fact is material if there is a substantial likelihood that a reasonable shareholder would consider it important in deciding whether to buy, sell, or hold his stock. Because this standard of materiality differs from what was used by both courts below, we remand the case for reconsideration as to whether summary judgment is appropriate under the facts in this record. Judgment vacated and remanded.

■ DISSENT

(White, J.) No. While I agree with the materiality standard adopted by the court in this case for a Rule 10b-5 action, I do not agree that the "fraud-on-the-market" theory should be applied. The majority's conclusion assumes that individuals rely on the integrity of the market price when buying or selling stock in impersonal, well-developed markets. Even if I could accept the assumption that most buyers and sellers act in response to the market price, the "fraud-on-the-market" theory goes further than that, also assuming that buyers and sellers rely on the *integrity* of that price. The meaning of that phrase eludes me. It wrongly suggests that stocks have some "true value" that is measurable by a standard other than their market price.

Analysis:

This case conclusively established two important points regarding litigation under Rule 10b-5. First, the Supreme Court adopted the case-by-case, fact-sensitive approach to determining the materiality of contingent facts that had been used by the Second Circuit in *Securities and Exchange Commission v. Texas Gulf Sulphur Co.*, 401 F.2d 833 (2d Cir.1968). Second, the Court determined that a rebuttable presumption of reliance was appropriate in the context of a material misstatement regarding a publicly traded security. The Court explained that anyone buying or selling stock in an organized market relies on the integrity of the price of that stock in the market. Finding that the price reflected all public information about the stock, the Court concluded that a buyer or seller can therefore logically be presumed to have relied on whatever public statements have been made about the stock in deciding whether to buy or sell. The Court did suggest that such a presumption could be rebutted by a defendant if, for example, it could be shown that a misrepresentation did not actually distort the price of the stock or that the shareholder would have traded anyway, despite the misrepresentation. As this case shows, the primary significance of permitting such a presumption is that it allows a class action for misrepresentation under Rule 10b-5 to be certified under the Federal Rules of Civil Procedure.

■ CASE VOCABULARY

CERTIFICATION: A requirement to bring a class action lawsuit that a trial court affirm that the class of plaintiffs is extremely large, that there are questions of law or fact common to the class, that the claims or defenses of the representative parties are typical of the class, and that the representative parties will fairly and adequately protect the interests of the class.

CLASS ACTION: A method under Rule 23 of the Federal Rules of Civil Procedure by which a few persons may sue as the representatives of a larger group of similarly injured persons.

FRAUD-ON-THE-MARKET THEORY: A theory which presumes that a false disclosure of fact that is disseminated to the public is a fraud on every person/entity who purchased stock after the false disclosure was made.

REBUTTABLE PRESUMPTION: A legal device which, in the absence of proof to the contrary, requires a fact finder to assume a particular fact is true.

Chiarella v. United States

(*Financial Printer*) v. (*Federal Government*)

445 U.S. 222 (1980)

U.S. SUPREME COURT REJECTS SECOND CIRCUIT'S EQUAL ACCESS THEORY AND NARROWS THE "DISCLOSE OR ABSTAIN" RULE

■ **INSTANT FACTS** An employee of a financial printing company appealed a criminal conviction for having violated § 10(b) of the Securities Exchange Act of 1934 by trading in the stock of several companies that were to be acquired, on the basis of information about the impending acquisitions he had learned from merger announcement documents.

■ **BLACK LETTER RULE** Under § 10(b) of the Securities Exchange Act of 1934, a duty to disclose material nonpublic corporate information or abstain from trading in the stock of the corporation which is the subject of that information requires a fiduciary relationship with the corporation that is the subject of the stock trade.

■ PROCEDURAL BASIS

Appeal following a grant of certiorari by the U.S. Supreme Court of a federal appeals court's affirmance of a criminal conviction on seventeen counts of having violated § 10(b) of the Securities Exchange Act of 1934 and SEC Rule 10b-5.

■ FACTS

Vincent Chiarella ("Chiarella") (D) worked as a financial printer for a company that was often hired by major corporations to print announcements of their mergers. When merger announcements were sent to the printer by the acquiring companies, the identities of the acquiring and target companies were left blank, to be filled in by the printer just before the final printing was to be done. Chiarella (D), however, was able to deduce the names of the companies from other information contained in the documents. Without disclosing his knowledge of the impending deals, Chiarella (D) bought stock in the target companies he had identified and then sold the stock immediately after the mergers were announced, realizing a sizeable profit. The Securities and Exchange Commission ("SEC") investigated Chiarella's (D) trading activities and Chiarella subsequently entered into a consent decree with the SEC in which he agreed to give up all of his trading profits. He also lost his job with the printing company. The United States Attorney (P) ultimately indicted Chiarella (D) for violating § 10(b) of the Securities Exchange Act of 1934 [legislation enabling the SEC to regulate the use of manipulative and deceptive devices in connection with purchase or sale of securities] and SEC Rule 10b-5 [regulation making it unlawful to defraud or deceive a person in connection with the purchase or sale of securities]. The trial court instructed the jury that Chiarella (D) should be found guilty if he traded on the basis of material nonpublic information, knowing that the other people trading in the market did not have access to the same confidential information. The jury convicted Chiarella (D) and the Second Circuit Court of Appeals affirmed his conviction. Chiarella (D) appealed to the U.S. Supreme Court, which granted certiorari.

■ ISSUE

Does a duty to disclose material nonpublic corporate information or abstain from trading in the stock of the corporation which is the subject of that information arise under § 10(b) of the Securities Exchange

Act of 1934 without the existence of a fiduciary relationship between the person trading and the corporation that is the subject of the stock trade?

■ DECISION AND RATIONALE

(Powell, J.) No. The trial court instructed the jury to convict Chiarella (D) if it found that he willfully failed to inform sellers of target company stock that he knew of an impending takeover bid that would make their shares more valuable. Chiarella (D) was not a corporate insider and he received no confidential information from the target company in whose stock he traded. At common law, one who fails to disclose material information prior to the consummation of a transaction commits fraud only when he is under a duty to disclose. That duty arises because of a fiduciary or other similar relation of trust and confidence between the parties. Chiarella's trades on the basis of information about the acquiring company was not fraud under § 10 of the Securities Exchange Act of 1934, unless he was subject to an affirmative duty to disclose the information before trading. The trial court's instructions failed to specify any such duty. In effect, the court instructed the jury that Chiarella (D) owed a duty to everyone; to all sellers and the market as a whole. The lower court ruling rested on the belief that the federal securities laws have created a system of equal access to investment information and that the use by anyone of material information that is not generally available is fraudulent because it gives certain buyers and sellers unfair advantages in the market. Not every instance of financial unfairness, however, constitutes fraudulent activity under § 10(b). Moreover, the element required to make silence fraudulent, a duty to disclose, is absent in this case. There can be no fraud absent a duty to speak. Here, no duty could arise from Chiarella's relationship with the sellers of the target companies' stock because Chiarella (D) had no prior relationship with them. He was not their agent, fiduciary, or anyone in whom those sellers had placed their trust. He was a stranger dealing with them only through impersonal market transactions. We cannot affirm the conviction here without finding a general duty for all market participants to forgo trading on material nonpublic information. Formulation of such a broad duty would depart from established doctrine that duty arises from a specific relationship between two parties and should not be undertaken in the absence of some evidence of explicit congressional intent. Neither Congress nor the SEC has ever adopted a rule of equal access to information. We hold that a duty to disclose does not arise from the mere possession of nonpublic market information. The United States (P) has offered an alternative theory to support the conviction, arguing that Chiarella (D) breached a duty to the acquiring corporations when he acted on information he obtained through his position as an employee of a printer employed by the acquiring corporations. We need not decide whether such a theory has merit because it was never submitted to the jury and thus we will not speculate as to whether such a duty exists. Reversed.

■ DISSENT

(Burger, C.J.) I would read § 10(b) and Rule 10b-5 to mean that a person who has misappropriated material nonpublic information has an absolute duty to disclose that information or refrain from trading. The majority leaves open this issue, apparently concluding that this theory of the case was not submitted to the jury. I believe that the jury instructions did properly charge a violation of § 10(b) and Rule 10b-5. By their terms, those provisions reach any person engaged in any fraudulent scheme. This broad language negates the majority's suggestion that congressional concern was limited to trading by corporate insiders or to deceptive practices related to information obtained from within the corporation. The antifraud provisions were designed to assure that dealing in securities is fair and without undue advantages among investors. An investor who purchases stock on the basis of misappropriated nonpublic information possesses such an undue trading advantage. His conduct clearly serves no useful function except his own enrichment at the expense of others. Chiarella (D) stole valuable nonpublic information entrusted to him in confidence and then exploited his ill-gotten informational advantage by buying stock in the market. I would affirm the conviction.

Analysis:

In this case, Justice Powell and Chief Justice Burger set the stage for a lively debate regarding the scope of the duty to disclose material nonpublic information about a corporation or abstain from trading in that corporation's stock under § 10(b) and Rule 10b-5. Justice Powell's opinion for the majority narrowed the reading of Rule 10b-5 by finding that, in order for a "disclose or abstain" duty to apply, there must be some kind of fiduciary relationship between the person possessing the material nonpublic information and the corporation that is the subject of the information and the stock trading. Since Chiarella (D) had no fiduciary relationship with the target corporations whose stock he was buying and selling, the majority believed that there was no basis to impose a "disclose or abstain" duty upon him. In dissent, Chief Justice Burger adopted what has since come to be known as the "misappropriation theory," arguing that a "disclose or abstain" duty should apply to anyone who "misappropriates" (steals) nonpublic information, regardless of a fiduciary relationship.

■ CASE VOCABULARY

JURY INSTRUCTIONS: The directions given by a trial judge to the jury regarding how they should apply the law to the facts of the case. The jury is required to follow the statement of the law the judge gives to them.

Dirks v. Securities and Exchange Commission

(*Investment Analyst*) v. (*Government Agency*)

463 U.S. 646 (1983)

U.S. SUPREME COURT EXPLAINS TIPPEE LIABILITY UNDER RULE 10b-5

■ **INSTANT FACTS** An investment analyst appealed his administrative censure for allegedly violating SEC Rule 10b-5 by disclosing material nonpublic information about fraudulent activity at an insurance company which he learned from corporate insiders at the insurance company to his investor clients, who sold their stock in the insurance company before the information became public.

■ **BLACK LETTER RULE** A person receiving a stock tip from a corporate insider violates SEC Rule 10b-5 when the corporate insider has breached his fiduciary duty to the corporation's shareholders by tipping information for his own personal benefit and the person receiving the tip knows or should know that the tip was a breach of the corporate insider's fiduciary duty.

■ PROCEDURAL BASIS

Appeal following a grant of certiorari by the U.S. Supreme Court of an appeals court's affirmance of an investment analyst's SEC disciplinary censure for violations of SEC rules.

■ FACTS

Raymond Dirks ("Dirks") (D) was an investment analyst for a brokerage company. He specialized in the analysis of insurance company stocks for institutional investors. Dirks (D) was given information by Ronald Secrist ("Secrist"), a former officer of Equity Funding, an insurance company, that the company had vastly overstated its assets and engaged in fraudulent activities. Secrist urged Dirks (D) to investigate the charges and disclose the fraud. Dirks conducted an investigation, visiting Equity Funding and interviewing several employees who corroborated the fraud charges. While neither Dirks (D) nor his brokerage firm owned or traded any Equity Funding stock, during his investigation, Dirks discussed the information he had obtained with several clients and other investment analysts who subsequently sold all of their Equity Funding stock. Dirks urged the Wall Street Journal to write a story on the alleged fraud, but the newspaper did not believe that such extensive fraud was possible and would not print the story. Over the two-week period of Dirks' investigation, Equity Funding's stock price fell sharply. Eventually, the New York Stock Exchange halted trading of the stock and California authorities impounded Equity Funding's records, uncovering direct evidence of the fraud. The Securities and Exchange Commission ("SEC") (P) then filed a complaint against Equity Funding, which went into receivership. Subsequently, the SEC (P) investigated Dirks' (D) role in the exposure of the fraud. After an administrative disciplinary hearing, the SEC (P) ruled that Dirks (D) had aided and abetted violations of Rule 10b-5 [SEC (P) regulation making it unlawful to defraud or deceive a person in connection with the purchase or sale of securities] by repeating the fraud allegations to his clients and other investors who later sold their Equity Funding stock. The SEC (P) concluded that those who receive a selective disclosure of material inside information that they know is confidential and that they know or should know came from a corporate insider must publicly disclose that information or abstain from trading. Recognizing Dirks' (D) role in bringing the fraud to light, the SEC (P) merely censured him, Dirks (D) appealed that censure to the D.C. Court of Appeals, which affirmed the SEC's (P) ruling. Dirks (D) then appealed to the U.S. Supreme Court, which granted certiorari.

■ ISSUE

Does a person receiving a stock tip from a corporate insider violate SEC Rule 10b-5 only when the corporate insider has breached his fiduciary duty to the corporation's shareholders by tipping information for his own personal benefit and the person receiving the tip knows or should know that the tip was a breach of the corporate insider's fiduciary duty?

■ DECISION AND RATIONALE

(Powell, J.) Yes. The SEC (P) asserts that a tippee inherits a corporate insider's obligation to shareholders whenever he receives inside information from an insider. This position conflicts with the principle set out in *Chiarella v. United States* [holding that a "disclose or abstain" duty requires a fiduciary relationship with the corporation that is the subject of the stock trade] that only some persons, under some circumstances, will be barred from trading while in possession of material nonpublic information. We reaffirm today that a duty to disclose arises from the relationship between parties and not merely from one's ability to get information because of his position in the market. This conclusion does not mean that tippees are always free to trade on the information they have received. The need for a ban on some tippee trading is clear. Insiders are forbidden by their fiduciary relationship from personally using undisclosed corporate information to their advantage and should also be unable to give such information to an outsider for the same improper purpose of exploiting the information for their personal gain. The tippee's "disclose or abstain" duty is derivative from that of the insider. A tippee assumes a fiduciary duty to the corporation's shareholders not to trade on material nonpublic information only when the tipper/insider has breached his fiduciary duty to the shareholders by disclosing the information to the tippee and the tippee knows or should know that there has been a breach, Whether the disclosure by the insider is a breach of his fiduciary duty will depend on the purpose of the disclosure. If the insider will directly or indirectly personally benefit from the disclosure, then there is a breach. Here, we find no violation by Dirks (D). Dirks (D) was a stranger to Equity Funding, with no direct fiduciary duty to shareholders. Unless the insiders breached their fiduciary duty to the shareholders in disclosing the material nonpublic information about the fraud to Dirks (D), he breached no duty by passing the information to investors and the press. Neither Secrist nor the Equity Funding employees who told Dirks (D) of the fraud violated their duty to the shareholders by tipping off Dirks (D). The tippers received no monetary or personal benefit for revealing the secrets and were not trying to make a gift of the information to Dirks (D). The facts show they were simply out to expose the fraud at the company. With no breach of duty by the insiders, Dirks (D) can have committed no derivative breach. Reversed.

■ DISSENT

(Blackmun, J.) In disclosing the fraud information to Dirks (D), Secrist intended that Dirks (D) would disseminate the information to his clients, those clients would unload their Equity Funding stock on the market, the price would fall precipitously, and that this would trigger a reaction from the SEC (P). No one questions that Secrist could not himself have traded on the inside information to the disadvantage of uninformed shareholders and purchasers of Equity Funding stock. Secrist had a fiduciary duty to them. The majority acknowledges that Secrist could not do by proxy what he was prohibited from doing personally. But this is exactly what Secrist did. He used Dirks (D) to disseminate information to Dirks' (D) clients, knowing they would dump their stock, and thus intending to injure the purchasers of Equity Funding stock to whom Secrist had a duty to disclose. The majority says that Dirks (D) is not liable because Secrist had no improper purpose of personal gain. I disagree with this new, subjective limitation on the scope of the duty owed by insiders to shareholders. The fact that the insider himself does not benefit from the breach does not eradicate the shareholder's injury. The insider's duty is addressed not to his own motives, but to the consequences of his actions on the shareholders. Personal gain is not an element of the breach of duty. In my view, Secrist violated his duty to the Equity Funding shareholders by giving material nonpublic information to Dirks (D) with the intent to cause Dirks' (D) clients to trade on that information. Dirks (D) was thus under a duty to disclose the information or refrain from actions he knew would lead to trading at the expense of purchasers of Equity Funding stock. I would find that Dirks (D) violated Rule 10b-5 and affirm the appeals court.

Analysis:

The SEC's (P) approach in going after Dirks (D) was to argue that anyone who obtains information from an insider picks up the insider's duty to disclose the information or refrain from trading. The Supreme Court, however, refused to accept such a blanket prohibition, finding a "disclose or abstain" duty only where the tippee was acting as an after-the-fact participant in the insider's breach of his duty to the shareholders of the corporation. Noting that an insider cannot trade on the basis of material nonpublic corporate information, the Court believed that it should also be illegal for the insider to profit indirectly by passing the information to other persons for their use. Thus, under the rule established in this case, a tippee violates Rule 10b-5 when the tipper/insider breaches his fiduciary duty to the shareholders by tipping information for his own personal benefit and the tippee knows or should know that the tip was a breach of the tipper/insider's fiduciary duty.

■ CASE VOCABULARY

CENSURE: An formal and official reprimand issued against a party by an administrative agency regulating that party. In general, such reprimands are viewed as a very minor form of punishment for wrongful behavior.

INSTITUTIONAL INVESTORS: Organizations such as mutual funds, pension plans, and labor unions that are significant investors of money they are employed to manage and invest in public corporations.

RECEIVERSHIP: When a court has appointed a person to control and preserve the assets of an insolvent corporation in order to preserve those assets for the benefit of the creditors of the corporation.

TIPPER: A person who provides information (a tip) to another person with the expectation that the other person will trade stock on the basis of that information.

TIPPEE: A person who receives information (a tip) from a person who provides the information with the expectation that the tippee will trade stock based on the information provided.

United States v. O'Hagan

(Federal Government) v. *(Attorney)*

521 U.S. 642 (1997)

U.S. SUPREME COURT UPHOLDS A CRIMINAL CONVICTION FOR VIOLATING RULE 10b-5 UNDER A MODIFIED "MISAPPROPRIATION THEORY"

■ **INSTANT FACTS** An attorney who worked for a law firm that represented the potential acquirer in a takeover bid of a target corporation was convicted of criminal charges for violating SEC Rule 10b-5 by trading in the stock of the target corporation on the basis of information he had learned from his firm's representation of the acquirer.

■ **BLACK LETTER RULE** A person can commit fraud in connection with a securities transaction and thereby violate Rule 10b-5, by misappropriating material nonpublic information for trading purposes in breach of a duty owed to the source of that information.

■ PROCEDURAL BASIS

Appeal following a grant of certiorari by the U.S. Supreme Court of a federal appeals court's reversal of a criminal conviction for violations of SEC Rule 10b-5.

■ FACTS

James Herman O'Hagan ("O'Hagan") (D) was a partner in a Minnesota law firm. The firm was hired to represent a British company, Grand Metropolitan PLC ("Grand Met") regarding a potential takeover of Pillsbury Corporation ("Pillsbury"). O'Hagan (D) was not involved in the actual representation of Grand Met. Both Grand Met and O'Hagan's (D) firm took precautions to protect the confidentiality of the takeover plans. O'Hagan (D) learned of the deal and began purchasing call options for Pillsbury stock, which gave him the right to purchase shares of Pillsbury at a set price in the future. Eventually, O'Hagan (D) had purchased more options than any other Pillsbury investor. He also purchased Pillsbury stock at $39 a share. Subsequently, Grand Met announced a tender offer for the stock of Pillsbury. Pillsbury's stock price rose to almost $60 a share. O'Hagan (D) then sold his call options and his stock for a profit of more than $4.3 million. The Securities and Exchange Commission investigated O'Hagan's (D) trading and the U.S. Attorney (P) eventually indicted him for, among other things, criminal violation of SEC Rule 10b-5 [regulation making it unlawful to defraud or deceive a person in connection with the purchase or sale of securities] for defrauding his law firm and its client, Grand Met, by misappropriating nonpublic information about the takeover plan and using that information for his own trading benefit. A jury convicted O'Hagan (D). On appeal, the Eighth Circuit Court of Appeals reversed his conviction, concluding that Rule 10b-5 liability could not be based on the "misappropriation theory" of securities fraud on which the prosecution had relied. The U.S. Attorney (P) then appealed to the U.S. Supreme Court, which granted certiorari.

■ ISSUE

Can a person commit fraud in connection with a securities transaction and thereby violate Rule 10b-5, by misappropriating material nonpublic information for trading purposes in breach of a duty owed to the source of that information?

■ DECISION AND RATIONALE

(Ginsburg, J.) Yes. In *Chiarella v. United States* [holding that a duty to disclose material nonpublic corporate information or abstain from trading in the stock of the corporation which is the subject of that information requires a fiduciary relationship with the corporation that is the subject of the stock trade], we were presented with the question of whether criminal liability for violation of Rule 10b-5 may be based on a misappropriation theory. In that case, the jury had received no misappropriation theory instructions, so we declined to address the question. We now hold that criminal liability under Rule 10b-5 may be based on misappropriation theory. Section 10(b) of the Securities Exchange Act of 1934 [legislation enabling the SEC to regulate the use of manipulative and deceptive devices in connection with purchase or sale of securities] prohibits using any deceptive device in connection with the purchase or sale of stock in violation of the rules of the SEC. The "classical" theory of insider trading liability says that Rule 10b-5 is violated when a corporate insider trades in his company's stock on the basis of material nonpublic information. Trading on the basis of such information is a "deceptive device" under § 10(b) because of the fiduciary relationship between the insider and his company's shareholders. Under the "misappropriation theory," a person commits fraud in connection with a securities transaction and thereby violates Rule 10b-5, when he misappropriates confidential information for trading purposes in breach of a duty owed to the source of that information. The theory is designed to protect the integrity of the securities markets against abuses by corporate "outsiders" who have access to material nonpublic corporate information, but who owe no fiduciary duty or other duty to that corporation's shareholders. In place of premising liability on a fiduciary relationship between a company insider and the purchaser or seller of the company's stock, the misappropriation theory bases liability on a fiduciary/trader's deception of those who have trusted him with access to the confidential information. Here, O'Hagan (D) could not have been prosecuted under the classical theory, because he was not an "insider" of Pillsbury, the corporation in whose stock he traded. O'Hagan (D), however, did breach a duty of trust he owed to his law firm and its client, Grand Met. We agree with the U.S. Attorney (P) that this misappropriation of information in breach of the duty owed to the source of the information satisfies § 10(b)'s requirement that chargeable conduct merely involves a deceptive device used in connection with the purchase or sale of securities. A misappropriation deals in deception. A fiduciary who pretends loyalty to his principal while secretly converting the principal's information for personal gain, defrauds his principal. When the fiduciary, without disclosure to his principal, trades on the basis of the converted information, his deceptive use of that information is used "in connection with the purchase or sale of a security" under § 10(b). This is so even though the person or entity defrauded is not the other party to the trade, but instead, the source of the nonpublic information. Although information disparity is inevitable in the securities market, investors would surely hesitate to risk their capital in a market where trading was based on a use of misappropriated information, unchecked by law. Under such circumstances, the honest investor's information disadvantage cannot be overcome with research or skill. We believe that considering this inhibiting impact on market participation and the congressional purposes underlying § 10(b), it makes little sense to hold a lawyer like O'Hagan (D) a violator if he works for a firm representing the target of a takeover bid, but not if he works for a firm representing the bidder. The text of the statute requires no such result. We find that the Eighth Circuit was wrong to conclude that misappropriation theory could not form the basis for charges of violating Rule 10b-5. Reversed.

■ DISSENT

(Scalia, J.) I disagree with the majority's analysis of O'Hagan's (D) conviction under § 10(b) and Rule 10b-5. The majority's explanation of the scope of those provisions might be reasonable in some other context, but does not seem to accord with the principle of lenity that we apply to criminal statutes. I believe that lenity requires that we construe § 10(b)'s language to require the manipulation or deception of a party to the securities transaction, which did not occur in this case.

Analysis:

In *Chiarella v. United States*, 445 U.S. 222 (1980), the Supreme Court appeared to substantially narrow the scope of Rule 10b-5 from the broad, equal-access-to-the markets approach to a standard based solely on whether the person trading on the basis of the material nonpublic corporate information owed a fiduciary duty to the shareholders of the corporation in whose stock he was trading. In this case, the Court backtracks somewhat from what the SEC and many commentators believed was too narrow a standard. The Court held that O'Hagan (D) violated Rule 10b-5 even though he was not an insider of the corporation in whose stock he traded. Finding that his misappropriation of confidential information in order to trade for his own benefit constituted fraud, the Court read § 10(b) and Rule 10b-5 literally to conclude that this fraud was "in connection with the purchase or sale" of securities. In his dissent in *Chiarella*, Chief Justice Burger had called for a broad application of what came to be known as the "misappropriation theory" under Rule 10b-5. He argued that no breach of fiduciary duty to anyone was necessary in order to violate Rule 10b-5 and that all that should be needed was for a person to trade on the basis of misappropriated information, without disclosure. Here, the Court keeps an element of the fiduciary duty requirement, holding that a person can commit fraud in connection with a securities transaction and thereby violate Rule 10b-5 by misappropriating confidential information for trading purposes in breach of a duty owed to the source of that information.

■ CASE VOCABULARY

LENITY: A rule of statutory construction which provides that where there is ambiguity in the language of a criminal statute about what conduct has been criminalized, the statute should be read in the light most favorable to the defendant.

PRINCIPAL: A person who appoints or directs an agent to act on his behalf and under his control.

Santa Fe Industries, Inc. v. Green

(*Majority Stockholder*) v. (*Minority Stockholder*)

430 U.S. 462 (1977)

U.S. SUPREME COURT REFUSES TO PERMIT A RULE 10b-5 LAWSUIT FOR A MERL BREACH OF A MAJORITY SHAREHOLDER'S FIDUCIARY DUTY TO THE MINORITY SHAREHOLDERS OF A CORPORATION

■ **INSTANT FACTS** The minority shareholders of a corporate subsidiary brought an action in federal court claiming that an alleged breach of fiduciary duty by the majority shareholder of the corporate subsidiary regarding the price paid to cash out the minority shareholders in a short-form merger constituted a violation of SEC Rule 10b-5.

■ **BLACK LETTER RULE** A mere breach of fiduciary duty by a majority stockholder, without any deception, misrepresentation, or nondisclosure, does not violate SEC Rule 10b-5.

■ PROCEDURAL BASIS

Appeal following a grant of certiorari by the U.S. Supreme Court of a federal appeals court's reversal of a district court dismissal of a complaint alleging violations of SEC Rule 10b-5 for failure to state a claim on which relief could be granted.

■ FACTS

Santa Fe Industries, Inc. ("Santa Fe") (D) owned 95 percent of the stock of Kirby Lumber Corp. ("Kirby"), a Delaware corporation. Wishing to acquire the full 100 percent of Kirby's stock, Santa Fe (D) effected a short-form merger under Delaware law. Delaware law permitted a parent corporation owning at least 90 percent of its subsidiary's stock to merge with the subsidiary, requiring only the approval of the parent corporation's board of directors and a cash payment to the minority stockholders of the subsidiary for their shares. A parent did not need to have the consent of the subsidiary's minority stockholders and did not even have to provide advance notice of the merger. Within ten days after the merger, however, notice must be given to all stockholders and any stockholder dissatisfied with the terms of the merger may petition a court for an appraisal of his shares and payment of their appraised value. Santa Fe (D) got an independent appraisal of Kirby's physical assets, which valued the assets at $640 per share. Santa Fe (D) gave the appraisal and other financial information to an investment banking firm, which then valued Kirby's shares at $125 per share. Under the terms of the merger, Santa Fe (D) offered the Kirby minority shareholders $150 per share. On receiving notice of the merger and their right to an appraisal, Green (P) and the other minority shareholders of Kirby objected to the price offered them for their shares, but chose not to seek an appraisal in Delaware state court. Instead, they filed suit against Santa Fe (D) in federal district court, seeking to set aside the merger or recover what they claimed was the fair value of their shares. Green (P) and the other minority shareholders asserted that their Kirby stock was worth substantially more than they were being offered by Santa Fe (D) based solely on the value of the physical assets as determined by the independent appraisal of those assets which Santa Fe (D) had obtained. They alleged that Santa Fe's (D) purpose in effecting the merger was to obtain the difference between the high value of Kirby's physical assets and the much lower amount being offered to the minority shareholders for its own benefit. They argued that this conduct constituted a fraudulent device used in connection with the purchase or sale of stock and was a violation of SEC Rule 10b-5 [regulation making it unlawful to defraud or deceive a person in connection with the purchase or sale of securities]. The trial court dismissed their complaint for failure to state a claim on which relief could be granted. The Second Circuit Court of Appeals reversed that decision, finding that the allegation of a breach of fiduciary duty by the majority stockholder to the minority stockholders did state a viable cause of action under Rule 10b-5. Santa Fe (D) then appealed to the U.S. Supreme Court, which granted certiorari.

■ ISSUE

Can a mere breach of fiduciary duty by a majority stockholder, without any deception, misrepresentation, or nondisclosure, violate SEC Rule 10b-5?

■ DECISION AND RATIONALE

(White, J) No. Section 10(b) of the Securities Exchange Act of 1934 [legislation enabling the SEC to regulate the use of manipulative and deceptive devices in connection with purchase or sale of securities] makes it unlawful to use or employ an "manipulative or deceptive device" in connection with the purchase or sale of stock in violation of the rules of the SEC. Thus, Green's (P) claim of fraud and fiduciary breach states a viable cause of action under § 10(b) and Rule 10b-5 only if the conduct alleged in the complaint can be fairly viewed as "manipulative and deceptive" within the meaning of § 10(b). We find that the short-form merger transaction, if carried out as alleged in the complaint, was neither deceptive nor manipulative and did not violate § 10(b) and Rule 10b-5. The trial court specifically found that there was no omission or misstatement in the notice provided to the minority shareholders by Santa Fe (D). The minority shareholders were specifically told that they could accept the offer price or reject it and seek an appraisal in state court. Their choice was fairly presented and they were given all relevant information on which to make a decision. This Court has repeatedly described the purpose of the Securities Exchange Act of 1934 as implementing a philosophy of full disclosure. Once full and fair disclosure has occurred, the fairness of the terms of the transaction is at most a tangential concern of the statute. We find that a mere breach of fiduciary duty by a majority stockholder, without any deception, misrepresentation, or nondisclosure, does not violate the statute and the rule. The alleged conduct is also not "manipulative" within the meaning of § 10(b). "Manipulation" is a term of art referring to wash sales, matched order, rigged prices, and other practices intended to mislead investors by artificially affecting market activity. We do not think Congress would have chosen this term of art if it had meant to include within the scope of § 10(b) mere claims of unfair treatment by a fiduciary. This area has traditionally been relegated to state law. Absent a clear indication of congressional intent, we are reluctant to federalize the substantial portion of the law of corporations dealing with fiduciary self-dealing, particularly, as here, where established state policies of corporate regulation would be overridden. Reversed.

■ CONCURRENCE

(Stevens, J.) While I agree with the Court's decision, I believe it was unnecessary to discuss the extent to which Rule 10b-5 can intrude on areas of corporate governance traditionally regulated by state law. I also write to emphasize that the controlling stockholder in this instance, Santa Fe (D), did not breach any duty owed to the minority stockholders because there was complete disclosure of the relevant facts and the minority was entitled to receive the fair value of their shares.

■ CONCURRENCE

(Blackmun, J.) I agree with Justice Stevens' concurrence that it was unnecessary in reaching its decision for the Court to address the extent to which Rule 10b-5 can intrude on areas of corporate governance traditionally regulated by state law. I join the rest of the Court's opinion, however.

Analysis:

Perhaps worried about a large influx of federal lawsuits stemming from corporate mismanagement and breach of fiduciary duty cases normally brought in state court under state corporations statutes, the Supreme Court here refused to federalize such claims under Rule 10b-5. The Court concluded that

§ 10(b) and Rule 10b-5 were not violated so long as all of the material facts regarding an alleged breach of fiduciary duty have been disclosed. If the facts have been disclosed, the Court reasoned, there was no deception as required to state a claim under Rule 10b-5. Justice White's opinion suggests that Rule 10b-5 should not reach breaches of fiduciary duty by directors and controlling shareholders if state law provides a remedy for such breaches. Both Justice Stevens and Justice Blackmun wrote separate concurrences, suggesting that this portion of the opinion was dicta. Several lower courts have addressed the issue and have permitted Rule 10b-5 claims for breaches of fiduciary duty where the conduct constituting the alleged breach of duty was never disclosed or was misrepresented to the shareholders.

■ CASE VOCABULARY

SHORT-FORM MERGER: A special type of merger offered under the corporations statutes in many states meant to provide an inexpensive and faster method for a corporate parent owning a large percentage of a subsidiary corporation to acquire all of the stock of the subsidiary than through a regular merger. Often, short-form merger statutes permit a parent to effect the merger by simply passing its own resolution of merger or by filing merger articles with the secretary of state.

WASH SALE: A securities transaction which gives the appearance of being a purchase and sale but which avoids any actual change of beneficial ownership. Such a transaction might be used to attempt to artificially inflate the volume of trading for a stock on a stock exchange and has been outlawed by the Securities and Exchange Commission.

Gratz v. Claughton

(*Corporate Shareholder*) v. (*Corporate Insider*)

187 F.2d 46 (2d Cir.1951)

SECOND CIRCUIT ADOPTS A LOWEST PURCHASE PRICE HIGHEST SALE PRICE METHOD OF COMPUTING SHORT-SWING PROFITS UNDER § 16(b)

■ **INSTANT FACTS** A corporate insider, owning more than ten percent of the stock of a corporation, was sued by a shareholder of the corporation under § 16(b) of the Securities Exchange Act of 1934 to recover on behalf of the corporation alleged short-swing profits made by the insider by trading in the stock of the corporation.

■ **BLACK LETTER RULE** A lowest purchase price, highest sale price method of matching stock sales and purchases is the appropriate way to compute short-swing profits under § 16(b) of the Securities Exchange Act of 1934 when there is more than one purchase and sale transaction within a six-month period.

■ PROCEDURAL BASIS

Appeal of a judgment of a federal district court finding a violation of § 16(b) of the Securities Exchange Act of 1934 and awarding damages based on the findings of a special master.

■ FACTS

Stella Gratz ("Gratz") (P), a shareholder of the Missouri-Kansas-Texas Railroad Company ("MKT"), brought an action on behalf of MKT in federal district court under § 16(b) of the Securities Exchange Act of 1934 [statutory provision making officers, directors, and anyone who is an owner of ten percent or more of certain corporations strictly liable for any profits on the purchase and sale or sale and purchase of stock occurring within six months of each other] against Edward Claughton ("Claughton") (D), another MKT shareholder who owned more than ten percent of the company. Gratz (P) asserted that § 16(b) required Claughton (D) to turn over to MKT certain alleged profits he had made on the purchase and sale of corporate stock over a six month period. The district court referred the case to a special master to compute the amount of any profit made by Claughton (D) in trading the corporation's stock. Claughton (D) had made several purchases and sales of MKT stock during the relevant trading period. Applying a rule which did not match the purchase and subsequent sale of the actual securities traded, but instead sought to maximize the profits made through a lowest purchase price, highest sale price computation method, the special master found that Claughton's (D) trading had resulted in an illegal profit of over $300,000. The district court entered judgment for that amount and Claughton (D) appealed, asserting that the rule adopted by the special master in computing his profits was wrong because, in reality, he had suffered an actual net loss on the company stock during the relevant trading period of $400,000 and had not made a profit on his trading.

■ ISSUE

Is a lowest purchase price, highest sale price method of matching stock sales and purchases an appropriate way to compute short-swing profits under § 16(b) of the Securities Exchange Act of 1934 when there is more than one purchase and sale transaction within a six-month period?

■ DECISION AND RATIONALE

(Hand, C.J.) Yes. Section 16(b) of the Securities Exchange Act of 1934 requires that any profit of a more than ten percent shareholder realized from the purchase and sale or sale and purchase of his corporation's stock within a six month period shall go to the benefit of that corporation. The rule anticipates some method of matching purchases of stock against sales of stock or of sales against purchases, but does not expressly say what method should be used. At first glance, it might seem that § 16(b) limits recovery to profits from transactions in the same shares of stock. In other words, one could compute a trader's profit on the sale of a share of stock merely by subtracting what the trader paid for that share from what the trader got on a sale of that same share. This would allow an easy avoidance of the statute, however, and cannot be the right matching method. Using this method, a corporate insider could speculate freely, something which § 16(b) was meant to discourage, merely by holding a substantial block of stock for more than six months. Thus, if on January 1, the insider had 10,000 shares which he bought before October 1, he could buy 1000 shares on February 1 and sell 1000 shares at a profit on April 1, simply delivering as the sold shares stock from the 10,000 shares which he had purchased before October 1. After the two transactions, his position in the corporation's stock would be exactly what it had been on January 1, except that in two months, he would have made a profitable turnover of 1000 shares, the exact evil against which § 16(b) was directed. In the absence of exact matching, we can find no principle by which to select any two transactions which are to be matched. We have two choices, then. We can either match any given sale against any given purchase in such a way as to reduce profits to their lowest possible amount, or in such a way as to increase profits to their greatest possible amount. The special master chose the second method, matching sales by a lowest in, highest out method of computing profits, which increased profits to their highest possible amount. We think he was right. The statute makes all such dealings unlawful and makes the insider accountable to the corporation. Under the common law, where damages are not ascertainable below an acknowledged upper limit and the uncertainty of damages arises from the defendant's wrong, the upper limit was taken as the proper amount. This situation falls under that doctrine. It is true that this means that no insider may safely buy and sell or sell and buy shares of stock in his corporation except at intervals of six months. Whether that is too drastic a means of combating the evil the statute was meant to avoid, we do not have to decide. We simply can find no other way to administer the statute as enacted by Congress. The crushing liabilities which § 16(b) may impose are clear from this case in which the judgment was for over $300,000. It should certainly serve as a warning and may prove a deterrent. Affirmed.

Analysis:

This case requires a little math to understand the holding of the court. Assume that our insider, Claughton (D), bought 10 shares of his company's stock at $5 a share in January and sold those 10 shares at $3 a share in February. He then bought 10 shares at $2 a share in March and sold those 10 shares at $1 a share in April. A simple accounting would show that he lost a total of $30 over the course of his trading ($20 on the first sale in February and $10 on the second sale in April). The court says that for purposes of § 16(b), however, Claughton (D) would have a profit of $10. He would have to match the March purchase with the February sale ($20 purchase, $30 sale). This "profit" would have to be disgorged to the corporation under § 16(b). While recognizing that Congress had not expressly specified how to compute profits under the statute, the Second Circuit worried that under the method championed by Claughton (D), an insider could freely speculate in his company's stock and easily manipulate his trades to avoid ever having "profits" under § 16(b). The court's example shows clearly that, under Claughton's (D) proposed computation method, an insider would merely have to hold a substantial block of the company's stock for more than six months in order to have free reign to engage in speculative trading. In the court's view, § 16(b) was enacted to prevent such speculative abuses by corporate insiders in their company's stock.

■ CASE VOCABULARY

SHORT-SWING PROFITS: Under § 16(b) of the Securities Exchange Act of 1934, profits made within a six-month period from the purchase and sale or sale and purchase of a corporation's stock by a director, officer, or beneficial owner of more than ten percent of any class of that corporation's stock.

SPECIAL MASTER: A person, often an expert in a particular field, who is appointed by a court to serve as its representative in overseeing a particular transaction or addressing certain factual or legal issues in a case. The special master will generally prepare a report for the court that made the appointment, which can then either be adopted or rejected.

Kern County Land Co. v. Occidental Petroleum Corp.

(*White Knight's Subsidiary*) v. (*Takeover Bidder*)

411 U.S. 582 (1973)

APPLYING "PRAGMATIC" APPROACH, U.S. SUPREME COURT FINDS NO LIABILITY UNDER § 16(b) WHERE THERE IS AN INVOLUNTARY EXCHANGE OF STOCK PURSUANT TO A MERGER AND NO SPECULATIVE ABUSE OF INSIDER INFORMATION

■ **INSTANT FACTS** A corporation that had made an unsuccessful takeover bid for a target corporation was sued by a successor to the target corporation under § 16(b) to recover short-swing profits allegedly made from the exchange of its shares in the target corporation for shares in the corporation which successfully took over the target corporation.

■ **BLACK LETTER RULE** Where there is no reason to believe that there has been a speculative abuse of inside information, there has not been a "sale" within the meaning of § 16(b) of the Securities Exchange Act of 1934 when a statutory insider becomes irrevocably bound to exchange its shares in a corporation for new shares pursuant to a merger agreement over which the insider had no control.

■ PROCEDURAL BASIS

Appeal, following a grant of certiorari, of a federal appeals court decision reversing a grant of summary judgment by a federal district court which found a violation of § 16(b) of the Securities Exchange Act of 1934.

■ FACTS

Occidental Petroleum Corp. ("Occidental") (D) made a tender offer for the stock of Kern County Land Co. ("Old Kern"). By the close of the tender offer, Occidental (D) owned more than ten percent of the stock of Old Kern. Old Kern's management sought to frustrate Occidental's (D) takeover plan by agreeing to a merger proposal with a "white knight," Tenneco, Inc. ("Tenneco"). Under the agreement with Tenneco, all of the Old Kern shareholders (including Occidental (D)) would exchange their Old Kern stock for preferred shares in Tenneco. Fearing that it would be locked into a minority position in Tenneco, Occidental (D) negotiated an agreement with Tenneco under which, in return for $8.8 million, Occidental (D) granted a Tenneco subsidiary an option to purchase at a set price all of the Tenneco preferred shares to which Occidental would be entitled if the Old Kern-Tenneco merger occurred. Once the Old Kern-Tenneco merger went through, Tenneco exercised its option for Occidental's (D) shares. Occidental (D) exchanged its Old Kern stock for Tenneco preferred stock and then endorsed the Tenneco preferred stock over to Tenneco in return for cash, as dictated by the option agreement. Following the Old Kern-Tenneco merger, Old Kern was dissolved and Tenneco transferred its assets to a recently incorporated subsidiary corporation which it named Kern County Land Co. ("New Kern") (P). New Kern (P) then filed suit against Occidental (D) under § 16(b) of the Securities Exchange Act of 1934 [statutory provision making officers, directors, and anyone who is an owner of ten percent or more of certain corporations strictly liable for any profits on the purchase and sale or sale and purchase of stock occurring within six months of each other]. New Kern (P) alleged that the execution of the option agreement and the exchange of Old Kern shares for the preferred stock in Tenneco both constituted "sales" by Occidental (D) under § 16(b) and that since both transactions took place within six months of the date when Occidental (D) became an owner of more than ten percent of the stock of Old Kern, that Occidental (D) was required to surrender its profits in favor of New Kern (P). The trial court granted summary judgment in favor of New Kern (P). On appeal, the Second Circuit Court of Appeals reversed and ordered summary judgment in favor of Occidental (D), concluding that neither the option nor the share exchange were "sales" under § 16(b). New Kern (P) appealed to the U.S. Supreme Court, which granted certiorari.

■ ISSUE

Where there is no reason to believe that there has been a speculative abuse of inside information, has there been a "sale" within the meaning of § 16(b) of the Securities Exchange Act of 1934 when a statutory insider becomes irrevocably bound to exchange its shares in a corporation for new shares pursuant to a merger agreement over which the insider had no control?

■ DECISION AND RATIONALE

(White, J.) No. Section 16(b) of the Securities Exchange Act of 1934 was enacted for the purpose of preventing the unfair use of information which may have been obtained by a corporate insider by reason of his relationship to his company. Although traditional cash-for-stock transactions that result in a purchase and sale or a sale and purchase within the six-month statutory period clearly fall under the coverage of § 16(b), courts have debated whether to include or exclude certain "unorthodox" transactions. In deciding if a "sale" or "purchase" has occurred under the statute in certain borderline transactions, courts have asked if the transaction may serve as a vehicle for the evil Congress was seeking to prevent, speculative abuse through the realization of short-swing profits based on access to inside information. In this case, when the Old Kern-Tenneco merger agreement was signed, Occidental (D) became irrevocably entitled to exchange its Old Kern shares for Tenneco preferred shares. The transaction should be viewed as if Occidental (D) made the exchange on that day. We agree with the court of appeals that this exchange was not a "sale" of the Old Kern shares, however, within the meaning of § 16(b). It is totally unrealistic to believe that Occidental (D) had or was likely to have access to any inside information in this case. It was a business adversary of Old Kern and its "white knight," Tenneco, both of whom vigorously opposed Occidental's (D) efforts at merger. The exchange of shares took place and was required pursuant to the merger between Old Kern and Tenneco which was not engineered by Occidental (D), but was actually an attempt to stop Occidental (D) from gaining control of Old Kern. Once Old Kern and Tenneco came to a merger agreement, the course of subsequent events was totally out of Occidental's (D) hands. Occidental (D) was left with no real choice as to the future of its Old Kern shares. The involuntary nature of Occidental's (D) exchange and the absence of the possibility of speculative abuse of inside information convinces us that § 16(b) should not apply. Additionally, we hold that the option agreement, itself, should not be considered a "sale" under the statute. Occidental (D) wanted to avoid the position of a minority shareholder with a huge investment in a company over which it had no control and in which it had not chosen to invest. Tenneco did not want a possible troublesome minority shareholder, especially one it had just beaten in a takeover fight. Motivations like these do not smack of insider trading. It is simply not clear to us how the negotiation and execution of the option agreement gave Occidental (D) any possible opportunity to trade on inside information it might have gained from its position as a major stockholder of Old Kern. Occidental (D) granted a "call" option, giving Tenneco the right to buy after six months, but not forcing Tenneco to buy. The price was fixed. Occidental (D) could not share in a rising market for Tenneco stock. If the stock fell, the option might not be exercised and Occidental still risked a loss if it had to sell in such a market. Thus, the option does not appear to have been an instrument with potential for speculative abuse, whether or not Occidental (D) did possess inside information about Old Kern. Moreover, the option dealt with Tenneco stock, not Old Kern stock. Clearly, Occidental (D) had no inside information regarding Tenneco. Affirmed.

■ DISSENT

(Douglas, J.) I believe that the court's analysis of this case based on the possibility for the speculative abuse of inside information undermines the congressional purpose for § 16(b). The statute is written broadly and imposes strict liability for its violation. By its own terms the provision covers *all* transactions that are technically purchases and sales and applies regardless of any actual or potential use of inside information to gain a trading advantage. Here, the conclusion seems inescapable that Occidental (D) bought and sold shares of Old Kern within a six month period and that these transactions were covered by the literal terms of § 16(b). The term "sale," as used in the Securities Exchange Act, includes any contract to sell or otherwise dispose of an item. Clearly, Occidental (D) "disposed" of its Old Kern stock through the Old Kern-Tenneco merger. Its Old Kern shareholder status terminated and it became a shareholder of Tenneco. In my view we need look no further. The majority ignores the literal impact of § 16(b) by emphasizing the involuntary nature of Occidental's (D) action and its lack of access to inside information. Congress drafted § 16(b) as an objective rule, designed to have a preventative effect. The draftsmen of the rule recognized that, in some cases, an insider might have to give up profits even though his transactions did not lend themselves to the kinds of abuses that underlay the enactment of § 16(b). They opted for a bright-line rule, specifically acknowledging that in particular transactions such a rule might work a hardship. The majority's "pragmatic" approach to § 16(b) changes the provision from a section that is easy to administer to a section that fosters litigation by holding out the hope to an insider that he may be able to avoid liability. In my view, the majority improperly takes upon itself the task of refashioning the contours of § 16(b) and changes its essential thrust. I would reverse the court of appeals.

Analysis:

This case shows the clear split that has divided the courts regarding the scope of § 16(b). Section 16(b) is a strict liability provision and has been greatly criticized for imposing liability in situations where there has been no real trading on the basis of inside information. In such "unorthodox situations," some courts have taken the so-called "pragmatic" approach that Justice White and the majority take here, reading the provision so as to avoid imposing liability. Other courts have taken the so-called "objective" approach of Justice Douglas and the minority in this case, applying the statute literally, to cover all transactions regardless of whether there is any possibility of speculative abuse involved in the transaction. Since the *Kern* decision, most applications of the "pragmatic" approach have been limited to involuntary transactions involving exchanges of stock pursuant to a merger, where the statutory insider really had no access to any inside information.

■ CASE VOCABULARY

STRICT LIABILITY: Liability imposed under a statute without regard to fault or intent.

Diamond v. Oreamuno

(*Shareholder*) v. (*Inside Trader*)

24 N.Y.2d 494, 301 N.Y.S.2d 78, 248 N.E.2d 910 (1969)

NEW YORK COURT OF APPEALS PERMITS SHAREHOLDER DERIVATIVE ACTION UNDER STATE LAW FOR BREACH OF FIDUCIARY DUTY

■ **INSTANT FACTS** A shareholder of a corporation brought a derivative action on behalf of the corporation under state law against two corporate insiders, alleging that they had breached their fiduciary duty to the corporation by trading in the corporation's stock on the basis of material inside information.

■ **BLACK LETTER RULE** An insider can be liable to his corporation for breach of fiduciary duty as a result of trading corporate stock on the basis of material inside information, even in the absence of actual tangible harm to the corporation.

■ PROCEDURAL BASIS

Appeal of an appellate division decision reversing a dismissal by a trial court of a shareholder's derivative action for breach of fiduciary duty under state corporate law.

■ FACTS

Herman Diamond ("Diamond") (P), a shareholder of Management Assistance, Inc. (MAI), brought a shareholder derviative action under New York law against Walter Oreamuno ("Oreamuno") (D1), the chairman of MAI's board of directors, and Jorge Gonzalez ("Gonzalez") (D2), MAI's president. Diamond (P) asserted that Oreamuno (D1) and Gonzalez (D2) had used inside information about a sudden price increase in a service contract which would reduce MAI's net earnings, acquired through their positions in the company, to reap large profits from the sale of MAI shares before the information about the price increase was made public. Oreamuno (D1) and Gonzalez (D2) sold large blocks of their MAI stock at $28 a share before the information was announced. Once the information was announced, MAI stock fell from $28 a share to $11 a share. Diamond (P) sought to have Oreamuno (D1) and Gonzalez (D2) turn over the difference to MAI. The trial court granted a motion to dismiss the complaint for failure to state a cause of action made by Oreamuno (D1) and Gonzalez (D2). On appeal by Diamond (P), the Appellate Division reinstated the complaint. Oreamuno (D1) and Gonzalez (D2) then appealed to the New York Court of Appeals, the state's highest court.

■ ISSUE

Can an insider be liable to his corporation for breach of fiduciary duty as a result of trading corporate stock on the basis of material inside information in the absence of actual tangible harm to the corporation?

■ DECISION AND RATIONALE

(Fuld, C.J.) Yes. We must decide this case by assuming that the assertions alleged by Diamond (P) in his complaint are true. A person who acquires special information through a confidential or fiduciary relationship with another is not free to exploit that information for his own personal benefit but must account to his principal for any profits derived from the information. Oreamuno (D1) and Gonzalez (D2) assert that, although it is wrong for an officer or director to use his position to obtain trading profits for himself in his own corporation's stock, the actions they are accused of did not damage MAI in any way and thus, MAI should not be permitted to recover the proceeds through a derivative action. It is true that the complaint does not allege damages to the corporation, but this has never been considered essential for a cause of action based on a breach of fiduciary duty. This is because the function of such an action is not merely to compensate the plaintiff for wrongs committed by the defendant, but to *prevent* such wrongs in the first place, by removing from fiduciaries all incentive to attempt to deal for their own benefit in matters to which their fiduciary responsibility relates. The primary concern in such a case is not to determine whether the corporation has been damaged, but to decide, as between the corporation and the defendants, who has a higher claim to the proceeds from the exploitation of the information. In addition, as the Appellate Division recognized, there may be some damage to the corporation from such insider trading activity. When officers and directors abuse their position to gain personal profits, the effect may be to cast a cloud on the corporation's name and undermine public regard for its stock. The concept underlying such a derivative action is hardly new., Under federal law, for example, § 16(b) of the Securities Exchange Act of 1934 [statutory provision making officers, directors, and anyone who is an owner of ten percent or more of certain corporations strictly liable for any profits on the purchase and sale or sale and purchase of stock occurring within six months of each other] permits precisely the same remedy sought in this case. While here, Oreamuno (D1) and Gonzalez (D2) may be able to avoid liability under § 16(b) since they held the MAI shares for more than six months prior to the sales, as a court of equity, we should not hesitate to permit a state action to prevent unjust enrichment from the abuse of a fiduciary relationship. Affirmed.

Analysis:

In this case, the New York Court of Appeals holds that since insider trading constitutes a breach of fiduciary duty to the corporation, the corporation can recover the profits made from such trading through the device of a shareholder derivative action. Applying equitable principles, the court reasons that, given a choice between the corporation and the wrongdoer/insider, the corporation is entitled to the profits so that the insider is not unjustly enriched. Some commentators have criticized the holding of the case, arguing like Oreamuno (D1) and Gonzales (D2) that there is no tangible proof of actual harm to the corporation. The case was decided before an implied right to a shareholder action under Rule 10b-5 was commonplace in the federal courts, and the court may have stretched its reasoning in the interests of justice. With the advent of direct shareholder actions under federal law, there have been few cases pursued under the *Diamond* rationale and other jurisdictions have been reluctant to follow its reasoning.

■ CASE VOCABULARY

COURT OF EQUITY: A court sitting as a court of equity applies rules of fairness in an attempt to render the administration of justice more complete by providing a remedy in situations where a court of law could not. Equity courts arose in England as a method of dealing with what were perceived to be the harsh rules of common law. In most states today, a civil court can apply both sets of rules in a case.

DERIVATIVE ACTION: A lawsuit filed by a shareholder of a corporation on behalf of a corporation in order to assert the rights of the corporation.

Malone v. Brincat

(*Shareholder*) v. (*Director*)

722 A.2d 5 (Del.1998)

DELAWARE SUPREME COURT FINDS A BREACH OF FIDUCIARY DUTY RESULTING FROM DIRECTOR MISSTATEMENTS

■ **INSTANT FACTS** Several shareholders of a corporation brought a state law claim of breach of fiduciary duty against the corporation's board of directors, asserting that the directors had breached their fiduciary duties by overstating the corporation's earnings in their periodic reports to the shareholders.

■ **BLACK LETTER RULE** A director who knowingly disseminates false information that results in corporate injury or damage to an individual stockholder violates his fiduciary duty to the corporation or shareholder and may be held accountable under state law.

■ PROCEDURAL BASIS

Appeal of a dismissal with prejudice by the Delaware Court of Chancery of an action for breach of fiduciary duty under state corporate law.

■ FACTS

Doran Malone ("Malone") (P) and other shareholders of Mercury Finance Company ("Mercury") filed a suit against John Brincat ("Brincat") (D) and the other directors of Mercury alleging that Brincat (D) and the directors breached their fiduciary duty of disclosure by intentionally overstating Mercury's earnings on repeated occasions over a four-year period in documents issued to the company's shareholders. Malone (P) and the shareholders sought certification as a class action on behalf of themselves and all persons who owned Mercury stock over that four-year period. Malone (P) and the shareholders alleged simply that as a direct result of the false disclosures, Mercury had lost all or virtually all of its $2 billion value. The Delaware Court of Chancery dismissed the complaint with prejudice for failure to state a claim on which relief could be granted, accepting the directors' argument that directors have no fiduciary duty of disclosure under Delaware law in the absence of a request for shareholder action. The Chancery Court held that the only remedy a shareholder could pursue under such circumstances was a federal remedy. The shareholders appealed to the Delaware Supreme Court.

■ ISSUE

Has a director, who knowingly disseminates false information that results in corporate injury or damage to an individual stockholder, violated his state law fiduciary duty to the corporation or shareholder?

■ DECISION AND RATIONALE

(Holland, J.) Yes. This court has previously held that a board of directors is under a fiduciary duty to disclose material information when seeking shareholder action. This case requires us to decide if there may be a cause of action for disclosure violations only where directors seek shareholder action. We hold that directors who knowingly disseminate false information that results in corporate injury or damage to an individual stockholder violate their fiduciary duty and may be held accountable. Equitable principles act to protect beneficiaries who are not in a position to protect themselves. Fiduciary duties are imposed on the directors of Delaware corporations to regulate their conduct when they manage the business of a corporation for the benefit of its shareholders. Directors stand in a fiduciary relationship to both the stockholders and the corporation on whose board they serve. Shareholders are entitled to rely on their elected directors to discharge their fiduciary duties at all times. Whenever directors communicate publicly or directly with shareholders about the corporation's affairs, with or without a request for shareholder action, directors have a fiduciary duty to shareholders to exercise due case, good faith, and loyalty. Dissemination of false information could violate one of those duties. Directors must be honest with their shareholders. When directors are not seeking shareholder action, but are deliberately misinforming shareholders about the business of the corporation, there is a violation of fiduciary duty which may result in a derivative claim on behalf of the corporation or a cause of action for damages. Here, the complaint alleges an egregious violation of fiduciary duty by the directors in knowingly putting out materially false information about earnings. Then it alleges that the corporation lost about $2 billion dollars as a result. This allegation that the corporation lost all of its value, seems to be some kind of claim of injury to the corporation, but Malone (P) and the shareholders never expressly assert a derivative claim on behalf of the corporation in their complaint. If they assert such a derivative claim, they should be permitted to replead their complaint to assert such a claim on behalf of the corporation or replead to assert any individual cause of action that may be appropriate on behalf of the named plaintiffs or a properly recognizable class. Without well-pleaded allegations stating a derivative, class, or individual cause of action and a properly assertable remedy, the Chancery Court was right to dismiss the claim. Nevertheless, we disagree with the Chancery Court that such a claim cannot be articulated on these facts. Malone (P) and the plaintiffs should have been permitted to amend their complaint, if possible, to state a cognizable cause of action. Thus, the Chancery Court should have dismissed the complaint *without* prejudice. Affirmed as to dismissal. Reversed as to dismissal with prejudice.

Analysis:

In holding that directors may violate their fiduciary duties by materially misstating the corporation's financial condition even though the corporation does not engage in any specific transactions with shareholders or investors, the Delaware Supreme Court here finds a fiduciary duty of disclosure that some commentators have suggested parallels federal duties under Rule 10b-5. In previous cases, the court had held that there was a fiduciary duty of disclosure when the corporation was seeking shareholder action or approval. Here, the court clarified that the obligation of honesty exists whenever the corporation communicates with its shareholders. Given the large number of public corporations incorporated in Delaware, the fiduciary duty of disclosure found by the court could potentially become a competitor to Rule 10b-5 as a method of attacking director fraud.

■ CASE VOCABULARY

DISMISSAL WITH PREJUDICE: A court order disposing of a case and barring any future right to bring a suit on the same claim or cause of action.

DISMISSAL WITHOUT PREJUDICE: A court order that removes a case from proceeding further, but permits a new suit to be filed for the same cause of action, usually on the basis of amended pleadings.

CHAPTER ELEVEN

Shareholder Suits

Tooley v. Donaldson, Lufkin & Jenrette, Inc.

Instant Facts: Tooley (P) and other minority shareholders sued Donaldson, Lufkin & Jenrette, Inc. (D) for damages relating to a delay in paying out on a tender offer.

Black Letter Rule: Standing to assert a direct action depends on whether the individual, as opposed to the corporation, suffered the harm and would benefit from the recovery or remedy ordered.

Barth v. Barth

Instant Facts: A minority shareholder in a closely held corporation sued the majority shareholder in a direct action, accusing him of behavior that reduced the value of the corporate stock.

Black Letter Rule: Shareholders in a closely held corporation may be able to sue in a direct action (rather than being required to maintain a derivative action) for damage to the corporation.

Glenn v. Hoteltron Systems, Inc.

Instant Facts: Shareholder who brought derivative suit asked for individual recovery of misappropriated corporate assets.

Black Letter Rule: Recovery in derivative suits should go to the corporation, not to individual shareholders.

Bangor Punta Operations, Inc. v. Bangor & Aroostook R.R.

Instant Facts: A corporation brought an action against its former owner for mismanaging the corporation draining corporate assets when it controlled the corporation.

Black Letter Rule: Shareholders may not sue for harms to the corporation that happened prior to their ownership of the shares, and may not cause the corporation to sue its former owners in order to get around the contemporaneous-ownership requirement.

Rifkin v. Steele Platt

Instant Facts: New owners of a corporation caused it to bring suit against a former officer and director for damages caused by his breach of fiduciary duty.

Black Letter Rule: A newly acquired corporation may sue a former officer and director for damage to the corporation done before the acquisition—unless the purchase price reflected the damage.

Marx v. Akers

Instant Facts: Without first making a demand on the directors to initiate suit, a shareholder brought a derivative action against the board of directors for overcompensating the corporation's executives and outside directors.

Black Letter Rule: Since directors are self interested in their own compensation, any demand on the board to initiate a suit for overcompensation of the directors would be futile.

Auerbach v. Bennett

Instant Facts: A shareholder sued corporate directors for misappropriation of corporate funds, and a special litigation committee appointed by the board decided that the corporation should terminate the shareholder's action.

Black Letter Rule: The business judgment of the corporate directors will not be scrutinized by the court so long as the directors were disinterested and the investigation leading to the business decision was not a sham.

Zapata Corp. v. Maldonado

Instant Facts: Corporate directors took steps that enriched themselves but caused unnecessary expense to the corporation and then appointed an independent committee of directors, which determined that this action for breach of fiduciary duty should be dismissed.

Black Letter Rule: Where demand is excused because of director interest and the corporation moves to dismiss a shareholder's derivative action, the court should determine, applying its own independent business judgment, whether the motion should be granted.

Sugarland Industries v. Thomas

Instant Facts: The court ordered the corporation to pay $3.5 million to the shareholders' attorneys as attorneys' fees, $3 million of which represented a percentage of the benefit that the litigation had to the corporation.

Black Letter Rule: If attorneys' fees are based on a percentage of the benefit achieved, the percentage awarded should bear some relation to the influence that the attorneys had in procuring the benefit.

Alcott v. M.E.V. Corp.

Instant Facts: Defendants prevailed in a derivative action brought by corporate shareholders and were awarded their attorneys' fees, even thought the shareholders had not posted any security to cover the expenses of litigation.

Black Letter Rule: Attorneys' fees cannot be awarded to the defendants in a derivative action except out of the security for expenses.

Waltuch v. Conticommodity Services, Inc.

Instant Facts: A commodities trader who was sued for actions taken on behalf of his firm sued the firm for indemnification of the legal fees that were incurred in his defense.

Black Letter Rule: Before a corporation may indemnify an employee for legal expenses, he must have either been successful in defending against the suit or have taken in good faith the actions that gave rise to the suit.

Clarke v. Greenberg

Instant Facts: A shareholder who settled a derivative suit against corporate directors did not give to the corporation the money realized in the settlement.

Black Letter Rule: In a derivative suit, recovery belongs to the corporation regardless of the manner or method used in making the recovery.

Tooley v. Donaldson, Lufkin & Jenrette, Inc.

(*Shareholder*) v. (*Corporation*)
845 A.2d 1031 (Del.2004)

THE "SPECIAL INJURY" TEST IS DISAPPROVED FOR DETERMINING WHETHER A DIRECT ACTION EXISTS

■ **INSTANT FACTS** Tooley (P) and other minority shareholders sued Donaldson, Lufkin & Jenrette, Inc. (D) for damages relating to a delay in paying out on a tender offer.

■ **BLACK LETTER RULE** Standing to assert a direct action depends on whether the individual, as opposed to the corporation, suffered the harm and would benefit from the recovery or remedy ordered.

■ PROCEDURAL BASIS

On appeal to review a decision of the chancery court dismissing the plaintiffs' complaint for lack of standing.

■ FACTS

Tooley (P) was a minority shareholder in Donaldson, Lufkin & Jeanrette, Inc. (DLJ) (D). DLJ (D) was controlled by AXA Financial, Inc. (AXA), which owned seventy-one percent of DLJ (D) stock. When Credit Suisse Group acquired DLJ (D), AXA entered into a stockholder agreement whereby AXA agreed to exchange its DLJ stock for a mix of stock and cash. Credit Suisse then intended to acquire the minority interests through a cash tender offer, followed by a merger of DLJ (D) with one of its wholly owned subsidiaries. Credit Suisse set a tender offer price at ninety dollars per share, set to expire twenty days after it commenced. The merger agreement, however, allowed for an extension of that deadline under certain circumstances or by agreement with DLJ (D). After Credit Suisse unilaterally postponed the expiration of the offer as allowed under the agreement, DLJ (D) consented to a further extension. Tooley (P) and others filed suit challenging the second extension, which created a twenty-two-day delay, as improperly authorized and depriving the minority shareholders of the value of their money for AXA's benefit. The chancery court dismissed the complaint for lack of standing, reasoning that once the plaintiffs tendered their shares, they lost standing to bring a direct cause of action. At that point, any damages were not a "special injury" and thus only derivative claims existed.

■ ISSUE

Must a shareholder assert a special injury distinct from that suffered by other shareholders to maintain a direct action against the corporation?

■ DECISION AND RATIONALE

(Veasey, C.J.) No. Unlike a direct action, a derivative suit enables a shareholder to assert a claim for harm suffered by the corporation. It is brought on behalf of the corporation and any recovery is paid to the corporation. With a direct action, however, the shareholder himself is harmed and may sue in his individual capacity to recover for his losses. Under Delaware law, in order to bring a direct action, a plaintiff must experience a "special injury" that is "separate and distinct from that suffered by other shareholders, . . . or a wrong involving a contractual right of a shareholder, such as the right to vote, or to assert majority control, which exists independently of any right of the corporation." Using this test, the chancery court determined that the plaintiffs failed to establish standing after their shares had been tendered. The "special injury" concept, however, is unhelpful to the determination of a direct action and is disapproved. Instead, standing to assert a direct action depends on whether the individual, as opposed to the corporation, suffered the harm and would benefit from the recovery or remedy ordered. The shareholder need not establish an injury separate and distinct from that suffered by all other shareholders, such as a diminution of stock value, but rather need only show an injury separate from that suffered by the corporation for which he may individually recover.

Here, the complaint alleges no injury to the corporation, and therefore does not properly allege a derivative claim. But that alone does not properly allege a direct claim. The complaint purports to assert a direct claim, but in fact does not include any individual rights that have been infringed. The plaintiffs' contract claims, while individual and direct, are dependent upon the execution of the merger agreement, which has not yet occurred. Accordingly, the plaintiffs' complaint must be dismissed, but on different grounds. Reversed and remanded to correct the order of dismissal.

Analysis:

The distinction between a derivative action and a direct action has important implications for a corporation. Because individual shareholders may have similar causes of action against a corporation, such as a breach of fiduciary duty, the derivative action serves as a shareholder class action suit to consolidate all similar claims into one action, saving the corporation from duplicative lawsuits. When the action is direct and unique to a small number of shareholders, such duplication is not a concern.

■ CASE VOCABULARY

DERIVATIVE ACTION: A suit by a beneficiary of a fiduciary to enforce a right belonging to the fiduciary; especially, a suit asserted by a shareholder on the corporation's behalf against a third party (usually a corporate officer) because of the corporation's failure to take some action against the third party.

DIRECT ACTION: A lawsuit to enforce a shareholder's rights against a corporation.

Barth v. Barth

(*Minority Shareholder*) v. (*Majority Shareholder*)
659 N.E.2d 559 (Ind.1995)

POLICY CONCERNS DRIVE THE DISTINCTION BETWEEN DERIVATIVE AND DIRECT ACTIONS

■ **INSTANT FACTS** A minority shareholder in a closely held corporation sued the majority shareholder in a direct action, accusing him of behavior that reduced the value of the corporate stock.

■ **BLACK LETTER RULE** Shareholders in a closely held corporation may be able to sue in a direct action (rather than being required to maintain a derivative action) for damage to the corporation.

■ PROCEDURAL BASIS

Appeal from dismissal of a minority shareholder's direct action.

■ FACTS

Minority shareholder Robert Barth (P), who held 29.8% of the shares in a corporation, brought this direct action against the corporation, Barth Electric Co. (a closely held corporation), and its majority shareholder Michael Barth (D), who held 51% of the shares. The minority shareholder (P) alleged that the majority shareholder (D) took actions when managing the corporation that substantially reduced the value of the minority shareholder's (P) stock. The majority shareholder (D) moved to dismiss the action on the ground that the minority shareholder (P) should have brought a derivative action, rather than a direct action. The trial court granted the majority shareholder's (D) motion to dismiss. The court of appeals reversed, reasoning that the minority shareholder (P) could have satisfied the requirements for bringing a derivative action and that in this case, none of the policy reasons underlying the requirement for a derivative action were present.

■ ISSUE

May a minority shareholder in a closely held corporation bring a direct action where the same complaint against a publicly held corporation would require a derivative action?

■ DECISION AND RATIONALE

(Sullivan) Yes. At the discretion of the trial court, the shareholders in a closely held corporation may have a direct action. The well-established general rule is that shareholders in a corporation may not maintain actions in their own names to redress an injury to the corporation even if the value of their stock is impaired as a result of the injury. There are several reasons for the rule requiring a single derivative action to be brought rather than allowing for several individual actions: the rule conserves judicial resources by forbidding multiple litigation of the same issues; it ensures that parties give due regard to the corporate entity; it protects corporate creditors by putting any recovery back into the corporate treasury; it protects the interests of all of the shareholders, rather than just the one that filed suit; and it adequately compensates the suing shareholder by increasing the value of his shares in accord with the amount of recovery that is returned to the corporation. However, though we respect the general rule requiring derivative actions, there are two reasons why the general rule might not always apply to closely held corporations. First, shareholders in a closely held corporation stand in a fiduciary relationship to each other, and thus have direct personal obligations to the other shareholders. Second, shareholder litigation in the closely held corporation does not always implicate the same policy concerns that mandate derivative litigation in other contexts. For example, where there are only two or three shareholders, direct corporate recovery is not necessary to protect absent shareholders. However, other policies, such as protection of corporate creditors, are implicated even in closely held corporations. We believe that the trial court should have discretion in deciding whether to allow a shareholder of a closely held corporation to proceed in either derivative or direct action to remedy damage to the corporation. In doing so, we note that allowing a plaintiff to proceed by direct action will exempt him from the procedural requirements of maintaining a derivative action. Proceeding by direct action will also allow a defendant to make a counterclaim, which is generally prohibited in derivative actions. Finally, each side in a direct action will normally be responsible for its own legal fees, whereas in a derivative action a successful plaintiff can look to the corporation for attorney's fees. We vacate the opinion of the court of appeals. The judgment of the judgment of the trial court dismissing this action is reversed.

Analysis:

A derivative action is one to protect some right of the corporation, not the individual owners of the corporation. The court claims judicial economy as one of its purposes. Another policy of the derivative action is to protect all shareholders equally. Since the corporation recovers any benefit of a derivative action, one shareholder will not be able to benefit at the expense of all others. Not all jurisdictions have resolved the matter as this case did. Some jurisdictions have found that even in closely held corporations, a shareholder must bring a derivative action to remedy injury to the corporation. It is also worth noting that the American Law Institute's Principles of Corporate Governance (similar to a Restatement of the law of corporations) have adopted the position that shareholders may recover in a direct action for some harms done to the corporation, if the result would be fair to the corporation, its creditors, and the other shareholders.

■ CASE VOCABULARY

CLOSELY HELD CORPORATION: A corporation that has only a few shareholders whose shares are not traded on an open market.

CORPORATE CREDITORS: Include those who hold bonds issued by the corporation, as well as banks and credit card companies who loan money to the corporation.

FIDUCIARY: A duty to act in the best interests and for the benefit of another person and subordinate your interests to that of the other person - not just deal with them at arms length; fiduciary duties include fairness, honesty and candor.

Glenn v. Hoteltron Systems, Inc.

(*Shareholder*) v. (*Shareholder*)

74 N.Y.2d 386, 547 N.Y.S.2d 816, 547 N.E.2d 71 (1989)

DAMAGES AWARDED IN DERIVATIVE SUITS GO TO THE CORPORATION

■ **INSTANT FACTS** Shareholder who brought derivative suit asked for individual recovery of misappropriated corporate assets.

■ **BLACK LETTER RULE** Recovery in derivative suits should go to the corporation, not to individual shareholders.

■ PROCEDURAL BASIS

Appeal from a judgment in favor of the plaintiff.

■ FACTS

This is a dispute between Jacob Schachter (D) and Herbert Kulik (P), who founded Ketek Electric Corporation ("KEC"). Schachter (D) and Kulik (P) each own 50% of KEC's stock, and they serve as KEC's only corporate officers. The courts below found that Schachter (D) had diverted KEC assets and opportunities to Hoteltron Systems, Inc. ("Hoteltron") (D), which is wholly owned by Schachter (D). The trial court found that Hoteltron (D) had reaped profits of $362,242.84 from Schachter's (D) diversion of KEC assets and opportunities. The Appellate division concluded that these profits should be returned to KEC as the injured corporation, rather than to the innocent shareholder Kulik (P).

■ ISSUE

May an innocent shareholder get individual recovery in a derivative action?

■ DECISION AND RATIONALE

(Wachtler) No. The general rule is that, because a shareholder's derivative suit seeks to vindicate a wrong done to the corporation through enforcement of a corporate cause of action, any recovery obtained is for the benefit of the injured corporation. Kulik (P) argues that in this case there should be an exception to the rule because Schachter (D), who is the wrongdoer, will benefit from a return of the recovery to the corporation. However, this is true in any successful derivative action. An exception based on this ground alone would swallow the rule. In addition, the exception would not adequately protect corporate creditors, whose position would be compromised if misappropriated corporate assets were awarded to one shareholder. The fruits of a diverted corporate opportunity are properly a corporate asset. There is no need to invoke an exception to the general rule in this case. Affirmed.

Analysis:

The right to recover in a derivative suit belongs to the corporation and not the individual shareholders that brought suit. This makes sense in light of the corporation's status as an entity separate and distinct from its owners and the rule that a derivative cause of action belongs to the corporation. However, there are some situations where it would be most equitable to order recovery by individual shareholders. In those cases, the court has discretion to order recovery pro rata (in proportion to the number of shares that each holds). One example is where a great majority of the shareholders participated or acquiesced in the wrongdoing. Rather than order the wrongdoers to put the money back into the corporate treasury (where the wrongdoers would all benefit to an extent far greater than the minority shareholders), the court can order the recovery distributed pro rata to the injured shareholders. Another situation is where the wronged corporation was merged into another corporation. If the wronged shareholders are no longer shareholders of the new corporation, they were probably denied a fair price for their shares in the merger. Thus, they should be able to recover pro rata to the extent that they were injured.

■ CASE VOCABULARY

DIVERTED CORPORATE OPPORTUNITY: A business opportunity that should have gone to the corporation but was "stolen" by someone (often a director or officer) thereby denying the corporation the chance to benefit from the opportunity.

Bangor Punta Operations, Inc. v. Bangor & Aroostook R.R.

(Former Owner) v. *(Acquired Corporation)*

417 U.S. 703, 94 S.Ct. 2578, 41 L.Ed.2d 418 (1974)

SHAREHOLDERS CANNOT BRING A DERIVATIVE ACTION UNLESS THEY OWNED THE STOCK AT THE TIME OF THE INJURY

■ **INSTANT FACTS** A corporation brought an action against its former owner for mismanaging the corporation draining corporate assets when it controlled the corporation.

■ **BLACK LETTER RULE** Shareholders may not sue for harms to the corporation that happened prior to their ownership of the shares, and may not cause the corporation to sue its former owners in order to get around the contemporaneous-ownership requirement.

■ PROCEDURAL BASIS

Appeal from appellate decision to allow a derivative action to go forward.

■ FACTS

Prior to October 1964, Bangor & Aroostook Corporation ("B&A") owned 98.3% of the stock of the Bangor & Aroostook Railroad Company ("BAR") (P). In October 1964, B&A sold all of its stock in BAR (P) to Bangor Punta Operations, Inc. ("Bangor Punta") (D). Bangor Punta (D) at that time also agreed to assume all liabilities of B&A arising from the ownership and control of BAR (P). In October 1969, Bangor Punta (D) sold the stock to Amoskeag Co. ("Amoskeag"), which later bought additional stock and held over 99% of the stock in BAR (P) at the time this suit was filed. (The remaining stock was held by over 20 minority shareholders who together owned less than 1% of BAR (P).) In 1971, BAR (P) filed suit against Bangor Punta (D), alleging that Bangor Punta (D) was responsible for mismanagement, misappropriation and waste of BAR's (P) corporate assets between 1960 and 1967. The district court granted summary judgment to Bangor Punta (D), reasoning that the real plaintiff was Amoskeag, not BAR (P), because Amoskeag owned over 99% of BAR (P). Amoskeag, however, did not have contemporaneous ownership of the stock at the time that the alleged damage was done to BAR (P). Thus, Amoskeag would have been barred by both federal and state law from bringing a shareholder's derivative suit for damage to BAR (P). The district court found that equity prevented Amoskeag from using the corporate fiction to evade the contemporaneous ownership requirement. The First Circuit Court of Appeals reversed.

■ ISSUE

May the Court pierce the corporate veil to deny recovery to a corporation where its present shareholders would not be able to recover in a derivative action?

■ DECISION AND RATIONALE

(Powell) Yes. It is a well-settled principle of equity that a shareholder may not complain of acts of corporate mismanagement if he acquired his shares from those who participated or acquiesced in the mismanagement. This is especially true where the shareholder purchased all of its shares for a fair price, but then seeks to have the corporation recover against the seller for prior mismanagement. Dean Roscoe Pound, in *Home Fire Insurance Co.*, addressed exactly that situation. He reasoned that the new owner of the corporation should not be able to recover because it did not become a shareholder until after the damage had occurred, and thus sustained no injury. Therefore, any recovery by the new shareholders would constitute a windfall. They would be able to recover a large part of the purchase price even though they had gotten all that they bargained for. It would permit the new shareholders to reap profits from wrongs done to others. Dean Pound stated that it would be highly inequitable to allow any such recovery. The reasoning in *Home Fire* is especially pertinent in this case. Amoskeag, owner of over 99% of BAR's (P) stock, would be the principle beneficiary of any recovery by BAR (P), even though Amoskeag did not hold any stock in BAR (P) until two years after the alleged wrongs had occurred. In essence, Amoskeag is attempting to claim damages that it alleges BAR's (P) former owners did to themselves prior to Amoskeag's ownership of BAR (P). Amoskeag does not allege that it has been injured by the prior mismanagement, or that the prior mismanagement has caused any continuing harm. Yet if BAR (P) is successful, Amoskeag stands indirectly to recover the full $5,000,000 that it paid for BAR (P) plus an additional $2,000,000. Under the principles of *Home Fire Insurance Co.*, Amoskeag has no standing in equity to maintain the present action. Nor can Amoskeag hide behind the corporate fiction by bringing this action in the name of BAR (P) when Amoskeag itself would be barred from bringing the action. Although a corporation and its shareholders are deemed separate entities for most purposes, the corporate form may be disregarded in the interests of justice where it is used to defeat an overriding public policy. Where equity would preclude the shareholders from maintaining an action in their own right, the corporation would also be precluded. Finally, we reject the reasoning of the Court of Appeals that Amoskeag would not be the sole beneficiary of any recovery by BAR (P). First, the court noted that BAR (P) is a quasi-public entity because it is a railroad. Therefore, any recovery by BAR (P) would benefit the public through the improvement of BAR's (P) economic position and the quality of its services. However, that argument is flawed because there is no guarantee that the recovery to BAR (P) will be re-invested in the railroad. Second, the Court of Appeals overlooks the fact that Amoskeag will be unjustly enriched because it has sustained no injury. Finally, the Court of Appeals cited deterrence as a goal—to insure that Bangor Punta (D) would not be immune from liability for its wrongful conduct. However, deterrence cannot be the only goal. If it could, anybody could file the complaint and accept recovery from Bangor Punta (D). We decline to vary from the traditional rule that a plaintiff must have sustained an injury because of the defendant or the defendant must have violated a duty to the plaintiff before the plaintiff can bring suit. The Court of Appeals is Reversed.

■ DISSENT

(Marshall) Under *Home Fire Insurance Co.*, the case upon which the majority primarily relies, this case should be allowed to go forward. It is significant that in *Home Fire*, all of the shares of the plaintiff corporation had been acquired from the alleged wrongdoers after the transactions giving rise to the causes of action stated in the complaint. Since none of the corporation's shareholders held stock at the time of the alleged wrongdoing, equity barred a claim by the corporation where *none* of the shareholders could claim to have been injured. However, *Home Fire* went on to state that the corporation could maintain an action if any of the shareholders at the time of the action had also been shareholders at the time of the wrongdoing. The rationale for this distinction is simple. The sole shareholder who defrauds or mismanages his own corporation hurts only himself. However, where there are minority shareholders, the majority shareholder will harm them by misappropriating corporate assets. The directors of a corporation owe a fiduciary duty to all shareholders and are obliged to seek redress where a majority shareholder has drained the corporation's resources for his own benefit and to the detriment of the minority shareholders.

Analysis:

In order to have standing to bring a derivative action, a shareholder must have owned stock at the time of the wrong. The rationale for this requirement is that the purchase price of the corporation's shares after the wrongdoing ought to be lower because of the wrongdoing. Therefore, only contemporaneous owners are harmed by the lower value of their shares, whereas subsequent shareholders were not harmed because they purchased their shares at the lower price. In other words, the market should correct for the effects of any wrongdoing. Consider whether this makes much sense in situations where the wrongdoing does not come to light until much later or where the wrongdoing actually strengthens the corporation temporarily. In those cases, it seems entirely possible for later shareholders' stock to be affected every bit as much as that of contemporaneous shareholders' stock.

■ CASE VOCABULARY

CORPORATE FICTION: Phrase used when the court wants to exercise its equitable powers and ignore the separate legal existence of a corporation to get at the shareholders individually.

Rifkin v. Steele Platt

(*Corporation*) v. (*Officer*)
824 P.2d 32 (Colo.App.1991)

DAMAGE TO THE VALUE OF A BUYER'S STOCK THAT IS NOT REFLECTED IN THE PURCHASE PRICE MAY CREATE AN EXCEPTION TO THE CONTEMPORANEOUS OWNERSHIP REQUIREMENT FOR DERIVATIVE ACTIONS

■ **INSTANT FACTS** New owners of a corporation caused it to bring suit against a former officer and director for damages caused by his breach of fiduciary duty.

■ **Black Letter Rule** A newly acquired corporation may sue a former officer and director for damage to the corporation done before the acquisition - unless the purchase price reflected the damage.

■ PROCEDURAL BASIS

Appeal from judgment in favor of corporation on a breach of fiduciary duty claim.

■ FACTS

Steele Platt (D) and Fas-Wok, Inc. (D) ("the Sellers") sold their controlling shares of The Boiler Room, Inc. ("the corporation") (P) to the Buyers (P). All parties executed a Stock Purchase Agreement ("the Agreement"). After the closing, the Buyers (P) discovered inaccuracies in the financial representations made in the Agreement. The Buyers (P) caused the corporation (P) to file suit, alleging that Platt (D), who was an officer and director of the corporation (P), had breached his fiduciary duty to the corporation because he misappropriated corporate funds. After a trial to the court, judgment was entered in favor of the corporation (P). The Sellers (D) appealed, claiming that the corporation cannot be awarded damages for a breach of fiduciary duty for conduct that occurred prior to the Buyers' (P) acquisition of stock.

■ ISSUE

May a corporation recover for wrongs done to it by a prior owner?

■ DECISION AND RATIONALE

(Plank) Yes. The corporation (P) may recover if the purchase price does not reflect the prior wrongdoing. The *Bangor Punta* case raises issues that must be resolved here. In that case, the Supreme Court held that a corporation could not maintain an action for wrongs that occurred before the new shareholders' acquisition of the corporation. The Court reasoned that the real parties that would gain from a successful lawsuit were the new shareholders. It presumed that the purchase price that the new shareholders had paid reflected the prior wrongdoing. Thus, the shareholders would improperly receive a windfall if the corporation were allowed to recover damages. Here, the same reasoning should apply. The acts that support the corporation's (P) breach of fiduciary duty claim occurred prior to the Buyers' (P) acquisition of stock. However, in this case the parties dispute whether the purchase price reflected the prior wrongdoing of Platt (D). Therefore, the trial court must decide this issue. If the purchase price was lower because of the wrongdoing, then it must dismiss the breach of fiduciary duty claim. Otherwise, then trial court's damage award may stand. Reversed and Remanded.

Analysis:

In this case, the court focused on the effect that mismanagement had on the corporation's purchase price. The court does not simply presume that the market would automatically reflect the correct purchase price. Rather, the court holds that this is a fact question to be decided by the trial court. The court here seems to recognize that one exception to the contemporaneous ownership rule is where the corporation is sold and the prior mismanagement was not reflected in the purchase price. There are other exceptions to the contemporaneous-ownership requirement. If the shareholder got the shares "by operation of law" (e.g., he inherited them), then the shareholder may still have standing to maintain a derivative action by stepping into the dead person's shoes—the shareholder can bring the action if the dead person would have been able to bring it. There is also the continuing-wrong theory, where a shareholder may have standing to sue if he received the stock after a wrongful course of conduct has begun but before it has been completed.

Marx v. Akers

(*Shareholder*) v. (*Board of Directors*)

88 N.Y.2d 189, 644 N.Y.S.2d 121, 666 N.E.2d 1034 (1996)

IN A SHAREHOLDER'S DERIVATIVE SUIT, IF IT WOULD BE FUTILE TO MAKE A DEMAND ON THE BOARD TO TAKE ACTION, DEMAND IS EXCUSED

■ **INSTANT FACTS** Without first making a demand on the directors to initiate suit, a shareholder brought a derivative action against the board of directors for overcompensating the corporation's executives and outside directors.

■ **BLACK LETTER RULE** Since directors are self interested in their own compensation, any demand on the board to initiate a suit for overcompensation of the directors would be futile.

■ PROCEDURAL BASIS

Appeal from dismissal of a shareholder's derivative action.

■ FACTS

A shareholder (P) brought suit against IBM (D) and its board of directors ("the Board") (D), alleging that the Board (D) wasted corporate assets by granting excessive compensation to IBM's (D) executives and outside directors. The shareholder (P) did not first make a demand on the board to initiate a suit in the corporation's name. The Board (D) moved to dismiss the complaint because the shareholder (P) did not serve a demand on the Board (D) to initiate suit. The Board (D) also moved to dismiss for failure to state a cause of action. The trial court dismissed the action, finding that the shareholder (P) had failed to establish that a demand would have been futile and should therefore be excused. The Appellate Division affirmed the dismissal, concluding that the complaint did not contain any details from which the futility of demand could be inferred.

■ ISSUE

Does the doctrine of futility excuse a shareholder (P) from demanding that the board initiate suit?

■ DECISION AND RATIONALE

(Smith) Yes. A shareholder's derivative claims against corporate directors are claims that belong to the corporation. The New York statute codifies the common law rule requiring shareholders to first demand that the corporation initiate an action, unless such a demand would be futile, before the shareholder could bring a derivative action on the corporation's behalf. The statute requires that the shareholder's derivative complaint "set forth with particularity the efforts of the plaintiff to secure the initiation of such action by the board or the reasons for not making such effort." *Business Corporation Law § 626(c).* The purposes of the demand requirement are to allow directors the opportunity to address and correct alleged abuses; to protect directors from litigation of matters that are within their discretion; and to discourage "strike suits." In permitting a futility exception, the object is for the court to chart the course for the corporation that the directors should have selected and which it is presumed that they would have chosen if they had not been actuated by fraud or bad faith. There is a tension between preserving the rightful discretion of the directors to make business decisions about the corporation (reflected in the demand requirement) and permitting shareholders to bring derivative claims when it is obvious that directors will wrongfully refuse to act in the corporation's best interests (reflected in the futility exception). There are different approaches to demand futility. For example, one widely cited approach, developed by the Delaware courts, uses a two-pronged test to determine futility. Under that test, demand will be excused for futility only if the complaint alleges particularized facts that create a reasonable doubt that 1) the directors were disinterested and independent; and 2) that the challenged transaction was otherwise the product of a valid business judgment. Another approach, which has been adopted by statute in at least 11 states, is the universal demand approach. This approach generally requires shareholders to, in every case, make a demand on the board and then wait to file a derivative suit until either the demand is rejected or a specified time (usually 90 days) has passed without action by the board. We find both the Delaware approach and the Universal Demand approach to be instructive. However we cannot follow either approach. Under New York law, a demand is futile if a complaint alleges with particularity facts sufficient to establish any of the following: 1) that a majority of the directors are interested in the transaction; or 2) the directors failed to inform themselves to a degree reasonably necessary about the transaction; or 3) the directors failed to exercise their business judgment in approving the transaction. We emphasize that mere conclusory allegations will not be enough—facts that excuse a demand must be alleged with particularity. In the present case, the shareholder (P) has made two allegations that relate to futility of making a demand on the board: the Board (D) voted for excessive compensation of corporate executives and the Board (D) voted for excessive compensation of outside directors. First, regarding the compensation of the corporate executives, the shareholder (P) has failed to allege facts that would establish the futility of a demand. Only 3 of the Board's (D) 18 directors were executives who would benefit from the executive compensation (the other 15 were outside directors). Thus, the shareholder (P) has not alleged that a majority of directors was interested in the transaction. Furthermore, the shareholder (P) has failed to allege particular facts that would establish that members of the Board (D) did not deliberate or exercise their business judgment in setting executive compensation. The second set of allegations, however, fares differently. Regarding the allegations of excessive compensation to outside directors, we find that demand is excused because of director self-interest. Directors are self interested in a challenged transaction where they will receive a direct financial benefit from the transaction that is different from the benefit to shareholders generally. A director who votes him or herself a raise in directors' compensation is always interested because that person will receive a personal financial benefit from the transaction not shared in by stockholders. Since the outside directors make up a majority of the Board (D), a demand was excused because of director self-interest. However, the shareholder's (P) complaint will still be dismissed for failure to state a cause of action. By statute, the Board (D) is allowed to set the compensation levels of directors. To survive a motion to dismiss, a complaint that alleges excessive director compensation must allege some fact to establish one of the following: that the compensation rates were excessive on their face, that the compensation was unfair when approved, that the directors did not act in good faith in setting the compensation, or that the compensation that was set could not have been the product of a valid business decision. Here, the shareholder's (P) bare allegation that the compensation lacked a relationship to duties performed or the cost of living is insufficient to state a cause of action. The complaint was properly dismissed. Affirmed.

Analysis:

Due to the potential for abuse, Rule 23.1 imposes a number of procedural hurdles to bringing a derivative action. One of these hurdles is the requirement that a shareholder make a demand on the board of directors to remedy some wrong done to the corporation before the shareholder can bring a derivative action. In addition, since the derivative action belongs to the corporation and the board of directors is in charge of running the corporation, it is really the board's job to decide whether or not to pursue the claim. Thus, it is only logical that a shareholder should be required to bring a problem to the attention of the board. However, when the directors themselves have benefitted at the expense of the corporation, it is unlikely that they will take action to their own personal detriment and pursue a lawsuit against themselves. In such a situation, a demand would be a waste of time and it is sensible to excuse demand. This opinion explores the contours of the futility exception to the demand requirement. It sets out three different tests, which illustrate different methods of determining when it would be futile to make a demand on the board. First consider the N.Y. approach, which has three elements: (1) a majority of the directors are interested in the transaction, or (2) the directors failed to inform themselves to a degree reasonably necessary about the transaction, or (3) the directors failed to exercise their business judgment in approving the transaction. The third requirement is arguably broader than the second. However, one might argue that requirement 2 is really just a subset of requirement 3—that if a director acts as a rubber stamp (does not reasonably inform himself about the transaction), then he is not really exercising his business judgment in approving the transaction. If requirements 2 and 3 were merged, then it seems that the N.Y. approach is essentially the same as the Delaware approach, which will find futility where (1) the directors were disinterested and independent and (2) the challenged transaction was otherwise the product of a valid business judgment. Consider also the advantages of Universal Demand (always requiring demand, even if it would be futile). It seems that this requirement would benefit the plaintiff shareholders in that they would not file lawsuits without first making a demand, and thus would not have to guess whether the court would find demand to have been futile, thereby risking the court throwing out their case.

■ CASE VOCABULARY

INTERESTED DIRECTOR: If a director has some personal financial stake in a transaction, then he is interested in it; it will be difficult for him to decide objectively what the best interest of the corporation is with regard to that transaction, especially if the corporation's interest conflicts with the director's personal interest.

STRIKE SUIT: A derivative action of questionable merits that is brought primarily for its settlement value.

Auerbach v. Bennett

(*Shareholder*) v. (*Corporate Directors*)
47 N.Y.2d 619, 419 N.Y.S.2d 920, 393 N.E.2d 994 (1979)

A COURT SHOULD DEFER TO THE GOOD-FAITH BUSINESS JUDGMENT OF DISINTERESTED DIRECTORS

■ **INSTANT FACTS** A shareholder sued corporate directors for mis-appropriation of corporate funds, and a special litigation committee appointed by the board decided that the corporation should terminate the shareholder's action.

■ **BLACK LETTER RULE** The business judgment of the corporate directors will not be scrutinized by the court so long as the directors were disinterested and the investigation leading to the business decision was not a sham.

■ PROCEDURAL BASIS

Appeal from trial court's dismissal of a derivative action.

■ FACTS

In April 1976, General Telephone & Electronics Corporation ("GTE") (D) disclosed to shareholders that between 1971 and 1975 the corporation had paid bribes and kickbacks to government officials and political parties (both in the United States and abroad) in an amount totaling over $11 million. Shareholders also learned that a minority of GTE's directors (D) had been personally involved in some of the transactions. A shareholder (P) immediately instituted the present derivative action against GTE (D), Arthur Andersen & Co. ("Arthur Andersen") (the corporation's outside auditors) (D), and the four directors who were involved (D). The complaint alleged that the directors (D) and Arthur Anderson (D) breached their fiduciary duties to the corporation and should be made to account for the brides and kickbacks. On April 12, 1976, the full board of directors appointed a special litigation committee ("the committee") for the purpose of dealing with the shareholder litigation. The committee was comprised of three directors who were disinterested and had joined the board after the bribes and kickbacks had been given. The committee was vested with the power to determine what action the corporation should take with respect to the lawsuit. On November 22, 1976, after an investigation into the matter, the committee determined that Arthur Andersen (D) and the directors (D) had not acted improperly and had not breached any duty owed to the corporation. The committee also determined that the shareholder's (P) lawsuit had little chance of success, that the publicity of a continued lawsuit would damage the corporation's business, that the proceedings would waste the time and talent of senior management, and that the litigation would be inordinately expensive given the low probability of success. The committee decided that the corporation should terminate the prosecution of the present action. In December 1976 and January 1977, GTE (D), Arthur Andersen (D) and the individual directors (D) moved to dismiss the complaint or, in the alternative, for summary judgment. The trial court granted the motion to dismiss on the ground that the business judgment doctrine prevents the court from second-guessing the decision of the committee.

■ ISSUE

When a demand for legal action is made on a corporation, may the board appoint a committee of uninterested directors to determine if the corporation should take action?

■ DECISION AND RATIONALE

(Jones) Yes. The disposition of this case turns on the proper application of the business judgment doctrine, which bars judicial inquiry into actions of corporate directors taken in good faith and in the exercise of honest judgment in the lawful and legitimate furtherance of corporate purposes. The business judgment doctrine is grounded in the recognition that courts are ill equipped to evaluate the business judgments of corporate directors. The responsibility for business judgments must rest with the corporate directors, who are uniquely qualified to make such judgments by virtue of their individual capabilities and experience. Therefore, absent evidence or bad faith or fraud, the court must respect the decisions of the corporate directors. Derivative claims against the corporate directors belong to the corporation, and the decision to pursue such claims is within the judgment and control of the corporation's board of directors. In order to decide whether the corporation is best served by pursuing such an action, the directors must necessarily balance and weigh a variety of disparate considerations. This is the essence of a business judgment, into which a court should not intrude or interfere. Here the question is whether the business judgment rule applies to shield the committee, composed of three disinterested directors, in its determination not to prosecute the present action. The business judgment rule will not shield the committee if its members were not truly disinterested and independent. However, the record here contains nothing to cast doubt on the independence and disinterestedness of the committee members. The shareholder (P) contends that any committee will necessarily be legally infirm merely because some members of the board were interested in the challenged transactions. We must reject this contention. If such a principle were adhered to, the corporation would be powerless to make any decision, which would also adversely affect the corporation. The board in this instance prudently excluded the interested directors (who comprised 4 of the board's total 15 directors) while allowing the remaining members of the board to make decisions for the corporation. Courts have consistently held that the business judgment rule applies where some directors are charged with wrongdoing, so long as the remaining directors making the decision are disinterested and independent. Since we have determined that the special committee was independent and disinterested, we next turn to their action in deciding to terminate the litigation. There are two aspects to the decision, a substantive aspect and a procedural aspect. The substantive aspect involved the weighing and balancing of legal, ethical, commercial, promotional, public relations, fiscal and other factors familiar to the resolution of most corporate problems. As such, the substantive aspect of the decision to terminate the derivative suit was quintessential business judgment and should be shielded from judicial inquiry. The procedural component of the decision, however, is different. The procedural question is how to set about to gather the appropriate data to be used in making the substantive judgment. As to the methodologies and procedures best suited to investigate facts and determine legal liability, courts are well equipped by long and continuing experience and practice to review such determinations. However we will not overturn the committee's procedures unless there is proof that the investigation was so restricted in scope, so shallow in execution, or otherwise so pro forma or halfhearted as to constitute a pretext or a sham. We find nothing in the record that requires a trial of any material issue of fact concerning the sufficiency or appropriateness of the procedures chosen by the committee, nor is there anything in the record to raise a question of the committee's good faith. The order of the trial court dismissing the complaint is Affirmed.

Analysis:

This case is based on the principle that since the corporation owns the right to the derivative claims, the corporation has the right to decide whether to pursue those claims. The court here followed the general rule by allowing the disinterested directors to make the decision to terminate prosecution of a derivative action as inimical to the interests of the corporation. This result was acceptable because a minority of the directors on the board were interested in the action. When this happens, the directors will still be able to kill the action as long as a majority of the directors in good faith exercise their business judgment to find that the action is not in the best interests of the corporations. Here, the board gave its power to determine whether to pursue the lawsuit to a committee of disinterested directors. In effect, the committee was acting in place of the board. The court here is of the view that it can only look to see if the committee that was appointed by the directors was truly disinterested and whether its investigation was procedurally sufficient (its investigations were not a sham). The court refused to touch the substantive decision of the committee because that would interfere with the business judgment of the directors on the committee.

■ CASE VOCABULARY

BUSINESS JUDGMENT: It is the directors job to make decisions on behalf of the corporation, and they should consider all aspects of a situation (e.g., legal, ethical, commercial, promotional, public relations, fiscal) to determine what action is in the corporation's best interest.

EXECUTIVE COMMITTEE: The board of directors may chose two or more directors to serve on a committee that will act for a particular purpose and delegate its decision-making authority to the committee.

Zapata Corp. v. Maldonado

(*Corporation*) v. (*Shareholder*)

430 A.2d 779 (Del.1981)

COURTS MAY SOMETIMES SUBSTITUTE THEIR BUSINESS JUDGMENT FOR THAT OF THE BOARD OF DIRECTORS

■ **INSTANT FACTS** Corporate directors took steps that enriched themselves but caused unnecessary expense to the corporation and then appointed an independent committee of directors, which determined that this action for breach of fiduciary duty should be dismissed.

■ **Black Letter Rule** Where demand is excused because of director interest and the corporation moves to dismiss a shareholder's derivative action, the court should determine, applying its own independent business judgment, whether the motion should be granted.

■ PROCEDURAL BASIS

Interlocutory appeal from trial court's order denying motion to dismiss and motion for summary judgment.

■ FACTS

Pursuant to a 1970 stock option plan ("the plan"), certain senior officers (D) of Zapata (D) were granted the option to purchase Zapata (D) stock at $12.15 per share at specified times. The board was given the power to amend the plan freely. The final date that the option could be exercised was July 14, 1974. In 1974, when the stock was trading at $19 per share, the board voted to cause Zapata (D) to make a cash tender offer for its own stock at $25–30 per share. The tender offer would be publicly announced on July 2, 1974, after which it was anticipated that Zapata (D) stock would rise sharply. The board modified the stock option plan by accelerating the final stock option purchase date to July 2, 1974 (from July 14th). The accelerated purchase date saved the officers and directors (D) a good deal of personal tax liability while at the same time denying Zapata (D) a substantial tax write-off. The modification also authorized Zapata (D) to make interest-free loans to the senior officers (D) to cover the purchase price of the options and the tax liability they would incur by exercising the options. These interest-free loans benefitted the officers and directors (D) at the expense of the corporation. Based on these actions, Maldonado, a shareholder (P), sued Zapata (D) and ten officers and directors (D), alleging breaches of fiduciary duty. The shareholder (P) did not first demand that the board bring an action in the name of the corporation; instead, the shareholder (P) alleged that the demand would be futile because all of Zapata's directors (D) had been named as defendants and had participated in the alleged wrongdoing. Four years after this suit was initiated, four of the directors (D) had quit the board. The remaining directors (D) appointed two new outside directors and formed an "independent investigation committee" ("the committee"), comprised solely of the new directors. The committee's function was to investigate the lawsuits and determine whether Zapata (D) should continue to prosecute the derivative action. After investigation, the committee decided it would be in Zapata's (D) best interest to terminate the action. Zapata (D) then moved to dismiss or for summary judgment. The Court of Chancery denied the motions.

■ ISSUE

Does a committee, at its sole discretion in exercise of its business judgment, have the power to terminate a derivative action brought by a shareholder?

■ DECISION AND RATIONALE

(Quillen) No. A board has the power to choose not to pursue litigation when demand is made upon it, so long as the decision is not wrongful. Even when demand is excusable, the continuation of a shareholder's litigation may not necessarily be in the corporation's best interest. Thus, it may sometimes be desirable for the corporation to end such litigation. As in this case, the question becomes how best to do this while still safeguarding the corporation from abuse by the board. In the present case, we are faced with the question of whether the board (D), tainted by the self-interest of a majority of its members, can legally delegate its authority to a committee of two disinterested directors. We note that under our statutes, a board may delegate to a committee of disinterested directors the power to make decisions that will bind the corporation. We do not think that the interest taint of the board majority is per se a legal bar to the delegation of the board's power to an independent committee composed of interested board members. The committee can properly act for the corporation to move to dismiss derivative litigation that is believed to be detrimental to the corporation. We now turn our attention to the situation before us—where we have a shareholder (P) asserting that a derivative action should be allowed to continue for the benefit of the corporation, and the corporation (D), through the committee, asserting that it would best be served by dismissing the suit. It appears desirable to us to find a balancing point where bona fide stockholder power to bring corporate causes of action cannot be unfairly trampled on by the board of directors, but the corporation can still rid itself of detrimental litigation. Some courts have made the balance turn on the "business judgment" of the board committee. According to those courts, if a committee, composed of independent and disinterested directors, conducted a proper review of the matters before it, considered a variety of factors and reached, in good faith, a business judgment that the action was not in the best interest of the corporation, then the action must be dismissed. We refuse to apply the business judgment rule here; we believe that in this context, where the demand against the directors (D) was excused, some tribute must be paid to the fact that the lawsuit was properly initiated. We are also mindful that the committee, composed of directors, may be unduly sympathetic when passing judgment on other directors in the same corporation. We also question whether the inquiry into the independence, good faith, and reasonable investigation of the committee is sufficient safeguard against abuse. We believe that the Court of Chancery should have the discretion to determine whether the committee properly exercised its power in seeking dismissal of this suit. We recognize that the decision of a corporation to terminate a derivative action requires a balance of many factors—ethical, commercial, promotional, public relations, employee relations, fiscal and legal. However, we believe that the Court of Chancery, which deals regularly with such questions, is capable of reaching the proper conclusion. Therefore, after a thorough and objective investigation of a derivative suit, if an independent committee decides that it is in the best interest of the corporation to dismiss the suit, the court shall treat such motion as one for summary judgment. The court shall examine all evidence and apply the following two-part test. First, the corporation has the burden of proving the independent committee's independence, good faith, and reasonable investigation. Only if the corporation has established this, may the court move on to the next step. Second, the court should determine, applying its own independent business judgment, whether the motion should be granted. This second step is intended to thwart instances where corporate actions meet the criteria of step one, but the result does not appear to satisfy its spirit, or where corporate actions would simply prematurely terminate a stockholder grievance deserving of further consideration in the corporation's interest. The order of the Court of Chancery is Reversed, and this action is Remanded for further proceedings consistent with this opinion.

Analysis:

When all directors are named as defendants in the derivative suit, they are all interested in the outcome of the litigation and will not be allowed to end it. However, when only a minority of the directors is interested in the suit, the board as a whole could decide to end the litigation. The statutes controlling such a situation vary among jurisdictions. Some jurisdictions allow the entire board (including the interested directors) to vote on whether to kill the derivative action, while others allow only the disinterested directors to vote. Note that the court here applies a different rule regarding the business judgment of the board. The Delaware court finds that the Court of Chancery may substitute its own business judgment to determine if the committee reasonably decided that termination of the derivative suit was in the best interests of the corporation. Since a great many corporations are incorporated in Delaware, the Court of Chancery has an expertise in business and corporate decision-making that other courts are probably lacking.

■ CASE VOCABULARY

INTERLOCUTORY APPEAL: An appeal of a lower court's decision that usually could not be appealed because it is not final, but an appellate determination in this instance is necessary in order to conduct a proper adjudication on the merits.

Sugarland Industries v. Thomas

(*Corporation*) v. (*Shareholders*)

420 A.2d 142 (Del.1980)

THE COURT HAS DISCRETION TO AWARD REASONABLE ATTORNEYS' FEES IN A DERIVATIVE ACTION

■ **INSTANT FACTS** The court ordered the corporation to pay $3.5 million to the shareholders' attorneys as attorneys' fees, $3 million of which represented a percentage of the benefit that the litigation had to the corporation.

■ **BLACK LETTER RULE** If attorneys' fees are based on a percentage of the benefit achieved, the percentage awarded should bear some relation to the influence that the attorneys had in procuring the benefit.

■ PROCEDURAL BASIS

Appeal from Court of Chancery's award of attorneys' fees to shareholders' attorney in derivative litigation.

■ FACTS

Sugarland Industries ("Sugarland") (D) is a Delaware corporation that is controlled by members of the Kempner family. Lyda and J. Redmond Thomas ("the Thomases") (P) are members of the Kempner family and shareholders in Sugarland (D). This dispute revolves around the sale of some land south of Houston, Texas that Sugarland (D) owned. Sugarland (D) was going to sell land (known as the South Tract) to the partnership White and Hill for a price of $23.8 million. The Thomases (P) objected to the sale because they thought the price was too low. They hired the Prappas firm, which organized a syndicate, R-S-C, to compete with White and Hill. R-S-C offered $27 million for the South Tract. When it became clear that Sugarland (D) intended to sell the South Tract to White and Hill despite the higher offer, the Thomases (P) filed this derivative action to enjoin the sale. Thus began Phase I of this litigation—the injunctive phase. The Court of Chancery enjoined the sale to White and Hill and ordered competitive bidding for the property. The highest bidder was Gerald D. Hines Interests ("Hines") at $37.2 million. In a subsequent negotiation, Hines also agreed to buy Sugarland (D) property known as the North Tract for $6.8 million, which was $1.2 million more than the second highest bidder. While Phase I was still pending, the Thomases (P) and the Prappas firm began Phase II of the litigation by filing a supplemental complaint for damages against the Sugarland directors (D). Phase II took three years and 13,000 hours of the Prappas firm's time. Phase II resulted in a settlement, whereby the management of various other business entities owned by the Kempner family was reorganized. The court approved the settlement. The Prappas firm then petitioned the court to have Sugarland (D) pay $6 million in attorneys' fees for its work on behalf of the Thomases (P) during both phases of the litigation. At this point the Bank of Galveston, which owns 23% of Sugarland's (D) stock, intervened and objected to the attorneys' fees. The court awarded the Prappas firm $3.5 million in attorneys' fees. For Phase I of the litigation, the Prappas firm was awarded 20% of the benefit created by the firm's efforts to get a better price for the land, with a cap of $3 million. For Phase II, the court approved $500,000 for time expended on the settlement. Sugarland (D) and the Bank appealed that award.

■ ISSUE

Did the Court of Chancery correctly determine the amount of attorneys' fees?

■ DECISION AND RATIONALE

(Duffy) No. We first address the Bank of Galveston's argument that Sugarland (D) did not benefit from Phase II of the litigation, and therefore the corporation should not have to pay the Prappas firm (which represented the Thomases (P)) for any work that it did in Phase II. It is true that Phase II produced no fund or tangible benefit for Sugarland (D). The reorganization from the settlement of Phase II created harmony in the Kempner family, which, at best, was an indirect benefit to Sugarland (D). However, the settlement also benefitted the corporation directly in that it put an end to the litigation and settled all claims against Sugarland (D). We also accord some weight to the settlement stipulation, in which Sugarland (D) represented to the court that "Sugarland (D) has determined that this settlement is beneficial to it and in the best interests of Sugarland (D) and its stockholders." We are satisfied that the Chancellor properly ordered Sugarland (D) to pay the Prappas firms' attorneys' fees in Phase II of the litigation. Next, Sugarland (D) claims that $3 million in attorneys' fees for Phase I is grossly excessive and that the percentage-of-the-benefit approach adopted by the Chancellor was arbitrary. In determining attorneys' fees (to be paid by the corporation to the shareholder's attorney who prosecuted a derivative action for the benefit of the corporation), the relevant factors to consider are: the results achieved, the time and effort expended, the complexity of the litigation, the contingency factor, and the [community] standing and ability of counsel. Sugarland (D) contends that the Chancellor should have placed more emphasis on the time that the attorneys spent on the case, rather than results achieved, because the Prappas firm's entire fee was not at risk. We believe that time should not necessarily be the principal factor in determining attorneys' fees. We agree with the Chancellor that the Prappas firm is entitled to a percentage of the benefit that it created. However, we disagree as to how that benefit should be measured and compensated. The South Tract was originally going to be sold to White and Hill for $23.8 million. But, due to the Prappas firm's involvement, R-S-C offered $27 million for the same land. This increase in the amount offered was undoubtedly due to the active efforts of the Prappas firm. Therefore, we find that the 20% of the benefit figure is reasonable as applied to the $3.2 million difference between the White and Hill offer and the R-S-C offer. However, any amount above $27 million is not so clearly the responsibility of the Prappas firm. The Prappas firm sought the best price attainable for the land, recognized the low price, and took initiative at the injunctive stage. Thus, there is some cause and effect between its efforts and the ultimate price received. However, the Prappas firm is not a real estate agency. The price that Hines ultimately paid for both the South and North Tracts was neither caused nor influenced by the Prappas firm. Therefore, the Prappas firm cannot get full credit for that price. The Prappas firm should be compensated at 5% (rather than 20%) of the $10.2 million in excess of R-S-C's offer that Hines bid for the South Tract. The Prappas firm should also get 5% of the $1.2 million that Hines paid for the North Tract that was above the offer of the next highest bidder. Finally, as to the adequacy of the $500,000 award of attorneys' fees for Phase II of the litigation, we find that the award is modest when considering the time expended, the difficulty of the litigation, and the purposes achieved by the settlement. This award stands. Reversed in part and Remanded.

Analysis:

In a derivative action, the corporation is responsible for paying the attorneys' fees of a successful shareholder. The "private attorney general" theory encourages the initiation of private litigation to promote important legal policies. Without an award of attorneys' fees, however, it would hardly pay for most shareholders to bring a derivative suit. Attorneys' fees can easily reach into the millions of dollars in a derivative action. Since the recovery in a derivative action goes to the corporation (not the shareholder), and since it is really the corporation that owns the derivative action, it is only fair that the corporation be the one to foot the bill. After all, the increase in share value from the action in and of itself would hardly justify the expense to an individual shareholder, who may be one of thousands of shareholders. There is also a free-rider problem, it is unfair for the other shareholders to benefit at the expense of the one shareholder who brought action. In order to allow shareholders to bring derivative actions, then, the plaintiff-shareholder's attorneys' fees are paid by the corporation. There are safeguards to insure that shareholders don't bring suits with very little chance of success. One safeguard is that the court must approve all settlement agreements. Another is that attorneys' fees will only be awarded if the plaintiff-shareholder was successful. In measuring success and determining the amount of attorneys' fees to be paid, it is easiest if the resolution resulted in the payment of money. Payment of money both guarantees that there was success and makes it easier for the court to decide that the action was worth something to the corporation. However, even if no money was recovered, attorneys' fees may still have to be paid if the corporation incurred some nonmonetary benefit. This ties in to another theory for recovery of attorneys' fees—the "common fund" theory. Since the derivative action was maintained for the benefit of all the shareholders and creditors of the corporation, everyone should have to share in the expense of bringing the successful suit.

■ CASE VOCABULARY

ATTORNEYS' FEES: At the discretion of the court, the corporation may have to pay the fee of the plaintiffs' (shareholders') attorneys if they successfully prosecute a derivative action and obtain some benefit for the corporation.

CONTINGENCY FACTOR: Whether counsel is getting a fixed fee from the plaintiff (shareholder), or whether the fee is contingent upon the outcome of the case—i.e. how much personal risk did the counsel take on in taking this case?

Alcott v. M.E.V. Corp.

(*Shareholder*) v. (*Corporation*)
193 Cal.App.3d 797, 238 Cal.Rptr. 520 (1987)

IF SECURITY FOR EXPENSES IS POSTED, IT COVERS ATTORNEYS' FEES OF PREVAILING DEFENDANTS

■ **INSTANT FACTS** Defendants prevailed in a derivative action brought by corporate shareholders and were awarded their attorneys' fees, even thought the shareholders had not posted any security to cover the expenses of litigation.

■ **BLACK LETTER RULE** Attorneys' fees cannot be awarded to the defendants in a derivative action except out of the security for expenses.

■ PROCEDURAL BASIS

Appeal from award of attorneys' fees to defendants in a shareholders' derivative action.

■ FACTS

Shareholders (P) filed a derivative action against M.E.V. Corp. (D) and others (D). The shareholders (P) did not post any security during the suit, nor was any sought. The action collapsed at the pretrial stage when each defendant was either dismissed or granted summary judgment. The defendants then made requests for attorneys' fees from the shareholders (P), which the court granted. The shareholders (P) appealed the award of attorneys' fees.

■ ISSUE

Can successful defendants in a derivative action collect attorneys' fees if the shareholder-plaintiffs did not post security?

■ DECISION AND RATIONALE

(Brauer) No. The statutory basis for the award of attorneys' fees to the prevailing defendants is Section 800 of the Corporations code. Section 800 is susceptible of two constructions: (1) Attorneys' fees are recoverable only out of the security, if posted; or (2) Prevailing defendants are entitled to their attorneys' fees. The California Supreme Court, in interpreting the predecessor to Section 800, held that the prevailing defendants could not get attorneys' fees where security was not furnished. Section 800 is identical to its predecessor in all respects. The attorneys' fees were improperly awarded. Reversed.

Analysis:

The "American Rule" is that each side to a lawsuit is expected to bear its own legal expenses. The rationale for the rule is that requiring the loser to pay the winner's expenses would deter people from bringing even meritorious cases, thereby effectively closing the courthouse door to all but the richest of people. However, legislatures have enacted many statutes that include "fee shifting." In this case, the fee shifting took the form of a security-for-expenses provision. The plaintiff is required to post a bond when he files the suit, and the corporation's liability is limited to the amount of the bond. Sometimes the plaintiff will only have to post security for expenses if he owns less than a certain percent of the total stock (e.g., less than 5%)—this is an effort to discourage strike suits. Sometimes the shareholder does not have to post security unless the corporation asks the court to order it. A corporation may be hesitant to do this, as it triggers the shareholder's right to a list of other shareholders in the corporation, who could then be notified about the pending lawsuit, which could be damaging to the corporation's image and stock value. In addition, there is also the fear that a motion to post security will cause the shareholders to dismiss the suit and file it in a friendlier jurisdiction that does not have a security-for-expenses statute.

■ CASE VOCABULARY

SECURITY-FOR-EXPENSES: Statutes may require shareholders who begin a derivative action to post a bond with the court, so that the corporation can recover some of the money expended in defending against the suit if the suit is ultimately found to be without merit.

Waltuch v. Conticommodity Services, Inc.

(*Trader*) v. (*Firm*)

88 F.3d 87 (2d Cir.1996)

A CORPORATION MAY BE OBLIGATED TO PAY THE ATTORNEY FEES OF AN EMPLOYEE CHARGED WITH WRONGDOING IF HE WAS ACTING ON BEHALF OF THE CORPORATION

■ **INSTANT FACTS** A commodities trader who was sued for actions taken on behalf of his firm sued the firm for indemnification of the legal fees that were incurred in his defense.

■ **BLACK LETTER RULE** Before a corporation may indemnify an employee for legal expenses, he must have either been successful in defending against the suit or have taken in good faith the actions that gave rise to the suit.

■ PROCEDURAL BASIS

Appeal from a judgment of the District Court.

■ FACTS

Waltuch (P) was chief metals trader for Conticommodity Services, Inc. ("Conti") (D). While working at Conti (D), Waltuch (P) was accused of participating in a scheme that caused the silver market to first spike upwards sharply and then crash. Waltuch (P) and Conti (D) were sued by numerous speculators for fraud, market manipulation and antitrust violations. Conti (D) paid over $35 million to settle these suits. As a result of Conti's (D) settlement the cases were also dropped against Waltuch (P), who did not have to contribute anything to the settlement amount. Waltuch (P) incurred $1.2 million in attorneys' fees defending against these private lawsuits. Next the Commodity Futures Trading Commission ("CFTC") brought an enforcement proceeding against Waltuch (P) for fraud and market manipulation. Waltuch (P) spent $1 million in legal fees for his defense in the CTFC proceedings, which resulted in a fine and a six-month suspension from trading. Waltuch (P) now brings this suit against Conti (D) for the $2.2 million in unreimbursed legal expenses. There are two claims to consider on this appeal. First, Waltuch (P) contends that Article 9 of Conti's (D) Articles of Incorporation require it to indemnify Waltuch (P) for his expenses in both actions. Conti (D) contends that, under Delaware statute, Waltuch (P) can recover his expenses only if he acted in "good faith." Waltuch does not claim that he acted in good faith, only that good faith is irrelevant under Article 9. Second, Waltuch (P) contends that Delaware statute requires Conti (D) to indemnify him for the $1.2 million that he spent in the private suits because he was successful. The District Court found that Waltuch (P) did not achieve success because Conti (D) made payments on Waltuch's (P) behalf.

■ ISSUE

Is one who is acting on behalf of a corporation when he is accused of violating of the law, entitled to indemnification by the corporation?

■ DECISION AND RATIONALE

(Jacobs) Yes. Waltuch (P) first claims that Article 9 of Conti's (D) Articles of Incorporation require Conti (D) to indemnify him for his legal expenses, regardless of whether he acted in good faith while doing the acts that gave rise to the legal proceedings. Indeed, Article 9 on its face requires indemnification without mentioning good faith. However, Conti (D) argues that Article 9 is invalid to the extent that it requires indemnification of officers who have acted in bad faith because such a requirement is beyond the scope of Delaware General Corporate Law § 145(a) [giving corporations the power to indemnify their directors, officers, employees or agents who are threatened with or made parties to legal action because of some act that they did in the scope of employment if it was done in good faith or reasonably believed to be in the best interest of the corporation.] Waltuch (P) counters that, § 145(a) notwithstanding, corporations have a broader power of indemnification under § 145(f) [indemnification rights under § 145 shall not be deemed exclusive of any other rights that the corporation may give to one who was acting on behalf of the corporation.] Conti (D) responds that public policy requires indemnification to be limited to situations where the corporate officer was acting in good faith. No Delaware court has decided this issue, but we find that the applicable cases tend to support Conti's (D) arguments—the indemnification rights of corporations cannot be inconsistent with the provisions of § 145, notwithstanding the language of § 145(f). Under § 145(f), a corporation may grant indemnification rights beyond the scope of § 145(a). However, such additional indemnification rights may not be inconsistent with any of the limitations in § 145(a). We believe that the rule of consistency is reinforced by our reading of § 145 as a whole. By its own terms, § 145(a) limits the power of a corporation to indemnify its officers and directors to those who have acted in good faith. Subsection (f) does nothing more than acknowledge that those seeking indemnification may be entitled to other rights; it cannot be read to erase the requirement of good faith. Otherwise § 145(f) would require us to ignore the explicit terms of § 145 (a), and a corporation could indemnify whomever and however it wished, regardless of the good-faith requirement. When the legislature meant to augment the power of indemnification beyond the limits of § 145(a), it did so expressly—as it did, for example, in § 145(g) [a corporation may maintain liability insurance for an officer, director, employee or agent of the corporation against any liability incurred while acting in that capacity regardless of whether the corporation itself would have the power to indemnify the loss directly.] The legislative history of § 145 also supports the consistency requirement. It reveals that § 145(a) was intended to clarify the circumstances under which a corporation could indemnify those acting on its behalf. Limitations to indemnification were considered necessary to avoid undermining provisions of the criminal law and corporation law. It was ultimately decided that the way to best do this would be to limit indemnity to those situations where the person seeking indemnification acted in good faith. Waltuch (P) argues that our reading of the statute will render § 145(f) meaningless. We disagree. There are various other indemnification rights that are beyond those provided by § 145(a) and yet are still consistent with that subsection. We hold that Conti's (D) Article 9 is inconsistent with § 145(a) to the extent that it would require Conti (D) to indemnify Waltuch (P) even if he had not acted in good faith. Thus, since Waltuch (P) does not claim that he acted in good faith, he cannot be indemnified for any of the $2.2 million in legal fees incurred during the private lawsuits and CTFC proceeding under the terms of Article 9. Waltuch's (P) second claim fares much better: He is entitled to indemnification under § 145(c) [corporations must indemnify their officers and directors for the "successful" defense of certain claims.] Waltuch (P) argues that he was "successful" in the private lawsuits because they were dismissed against him without any payment or assumption of liability by him. Conti (D) argues that Waltuch (P) did not "succeed" because part of the $35 million that Conti (D) paid to settle the private lawsuits was paid on Waltuch's (P) behalf. We find Conti's (D) argument to be lacking. "Success" under § 145(c), does not mean moral exoneration. Escape from an adverse judgment or other detriment, for whatever reason, is determinative. The only question a court may ask is *what* the result was, not why it was. Once Waltuch (P) achieved his settlement gratis, he was successful in defense of the private lawsuits. In addition, Waltuch (P) apparently had no say in Conti's (D) settlement arrangements. An indemnifying corporation cannot escape mandatory indemnification of § 145(c) by paying a sum in settlement on behalf of an unwilling indemnitee. Thus, Waltuch is entitled to indemnification under § 145(c) for his expenses in the private lawsuits. Reversed.

Analysis:

Today all states have statutes whereby a corporation may indemnify its directors, officers, employees, or other agents. However, even prior to these statutes, the common law recognized the right of a vindicated director to recover the expenses in defending against suits for actions that he took on behalf of the corporation. There are several reasons that a corporation would want to be able to indemnify those working on its behalf. Indemnification will encourage those in charge of the corporation to take acceptable risks in making aggressive decisions that will hopefully benefit the corporation. Indemnification will encourage directors and officers to fight frivolous lawsuits, knowing that they won't have to pay the legal fees personally if they acted in good faith. On the flip-side, however, there is also the concern that immunizing directors and employees from personal liability for legal fees will encourage them to act recklessly and in a way that might injure the corporation. It is this concern that gives rise to the requirement in the present case that those who seek to be indemnified must have acted in good faith or in the belief that the action would benefit the corporation. To insure such action, the statute adopts the objective standard that a defendant must have been "successful" in defending against the suit. This court defines success very broadly as anything that does not result in money being paid by the defendant. However, other courts will only allow indemnification where there was success on the merits—that is, the defendant was exonerated from wrongdoing.

■ CASE VOCABULARY

ARTICLES OF INCORPORATION: A contract between the corporation and the state, and the corporation and its shareholders, where the corporation promises that it will act in a certain fashion.

INDEMNIFICATION: When the corporation pays the legal expenses incurred by a person who got sued for doing something on the corporation's behalf.

LEGISLATIVE HISTORY: A contemporaneous account of the creation of the statute that will give some clue as to what the legislature intended when it enacted the statute.

READING A STATUTE AS A WHOLE: A method of statutory interpretation where the court discerns the meaning of one provision in a statute by looking at the surrounding provisions.

SUCCESSFUL DEFENSE: Here success is defined broadly as any escape from liability, even if the escape was for technical reasons; however, some courts find success only where the defendant has been cleared of wrongdoing.

Clarke v. Greenberg

(*Corporate Trustee*) v. (*Shareholder*)
296 N.Y. 146, 71 N.E.2d 443 (1947)

DERIVATIVE ACTION RECOVERY BELONGS TO THE CORPORATION, EVEN IF THE PLAINTIFF SETTLED ONLY HIS/HER PERSONAL CLAIM

■ **INSTANT FACTS** A shareholder who settled a derivative suit against corporate directors did not give to the corporation the money realized in the settlement.

■ **BLACK LETTER RULE** In a derivative suit, recovery belongs to the corporation regardless of the manner or method used in making the recovery.

■ PROCEDURAL BASIS

Appeal from dismissal of a complaint.

■ FACTS

In a prior proceeding, Greenberg (D), a shareholder, commenced a derivative action on behalf of Associated Gas & Electric Company ("AGECO") alleging that the officers and directors had mismanaged the corporation for their own benefit. That action was settled and discontinued before trial without notice to the other shareholders and without approval of the court. Under the terms of the private settlement, Greenberg (D) sold his stock worth $51.88 to the directors of AGECO and received in return $9,000.00. A trustee (P) of AGECO then filed the present action against Greenberg (D) alleging that the amount received in excess of the stock value ($8,948.12) had been received for the benefit of the corporation, that Greenberg (D) had been holding that money in constructive trust for the corporation, and that he should now turn the money over to the corporation. The trial court and appellate court dismissed the complaint for failure to state a cause of action.

■ ISSUE

If a shareholder privately settles a derivative action must he turn the settlement monies over to the corporation?

■ DECISION AND RATIONALE

(Dye) Yes. The very nature of a derivative suit suggests the application of the fiduciary principle to the proceeds realized, regardless of whether they are received by judgment, settlement with approval of the court, or private settlement. A derivative action belongs to the corporation and any proceeds from the settlement of such action belong to the corporation as well. It is therefore logical that Greenberg (D) be required to account to AGECO for all benefit that he received in the settlement. The trustee's (P) complaint does state a cause of action. Reversed.

Analysis:

Aside from the recognition of the corporation's separate legal existence, the court here is also concerned about a collusive settlement. At common law, a plaintiff-shareholder who brought a derivative action was free to do as the shareholder did here—to bring an action, settle it with respect to himself, and then leave the other shareholders to fend for themselves. However, this rule defeated several of the purposes of derivative actions—to avoid multiplicity of actions, to recognize the corporate entity, and to protect the interests of all shareholders. Furthermore, the common law practice invited abuse. Private settlements encouraged the bringing of less meritorious suits for their settlement value to the individual plaintiff. They also allowed directors and officers to quietly and cheaply get rid of meritorious lawsuits before the full extent of their exposure could be realized. The rule here, forcing plaintiffs to disgorge settlement funds to the corporation takes away a good deal of incentive for private settlements. In addition, court rules, such as Federal Rule of Civil Procedure 23.1, which have been adopted in most states, attempted to address the problems of the common law rule. These court rules require judicial approval of settlements. The theory behind judicial approval is that courts are supposed to scrutinize the settlements to insure that the corporation and absent shareholders are adequately protected.

■ CASE VOCABULARY

CONSTRUCTIVE TRUST: When one person has money that in all fairness belongs to another, the court will find that the first person is merely holding the money for the other's benefit, and must account to the other for the money.

CHAPTER TWELVE

Structural Changes: Corporate Combinations and Tender Offers

Hollinger, Inc. v. Hollinger International, Inc.

Instant Facts: Hollinger, Inc. (P) sought a preliminary injunction against the sale of the *Telegraph* Group, a wholly owned subsidiary of Hollinger International, Inc. (D).

Black Letter Rule: Shareholders must be afforded the right to vote on a sale if it involves "all or substantially all" of the corporation's (D) assets.

Hariton v. Arco Electronics, Inc.

Instant Facts: Asserting that an agreement by a corporation to sell all of its assets in return for an acquirer's stock, followed by the corporation's dissolution and the pro rata distribution of the acquirer's stock to its shareholders, constituted a de facto merger which permitted him appraisal rights for his shares, a shareholder sued who had not been granted appraisal rights.

Black Letter Rule: Where a corporation sells its assets in exchange for an acquiring company's stock, dissolves, and then distributes the acquirer's stock, pro rata, to its shareholders, achieving the same substantive result as if the two companies had merged, the shareholders of the dissolving corporation need not be given the appraisal rights that the shareholders of a merging corporation would receive under a merger statute.

Farris v. Glen Alden Corp.

Instant Facts: Arguing that the transaction constituted a de facto merger for which he should have been notified of his appraisal rights under Pennsylvania law, a shareholder sued to enjoin the execution of an agreement between two corporations under which one of the corporations agreed to purchase all of the assets of the other corporation in return for its stock and the other corporation agreed to dissolve and distribute the acquirer's stock to its shareholders.

Black Letter Rule: Where a corporation purchases the assets of another corporation which then dissolves and distributes the acquirer's stock to its shareholders, achieving the same substantive result as if the two companies had merged, the shareholders of the acquiring corporation must be given the same rights that the shareholders of a merging corporation would have received in a statutory merger.

Terry v. Penn Central Corp.

Instant Facts: The shareholder of the corporate parent of a subsidiary holding company sought a declaratory judgment finding that, under a proposed forward triangular merger of another company into the subsidiary holding company, the shareholders of the holding company's parent were entitled to dissent and appraisal rights for their parent company stock under the de facto merger doctrine.

Black Letter Rule: The de facto merger doctrine does not apply to give the shareholders of a parent corporation dissent and appraisal rights in the event of a forward triangular merger of another company into a subsidiary of the parent.

Weinberger v. UOP, Inc.

Instant Facts: A class of minority shareholders of a subsidiary corporation challenged the terms of a cash-out merger of the subsidiary into its corporate parent asserting that the terms of the merger were unfair.

Black Letter Rule: A majority shareholder in a cash-out merger has the burden to show that it completely disclosed to the minority shareholders all material facts relevant to the transaction, in order to uphold a majority vote of the minority shareholders approving the merger.

Glassman v. Unocal Exploration Corp.

Instant Facts: Unocal Corporation (D) filed a short-form merger to eliminate the minority shareholders of its subsidiary corporation.

Black Letter Rule: With a statutory short-form merger, controlling fiduciaries of the parent corporation do not owe a duty of entire fairness to the corporate subsidiary's minority shareholders.

Solomon v. Pathe

Instant Facts: Solomon (P) sued Pathe (D) to challenge a tender offer as coercive.

Black Letter Rule: Tender offers are voluntary absent specific evidence of coercion or lack of complete disclosure.

Unocal Corp. v. Mesa Petroleum Co.

Instant Facts: A minority shareholder that had made a tender offer to take over a corporation sued to prevent the corporation's board of directors from defending against the takeover bid by making its own tender offer for the corporation's stock.

Black Letter Rule: A corporate board can oppose a takeover threat it reasonably perceives to be harmful to the corporation.

Moran v. Household International, Inc.

Instant Facts: A corporate director who had voted against the adoption of a "poison pill" defensive measure sued to invalidate the plan after he lost the vote 14 to 2.

Black Letter Rule: A board of directors can adopt a poison pill plan as a defensive measure in response to its reasonable fear of a possible future hostile takeover of the corporation.

Quickturn Design Systems, Inc. v. Shapiro

Instant Facts: A hostile bidder conducting a proxy contest for control of the board of directors of a target corporation sued to invalidate a recently-adopted provision of the target's "poison pill" rights plan which would have delayed the ability of a newly-elected target board of directors, controlled by the hostile bidder, to cancel the "poison pill" rights plan.

Black Letter Rule: A defensive measure to a hostile takeover that restricts the ability of a board of directors to perform its statutory and fiduciary duties is invalid.

Revlon, Inc. v. Macandrews & Forbes Holdings, Inc.

Instant Facts: A hostile bidder for a target corporation sued to enjoin certain defensive measures taken by the target's board against its bid and to enjoin a competing bid by another corporation that had been approved by the target board.

Black Letter Rule: Once a corporation is to be sold, the primary duty of the board of directors is to obtain the highest possible sale price for the benefit of the corporation's shareholders.

Paramount Communications, Inc. v. QVC Network

Instant Facts: A hostile bidder for a target corporation sued to enjoin an agreement by the target's board of directors to merge with another corporation in a transaction that would cause the corporation to change from being a company owned by an unaggregated group of unaffiliated shareholders to a company controlled by a single shareholder.

Black Letter Rule: When a board of directors agrees to a sale or change in control of a corporation, the board has a duty to act reasonably to seek the best value reasonably available to the shareholders.

Hilton Hotels Corp. v. ITT Corp.

Instant Facts: Hilton Hotels (P), which sought to acquire ITT Corp. (D), sued to obtain an injunction precluding implementation of the targeted company's comprehensive plan.

Black Letter Rule: A targeted corporation's attempts to restructure itself in order to preclude an acquiring corporation from obtaining a majority on the board impermissibly restricts its shareholders' rights to vote for directors.

Omnicare, Inc. v. NCS Healthcare, Inc.

Instant Facts: NCS Healthcare, Inc. (D) agreed to defensive devices in a merger transaction with Genesis Health Ventures, Inc. that precluded the NCS (D) board's consideration of Omnicare, Inc.'s (P) subsequent superior offer.

Black Letter Rule: A proposed merger transaction that prevents the board from discharging its fiduciary duties is invalid and unenforceable.

Hollinger Inc. v. Hollinger International, Inc.

(*Stockholder*) v. (*Corporation*)
858 A.2d 342 (Del.Ch.Ct.2004)

WHETHER A SALE INVOLVES SUBSTANTIALLY ALL OF A CORPORATION'S ASSETS REQUIRES A QUANTITITAVE AND QUALITATIVE ANALYSIS

■ **INSTANT FACTS** Hollinger, Inc. (P) sought a preliminary injunction against the sale of the *Telegraph* Group, a wholly owned subsidiary of Hollinger International, Inc. (D).

■ **BLACK LETTER RULE** Shareholders must be afforded the right to vote on a sale if it involves "all or substantially all" of the corporation's (D) assets.

■ PROCEDURAL BASIS

Chancery court consideration of the plaintiff's motion for a preliminary injunction.

■ FACTS

The *Telegraph* Group was an indirect, wholly owned subsidiary of Hollinger International, Inc. ("International") (D). Hollinger, Inc. ("Hollinger") (P) owned eighteen percent of International's (D) total equity, but maintained sixty-eight percent of the defendant's voting power. After a lengthy auction process, International (D) agreed to sell *Telegraph* to Press Holdings International without shareholder approval. Hollinger (P) sought a preliminary injunction against the sale.

■ ISSUE

Must shareholders of a parent corporation be afforded the opportunity to vote on the sale of an indirect wholly owned subsidiary when the parent corporation will remain profitable after the sale?

■ DECISION AND RATIONALE

(Strine, Vice Ch.) No. Although International (D) does not own *Telegraph* directly, it directly negotiated and controlled the sale and is the sole signatory to the sale agreement. Based on this control, 8 Del. C. § 271 applies to the sale of the indirect wholly owned subsidiary. Under § 271, International's (D) shareholders must be afforded the right to vote on the sale if it involves "all or substantially all" of International's (D) assets. Under this test, a stockholder vote is required if the assets to be sold "are quantitatively vital to the operation of the corporation and substantially affect the existence and purpose of the corporation." Here, *Telegraph* is not quantitatively vital to International's (D) operations. It comprises less than fifty percent of International's (D) asset value, and International (D) will retain other significant assets that have a strong history of profit. While *Telegraph* may be International's most valuable asset, it is not quantitatively vital to its operations.

The second part of the test—whether the sale substantially affects the existence and purpose of International (D)—requires a look at *Telegraph*'s qualitative importance to International. Qualitative importance, however, is not based on social, moral, or political importance. It turns on the economic importance of the sale to the resulting quality of investors' investments. If the sale leaves stockholders with an economic investment qualitatively different than that held before the sale, § 271 may be implicated. Only those transactions that "strike at the heart of the corporate existence" are subject to shareholder vote. Here, the *Telegraph* sale does not strike at the heart of International's (D) existence. After the sale, International (D) shareholders remain shareholders in a corporation engaged in the same business with profit and other valuable assets. Since, the *Telegraph* sale does not involve the sale of substantially all of International's (D) assets, no shareholder vote is required under § 271. Motion denied.

Analysis:

Although corporate statutes generally suggest a quantitative standard, most courts construe the phrase "all or substantially all" to include the qualitative component suggested by the court here. Because the purpose of the shareholder vote is to protect the expectations of their initial investment, a sale of assets, although less than half of the corporate assets, will require shareholder approval if it changes the manner in which the corporation operates or otherwise frustrates the shareholders' reasonable expectations of their initial investment.

Hariton v. Arco Electronics, Inc.

(*Shareholder*) v. (*Dissolving Corporation*)

41 Del.Ch. 74, 188 A.2d 123 (1963)

DELAWARE SUPREME COURT REJECTS DE FACTO MERGER DOCTRINE

■ **INSTANT FACTS** Asserting that an agreement by a corporation to sell all of its assets in return for an acquirer's stock, followed by the corporation's dissolution and the pro rata distribution of the acquirer's stock to its shareholders, constituted a de facto merger which permitted him appraisal rights for his shares, a shareholder sued who had not been granted appraisal rights.

■ **BLACK LETTER RULE** Where a corporation sells its assets in exchange for an acquiring company's stock, dissolves, and then distributes the acquirer's stock, pro rata, to its shareholders, achieving the same substantive result as if the two companies had merged, the shareholders of the dissolving corporation need not be given the appraisal rights that the shareholders of a merging corporation would receive under a merger statute.

■ PROCEDURAL BASIS

Appeal of a grant of summary judgment by the Delaware Chancery Court, dismissing a complaint contending that a sale of corporate assets was illegal.

■ FACTS

Arco Electronics, Inc. ("Arco") (D) entered into an agreement with Loral Electronics Corporation ("Loral") under which Arco (D) would: (1) sell all its assets to Loral in exchange for Loral stock; (2) call a shareholder meeting to dissolve Arco (D); and (3) distribute to its shareholders the Loral stock Arco (D) had received for its assets. After these steps were accomplished and 80% of the Arco (D) shareholders had approved the dissolution of the company, Martin Hariton ("Hariton") (P), an Arco (D) shareholder who had not voted sought to enjoin the sale and dissolution. Hariton (P) contended that the result of the agreement's three steps was the same substantive result that would have occurred if Arco (D) and Loral had merged under Delaware law. Hariton (P) argued that, had the two companies merged, he and the other Arco (D) shareholders would have been entitled to have their shares appraised and bought at fair value by the company under Delaware's merger statute, an opportunity Arco (D) had not provided to the shareholders. Arguing that the Arco (D)—Loral agreement was a de facto merger, Hariton (P) sought appraisal rights for his shares. Arco (D) obtained summary judgment dismissing Hariton's (P) complaint in the Chancery Court and Hariton (P) appealed.

■ ISSUE

If a corporation sells its assets in exchange for an acquiring company's stock, dissolves, and then distributes the acquirer's stock, pro rata, to its shareholders, achieving the same substantive result as if the two companies had merged, must the shareholders of the dissolving corporation be given the appraisal rights that the shareholders of a merging corporation would receive under the merger statute?

■ DECISION AND RATIONALE

(Southerland, C.J.) No. Hariton (P) is correct that the results of the sale of assets here are the same as if a statutory merger had occurred between Arco (D) and Loral. This result is possible because of the overlapping scope of Delaware's merger statute and the Delaware statute authorizing a sale of assets in return for stock. Despite the overlap, however, the sale-of-assets statute and the merger statute are independent of each other and are of equal dignity. Thus, the framers of a corporate reorganization may choose either method to achieve their desired end. Both methods are valid acts of independent legal significance. We will not recognize a de facto merger doctrine and will not require Hariton (P) to be given the appraisal rights he would have received if Arco (D) had chosen to effect its reorganization through a merger. Affirmed.

Analysis:

The Delaware Supreme Court here adopts the majority approach, rejecting the de facto merger doctrine in favor of the doctrine of independent legal significance. The de facto merger doctrine holds that, since a sale of assets for stock, followed by a dissolution of the selling company and a distribution of the acquired stock, achieves the same result as an actual statutory merger of the selling company and the acquirer, the shareholders of the companies involved in the transaction should be entitled to the same rights they would have had if the companies had merged. In particular, the shareholders want appraisal rights, permitting them to have their shares priced at market value and purchased by the corporation in the event they dislike the result of the proposed corporate reorganization. In rejecting this approach, the Delaware Supreme Court reasons that the state's statutory provisions authorizing a sale of assets and a merger are of "equal dignity" and that, since the legislature has provided alternative means of achieving the same result, corporations are entitled to choose whichever means they prefer to achieve that end result. The court strictly enforces the terms of the two statutory provisions, finding them equal and independent of each other.

■ CASE VOCABULARY

APPRAISAL RIGHT: The ability of a shareholder of a corporation to opt out of a plan or agreement to restructure the corporation by obtaining a valuation of his stock at its fair market price at which the corporation is then required to purchase his shares.

DE FACTO: Something that is in form one thing, while in actuality, it is really something else.

PRO RATA: Proportionately, according to the percentage of stock owned.

STATUTORY MERGER: The absorption of one corporation by another corporation under the terms of a state statute authorizing such a combination, which results in the automatic transfer of the absorbed corporation's assets and liabilities by operation of law.

Farris v. Glen Alden Corp.

(*Shareholder*) v. (*Acquiring Corporation*)

393 Pa. 427, 143 A.2d 25 (1958)

PENNSYLVANIA SUPREME COURT ADOPTS THE DE FACTO MERGER DOCTRINE

■ **INSTANT FACTS** Arguing that the transaction constituted a de facto merger for which he should have been notified of his appraisal rights under Pennsylvania law, a shareholder sued to enjoin the execution of an agreement between two corporations under which one of the corporations agreed to purchase all of the assets of the other corporation in return for its stock and the other corporation agreed to dissolve and distribute the acquirer's stock to its shareholders.

■ **BLACK LETTER RULE** Where a corporation purchases the assets of another corporation which then dissolves and distributes the acquirer's stock to its shareholders, achieving the same substantive result as if the two companies had merged, the shareholders of the acquiring corporation must be given the same rights that the shareholders of a merging corporation would have received in a statutory merger.

■ PROCEDURAL BASIS

Appeal of a decision on the pleadings by a Pennsylvania trial court granting injunctive relief that voided a shareholder vote on a plan of reorganization.

■ FACTS

Glen Alden Corporation ("Glen Alden") (D), a coal mining company, entered into an agreement with List Industries Corporation ("List"), a diversified holding company, in which Glen Alden (D), the smaller company, agreed to acquire all of List's assets and liabilities in exchange for Glen Alden (D) stock. List would then dissolve and distribute the Glen Alden (D) stock to its shareholders. Following the execution of the agreement, Glen Alden (D) sent out notice of its annual shareholders' meeting along with a proxy statement recommending approval of the reorganization agreement with List. At the shareholders' meeting, holders of a majority of the outstanding shares of Glen Alden (D) voted to approve the plan. Farris (P), a Glen Alden (D) shareholder, filed suit against Glen Alden (D) and its officers seeking a preliminary injunction preventing execution of the agreement. Farris (P) argued that the reorganization agreement was actually a merger between Glen Alden (D) and List and that Pennsylvania's corporate law statutes required that in the event of a merger, proper notice be given to the shareholders of the merging corporations of their right to dissent from the merger and obtain an appraisal of their shares. [Sounds familiar.] Glen Alden (D) asserted that the agreement between the corporations was merely an agreement for the purchase of corporate assets for which Pennsylvania law did not provide a right of dissent and appraisal. The trial court ruled that the reorganization plan was a plan for a de facto merger and that, because Glen Alden (D) had not provided notice of dissent and appraisal rights, the shareholder vote and agreement were void. Glen Alden (D) appealed.

■ ISSUE

Where a corporation purchases the assets of another corporation which then dissolves and distributes the acquirer's stock to its shareholders, achieving the same substantive result as if the two companies had merged, should the shareholders of the acquiring corporation be given the same rights that the shareholders of a merging corporation would have received in a statutory merger?

■ DECISION AND RATIONALE

(Cohen J.) Yes. We believe that you must look to the substance of a transaction over its form, examining not merely the formal provisions of a plan of reorganization, but also the consequences of the transaction and the purposes of the corporate law provisions that are applicable. Under Pennsylvania's merger statute, shareholders are granted the right to dissent from a merger plan and obtain the fair value of their shares. The idea of that law was that when a corporation combines with another so as to lose its essential nature and alter the original fundamental relationships among the shareholders, a shareholder who does not approve of such change should be allowed to end his participation in the corporation and receive fair value for his shares. Here, the agreement between Glen Alden (D) and List so fundamentally changes the corporate character of Glen Alden (D) and the interest of Farris (P) that it constitutes a merger and Farris (P) should have been granted the rights accorded to shareholders under the state's merger statute. The company resulting from the transaction would be very different than the Glen Alden (D) company that existed before the transaction. Glen Alden's (D) business would change from a coal mining company to a diversified holding company. There would be a substantial increase in the corporation's debt. Moreover, control of the board of directors would pass to the former directors of List. Thus, if the deal is permitted to occur, Farris (P) would essentially have his stock in Glen Alden (D) taken away and a new stock thrust upon him in its place. He would be forced into a new enterprise under terms not of his own choosing. This was what the Pennsylvania legislature tried to avoid by creating an appraisal right in the event of a merger. Glen Alden (D) asserts that Pennsylvania's merger statute specifically provides that the shareholders of a corporation purchasing assets shall not have dissenter rights and that this precludes a finding in favor of Farris (P). We disagree. There is no evidence that the legislature intended that a transaction having the effect of a merger but which includes a purchase of assets should be exempt from appraisal requirements. Furthermore, while it is technically true that Glen Alden (D) is acquiring List, we will not blind our eyes to the realities of the transaction. Despite the designation of the parties and the form employed, we can see that List is really acquiring Glen Alden (D), and in that event, the Glen Alden (D) shareholders would be entitled to dissent rights under Pennsylvania law. We hold that the proposed reorganization is a merger of the two companies and thus required notification to the Glen Alden (D) shareholders of their statutory rights of dissent and appraisal. Affirmed.

Analysis:

In this case, the Pennsylvania Supreme Court adopts the de facto merger doctrine to find that a transaction that on its face appeared to be a stock-for-assets purchase should be treated as if it were a statutory merger. Glen Alden (D) was a much smaller company than List. By structuring the deal as a purchase by Glen Alden (D) of List's assets, the companies were attempting to take advantage of what appeared to be the law in Delaware and Pennsylvania regarding such an asset purchase. List was a Delaware corporation and, under Delaware law, shareholders of a corporation selling substantially all of its assets were not entitled to appraisal rights. The companies read Pennsylvania law to require appraisal rights for the shareholders of a corporation selling its assets, but not for the shareholders of a corporation buying the assets of another corporation. In finding that this transaction amounted to a de facto merger, however, the Pennsylvania Supreme Court concluded that the acquiring company's shareholders were also entitled to appraisal rights because of the fundamental change in the nature of the acquiring corporation after the transaction.

■ CASE VOCABULARY

HOLDING COMPANY: A corporation that owns the stock of subsidiary corporations that operate businesses.

LIABILITIES: The debts of a corporation.

Terry v. Penn Central Corp.

(*Shareholder*) v. (*Parent of Holding Company*)

668 F.2d 188 (3d Cir.1981)

FEDERAL COURT FINDS THAT DE FACTO MERGER DOCTRINE WOULD NOT APPLY TO A TRIANGULAR MERGER UNDER PENNSYLVANIA LAW

■ **INSTANT FACTS** The shareholder of the corporate parent of a subsidiary holding company sought a declaratory judgment finding that, under a proposed forward triangular merger of another company into the subsidiary holding company, the shareholders of the holding company's parent were entitled to dissent and appraisal rights for their parent company stock under the de facto merger doctrine.

■ **BLACK LETTER RULE** The de facto merger doctrine does not apply to give the shareholders of a parent corporation dissent and appraisal rights in the event of a forward triangular merger of another company into a subsidiary of the parent.

■ FACTS

Penn Central Corporation ("Penn Central") (D1), sought to acquire a number of profitable corporations in an attempt to be able to use its own large federal tax loss carry-forward. To acquire the businesses, Penn Central (D1) created a wholly-owned subsidiary corporation, known as PCC Holdings, Inc. ("Holdings"). One company that Penn Central sought to acquire was Colt Industries, Inc. ("Colt") (D2). The management and directors of Colt (D2) and Penn Central (D1) agreed that Colt (D2) would merge into Holdings in return for the issuance of Penn Central (D1) stock to the Colt (D1) shareholders. This kind of merger is a "forward triangular merger." Terry (P), a shareholder and member of the Penn Central (D) board of directors, opposed the deal and filed suit to prevent the merger. A federal trial court ruled for Penn Central (D1) and Colt (D2) and Terry (P) appealed. Following the appeal, Penn Central (D1) and Colt (D2) called off the merger agreement. While the request for injunctive relief preventing the merger therefore became moot, Terry (P) still sought a declaratory judgment that in the event of a future merger under Penn Central's (D1) plan of acquisitions, he would be entitled to dissenters' rights.

■ ISSUE

Does the de facto merger doctrine apply to give the shareholders of a parent corporation dissent and appraisal rights in the event of a forward triangular merger of another company into a subsidiary of the parent?

■ DECISION AND RATIONALE

(Adams J.) No. Terry (P) contends that the proposed merger between Holdings and Colt (D2) constitutes a de facto merger between Colt (D2) and Penn Central (D1) and that Penn Central (D1) shareholders are therefore entitled to the protections accorded dissenting shareholders in a merger under Pennsylvania law. While this reasoning may be attractive from a policy standpoint, we believe that it contravenes the language used by the Pennsylvania legislature in its corporate law statutes. Under the Pennsylvania merger statute, shareholders of corporations that are parties to a merger plan are entitled to dissent and appraisal rights. Under the statute, the "parties to a merger" are those companies that are *actually* combined in the transaction. Here, Penn Central (D1) and Holdings would both exist as separate entities after the merger of Colt (D2) into Holdings. Thus, Penn Central (D1) is not a party to the merger. As for the de facto merger doctrine, following the case of *Farris v. Glen Alden* [where the Pennsylvania Supreme Court held that a transaction having the effect of a merger would be treated as a statutory merger], the legislature enacted a law which appears to have abolished the doctrine of de facto merger in Pennsylvania. We do not think that a Pennsylvania court would apply the de facto merger doctrine to the situation in this case. Neither fraud nor fundamental unfairness have been shown to result from this proposed merger. At worst, the deal might be bad business judgment by management as Terry (P) suggests. Poor business judgment is not enough to constitute unfairness cognizable by a court. We therefore rule that Terry (P) would not possess dissent and appraisal rights in the event of a transaction such as the one involved in this case. Affirmed.

Analysis:

A forward triangular merger occurs when a target corporation merges into a subsidiary of a parent corporation in return for stock of the parent corporation, which is then distributed to the target corporation's shareholders. An acquiring corporation might use this approach to try to shield itself from direct responsibility for the target's potential liabilities. As shown here, the forward triangular merger structure also can allow an acquisition without the requirement of a vote (or dissent and appraisal rights) by the shareholders of the acquiring corporation. By finding that the de facto merger doctrine would not apply to a forward triangular merger under Pennsylvania law, the U.S. Court of Appeals for the Third Circuit makes it relatively easy for the management and directors of an acquiring corporation to avoid a vote of the acquirer's own shareholders. Some states, such as California, and certain stock exchanges, like the New York Stock Exchange, place restrictions on the ability of an acquiring corporation to avoid a vote or appraisal rights for its own shareholders.

■ CASE VOCABULARY

FORWARD TRIANGULAR MERGER: A merger that occurs when a target corporation merges into a subsidiary of a parent corporation in return for stock of the parent corporation, which is then distributed to the target corporation's shareholders, sometimes called a forward subsidiary merger.

PARENT CORPORATION: A corporation owning a majority of the stock of a subsidiary corporation.

TARGET CORPORATION: The corporation that is sought to be acquired by an acquiring corporation through a merger, reorganization, stock purchase, or asset purchase.

Weinberger v. UOP, Inc.

(*Minority Shareholder in Subsidiary Corporation*) v. (*Subsidiary Corporation*)
457 A.2d 701 (Del.1983)

MAJORITY'S LACK OF DISCLOSURE TO MINORITY OF MATERIAL INFORMATION RELEVANT TO A CASH-OUT MERGER VOIDS THE MINORITY'S VOTE APPROVING THE MERGER

■ **INSTANT FACTS** A class of minority shareholders of a subsidiary corporation challenged the terms of a cash-out merger of the subsidiary into its corporate parent asserting that the terms of the merger were unfair.

■ **BLACK LETTER RULE** A majority shareholder in a cash-out merger has the burden to show that it completely disclosed to the minority shareholders all material facts relevant to the transaction, in order to uphold a majority vote of the minority shareholders approving the merger.

■ PROCEDURAL BASIS

Appeal of a judgment of the Delaware Court of Chancery finding that the terms of a cash-out merger were fair to the minority shareholders.

■ FACTS

After selling one of its subsidiaries for a large amount of cash, The Signals Company, Inc. ("Signal") (D1) sought to invest the cash by acquiring a controlling interest in UOP, Inc. ("UOP") (D2) and successfully acquired 50.6 percent of the company. Signal (D1) was then able to nominate and elect six of the thirteen members of the UOP (D2) board and eventually was able to replace the UOP (D2) president and CEO with a Signal (D1) employee, James Crawford ("Crawford"), who also became a director of both the UOP (D2) and Signal (D1) boards. Subsequently, Signal's (D1) chairman and its president, who were both members of the UOP (D2) board, ordered Signal's (D1) director of planning and chief financial officer, both of whom were also members of the UOP (D2) board, to conduct a feasibility study on the issue of whether it would be a good investment for Signal (D1) to acquire the rest of the UOP (D2) stock and at what price the deal would make sense for Signal (D1). The feasibility study concluded that the deal would be a good investment at a price of up to $24 a share. Signal (D1) then proposed a cash-out merger, in which Signal (D1) would acquire the remaining stock of UOP (D2) for $21 a share. Over the succeeding four business days, UOP (D2) reviewed the proposed terms. Crawford hired Lehman Brothers, an investment banking firm that had been UOP's (D2) longstanding business adviser, to render a fairness opinion on the price offered by Signal (D1) to the UOP (D1) minority shareholders. Lehman Brothers conducted a very hurried review and found the $21 price to be fair. At a joint meeting of the Signal (D1) and UOP (D2) boards just four business days after the initial price offer by Signal (D1), Signal's (D1) board voted to propose a cash-out merger for $21 per share, contingent on the approval of the merger by a majority of the UOP (D2) minority shareholders. UOP's (D2) board then considered the proposal, reviewing the company's financial data and the Lehman Brothers fairness opinion letter. The outside members of the UOP (D2) board were never told about the feasibility study done by Signal (D1) management. With the Signal (D1)—appointed directors of the UOP (D2) board abstaining, the UOP (D2) outside directors approved the proposal. Subsequently, UOP (D2) scheduled a shareholder vote and issued a proxy statement to its shareholders recommending approval of the merger and indicating that the price had been determined after discussions between Crawford and Signal (D2) management and that Lehman Brothers had approved the price as fair. The plan was approved by the UOP minority shareholders and went into effect immediately. William Weinberger (P), a minority shareholder of UOP (D2), filed a class-action lawsuit, challenging the fairness of the cash-out merger and asserting that a business purpose was required for a cash-out merger. At trial, the Delaware Chancellor held in favor of Signal (D1) and UOP (D2), finding that the terms of the transaction were fair. Weinberger (P) appealed.

■ ISSUE

Does a majority shareholder in a cash-out merger have the burden to show that it completely disclosed to the minority shareholders all material facts relevant to the transaction, in order to uphold a majority vote of the minority shareholders approving the merger?

■ DECISION AND RATIONALE

(Moore J.) Yes. The Chancellor found that the ultimate burden of proof in a suit challenging a cash-out merger rests with the majority shareholder to show that the terms are fair to the minority, but that it is first the burden of the minority shareholder attacking the transaction to show some basis for invoking the fairness obligation. While we agree with that conclusion, we find that, where corporate action has been approved by an informed vote of a majority of the minority shareholders, the burden shifts entirely to the complaining minority shareholders to show the unfairness of the transaction. The burden remains on the majority shareholder however, to show that it completely disclosed all material facts relevant to the transaction. In this case, the UOP (D2) minority shareholder vote was not an informed vote. Material information necessary to understand the bargaining positions of Signal (D1) and UOP (D2), was withheld by Signal (D1), the majority shareholder, under circumstances amounting to a breach of its fiduciary duty to the minority. Senior management of Signal (D1), including its chairman, its president, its director of planning, and its chief financial officer, all of whom were also members of the UOP (D2) board of directors, had a feasibility study done which concluded that it would be a good investment for Signal (D1) to acquire the rest of the UOP (D2) stock at a price of up to $24 a share. This study was never disclosed to the UOP (D2) outside directors by these Signal (D1)—appointed directors. This conduct does not meet the fiduciary standard required in a self-interested combination. The study found that the difference between $21 a share and $24 a share would have produced a change in Signal's (D2) investment return of only two-tenths of one percent, while it meant over $17,000,000 to the UOP (D2) minority shareholders. We find that the fact that Signal (D1) could have paid an even higher price and still had a "good investment" was a matter of material significance to the UOP (D2) minority shareholders. In addition, the minority was misled into thinking that the Lehman Brothers opinion was a careful study of the fairness of the price. There was no disclosure of the hurried method of review by Lehman Brothers. We find that this merger does not meet the fairness test and no burden of proof shifted to the complaining minority shareholders following the minority shareholder vote. Weinberger (P) has also raised the issue of whether a business purpose is required for a freeze-out merger other than the elimination of the minority shareholders. Although recent Delaware case law has found such a requirement, given the protection offered to minority shareholders through the entire fairness test, we now hold that no business purpose is required. Reversed.

Analysis:

Signal (D1), as the majority shareholder in UOP (D2), stood on both sides of the proposed freeze-out merger transaction in this case and was required to either disclose all material terms of the transaction and obtain the approval of a majority of the minority shareholders or prove that the transaction was entirely fair. Here, because Signal (D1) did not disclose material information about the price to the minority shareholders, the vote of the minority approving the transaction could not stand. The case does not establish that a majority shareholder must always disclose the highest price it will pay the minority in a cash-out merger, however. The difficulty here was that Signal (D1) had its own management on the board of UOP (D2) that was aware of the feasibility study and the price Signal (D1) could afford while still making a worthwhile return on its investment. The case also establishes that no business purpose is necessary for a freeze-out merger in Delaware, finding that the entire fairness test offers enough protection to minority shareholders to make a business purpose test unnecessary. Other states, including New York and Massachusetts, require a valid business purpose beyond the elimination of minority shareholders for a freeze-out merger, asserting that the great danger of an abuse of fiduciary duty justifies such a requirement.

■ CASE VOCABULARY

CASH-OUT MERGER: A type of freeze-out merger in which the minority shareholders will receive cash (or sometimes debt securities) from the majority shareholder in return for their shares of stock.

FREEZE-OUT MERGER: When a controlling shareholder of a corporation seeks to acquire 100 percent of the corporation's stock by eliminating the stock ownership of the minority shareholders through the use of a merger.

OUTSIDE DIRECTOR: A member of the board of directors of a corporation who is neither employed by the corporation nor by its controlling shareholder.

Glassman v. Unocal Exploration Corp.

(*Shareholder*) v. (*Corporation*)
777 A.2d 242 (Del.2001)

MINORITY SHAREHOLDERS ARE ENTITLED TO AN APPRAISAL TO ENSURE FAIR VALUE FOR THEIR SHARES

■ **INSTANT FACTS** Unocal Corporation (D) filed a short-form merger to eliminate the minority shareholders of its subsidiary corporation.

■ **BLACK LETTER RULE** With a statutory short-form merger, controlling fiduciaries of the parent corporation do not owe a duty of entire fairness to the corporate subsidiary's minority shareholders.

■ PROCEDURAL BASIS

On appeal to review a decision of the chancery court in favor of the defendants.

■ FACTS

Unocal Corporation (D) owned approximately ninety-six percent of the stock of Unocal Exploration Corp. (UXC) (D). In response to low revenues, Unocal (D) decided that by eliminating the UXC (D) minority, it would reduce taxes and overhead expenses. Unocal (D) and UXC (D) thereafter voted to form special committees to consider a possible merger. The UXC (D) committee was made up of three directors who were Unocal (D) directors, but not employees or officers. The merger involved the exchange of one Unocal (D) share for every .54 UXC (D) share. After agreeing to the "short-form" merger, UXC (D) notified its shareholders of their appraisal rights. The plaintiffs filed a class action on behalf of UXC's (D) minority shareholders, asserting that Unocal (D) and its directors breached their fiduciary duties of entire fairness and full disclosure to the minority shareholders. The chancery court concluded that the prospectus contained no material misstatements or omissions, that the duty of entire fairness did not apply to a short-form merger, and that the plaintiff's only remedy was an appraisal.

■ ISSUE

Are stockholders of a merged subsidiary entitled to equitable relief when objecting to a short-form merger?

■ DECISION AND RATIONALE

(Berger, J.) No. Under Delaware's short-form merger statute, a parent corporation is authorized to merge with a subsidiary by filing and recording a certificate evidencing the merger resolution. The statute applies when the parent corporation owns at least ninety percent of the subsidiary's stock and authorizes the parent corporation to pay cash for minority shares, thereby eliminating the minority. The statute affords the stockholders of the acquired subsidiary the right of appraisal.

In a merger situation, the parent corporation generally owes the subsidiary's minority shareholders the fiduciary duty of entire fairness. This duty involves both fair dealing in the manner in which the transaction is conducted and a fair price. In challenging the merger, the shareholders may seek both an accounting and money damages if the merger is undervalued. The short-form merger statute, however, authorizes a summary procedure that directly conflicts with these fiduciary requirements. With a short-form merger, the self-dealing fiduciary invokes the statute for the purpose of eliminating the minority shareholders' interests. The short-form merger is not subject to prior notice to the minority shareholders and they are entitled to no vote on the merger. The only protection offered by the statute is the right of appraisal to ensure that they receive fair value for their shares. By following the procedure outlined in the short-form merger statute, the parent corporation is incapable of satisfying the duty of entire fairness otherwise expected of it. If such a duty is expected, the benefits derived from the short-form merger statute are lost. Accordingly, the only remedy available to shareholders in a short-form merger is an appraisal, which can ensure they receive fair value based on all relevant factors. Although the parent corporation is not bound by the duty of entire fairness, it is bound by the duty of full disclosure to enable shareholders to determine whether to accept the merger consideration or seek an appraisal. Affirmed.

Analysis:

Short-form merger statutes underscore that no individual has a general right to invest in a particular corporation. With a short-form merger, a parent corporation may legally compel shareholders of a subsidiary to sell their shares to the corporation. The result of the merger is not an exchange of stock in the surviving corporation, but rather cash for their existing shares, resulting in no interest in the newly merged corporation. The right of appraisal, however, protects shareholders from undervaluation to ensure they receive a fair price for their investment.

■ CASE VOCABULARY

APPRAISAL: The determination of what constitutes a fair price; valuation; estimation of worth.

Solomon v. Pathe

(*Shareholder*) v. (*Corporation*)
672 A.2d 35 (Del.1996)

SHAREHOLDERS HAVE NO RIGHT TO RECEIVE ANY PARTICULAR COMPENSATION FROM A TENDER OFFER

■ **INSTANT FACTS** Solomon (P) sued Pathe (D) to challenge a tender offer as coercive.

■ **BLACK LETTER RULE** Tender offers are voluntary absent specific evidence of coercion or lack of complete disclosure.

■ PROCEDURAL BASIS

On appeal to review a decision of the chancery court dismissing the plaintiffs' complaint.

■ FACTS

Pathe (D) borrowed nearly one billion dollars from Credit Lyonnais Banque Nederland N.V. ("CLBN") (D) to purchase MGM/UA Communications Corporation ("MGM"). In return, CLBN (D) took a security interest in eighty-nine percent of Pathe's (D) stock and ninety-eight percent of MGM's stock. Thereafter, CLBN (D) submitted a tender offer to purchase nearly six million outstanding shares of Pathe (D) stock at $1.50 per share. Solomon (P) is a shareholder representing a class of shareholders holding ten percent of Pathe (D) stock. The class sued to challenge the tender offer, alleging that it was unfair to those shareholders who tendered their shares in response to the offer because the tender offer price was coercive. CLBN (D) moved to dismiss the complaint, which motion was granted with prejudice.

■ ISSUE

Did the plaintiff state a claim for which relief could be granted by alleging that the price of a tender offer was coercive?

■ DECISION AND RATIONALE

(Hartnett, J.) No. With voluntary tender offers, shareholders do not have a right to receive any particular compensation. Only when coercion exists or there are "materially false or misleading disclosures made to shareholders in connection with the offer" is an offer considered involuntary. Here, the only allegation of coercion in the complaint is the price offered. This allegation is conclusory, and there are no other allegations that allow for an inference of coercion or nondisclosure. The complaint fails to state a claim for which relief can be granted. Affirmed.

Analysis:

In re Pure Resources, Inc. Shareholders Litigation, 808 A.2d 421 (Del. Ch. 2002), established a test for establishing shareholder coercion. There, the court determined that no actionable coercion exists if a majority shareholder (1) conditions the tender offer on the approval of a majority of the minority shareholders, (2) promises to effect a short-form merger at the same price if it obtains more than ninety percent of the shares, and (3) has not made threats of retribution if minority shareholders withhold approval.

Unocal Corp. v. Mesa Petroleum Co.

(*Target Corporation*) v. (*Bidder*)
493 A.2d 946 (Del.1985)

BOARD MAY ACT TO OPPOSE TAKEOVER THREAT IT REASONABLY PERCEIVES TO BL HARMFUL TO THE CORPORATION

■ **INSTANT FACTS** A minority shareholder that had made a tender offer to take over a corporation sued to prevent the corporation's board of directors from defending against the takeover bid by making its own tender offer for the corporation's stock.

■ **BLACK LETTER RULE** A corporate board can oppose a takeover threat it reasonably perceives to be harmful to the corporation.

■ PROCEDURAL BASIS

Appeal of a grant of a preliminary injunction by the Delaware Court of Chancery, enjoining a self-tender offer by a corporation for its own stock.

■ FACTS

Mesa Petroleum Co. ("Mesa") (P) owned 13% of the stock of Unocal Corp. ("Unocal") (D). Mesa (P) sought to acquire the rest of Unocal's (D) stock through a two-tier, "front-loaded" tender offer. First, Mesa (P) would offer $54 a share in cash for 37 percent of the stock of Unocal (D). Once that step was completed, the rest of the publicly held shares of Unocal (D) were to be acquired in return for highly subordinated junk bonds. Following the announcement of the tender offer by Mesa (P), Unocal's (D) board, made up of eight outside directors and six inside directors, met to consider the offer. The board received a presentation from an investment banker who told them that he viewed the Mesa (P) offer as too low, given that the liquidation value of Unocal (D) was in excess of $60 per share. The investment banker also suggested a defensive strategy the board could employ if it wanted to oppose the Mesa (P) proposal. The board could authorize a self-tender by Unocal (D) for its own stock for a price between $70 and $75 a share, which would require the company to incur more debt, but the company would remain viable. Meeting separately, the eight Unocal (D) outside directors unanimously agreed to advise the board to reject the Mesa (P) offer as inadequate and that Unocal (D) should pursue a self-tender to give the shareholders a better priced alternative than the Mesa (P) proposal. The entire board then met and rejected the Mesa (P) offer, but made no decision on the self-tender defensive measure. Two days later, the board met again and heard a detailed presentation from Unocal's (D) financial and legal officers about the self-tender. The board then unanimously agreed to a self-tender offer for $72 a share. Under the plan, if Mesa (P) achieved the first step of its proposal and successfully acquired 37 percent of the Unocal (D) stock for cash, Unocal (D) would offer to buy the remaining 49 percent of its outstanding stock for an exchange of debt securities having a value of $72 a share. The board's plan excluded Mesa (P) from the terms of its offer. Mesa (P) filed suit for a preliminary injunction enjoining the Unocal (D) board from instituting its self-tender offer and challenging the right of the board to exclude Mesa (P) from the offer. The Chancery court granted a preliminary injunction to Mesa (P) and Unocal (D) appealed.

■ ISSUE

Can a corporate board oppose a takeover threat it reasonably perceived to be harmful to the corporation?

■ DECISION AND RATIONALE

(Moore J.) Yes. It is well established under Delaware law that in the acquisition of its shares, a Delaware corporation may deal selectively with its stockholders, provided the directors have not acted out of a sole or primary purpose to entrench themselves in office. The board has a fundamental duty to protect the corporate enterprise, which includes stockholders, from reasonably perceived harm, whatever its source. The business judgment rule applies in the context of a takeover. This is a presumption that in making a business decision, the directors acted on an informed basis, in good faith, and in the honest belief that the action was in the best interests of the company. A court will not substitute its judgment for the board's if the board's decision can be attributed to any rational business purpose. Thus, just like any other responsibility a corporate board has, when a board considers a pending takeover bid, it has an obligation to act in the best interests of the corporation and shareholders. In the takeover context, because of the strong possibility that the board might be acting to protect its own interests rather than the corporation's or the shareholders' interests, the board must show that it had reasonable grounds for believing a danger to corporate policy and effectiveness existed because of another person's stock ownership, before the protections of the business judgment will apply to the board's decision. They meet that burden, however, by showing good faith and reasonable investigation. Moreover, their position is greatly enhanced when they can show the approval of a board comprised of a majority of independent outside directors. Here, the Unocal (D) board, comprised of a majority of independent outside directors, were faced with a threat they reasonably viewed as a grossly inadequate coercive tender offer by Mesa (P) coupled with the threat of greenmail. The board sought to either defeat the inadequate offer or at least provide the shareholders who would otherwise have had to accept Mesa's (P) junk bonds, with more stable, senior debt securities. These purposes are valid reasons to defend against Mesa (P) as a bidder for the corporation. We find that the board's efforts to protect the Unocal (D) shareholders would be thwarted if Mesa (P) were permitted to participate in the self-tender offer. If Mesa (P) tendered its shares in the board's offer, Unocal (D) would effectively be subsidizing Mesa's (P) takeover effort. By definition. Mesa (P) could not fit within the class of shareholders being protected from its own coercive and inadequate tender offer. Reversed.

Analysis:

In this case, the Delaware Supreme Court established a two-part test to scrutinize the decision of a corporate board of directors to defend a corporate takeover. The first part of the test requires the board to show that it had reasonable grounds for believing that a threat to corporate policy or effectiveness existed. The second part of the test mandates that the defensive tactic employed by the board be reasonable in relation to the threat posed by the takeover. While the normal business judgment rule does not place the burden of proof on the board to justify its conduct, the test set out here requires the directors to justify their conduct, in a manner similar to the fairness standard applied when a director engages in a transaction in which he has a conflict of interest. Here, the court concluded that Mesa's (P) tender offer was a coercive bid that was unfair to the Unocal (D) shareholders. Under Mesa's (P) scheme, the Unocal (D) shareholders would be forced to tender their shares out of the fear that if they did not, they would be left with high-risk, junk bonds, in the second stage of the proposed merger. The court found it proper for the Unocal (D) board to act to protect such shareholders. In the court's view, the Unocal (D) board's proposed defensive measure, the self-tender offer which excluded Mesa (P), was a reasonable defense in the face of the threat posed by Mesa (P) to the other shareholders.

■ CASE VOCABULARY

BIDDER: An individual or corporation attempting to obtain control of a corporation through the use of a tender offer.

GREENMAIL: When a target corporation pays a bidder a premium in return for the bidder's shares in the target corporation and the bidder's agreement to abandon its attempt to take over the target corporation.

JUNK BOND: A bond with a very high risk of default, but which carries an extremely high rate of interest. In general, these bonds are considered to be of very low investment quality.

SELF-TENDER OFFER: A tender offer made by a corporation to its shareholders for the corporation's own stock.

TENDER OFFER: A public offer of cash, debt, stock, or some combination of the three, made to the shareholders of a target corporation for some or all of the corporation's stock, generally at a price above the current market price for the stock. Such offers are generally governed by federal securities laws.

Moran v. Household International, Inc.

(*Director*) v. (*Corporation*)
500 A.2d 1346 (Del.1985)

CORPORATE BOARD MAY EMPLOY A POISON PILL PLAN TO COUNTER A GENERAL THREAT OF A COERCIVE TAKEOVER

■ **INSTANT FACTS** A corporate director who had voted against the adoption of a "poison pill" defensive measure sued to invalidate the plan after he lost the vote 14 to 2.

■ **BLACK LETTER RULE** A board of directors can adopt a poison pill plan as a defensive measure in response to its reasonable fear of a possible future hostile takeover of the corporation.

■ PROCEDURAL BASIS

Appeal of a judgment of the Delaware Court of Chancery.

■ FACTS

The board of directors of Household International, Inc. ("Household") (D) adopted a "poison pill" plan. Under the plan, if either a bidder made a tender offer for 30 percent of Household's (D) shares and then merged with Household (D), or, a single entity or group acquired 20 percent of Household's (D) shares and then merged with Household (D), the Household (D) shareholders would have a right to purchase stock in the surviving corporation at half price. The plan was thus designed to deter a takeover of Household (D) not supported by the Household (D) board. Although John Moran ("Moran") (P1), a Household (D) director and chairman of Dyson-Kissner-Moran Corporation ("D-K-M") (P2), the largest single stockholder in Household (D), had begun discussions concerning a possible leveraged buy-out of Household (D) by D-K-M (P2), the "poison pill" plan was not adopted as a specific response to a corporate raider, but instead as a general preventative mechanism to ward off any possible future hostile takeover attempts, with which the board was generally concerned. The board approved the plan by a vote of 14 to 2. The board consisted of ten outside directors and six members of Household's (D) management. Moran (P1) was one of the two board members to vote against the plan. Following its adoption, Moran (P1) and D-K-M (P2) brought suit to invalidate the "poison pill" plan. The Delaware Chancery Court upheld the plan as a legitimate exercise of business judgment by the Household (D) board. Moran (P1) and D-K-M (P2) appealed.

■ ISSUE

Can a board of directors adopt a poison pill plan as a defensive measure in response to its reasonable fear of a possible future hostile takeover of the corporation?

■ DECISION AND RATIONALE

(McNeilly J.) Yes. In *Unocal Corp. v. Mesa Petroleum Co.* [permitting a discriminatory self-tender offer by a corporation as a defensive measure in response to a hostile tender offer by a corporate shareholder], we held that a discriminatory self-tender offer was a reasonable response by the corporate board in that case to a pending coercive and inadequate tender offer made by one of the corporation's shareholders. Here, we have a defensive mechanism adopted to ward off possible future advances and not a specific threat as occurred in *Unocal.* This difference does not result in the board of directors losing the protection of the business judgment rule. To the contrary, pre-planning for the possibility of a hostile takeover might actually reduce the chance that management will fail to exercise reasonable judgment under the pressure of a hostile bid. Moran (P1) and D-K-M (P2) contend that no provision of Delaware law authorizes a board to adopt a "poison pill" plan. They assert that, while Delaware corporate law provides for the issuance of options to purchase shares, the legislature intended this power to apply only as a device to finance the corporation and not for use as a defensive measure to a takeover bid. We disagree. Nothing in the statutes limits the right to issue such options only to the purpose of corporate financing. Without affirmative evidence showing that the legislature meant to confine the statute to corporate financing, we decline to impose such a limit on a board. Moran (P1) and D-K-M (P2) also assert that the "poison pill" plan would effectively block any hostile tender offer. Again, we disagree. The plan is not absolute. When the board is faced with a hostile tender offer, they will not be able to arbitrarily reject the offer. They will be held to the same fiduciary standards any other board of directors would be held to in deciding to adopt a defensive mechanism, the same standard they were held to in initially approving the "poison pill" plan. *Unocal* says that the board must show that it had reasonable grounds for believing a danger to corporate policy and effectiveness existed, but can do this by showing good faith and reasonable investigation. The board must also show that the defensive mechanism established was reasonable in relation to the threat posed. That proof is materially enhanced where, as here, a majority of the board favoring the proposal consisted of outside independent directors. Here, there is no claim of bad faith or that the board took its action in order to preserve its own power. Household (D) has adequately demonstrated that the adoption of the "poison pill" plan was a reaction to what it perceived to be the threat in the marketplace of coercive two-tier tender offers. The board reviewed adequate information to make its decision. Their response was reasonable. We conclude that the board receives the benefit of the business judgment rule in the adoption of this defensive measure. Affirmed.

Analysis:

This case involves a so-called "flip over poison pill" provision. In general, a "poison pill" is a device adopted by a corporation to make its stock less attractive to a potential takeover bidder. The "flip-over" variety of "poison pill" is meant to scare off potential hostile takeovers of a corporation by the threat that shareholders will be permitted to purchase stock in the surviving company after a merger with the hostile acquirer at a very reduced price. Moran (P1) argued that this mere threat would be enough to deter all potential hostile takeovers to the detriment of corporate shareholders. The court rightly recognized that, should a takeover bid be made, the board could not simply rubber stamp a veto of it, but would be required to carefully examine the bid under its general fiduciary obligations to shareholders.

■ CASE VOCABULARY

FLIP-OVER POISON PILL: A device adopted by a target (or potential target) corporation in which, in the event of a takeover of the target corporation in which the bidder merges with the target, the target's shareholders will have the right to purchase the stock of the surviving corporation at a bargain price.

POISON PILL: A device adopted by a corporation to make its stock less attractive to a potential takeover bidder. In general the idea is to make more difficult and expensive for a bidder to acquire the corporation than it would be without the existence of the device.

Quickturn Design Systems, Inc. v. Shapiro

(*Target Corporation*) v. (*Stockholder in Target*)

721 A.2d 1281 (Del.1998)

DELAWARE SUPREME COURT STRIKES DOWN NO-HAND PROVISION AS VIOLATION OF BOARD'S OBLIGATION TO MANAGE THE CORPORATION'S BUSINESS

■ **INSTANT FACTS** A hostile bidder conducting a proxy contest for control of the board of directors of a target corporation sued to invalidate a recently adopted provision of the target's "poison pill" rights plan which would have delayed the ability of a newly elected target board of directors, controlled by the hostile bidder, to cancel the "poison pill" rights plan.

■ **BLACK LETTER RULE** A defensive measure to a hostile takeover that restricts the ability of a board of directors to perform its statutory and fiduciary duties is invalid.

■ PROCEDURAL BASIS

Appeal of an order of the Delaware Court of Chancery, invalidating a delayed redemption provision to a "poison pill" rights plan.

■ FACTS

Mentor Graphics Corporation ("Mentor") (P1) made a hostile takeover bid for Quickturn Design Systems, Inc. ("Quickturn") (D) in an effort to stop certain patent litigation by Quickturn (D) against Mentor (P1). Mentor (P1) also engaged in a proxy contest, seeking to replace Quickturn's (D) board of directors. Following the Mentor (P1) tender offer, Quickturn's (D) board of directors met several times to review the bid. The board retained financial advisors to help evaluate the bid. The advisors analyzed the bid and explained to the board that the price offered by Mentor (P1) was too low given their valuation of Quickturn (D). On the basis of the advisors' report and the fact that the company was expected to quickly rebound from temporary market problems that had recently reduced its stock price, the Quickturn (D) board recommended a rejection of the offer to the Quickturn (D) shareholders. At a subsequent meeting, the Quickturn (D) board adopted a defensive measure against the hostile bid. They amended Quicktum's (D) "poison pill" rights plan to include a deferred redemption provision, under which no newly elected board could redeem the "poison pill" rights of shareholders until six months after taking office if the purpose of the redemption would be to facilitate a transaction with an "interested person," defined as someone who proposed, nominated or financially supported the election of the new directors to the board. The effect of this amendment would be to delay the ability of a newly-elected, Mentor (P1) nominated board to redeem the "poison pill" for six months. In response, Mentor (P1) and a Quickturn (D) shareholder, Howard Shapiro (P2), brought an action for declaratory and injunctive relief requiring the Quickturn (D) board to remove the defense. The Delaware Chancery Court concluded that the delayed redemption provision was a violation of the fiduciary obligations of the board to the Quickturn (D) shareholders. Quickturn (D) appealed.

■ ISSUE

Is a defensive measure to a hostile takeover that restricts the ability of a board of directors to perform its statutory and fiduciary duties invalid?

■ DECISION AND RATIONALE

(Holland J.) Yes. It is undisputed that the delayed redemption provision or "no hand provision" would prevent Mentor's (P1) slate of directors, if elected as the new board majority, from redeeming the "poison pill" rights plan for six months following their election, because a redemption would have the effect of facilitating a transaction (the tender offer) with Mentor (P1), a party that proposed, nominated, or financially supported the election of the new board. When a board takes action to resist a hostile bid for control, the defensive actions are subject to enhanced scrutiny by a court. The board must establish that it had reasonable grounds to believe a threat existed to corporate policy and effectiveness and must show that the response was proportionate in relation to the perceived threat. The Chancery Court found that the Mentor (P1) combined tender offer and proxy contest were coercive and therefore constituted a threat. However, the Chancery Court concluded that the delayed redemption provision response was not a proportionate response to the threat. We agree. One of the basic principles of Delaware corporate law is that the board of directors has the ultimate responsibility for managing the affairs of a corporation. The only way a board's power may be limited under Delaware law is through a provision in the corporation's certificate of incorporation. There was no such limitation on the board's power in this case. Here, the delayed redemption provision would prevent a newly elected board from completely discharging its fundamental management duties to the corporation and shareholders for at least six months. It restricts the board's power in an area of fundamental importance to the shareholders—negotiating a possible sale of the corporation. We therefore hold the provision invalid under our corporation statute's provision conferring upon any newly elected board the power manage and direct the corporation. No defensive measure can be sustained which would require a new board of directors to breach its fiduciary duty. We hold the delayed redemption provision to be invalid. Affirmed.

Analysis:

In *Moran v. Household International, Inc.*, 500 A.2d 1346 (Del.1985), the Delaware Supreme Court reasoned that the adoption of a "poison pill" rights plan, a defensive device adopted by a corporation to make its stock less attractive to a potential takeover bidder, was permissible in part because a hostile bidder could engage in a proxy contest, take over the board with its own new slate of directors, and eventually cancel the "poison pill." Following that case, however, several target board tried to employ so-called "dead-hand" and "no-hand provision" provisions that would prevent cancellation of the "poison pill" by anyone other than the board that had adopted the plan or would, as here, delay a new board's ability to cancel the plan. The Delaware courts have consistently invalidated such provisions. Here, the court explains that such limitations on a new board's powers are inconsistent with any board's legal obligations to manage the company in the best interests of the shareholders.

■ CASE VOCABULARY

DEAD-HAND PROVISION: A clause attached to a "poison pill" rights plan which permits only the exact board of directors who authorized the "poison pill" rights plan to cancel the plan.

NO-HAND PROVISION: A clause attached to a "poison pill" rights plan which delays the ability of new directors (i.e. those who did not authorize the "poison pill" plan) to cancel the plan.

PROXY CONTEST: A competition between groups of shareholders over the election of the directors of a corporation or over management or shareholder policy proposals. Such contests are closely regulated by the Securities and Exchange Commission.

Revlon, Inc. v. MacAndrews & Forbes Holdings, Inc.

(Target Corporation) v. *(Controlling Stockholder of Hostile Bidder)*
506 A.2d 173 (Del.1985)

ONCE A CORPORATE BOARD DECIDES A COMPANY IS "FOR SALE," THE BOARD HAS A DUTY TO MAXIMIZE THE SALE PRICE FOR THE BENEFIT OF THE SHAREHOLDERS

■ **INSTANT FACTS** A hostile bidder for a target corporation sued to enjoin certain defensive measures taken by the target's board against its bid and to enjoin a competing bid by another corporation that had been approved by the target board.

■ **BLACK LETTER RULE** Once a corporation is to be sold, the primary duty of the board of directors is to obtain the highest possible sale price for the benefit of the corporation's shareholders.

■ PROCEDURAL BASIS

Appeal of a temporary restraining order by the Delaware Court of Chancery, enjoining provisions of a merger agreement.

■ FACTS

Pantry Pride, Inc. ("Pantry Pride") approached the management of Revlon, Inc. ("Revlon") (D1) with a proposal to acquire Revlon (D1) for $45 a share. Advised by their investment bankers that the Pantry Pride offer was "grossly inadequate" due to its use of junk bond financing, the Revlon (D1) board of directors adopted a "poison pill" rights plan meant to scare off Pantry Pride's bid. Pantry Pride went ahead with a hostile bid, however, offering $47.50 cash for all Revlon (D1) common shares, subject to the recission of the "poison pill" plan by the Revlon (D1) board. The Revlon (D1) board advised the shareholders to reject the Pantry Pride offer and, as another defensive measure against Pantry Pride, made its own offer to exchange notes valued at $47.50 and preferred stock for ten million shares of Revlon (D1) common stock. The notes to be exchanged contained covenants which limited Revlon's ability to borrow, sell assets, or pay dividends unless otherwise approved by the independent members of Revlon's (D1) board. Revlon (D1) shareholders tendered their stock for this offer and the board exchanged the notes and preferred stock for ten million common shares. Subsequently, Pantry Pride made a $53 a share cash bid for Revlon (D1), which was rejected by the Revlon (D1) board. The Revlon (D1) board then authorized company management to negotiate with other parties interested in acquiring Revlon (D1). Revlon (D1) management met with a proposed "white knight," Forstmann Little & Co. ("Forstmann") (D2), that offered to do a leveraged buyout of Revlon (D1), if the Revlon (D1) board cancelled the "poison pill" plan and waived the covenants attached to the notes. Under the Forstmann (D2) proposal, each shareholder would get $56 a share. The Revlon (D1) board accepted the Forstmann (D2) proposal, but on the announcement of the acceptance of the bid, which meant that the special note covenants would be waived by the board, the market value of the notes began to fall. Noteholders then threatened litigation against Revlon (D1). Pantry Pride made another new bid, raising its cash offer to $56.25 a share, subject to the cancellation of the "poison pill" and the waiver of the special note covenants. Pantry Pride also told the Revlon (D1) board that it would continue to top any offer made by Forstmann (D2) by a slightly higher fractional bid. Given special access to Revlon (D1) financial data that was not available to Pantry Pride, Forstmann (D2) made a new bid for $57.25 a share, with several conditions attached, including: (1) a "lock-up" option to purchase two Revlon (D1) divisions at a bargain price, if another bidder were to acquire 40 percent of Revlon's (D1) shares; (2) a $25 million cancellation fee, if the deal fell through or another bidder acquired 20% of Revlon's (D1) shares; (3) a "no-shop" provision, under which Revlon (D1) would agree not to deal with any other bidder; and (4) the cancellation of the "poison pill" and special note covenants. If the Revlon (D1) board agreed to the plan, Forstmann (D2) would agree to exchange new notes for the notes the board had previously exchanged with shareholders and which had fallen in value, in an effort to raise the current value of the notes in the market. The Revlon (D1) board accepted Forstmann's (D2) proposal, reasoning that it was for a higher price than the Pantry Pride bid and that it protected the noteholders. MacAndrews & Forbes Holdings, Inc., ("MacAndrews") (P), the controlling shareholder of Pantry Pride, sought a preliminary injunction against the adoption of the "poison pill," the lock-up provision, the no-shop provision, and the cancellation fee in the Forstmann (D2) proposal, as well as against the exercise of the note covenants. Pantry Pride also raised its bid to a cash offer of $58 a share, conditioned upon the cancellation of the "poison pill," waiver of the note covenants, and the issuance of an injunction against the Forstmann (D2) lock-up option. The Delaware Chancery Court enjoined the lock-up provision, the no-shop provision, and the cancellation fee, and prohibited any transfer of Revlon (D1) assets to Forstmann (D2). The Chancery Court concluded that the Revlon (D1) directors had breached their fiduciary duty of loyalty to the shareholders by making concessions to Forstmann (D2), concerned with their liability to the noteholders, rather than with obtaining the highest sale price for the Revlon (D1) stockholders. Revlon (D1) and Forstmann (D2) appealed.

■ ISSUE

Once a corporation is to be sold, is the primary duty of the board of directors to obtain the highest possible sale price for the benefit of the corporation's shareholders?

■ DECISION AND RATIONALE

(Moore J.) Yes. Both the "poison pill" plan and Revlon's (D1) own exchange offer of notes for 10 million of its own common shares were approved after the Revlon (D1) board was advised by its investment banker that the Pantry Pride offer was "grossly inadequate" due to its use of "junk bond" financing. To that extent, the board acted with good faith and reasonable investigation. Under those circumstances, the defensive measures adopted were not unreasonable given the threat thought to be posed by Pantry Pride's bid. However, once Pantry Pride increased its offer to $53 a share, it became apparent that a break-up of the company was inevitable. The Revlon (D1) board's authorization to management to negotiate a merger or buyout with a third party was a recognition that the company was now officially "for sale." At that moment, the duty of the board changed from the preservation of Revlon (D1) as a corporate entity to the maximization of the company's value at a sale for the benefit of the stockholders. The directors' roles changed from defenders of the corporation to auctioneers charged with getting the best price for the shareholders from a sale of the company. The subsequent lock-up with Forstmann (D2) and its emphasis on shoring up the sagging market value of the notes in the face of threatened litigation by the noteholders was a response that was inconsistent with the changed duties of the directors at this point in time. The directors made the fear of litigation by the noteholders a primary concern even though their primary responsibility was to the stockholders under these circumstances. Such concern for non-stockholder interests is inappropriate when an auction among active bidders is in progress and the object is to sell the enterprise to the highest bidder. The Forstmann (D2) lock-up provision, no-shop clause, and cancellation fee are not per se illegal. Sometimes such provisions can have the benefit of enticing new bidders into an auction to make a bid and raise a price for the benefit of corporate shareholders. However, when such measures end an active auction and foreclose further bidding to the detriment of shareholders, they cannot be permitted. Market forces must be allowed to operate freely to bring the target's shareholders the best price available for their stock. Here, the Revlon (D1) board ended an active auction of the company for very little improvement in the final bid. This was done for the board's own perceived benefit and to the detriment of Revlon's (D1) shareholders. Under these circumstances, the measures were properly enjoined by the Chancery Court. Affirmed.

Analysis:

Once it is clear that a corporation will be sold, a board is not simply able to engage in defensive measures meant to protect the corporation's existence, but is under an affirmative duty to engage in action that will obtain the best sale price for the benefit of the corporation's shareholders. Here, once the Revlon (D1) board authorized its management to enter into a merger or buyout agreement with a third party as a response to the Pantry Pride bids, the board was agreeing to sell the company. At that point, its actions began to be judged under its obligation to obtain the best sale price. In this instance, the board's actions were inconsistent with its obligation. By agreeing to the lock-up provision, the no-shop clause, and the cancellation fee, the Revlon (D1) board was acting in its own interest, to the detriment of the shareholders. The board members feared personal liability to noteholders who were threatening litigation over the falling value of their notes and had negotiated with Forstmann (D2) to support the notes in return for their agreement on those provisions. The result of the board's action was to effectively end an active bidding process for the company. Pantry Pride had expressed a willingness to keep bidding higher, but only on the condition that the substantial bidding advantages and subsidies given by the board to Forstmann (D2) were stopped. By giving its "white knight," Forstmann (D2), such a substantial bidding advantage, the Revlon (D1) board hurt its shareholders' chance to get an even higher price for the company. The court rightly found this to be a violation of the board's duty to its shareholders.

■ CASE VOCABULARY

COVENANT: A provision of a contract in which one party promises or agrees to do or not do some action for the benefit of another party to the contract.

LEVERAGED BUYOUT: The acquisition of a target corporation funded largely by debt, secured by the target corporation's assets, which the acquirer hopes to pay off using the future earnings of the target corporation.

LOCK-UP PROVISION: A clause in a merger or acquisition agreement intended to protect or give advantage to one bidder over other bidders in a takeover contest. These provisions can take several forms, including an option to purchase valuable target assets at a bargain price and an option to directly purchase treasury stock of the target corporation at a reduced price.

NO-SHOP PROVISION: A clause in a merger of acquisition agreement in which the board of directors and management of the target corporation agree that they will not seek a more attractive offer for the corporation from other bidders.

WHITE KNIGHT: A bidder in a corporate takeover contest who has been solicited to bid for the target corporation by the management of the target corporation so that the target will not be acquired by a competing hostile bidder.

Paramount Communications Inc. v. QVC Network

(*Target Corporation*) v. (*Hostile Bidder*)
637 A.2d 34 (Del.1994)

DELAWARE SUPREME COURT FINDS THAT A COMPANY'S MERGER PROPOSAL WHICH WOULD HAVE CHANGED THE CONTROL OF THE COMPANY PUT THE COMPANY UP FOR SALE AND OBLIGATED THE COMPANY'S BOARD TO PURSUE THE BEST PRICE FOR THE SHAREHOLDERS

■ **INSTANT FACTS** A hostile bidder for a target corporation sued to enjoin an agreement by the target's board of directors to merge with another corporation in a transaction that would cause the corporation to change from being a company owned by an unaggregated group of unaffiliated shareholders to a company controlled by a single shareholder.

■ **BLACK LETTER RULE** When a board of directors agrees to a sale or change in control of a corporation, the board has a duty to act reasonably to seek the best value reasonably available to the shareholders.

■ PROCEDURAL BASIS

Appeal of an order of the Delaware Court of Chancery, enjoining the consummation of a merger agreement.

■ FACTS

Paramount Communications, Inc. ("Paramount") (D1) agreed to merge with Viacom Inc. ("Viacom") (D2). Under the merger agreement, control of Paramount (D1) would change after the merger from a group of unaffiliated shareholders to a controlling shareholder, Sumner Redstone, the chairman and controlling shareholder of Viacom (D2). The merger agreement contained several provisions intended to preempt a hostile bid by other companies interested in Paramount (D1). These provisions included: (1) a no-shop clause, preventing Paramount (D1) from encouraging or discussing a competing bid; (2) a termination fee, under which Viacom (D2) would receive $100 million if Paramount (D1) did not go through with the deal; and (3) a stock option lock-up provision, which granted Viacom (D2) the right to buy 19.9 percent of Paramount's (D1) stock at a bargain price. Following the announcement of the merger, QVC Network, Inc. ("QVC") (P) made a tender offer to acquire Paramount (D1) in a two-tier transaction with the initial 51 percent of Paramount's (D1) stock purchased for cash in the first step and the remaining shares converted into QVC (P) stock in the second step. The QVC (P) bid was valued at $10 a share more than the Viacom (D2) bid. Viacom (D2) and Paramount (D1) then amended their original merger agreement, raising Viacom's (D2) bid to match QVC's (P) bid. Subsequently, Viacom (D2) raised its bid to top QVC's (P) bid. QVC (P) responded by topping Viacom's (D2) bid. The Paramount (D1) board then met and voted down the QVC (P) offer, concluding on the basis of a Paramount (D1) management report that the offer had too many conditions attached to it. The board believed that it could not communicate with QVC (P) to discuss the status of the conditions of the bid because of the no-shop provision in the agreement with Viacom (D2). The only analysis of the two competing bids that the board reviewed was based on current market values of the securities involved and not on the anticipated value of the securities at the time when the shareholders would receive them. QVC (P) and certain Paramount (D1) shareholders then sought injunctive relief from the Delaware Court of Chancery preventing the Paramount (D1) merger with Viacom (D2). The Chancery Court found that

Paramount's (D1) board had violated its fiduciary duties to the company shareholders by favoring the Viacom (D2) deal over a more valuable QVC (P) offer. Paramount (D1) and Viacom (D2) appealed.

■ ISSUE

Does a board of directors have a duty to seek the transaction offering the best value reasonably available to the stockholders when it agrees to a sale or change in control of the corporation?

■ DECISION AND RATIONALE

(Veasey, C.J.) Yes. The Paramount (D1) merger with Viacom (D2) will effect a sale or change in control of Paramount (D1). Prior to the merger, control of the corporation would be vested in a fluid aggregation of unaffiliated stockholders. After the merger, however, there would be a controlling shareholder with the power to elect directors, break up the company, merge it with another company, cash out the minority, sell company assets, and greatly affect the public shareholder interests. Since the proposed merger will effect a sale or change in control, the Paramount (D1) board had one primary objective: to act reasonably to seek the transaction offering the best value reasonably available to the stockholders. In pursuing this objective the board was required to be especially diligent and adequately informed. In reviewing competing bids, the board had a duty to try to quantify the values of the competing offers and compare them. A court must examine the board's decision under an enhanced scrutiny test, which requires a determination of the adequacy of the directors' decision making process and the reasonableness of their action in light of existing circumstances. The directors have the burden of proving they were adequately informed and acted reasonably. Since a board is the corporate decision making body best equipped to make value judgments for a company, a court should merely decide if the directors made a reasonable decision, not a perfect decision. Here, the Paramount (D1) board's process, once it had decided to sell the company, was not reasonable under the circumstances. Paramount (D1) agreed to the no-shop clause, the lock-up provision, and the termination fee, all of which inhibited other, better bids for the company. Once another bid did occur, Paramount (D1) could have negotiated to remove those defensive provisions from the Viacom (D2) agreement, but did not. It should have been clear to the Paramount (D1) board that those provisions were impeding the realization of the best value possible for the shareholders. In addition, the Paramount (D1) board relied on advice from Paramount (D1) management that the QVC (P) offer was "conditional" and used the no-shop provision as a reason for not seeking more information about the deal or negotiating further with QVC (P). The final QVC (P) offer exceeded the Viacom (D2) offer by over $1 billion. This significant disparity of value cannot be justified on the basis of the directors' vision of future strategy, primarily because the control change would remove the current board's ability to continue to hold and implement a strategic vision. Additionally, the board's uninformed process deprives their claim of a strategic vision of much of its credibility. The board's initial hope for a strategic alliance with Viacom (D2) was allowed to dominate their decision making process to the point where it unreasonably caused the board to ignore opportunities to obtain significantly greater value for the shareholders of the company. Affirmed.

Analysis:

The court notes in this case that there would be a "sale or change of control" under the facts presented. Prior to the proposed Viacom (D2) deal, Paramount (D1) was owned by unaffiliated public shareholders. After such a merger, however, a single individual would control the merged corporation. For the court, this constituted a "sale" and triggered the duties of *Revlon, Inc. v. MacAndrews & Forbes Holdings, Inc.*, 506 A.2d 173 (Del.1985). Second, the court disapproved of the process by which the Paramount (D1) board reviewed the competing proposals. The Paramount (D1) board was sloppy. It did not take steps to try to get as much information about the proposals as it could. It hid behind defensive provisions in the Viacom (D2) merger agreement, which it could probably have caused Viacom (D2) to remove. For the court, the board's lack of exploration of the QVC (P) offer was unreasonable.

■ CASE VOCABULARY

TERMINATION FEE: A defensive measure in a merger agreement meant to discourage a hostile takeover bid by providing the favored merger partner with such a substantial payment of cash or property in the event the merger agreement did not go through that the target company becomes less attractive to a hostile bidder seeking to prevent the merger agreement.

Hilton Hotels Corp. v. ITT Corp.

(*Acquiring Company*) v. (*Targeted Company*)
978 F.Supp. 1342 (D.Nev.1997)

A TARGETED COMPANY MAY NOT UNREASONABLY RESTRUCTURE ITSELF

■ **INSTANT FACTS** Hilton Hotels (P), which sought to acquire ITT Corp. (D), sued to obtain an injunction precluding implementation of the targeted company's comprehensive plan.

■ **BLACK LETTER RULE** A targeted corporation's attempts to restructure itself in order to preclude an acquiring corporation from obtaining a majority on the board impermissibly restricts its shareholders' rights to vote for directors.

■ PROCEDURAL BASIS

Before the court on a motion for an injunction.

■ FACTS

Hilton Hotels Corp. (P) proposed a fifty-five-dollar-per-share tender offer for ITT's (D) stock and announced a plan to engage in a proxy contest at ITT's (D) next annual meeting. ITT (D) rejected Hilton's (P) offer, sold some of its non-core assets, and held off its annual meeting. Hilton (P) filed a motion to compel the meeting. The court determined that under Nevada law, ITT (D) had eighteen months from the last meeting to schedule the next meeting. ITT (D) announced a Comprehensive Plan to split ITT (D) into three entities: ITT Destinations, which would include the hotel and gaming business and hold ninety-three percent of the company's assets; ITT Educational Services, which would consist of the current technical schools; and ITT's European Yellow Pages Division, which would remain with the current ITT (D) as ITT World Directories. Although members of ITT's (D) current board would run ITT Destinations, the memberships would be staggered so that a third of the directors would be elected each year for a three-year term. Eighty percent of the company's shareholders were required to approve any measures repealing this provision. The Comprehensive Plan also included a poison-pill provision creating a $1.4 billion tax liability for Hilton (P) upon its successful acquisition of ITT Destinations. ITT (D) tried to implement the plan without shareholder approval. Notwithstanding the plan, Hilton (P) amended its tender offer to seventy dollars per share, but ITT (D) rejected the offer. Hilton (P) then brought an action asking the court to enjoin ITT (D) from implementing the Comprehensive Plan, holding that the ITT (D) board had breached its fiduciary duties to ITT (D) and its shareholders, and barring ITT (D) from implementing the plan without shareholder approval.

■ ISSUE

In the face of an attempted hostile takeover, may a targeted corporation eliminate its shareholders' right to elect a board of directors?

■ DECISION AND RATIONALE

(Pro, J.) No. Hilton (P) must show irreparable injury and must actually succeed on the merits of its claims to justify an injunction. A tender offer coupled with a proxy fight puts the board in a tough position. Poison pills can frustrate many hostile takeovers, but proxy fights are an effective means to circumvent them. Nevada case law does not address the issue, but Delaware case law provides some guidance. Under Delaware law, any defensive reaction to a takeover bid must be evaluated in terms of the board's overall response, the measure's justification, and the results. Shareholders need to be assured free exercise of their voting rights, and any measure that disenfranchises the shareholders is strongly suspect and can be upheld only upon compelling justification.

Implementation of a plan like the one proposed here is not generally subjected to a shareholder vote. However, this plan allows the board to adopt measures that will affect the shareholders' right to vote for the board's members. Therefore, it must be enjoined. Although Nevada law allows a board to resist changes in control, the powers granted to the board under the plan cannot be reconciled with those rights. A company's shareholders' right to vote for the board limits the board's powers, so a board must have a compelling justification for limiting that right. ITT (D) argues that its plan is better for its shareholders than the Hilton (P) offer, but "better" is not the issue. The defendant must prove that Hilton's (P) offer threatens corporate policy, and ITT (D) has failed to establish such a threat. Also, there is no proof that ITT's (D) board conducted a good faith and reasonable investigation and, although an inadequate price may present a threat, ITT (D) has not demonstrated resulting harm to the company.

Furthermore, even if Hilton's (P) offer is a threat, ITT's (D) response must be reasonable. Although a corporation may adopt a classified board structure, it cannot adopt the measure simply to prohibit shareholders from engaging in a proxy contest. Here, the timing of the Comprehensive Plan with the staggered board is suspect. The ITT (D) directors approving the plan are the same ones who would fill the positions on the ITT Destinations board. There is no justification for not seeking shareholder approval of the plan. By classifying the board, the shareholders are prevented from electing a majority of the directors at their next meeting. And finally, ITT (D) did not seek an opinion from the IRS on the effect of the split, and proper business practice requires tax issues to be investigated before embarking on a venture. The primary purpose of ITT's (D) adoption of the Comprehensive Plan is to impede the shareholders' right to vote for directors. Motion for permanent injunctive relief granted.

Analysis:

ITT's (D) reaction to Hilton's (P) bid is similar to Paramount's reaction in *Paramount Communications Inc. v. QVC Network Inc.*, 637 A.2d 34 (Del. 1994). Without fully examining the QVC bid, Paramount rejected it as inferior to its agreement with Viacom. ITT's (D) reaction here was also extreme. ITT (D) failed to make its decision in a manner such that it would be protected by the business judgment rule. Also, the court noted that ITT's (D) plan seemed to adopt some of Hilton's plan's features, serving as more evidence that Hilton's proposal had some merit that ITT (D) simply chose to overlook.

■ CASE VOCABULARY

PERMANENT INJUNCTION: An injunction granted after a final hearing on the merits. Despite its name, a permanent injunction does not necessarily last forever.

Omnicare, Inc. v. NCS Healthcare, Inc.

(*Potential Purchaser*) v. (*Corporation*)
818 A.2d 914 (Del.2003)

DEFENSIVE DEVICES IN A MERGER MUST BE REASONABLY RELATED TO A PERCEIVED THREAT

■ **INSTANT FACTS** NCS Healthcare, Inc. (D) agreed to defensive devices in a merger transaction with Genesis Health Ventures, Inc. that precluded the NCS (D) board's consideration of Omnicare, Inc.'s (P) subsequent superior offer.

■ **BLACK LETTER RULE** A proposed merger transaction that prevents the board from discharging its fiduciary duties is invalid and unenforceable.

■ PROCEDURAL BASIS

On appeal to review an undisclosed lower court order.

■ FACTS

Facing financial problems, NCS Healthcare, Inc. (D) invited Omnicare, Inc. (P) to acquire NCS (D) in a bankruptcy sale. Several months later, NCS (D) formed an independent committee of board members to explore transactions that could potentially increase its stock value, believing such action to be owed under its fiduciary duty to the corporation. Two NCS (D) directors, Sells and Osborne, served on the independent committee, but the full NCS (D) board retained authority to approve any transaction. After agreeing to explore a merger to increase stock value, independent committee members met with representatives of Genesis Health Ventures, Inc. to negotiate a merger. After some negotiation, Genesis demanded an exclusivity agreement to restrict NCS (D) from negotiating a merger with Omnicare (P). Before the exclusivity agreement was executed, however, Omnicare (P) submitted to NCS (D) a proposal for merger conditioned on the negotiation of a merger agreement. Because of the exclusivity agreement, NCS (D) did not respond to the proposal or return Omnicare's (P) calls. Instead, NCS (D) used the Omnicare (P) proposal to successfully persuade Genesis to improve the terms of its merger proposal.

Facing a deadline for approval demanded by Genesis, the NCS (D) board of directors met and determined that approval of the Genesis merger was the only reasonable alternative given uncertainties surrounding the Omnicare (P) proposal. Included in the approval were stockholder voting agreements with two NCS (D) directors, Outcalt and Shaw, to compel them to vote in favor of the merger in their capacity as stockholders rather than as directors. After executing the voting agreements, the board approved the merger agreement and resolved that it be presented to the shareholders for a vote. The merger agreement did not include a "fiduciary out," which would have provided that any term in the agreement restricting the discretion of the board did not apply if the restriction would result in a breach of fiduciary duty owed by the acquired corporation's board to the corporation or its stockholders.

Several months later, Omnicare (P) irrevocably committed itself to acquiring NCS (D) through a tender offer valued at twice the market value to be received in the Genesis merger. The terms of the Genesis merger agreement required the agreement to be submitted to a shareholder vote, even if the board no longer recommended the merger. As a result of the irrevocable Omnicare (P) offer, the NCS (D) board withdrew its recommendation to the shareholders of the Genesis merger.

■ ISSUE

Is a proposed merger transaction that prevents the board of directors of a corporation from discharging its fiduciary duties valid and enforceable?

■ DECISION AND RATIONALE

(Holland, J.) No. By statute, a board's decision to enter into and recommend a merger transaction can be final only when approved by a vote of the shareholders. Board action that effectively interferes with the shareholders' right to vote on a merger transaction creates a conflict of interest between the board's interest in protecting the merger transaction, the stockholders' statutory right to vote on the transaction, and the board's subsequent fiduciary duties after the merger agreement is executed. Accordingly, defensive devices approved by the board are valid only when they fall within the board's statutory authority and are consistent with the fiduciary duties owed to the shareholders. The Genesis merger agreement included a defensive device when Genesis insisted on the omission of an effective "fiduciary out" clause. Combined with the non-negotiable voting agreements, the fiduciary out clause and the withholding of shareholder approval stood to protect Genesis from competing suitors.

To withstand enhanced judicial scrutiny, NCS (D) must first establish "that they had reasonable grounds for believing that a danger to corporate policy and effectiveness existed," acting in good faith after conducting a reasonable investigation. NCS (D) must then demonstrate that the defensive devices were not preclusive or coercive and were within "a range of reasonable responses" to the perceived threat. A response is coercive if "it is aimed at forcing upon stockholders a management-sponsored alternative to a hostile offer." Likewise, a response is preclusive "if it deprives stockholders of the right to receive all tender offers or precludes a bidder from seeking control by fundamentally restricting proxy contests or otherwise." Here, the defensive devices were both coercive and preclusive. By agreeing to the devices, NCS (D) effectively deprived the shareholders of their right to vote on the merger because the voting agreements gave Genesis all the voting strength needed to gain shareholder approval. Similarly, the defensive devices precluded shareholder consideration of the Omnicare (P) transaction because it was mathematically impossible to gain majority approval. The devices were designed to coerce the shareholders into accepting the Genesis transaction and preclude the consideration of any other offer. They were not within the range of reasonable responses to the threat of losing the Genesis transaction and are unenforceable.

Not only do the devices fail to survive enhanced judicial scrutiny because they are coercive and preclusive, but they also fail because they prevented the board from fulfilling its fiduciary duties to the minority shareholders when Omnicare (P) presented a superior offer. A proposed merger transaction that prevents the board from discharging its fiduciary duties is invalid and unenforceable. Because the irrevocable voting agreements with the majority shareholders foreclosed an effective shareholder vote on the Genesis transaction, the board owed a fiduciary duty to protect the interests of minority shareholders. By failing to include a fiduciary out clause, the board "disabled itself from exercising its own fiduciary obligations at a time when the board's own judgment is most important, i.e. receipt of a subsequent superior offer." The board is free to extend defensive measures to protect a merger transaction, but they must be reasonable under the circumstances and may not limit the board's fiduciary duties. Because the transaction, through the defensive devices employed, is inconsistent with the board's fiduciary duties to the shareholders, the merger agreement and voting agreements are invalid an unenforceable.

■ DISSENT

(Veasey, C.J.) In determining the validity of the board's defensive devices, the court should not consider them in a vacuum, but must consider the entire context from which they arose. NCS (D) had sought potential merger partners for some time before the Genesis offer and had received only the initial bid from Omnicare (P). Because that bid would have resulted in insufficient returns on the value of the shareholders' stock and little funds to pay off debts, NCS (D) rejected that proposal. The Genesis offer, in contrast, ensured the shareholders some return on their investments and full repayment of all debts. The defensive devices were required to protect Genesis in the event of a superior offer. Given that Omnicare (P) had outbid Genesis at the eleventh hour on a prior merger, these demands were not unreasonable to enable Genesis to protect the time and effort it invested in the merger. As predicted, Omnicare (P) indeed made an eleventh-hour superior offer. The offer, however, was conditional on

Omnicare's (P) due diligence examination and would have left NCS (D) without a merger partner if it did not go forward. Balancing these considerations, NCS (D) opted as a matter of business judgment to forgo the conditional superior offer in the best interests of the corporation and the shareholders. The rule the court adopts does not take into account such context and is unwise in application.

Likewise, there is nothing coercive about the defensive devices. The two majority shareholders agreeing to the irrevocable voting agreements did so after an independent review of the merits of the transaction. Minority stockholders are on notice that the majority shareholders, who necessarily always have sufficient voting strength to render a shareholder vote meaningless, will carry a shareholder vote on any issue. The transaction was neither coercive nor preclusive. The proportionality requirement of judicial scrutiny requires the court to consider the contextual history underlying the board action. Here, the board's decision to accept the only certain bid that will satisfy the creditors and benefit the stockholders was reasonable and proportionate to the threat of losing the Genesis merger.

Analysis:

It is clear from the court's decision that the fiduciary duties owed to the shareholders are paramount to any defensive device included in a merger agreement. The requirement of a fiduciary out clause often places a board of directors in a difficult position. While the benefit of hindsight may indicate that a board's decision was ultimately not in the shareholders' best interests, its business judgment must be afforded some deference.

■ CASE VOCABULARY

FIDUCIARY: One who owes another the duties of good faith, trust, confidence, and candor.

CHAPTER THIRTEEN

Distributions to Shareholders

Klang v. Smith's Food & Drug Centers, Inc.

Instant Facts: Stockholders in the defendant's corporation sued, claiming that the corporation's repurchase of its shares caused an impairment of capital.

Black Letter Rule: A corporation may not repurchase its shares if, in so doing, it would cause an impairment of capital, unless expressly authorized by statute.

Klang v. Smith's Food & Drug Centers, Inc.

(*Shareholder*) v. (*Grocery Store*)

702 A.2d 150 (Del.1997)

A CORPORATION MAY REPURCHASE OR REDEEM ITS OWN SHARES ONLY OUT OF "SURPLUS"

■ **INSTANT FACTS** Stockholders in the defendant's corporation sued, claiming that the corporation's repurchase of its shares caused an impairment of capital.

■ **BLACK LETTER RULE** A corporation may not repurchase its shares if, in so doing, it would cause an impairment of capital, unless expressly authorized by statute.

■ PROCEDURAL BASIS

Appeal from the Court of Chancery's Memorandum Opinion dismissing the plaintiff's class action suit.

■ FACTS

Smith's Food & Drug Centers, Inc. ("SFD") (D) owns and operates a chain of supermarkets in the Southwestern United States. Jeffrey Smith, the CEO, began to entertain suitors with an interest in acquiring SFD (D). At the time, and until the transactions at issue, Mr. Smith and his family held common and preferred stock constituting 62.1% voting control of SFD (D). Klang (P) and the class he purports to represent are holders of common stock in SFD (D). Two years later, SFD (D) entered into an agreement with The Yucaipa Companies ("Yucaipa"), a California partnership also active in the supermarket industry. Under the agreement, Smitty's Supermarkets, a wholly-owned subsidiary of Yucaipa was to merge into Cactus Acquisition, Inc., a subsidiary of SFD (D), in exchange for which SFD (D) would deliver over 3 million newly-issued shares of SFD (D) common stock. Additionally, SFD was to undertake a recapitalization, assume a sizable amount of new debt, retire old debt, and offer to repurchase up to fifty percent of its outstanding shares (other than those issued to Yucaipa) for $36 per share. Finally, SFD (D) was to repurchase 3 million shares of preferred stock from Mr. Smith and his family. SFD (D) hired an investment firm to examine the transactions and render a solvency opinion. The firm issued a report to the SFD (D) Board replete with assurances that the transactions would not endanger SFD's (D) solvency, and would not impair SFD's (D) capital in statutory violation. In reliance on this opinion, SFD's (D) Board determined there existed sufficient surplus to consummate the transactions, and enacted a resolution proclaiming as much. SFD's (D) stockholders voted to approve the transactions, which closed on that day. The self-tender offer was over-subscribed [oops], so SFD (D) repurchased fully fifty percent of its shares at the offering price of $36 per share.

■ ISSUE

Did Smith's (D) stock repurchases violate the statutory prohibition against the impairment of capital?

■ DECISION AND RATIONALE

(Veasey, C.J.) No. A corporation may not repurchase its shares if, in so doing, it would cause an impairment of capital, unless expressly authorized by statute. A repurchase impairs capital if the funds used in the repurchase exceed the amount of the corporation's "surplus." Klang (P) asked the Court of Chancery to rescind the transactions SFD (D) made as violative of 8 Del. C. Section 160. First, he contends that SFD's balance sheets constitute conclusive evidence of capital impairment. Second, he suggests that even allowing the Board to go behind the balance sheet to calculate surplus does not save the transactions from violating Section 160. We hold that each of these claims is without merit. Klang (P) argues that the negative net worth that appeared on SFD's (D) books following the repurchase compels us to find a violation of Section 160. A balance sheet the SFD (D) Board issued shortly after the transactions confirmed that the merger and self-tender offer resulted in a deficit to surplus on SFD's (D) books of more than $100 million. SFD (D) does not dispute that the books showed a negative net worth in the wake of the transactions, but argue that corporations should have the presumptive right to revalue assets and liabilities to comply with Section 160. We understand that the books of a corporation do not necessarily reflect the current values of its assets and liabilities. It is unrealistic to hold that a corporation is bound by its balance sheets for purposes of determining compliance with Section 160. Accordingly we adhere to the principles allowing corporations to revalue properly its assets and liabilities to show a surplus and thus conform to the statute. Klang (P) also contends that the SFD Board was not entitled to rely on the solvency opinion of the investment firm, which showed that the transactions would not impair SFD's (D) capital given a revaluation of corporate assets. The argument is that the methods that underlay the solvency opinion were inappropriate as a matter of law because they failed to take into account all of SFD's (D) assets and liabilities. In fact, Klang (P) has misunderstood the investment firm's methods. The statute simply defines "net assets" in the course of defining "surplus." It does not mandate a "facts and figures balancing of assets and liabilities" to determine by what amount, if any, total assets exceeds total liabilities. The statute is merely definitional. Thus we are satisfied that the investment firm's opinion adequately took into account all of SFD's (D) assets and liabilities. We hold that, on this record, the Court of Chancery was correct in finding that there was no impairment of capital and there were no disclosure violations. Accordingly, the judgment of the Court of Chancery is affirmed.

Analysis:

No corporation may repurchase or redeem its own shares except out of surplus, as statutorily defined, or except as expressly authorized by provisions of the applicable statute. Balance sheets are not, however, conclusive indicators of surplus or a lack thereof. Corporations may revalue assets to show surplus, but perfection in that process is not required. Directors have reasonable latitude to depart from the balance sheet to calculate surplus, so long as they evaluate assets and liabilities in good faith, on the basis of acceptable data, and by methods that they reasonably believe reflect present values, and arrive at a determination of the surplus that is not so far off the mark as to constitute actual or constructive fraud. It is helpful in this case to recall the purpose behind Section 160. The General Assembly enacted the statute to prevent boards from draining corporations of assets to the detriment of creditors and the long-term health of the corporation. That a corporation has not yet realized or reflected on its balance sheet the appreciation of assets is irrelevant to this concern. Regardless of what a balance sheet that has not been updated may show, an actual, though unrealized, appreciation reflects real economic value that the corporation may borrow against or that creditors may claim or levy upon. Allowing corporations to revalue assets and liabilities to reflect current realities complies with the statute and serves well the policies behind this statute.

■ CASE VOCABULARY

BALANCE SHEET: Financial statement evaluating assets and liabilities.

CAPITAL IMPAIRMENT STATUTE: Focuses on whether the corporation's assets exceed its liabilities plus its capital

EN BANC: By the full court; a decision whereby the entire panel of judges hears the case.

PAR VALUE: The expected sale price of the share of the corporation's stock.

SURPLUS: The excess of net assets over the par value of the corporation's issued stock.

CHAPTER FOURTEEN

The Public Distribution of Securities

Reves v. Ernst & Young

Instant Facts: A Co–Op sold over $10 million in demand notes under the guise of an "Investment Program," and subsequently filed bankruptcy.

Black Letter Rule: A note is presumed to be a "security," and that presumption may be rebutted only by a showing that the note bears a strong resemblance to one of the enumerated categories of instrument.

Securities and Exchange Commission v. Edwards

Instant Facts: The SEC (P) filed a civil action against Edwards (D) for violations of federal securities law related to an investment scheme promising a fixed rate of return.

Black Letter Rule: An investment scheme promising a fixed rate of return can be an investment contract subject to federal securities law.

S.E.C. v. Ralston Purina Co.

Instant Facts: Ralston (D) sold stock to employees without registration, claiming a private offering exemption to the registration requirement of the Securities Act of 1933.

Black Letter Rule: An offering to those shown to not need the protection of the Act is a transaction "not involving any public offering," and thus, is exempt from the registration requirements.

Escott v. Barchris Constr. Corp.

Instant Facts: Action by purchasers of convertible debentures of a construction company, alleging that the registration statement filed contained material false statements and omissions.

Black Letter Rule: To sustain the affirmative defense of due diligence, one must show that as regards any part of the registration statement not purporting to be made on the authority of an expert, he had, after reasonable investigation, reasonable ground to believe and did believe, at the time that such part of the registration statement became effective, that the statements therein were true and that there was no omission to state a material fact required to be stated therein or necessary to make the statements not misleading.

Reves v. Ernst & Young

(*Co-Op Investors*) v. (*Accountants*)

494 U.S. 56, 110 S. Ct. 945, 108 L.Ed.2d 47 (1990)

DEMAND NOTES SOLD AS INVESTMENTS ARE CONSIDERED "SECURITIES" WITHIN THE MEANING OF THE 1934 SECURITIES ACT

■ **INSTANT FACTS** A Co-Op sold over $10 million in demand notes under the guise of an "Investment Program," and subsequently filed bankruptcy.

■ **BLACK LETTER RULE** A note is presumed to be a "security," and that presumption may be rebutted only by a showing that the note bears a strong resemblance to one of the enumerated categories of instrument.

■ PROCEDURAL BASIS

Certiorari granted after the Court of Appeals reversed the trial court's judgment for the plaintiff.

■ FACTS

The Farmer's Cooperative of Arkansas and Oklahoma is an agricultural co-op that sold promissory notes payable on demand by the holder, in order to raise money to support its general business operations. Although the notes were uncollateralized and uninsured, they paid a high variable rate of interest that was adjusted monthly to keep it higher than the rate paid by local financial institutions. The Co-Op offered the notes to both members and non-members, marketing the scheme as an "Investment Program." The Co-Op subsequently filed for bankruptcy and, at the time of the filing, over 1,600 people held notes worth a total of $10 million [perfect timing!]. After the Co-Op filed for bankruptcy, Reves (P) and others, a class of holders of the notes, filed suit against Arthur Young & Co., the firm that had audited the Co-Op's financial statements (and the predecessor to Ernst & Young (D)). Reves (P) alleged, inter alia, that Arthur Young (D) had intentionally failed to follow generally accepted accounting principles in its audit, specifically with respect to the valuation of one of the Co-Op's major assets, a gasohol plant. Reves (P) claimed that Arthur Young (D) violated these principles in an effort to inflate the assets and net worth of the Co-Op, and that had Arthur Young (D) properly treated the plant in its audits, Reves (P) and the others would not have purchased demand notes because the Co-Op's insolvency would have been apparent. On the basis of these allegations, Reves (P) claimed that Arthur Young (D) had violated the antifraud provisions of the 1934 Securities Act as well as Arkansas' securities laws. At trial, Reves (P) and the others were awarded a $6.1 million judgment. Arthur Young (D) appealed, claiming that the demand notes were not "securities" under either the 1934 Act or Arkansas law, and that the statutes' antifraud provisions therefore did not apply. A panel of the Eighth Circuit, agreeing with Arthur Young (D), reversed the trial court. This Court then granted certiorari to address the federal issue.

■ ISSUE

Are demand notes sold as investments considered "securities" within the meaning of the Securities Act?

■ DECISION AND RATIONALE

(Marshall, J.) Yes. A commitment to an examination of the economic realities of a transaction does not necessarily entail a case-by-case analysis of every instrument. Some instruments are obviously within the class Congress intended to regulate because they are by their nature investments. In Landreth Timber Co. v. Landreth, we held that an instrument bearing the name "stock" that, among other things, is negotiable, offers the possibility of capital appreciation, and carries the right to dividends contingent on the profits of a business enterprise is plainly within the class of instruments Congress intended the securities law to cover. We made clear in *Landreth Timber* that stock was a special case, explicitly limiting our holding to that sort of instrument. Although we refused finally to rule out a similar per se rule for notes, we intimated that such a rule would be unjustified. Unlike "stock," we said, "note" may now be viewed as a relatively broad term that encompasses instruments with widely varying characteristics, depending on whether issued in a consumer context, as commercial paper, or in some other investment context. Thus the phrase "any note" should not be interpreted to mean literally "any mote," but must be understood against the backdrop of what Congress was attempting to accomplish in enacting the Securities Acts. Because the *Landreth Timber* formula cannot sensibly be applied to notes, some other principle must be developed to define the term "note." The Second Circuit's "family resemblance" approach begins with the presumption that any note with a term of more than nine months is a "security." Recognizing that not all notes are securities, however, the Second Circuit has also devised a list of notes that it has decided are obviously not securities. Accordingly, the "family resemblance" test permits an issuer to rebut the presumption that a note is a security if it can show that the note in question bears a family resemblance to an item on the judicially crafted list of exceptions, or convinces the court to add a new instrument to the list. Because we think the family resemblance test provides the most promising framework for analysis, we adopt it. We thus begin with the presumption that every note is a security, and also recognize that this presumption is not irrebuttable. First, we examine the transaction to assess the motivations that would prompt a reasonable seller and buyer to enter into it. If the seller's purpose is to raise money for the general use of a business enterprise or to finance substantial investments and the buyer is interested primarily in the profit the note is expected to generate, the instrument is likely to be a "security." If the note is exchanged to facilitate the purchase and sale of a minor asset or consumer good, to correct for the seller's cash-flow difficulties, or to advance some other commercial or consumer purpose, on the other hand, the note is less sensibly described as a "security." Second, we examine the plan of distribution of the instrument to determine whether it is an instrument in which there is common trading for speculation or investment. Third, we examine the reasonable expectations of the investing public: The Court will consider instruments to be "securities" on the basis of such public expectations, even where an economic analysis of the circumstances of the particular transaction might suggest that the instruments are not "securities" as used in that transaction. Finally, we examine whether some factor such as the existence of another regulatory scheme significantly reduces the risk of the instrument, thereby rendering application of the Securities Acts unnecessary. We conclude, then, that in determining whether an instrument denominated a "note" is a "security," courts are to apply the version of the "family resemblance" test that we have articulated here: a note is presumed to be a "security," and that presumption may be rebutted only by a showing that the note bears a strong resemblance (in terms of the four factors we have identified) to one of the enumerated categories of instrument. If an instrument is not sufficiently similar to an item on the list, the decision whether another category should be added is to be made by examining the same factors. Applying the family resemblance approach to this case, we have little difficulty in concluding that the notes at issue here are "securities." The Co-Op sold the notes in an effort to raise capital for its general business operations, and purchasers bought them in order to earn a profit in the form of interest. From both sides, then, the transaction is most naturally conceived as an investment in a business enterprise rather than as a purely commercial or consumer transaction. As to the plan of distribution, the Co-Op offered and sold the notes over an extended period to a broad segment of the public, and that is all we have held to be necessary to establish the requisite "common trading" in an instrument. The third factor—the public's reasonable perceptions - also supports a finding that the notes in this case are "securities." We have consistently identified the fundamental essence of a "security" to be its character as an "investment." The advertisements for the notes here characterized them as "investments," and there were no countervailing factors that would have led a reasonable person to question this characterization. Finally, we find no risk-reducing factor to suggest that these instruments are not in fact securities. The notes are uncollateralized and uninsured, and would escape federal regulation entirely if the Acts were held not to apply. We therefore hold that the notes at issue here fall under the "note" category of instruments that are "securities" under the 1933 and 1934

Securities Acts. We also conclude that these demand notes do not fall within the exclusion for short-term notes. Accordingly, we reverse the judgment of the Court of Appeals and remand the case for further proceedings consistent with this opinion.

Analysis:

The fundamental purpose undergirding the Securities Acts is to eliminate serious abuses in a largely unregulated securities market. In defining the scope of the market that it wished to regulate, Congress painted with a broad brush. It recognized the virtually limitless scope of human ingenuity, especially in the creation of countless and variable schemes devised by those who seek the use of the money of others on the promise of profits. It determined that the best way to achieve its goal of protecting investors was to define the term "security" in sufficiently broad and general terms so as to include within that definition the many types of instruments that in the commercial world fall within the ordinary concept of a security. Congress therefore enacted a definition of "security" sufficiently broad to encompass virtually any instrument that might be sold as an investment. Congress did not, however, intend to provide a broad federal remedy for all fraud. Accordingly, the task has fallen to the Securities Exchange Commission and the federal courts to decide which of the myriad financial transactions in our society come within the coverage of these statutes.

■ CASE VOCABULARY

CERTIORARI: The means of gaining appellate review.

DEMAND NOTES: An instrument payable immediately upon presentation.

INTER ALIA: Among other things.

PER SE: Not requiring extraneous evidence or support to establish.

SECURITIES ACTS: Two major federal statutes regulating the issuing of and market trading in corporate securities.

Securities and Exchange Commission v. Edwards

(*Federal Agency*) v. (*Securities Laws Violator*)
540 U.S. 389, 124 S. Ct. 892 (2004)

"SECURITIES" IS BROADLY DEFINED UNDER THE FEDERAL SECURITIES LAWS

■ **INSTANT FACTS** The SEC (P) filed a civil action against Edwards (D) for violations of federal securities law related to an investment scheme promising a fixed rate of return.

■ **BLACK LETTER RULE** An investment scheme promising a fixed rate of return can be an investment contract subject to federal securities law.

■ PROCEDURAL BASIS

Certiorari to review a decision of a federal court of appeals reversing a judgment for the plaintiff.

■ FACTS

Edwards (D) was the chairman, chief executive officer, and sole shareholder of ETS Payphones, Inc. ETS sold payphones to the public in a package including a site lease, a five-year leaseback and management agreement, and a buy-back agreement. In return for their $7000 investment, investors were paid $82 per month and were guaranteed a full refund of their initial investment at the end of the lease term or at the earlier request of the investor. Due to insufficient revenue, ETS was unable to refund all investments and filed for bankruptcy. The SEC (P) filed a civil action against Edwards (D) for violations of the Securities Act of 1933 and Securities Exchange Act of 1934, including various registration and antifraud provisions. The district court concluded that the scheme constituted an "investment contract" within the meaning of federal securities laws. A federal court of appeals reversed, holding that the scheme did not constitute an investment contract because it offered a fixed rate of return and its success did not result "solely from the efforts of others."

■ ISSUE

Is a moneymaking scheme excluded from the meaning of "investment contract" simply because the scheme offered a contractual entitlement to a fixed, rather than variable, return?

■ DECISION AND RATIONALE

(O'Connor, J.) No. To accomplish its purpose of regulating investments, Congress broadly defined "security" to include "any instrument that might be sold as an investment." "Security" is defined as "any note, stock, treasury stock, security feature, bond, debenture, . . . investment contract, . . . [or any] instrument commonly known as a 'security.' " To determine whether a scheme constitutes an investment contract, courts look to whether the investment is expected to yield profits "solely from the efforts of others."

Because of the broad application of federal securities law, there is no basis to treat investments with a fixed rate of return differently from those with variable returns. Investments promising fixed returns are more attractive to the public and are therefore more susceptible to fraud and deception. Similarly, the scheme is no less an investment contract because the investors have bargained for a return on their investment. The bargain indicates the investors' expectations that their return will be derived solely from the efforts of others. "[A]n investment scheme promising a fixed rate of return can be an 'investment contract' and thus a 'security' subject to the federal securities laws." Reversed and remanded.

Analysis:

With the Court's broad interpretation of the term "security," many different transactions have been deemed to fall under federal securities laws. Such things as viatical settlements, promissory notes, and other transactions of similar substance have been considered securities implicating federal registration requirements and procedural protections. The broad application of the term indicates growing judicial awareness of securities fraud and is designed to enforce Congress's intent in enacting the laws.

S.E.C. v. Ralston Purina Co.

(*Government Agency*) v. (*Stock Selling Company*)
346 U.S. 119, 73 S.Ct. 981, 97 L.Ed. 1494 (1953)

STOCK SALE TRANSACTIONS NOT INVOLVING ANY PUBLIC OFFERING ARE EXEMPT FROM THE REGISTRATION REQUIREMENTS OF THE SECURITIES ACT OF 1933

■ **INSTANT FACTS** Ralston (D) sold stock to employees without registration, claiming a private offering exemption to the registration requirement of the Securities Act of 1933.

■ **BLACK LETTER RULE** An offering to those shown to not need the protection of the Act is a transaction "not involving any public offering," and thus, is exempt from the registration requirements.

■ PROCEDURAL BASIS

Certiorari granted in response to the Court of Appeals' affirmance of the District Court's dismissal of the complaint.

■ FACTS

Ralston Purina (D) has processing and distribution facilities scattered throughout the United States and Canada, staffed by about 7,000 employees [including cats and dogs]. The company has a policy of encouraging stock ownership among its employees, and has made authorized but unissued common shares available to some of them. During the period covered by the record in this case, Ralston Purina (D) sold nearly $2 million of stock to employees without registration and in so doing made use of the mails. In each of these years, a corporate resolution authorized the sale of common stock to employees who, without any solicitation by the company, inquire as to how to purchase stock in the company. A memorandum was issued to branch and store managers after the resolution was adopted, advising that the only employees to whom the stock would be available were those who took the initiative and are interested in buying stock at present market prices. The S.E.C. (P) brought a complaint under the Securities Act of 1933 seeking to enjoin Ralston Purina's (D) unregistered offerings. Ralston Purina (D) claims the offerings were exempt from registration, as the transactions did not involve any "public offering." The company bottoms its exemption claim on the classification of all offerees as "key employees" in its organization, thus it is a private offering. The District Court agreed with Ralston Purina (D), held the exemption applicable and dismissed the suit. The Court of Appeals affirmed. The question has arisen many times since the Act was passed, and an apparent need to define the scope of the private offering exemption prompted certiorari.

■ ISSUE

Are a corporation's offerings of treasury stock to its "key employees" within the exemption from the registration requirements of the Securities Act of 1933?

■ DECISION AND RATIONALE

(Clark, J.) No. Section 4(1) of the Securities Act of 1933 exempts "transactions by an issuer not involving any public offering" from the registration requirements of Section 5 of the Act. We must decide whether Ralston Purina's (D) offerings of treasury stock to its "key employees" are within this exemption. The problem was first dealt with in Section 4(1) of the House Bill, H.R. 5480, which exempted "transactions by an issuer not with or through an underwriter." The bill, as reported by the House Committee, added "and not involving any public offering." This was thought to be one of those transactions "where there is no practical need for the bill's application or where the public benefits are too remote." The exemption as thus delimited became law. It assumed its present shape with the deletion of "not with or through an underwriter" by Section 203(a) of the Securities Exchange Act of 1934, a change regarded as superfluous language. Decisions under comparable exemptions in the English Companies Acts and state "blue sky" laws, the statutory antecedents of federal securities legislation, have made one thing clear—to be public, an offer need not be open to the whole world. Therefore, we conclude that an offering to those shown to not need the protection of the Act is a transaction "not involving any public offering," and thus, is exempt from the registration requirements. To determine the distinction between "public" and "private" in any particular context, it is essential to examine the circumstances under which the distinction is sought to be established and to consider the purposes sought to be achieved by such distinction. The purpose of the statute is to protect investors. The participants in employee stock investment plans may be in as great a need of the protection afforded by availability of information concerning the issuer for which they work as are most other members of the public. Once it is seen that the exemption question turns on the knowledge of the offerees, the focus of the inquiry should be on the need of the offerees for the protections afforded by registration. The employees here were not shown to have access to the kind of information which registration would disclose. The obvious opportunities for pressure and imposition make it advisable that they be entitled to compliance with Section 5 of the Securities Act. Reversed.

Analysis:

The Securities Act nowhere defines the scope of Section 4(1)'s private offering exemption. Nor is the legislative history of much help in staking out its boundaries. The design of the statute is to protect investors by promoting full disclosure of information thought necessary to informed investment decisions. Since exempt transactions are those as to which there is no practical need for the bill's application, the applicability of the Securities Act should turn on whether the particular class of persons affected needs the protection of the Act. Thus, an offering to those who are shown to be able to fend for themselves is a transaction "not involving any public offering." Some employee offerings may come within the exemption such as one made to executive personnel who, because of their position, have access to the same kind of information that the Act would make available in the form of a registration statement. Absent such a showing of special circumstances, employees are just as much members of the investing "public" as any of their neighbors in the community. Since the employees who were made the offer to purchase Ralston Purina's (D) stock could not be shown to have had access to any of the kind of information registration would have provided, the Court was correct in deciding that they were not able to fend for themselves, and thus these offering should have been registered.

■ CASE VOCABULARY

"BLUE SKY" LAWS: Regulate the sales of corporate securities through investment companies.

ENJOIN: To suspend or refrain another from doing a certain act.

PRIVATE OFFERING: Any sale of securities in a corporation not subject to registration requirements.

REGISTRATION: Document describing the securities offered which must disclose, in detail, information on the nature of the business, accounting statements, identity of management and key stockholders, and the purpose of the offering, including the use to be made of profits.

TREASURY STOCK: Common or preferred stock issued by a company and later reacquired by it; earns no dividends and has no vote in company affairs.

Escott v BarChris Constr. Corp.

(*Debentures Purchaser*) v. (*Bowling Alley Builder*)

283 F.Supp. 643 (S.D.N.Y.1968)

THE AFFIRMATIVE DEFENSE OF DUE DILIGENCE REQUIRES REASONABLE INVESTIGATION

■ **INSTANT FACTS** Action by purchasers of convertible debentures of a construction company, alleging that the registration statement filed contained material false statements and omissions.

■ **BLACK LETTER RULE** To sustain the affirmative defense of due diligence, one must show that as regards any part of the registration statement not purporting to be made on the authority of an expert, he had, after reasonable investigation, reasonable ground to believe and did believe, at the time that such part of the registration statement became effective, that the statements therein were true and that there was no omission to state a material fact required to be stated therein or necessary to make the statements not misleading.

■ PROCEDURAL BASIS

Original action brought under Section 11 of the Securities Act of 1933 for material false statements and material omissions.

■ FACTS

BarChris (D) was engaged primarily in the construction of bowling alleys. This was an outgrowth of a business started as a partnership by Vitolo and Pugliese in 1946. BarChris's (D) sales increased dramatically from 1956 to 1960, and the business far exceeded the managerial capacity of its founders [not the sharpest crayons in the box]. In general, BarChris's (D) method of operation was to enter into a contract with a customer, receive from him at that time a comparatively small down payment on the purchase price, and proceed to construct and equip the bowling alley. When the work was finished and the building delivered, the customer paid the balance of the contract price in notes, payable in installments over a period of years. BarChris (D) discounted these notes with a factor and received part of their face amount in cash. The factor held back part as a reserve. In 1960 BarChris (D) began a practice which has been referred to as the "alternative method of financing." In substance this was a sale and leaseback arrangement which amounted to constructing and installing the equipment in a building, and then selling the interior to a factor, James Talcott Inc., who would pay BarChris (D) the full contract price therefor. The factor then proceeded to lease the interior either directly to BarChris's (D) customer or back to a subsidiary of BarChris (D). In the latter case, the subsidiary in turn would lease it to the customer. Under either financing method, BarChris (D) was compelled to expend considerable sums in defraying the cost of construction before it received reimbursement. As a consequence, BarChris (D) was in constant need of cash to finance its operations, a need which grew more pressing as operations expanded [so many bowlers, so few alleys]. In December 1959, BarChris sold 560,000 shares of common stock to the public at $3.00 per share. The issue was underwritten by Peter Morgan & Company (D), one of the present defendants, and was registered and filed with the S.E.C. By early 1961, BarChris (D) needed additional working capital. The proceeds of the sale of the debentures involved in this action were to be devoted, in part at least, to fill that need. Debentures are financial obligations of a corporation which are bought and sold as investments. The registration statement of the debentures, in preliminary form, was filed with the S.E.C. on March 30, 1961. A first amendment was filed on May 11 and a second on May 16. The closing of the financing took place on May 24, and on that day BarChris (D) received the net proceeds of the financing. By that time, BarChris (D) had begun experiencing difficulties in collecting amounts due from some of its customers, and as time went on those difficulties increased [uh,oh]. Some of them were in arrears in payments due to factors on their discounted notes. Although BarChris (D) continued to build alleys in 1961 and 1962, it became increasingly apparent that the industry was overbuilt. Operators of alleys, often inadequately financed, began to fail. BarChris (D) made an attempt to raise more money by selling more common stock. It filed a registration statement for the stock issue with the S.E.C. which it later withdrew. In October 1962, BarChris came to the end of the road and filed a petition for an arrangement under Chapter XI of the Bankruptcy Act. BarChris (D) defaulted in the payment of the interest due on the debentures on November 1, 1962. It later became clear that BarChris (D) had made various false statements and omissions in its 1961 debenture registration statement. BarChris (D) had overstated its sales by over a half million dollars, and its net operating income by over a quarter of a million dollars. It overstated its assets by over a half million dollars and understated it liabilities by over a half million dollars. BarChris (D) overstated its backlog by almost $4.5 million, and failed to disclose almost a half million dollars in officers' loans outstanding and unpaid. BarChris (D) also failed to disclose $1,160,000 use of proceeds, and over $1.35 million in customers' delinquencies for which BarChris is potentially liable. BarChris and the other defendants raised the affirmative defense of due diligence to the Section 11 action. Due diligence refers to one's attention to the matter at hand which is required to prevent liability. Section 11 requires one to show that as regards any part of the registration statement not purporting to be made on the authority of an expert, he had, after reasonable investigation, reasonable ground to believe and did believe, at the time that such part of the registration statement became effective, that the statements therein were true and that there was no omission to state a material fact required to be stated therein or necessary to make the statements not misleading. "Reasonable investigation," according to Section 11, is the standard of reasonableness required of a prudent man in the management of his own property.

■ ISSUE

Did the registration statement contain false statements of material facts, or did it omit to state material facts which should have been stated in order to prevent it from being misleading, and, if so, have the defendants established their affirmative defenses?

■ DECISION AND RATIONALE

(McLean, D.J.) Yes and No. It is a prerequisite to liability under Section 11 of the Act that the fact which is falsely stated in a registration statement, or the fact that is omitted when it should have been stated to avoid being misleading, be "material." I find that several misstatements and omissions in the debenture registration statement were material within the meaning of the Act. Thus the next question is whether each defendant has sustained their affirmative defense of due diligence in the matter. To sustain the affirmative defense of due diligence, one must show that as regards any part of the registration statement not purporting to be made on the authority of an expert, he had, after reasonable investigation, reasonable ground to believe and did believe, at the time that such part of the registration statement became effective, that the statements therein were true and that there was no omission to state a material fact required to be stated therein or necessary to make the statements not misleading. Each claims that (1) as to the part of the registration statement purporting to be made on the authority of an expert, he had no reasonable ground to believe and did not believe that there were any untrue statements or material omissions, and (2) as to the other parts of the registration statement, he made a reasonable investigation, as a result of which he had reasonable ground to believe and did believe that the registration statement was true and that no material fact was omitted. I will address each defendant's position separately. To begin with, these defenses are not available to BarChris (D), as the issuer. Russo, the chief executive officer of BarChris (D), acted on BarChris's (D) behalf in making the financing agreements with Talcott and he handled the negotiations with Talcott. In short, Russo knew all the relevant facts. He could not have believed that there were no untrue statements or material omissions in the prospectus. Russo has no due diligence defenses. Vitolo and Pugliese were the founders of the business who stuck with it to the end. Despite their titles of president and vice-president, respectively, their field of responsibility in the administration of BarChris's (D) affairs during the period in question seems to have been less all-embracing than Russo's. Vitolo and Pugliese are each men of limited education, however the liability of a director who signs a registration statement does not depend upon whether or not he read it or understood it. In any case, Vitolo and Pugliese were not as naive as they claim to be. They were members of BarChris's (D) executive committee, and attended meetings in which BarChris's (D) affairs were discussed at length. They must have known what was going on. Certainly they knew of the inadequacy of cash, as well as the large advances they had made which remained unpaid. All in all, the position of Vitolo and Pugliese is not significantly different, for present purposes, from Russo's. They could not have believed that the registration statement was wholly true and that no material facts had been omitted. And in any case, there is nothing to show that they made any investigation of anything which they may not have known about or understood. They have not proved their due diligence defenses. Kircher was treasurer of BarChris and its chief financial officer. He is a certified public accountant and an intelligent man. He was thoroughly familiar with BarChris's (D) financial affairs. He knew the terms of BarChris's (D agreements with Talcott. He worked on the preparation of the registration statement. He read the prospectus and understood it. Knowing the facts, he did not have a reasonable ground to believe it to be true. On the contrary, he must have known that in part it was untrue. Kircher has not proved his due diligence defenses. Auslander was an "outside" director (not an officer of BarChris). In considering Auslander's due diligence defenses, a distinction is to be drawn between the expertised and non-expertised portions of the prospectus. As to the former, Auslander knew that Peat, Marwick had audited the 1960 figures. He believed them to be correct because he had confidence in Peat, Marwick as independent public accountants. He had no reasonable ground to believe otherwise. As to the non-expertised portions, however, Auslander is in a different position. Auslander made no investigation of the accuracy of that portion of the prospectus. Thus, Auslander has not established his due diligence defense with respect to the misstatements and omissions in those portions of the prospectus other than the audited 1960 figures. Grant became a director of BarChris, and his law firm was counsel to BarChris in matters pertaining to the registration of securities. He drafted the registration statement for the debentures. Grant is sued as a director and as a signer of the registration statement. This is not an action against him for malpractice in his capacity as a lawyer. Nevertheless, in considering Grant's due diligence defenses, the unique position which he occupied cannot be disregarded. Grant was entitled to rely on Peat, Marwick for the 1960 figures, as he had no reasonable ground to believe them to be inaccurate. As to the rest of the prospectus, Grant was obliged to make a reasonable investigation. After making all due allowances for the fact that BarChris's (D) officers misled him, there are too many instances in which Grant failed to make an inquiry which he could easily have made which, if pursued, would have put him on his guard. I conclude that Grant has not established his due diligence defenses except as to the audited 1960 figures. The underwriters other than Drexel made no investigation of the accuracy of the prospectus. Drexel did make an investigation with the assistance of Coleman. After Coleman was elected a director, he made no further independent investigation of the accuracy of the prospectus. On the evidence in this case, I find that the underwriters' counsel did not make a reasonable investigation of the truth of those portions of the prospectus which were not made on the authority of Peat, Marwick as an expert. Drexel is bound by their failure. The other underwriters, who did nothing and relied solely on Drexel and on the lawyers, are also bound by it. It follows that although Drexel and the other underwriters believed that those portions of the prospectus were true, they had no reasonable ground for that belief, within the meaning of the statute. Hence, they have not established their due diligence defense, except as to the 1960 audited figures. The same conclusion must apply to Coleman. He made no investigation after he became a director. When it came to verification, he relied upon his counsel to do it for him. Since counsel failed to do it, Coleman is bound by that failure. Consequently, in his case also, he has not established his due diligence defense except as to the audited 1960 figures. The part of the registration statement purporting to be made upon the authority of Peat, Marwick as an expert was, as we have seen, the 1960 figures. But because the statute requires the court to determine Peat, Marwick's belief, and the grounds thereof, "at the time such part of the registration statement became effective," for the purposes of this affirmative defense, the matter must be viewed as of May, 1961, and the question is whether at that time Peat, Marwick, after reasonable investigation, had reasonable ground to believe that the 1960 figures were true and that no material fact had been omitted from the registration statement which should have been included in order to make the 1960 figures not misleading. Most of the work was performed by Berardi, and it is unnecessary to recount everything that Berardi did in the course of the audit. We are concerned only with the evidence relating to what Berardi did or did not do with respect to those items which I have found to have been incorrectly reported in the 1960 figures in the prospectus. Accountants should not be held to a standard higher than that recognized in their profession. I do not do so here. Berardi's review did not come up to that standard. He did not take some of the steps which Peat, Marwick's written program prescribed. He did not spend an adequate amount of time on a task of this magnitude. Generally accepted accounting standards required further investigation under these circumstances. I conclude that Peat. Marwick has not established its due diligence defense. The defendants' motions to dismiss this action, upon which decision was reserved at the trial, are denied. Motions made at various times during the trial to strike certain testimony are also denied, except so far as such motions pertain to evidence relating to the issues still undecided. Pursuant to Rule 52(a), this opinion constitutes the court's findings of fact and conclusions of law with respect to the issues determined herein. So ordered.

Analysis:

There is substantial case law supporting the court's decision in this case that the directors who claimed to know nothing about the prospectus (and even those who did not read it), but who relied on the statements of other company officials, were liable for its untrue statements. Additionally, Section 11 of the Securities Act imposes liability upon a director regardless of his duration at the position. He is presumed to know his responsibility when he becomes a director. He can escape liability only by using that reasonable care to investigate the facts that a prudent man would employ in the management of his own property. It seems logical to conclude that a prudent man would not act in an important matter without any knowledge of the relevant facts, in sole reliance upon representations of persons who are comparative strangers and upon general information that does not purport to cover the particular case. This decision is also in line with the fundamental purpose of Section 11, requiring full and truthful disclosure for the protection of investors.

■ CASE VOCABULARY

AFFIRMATIVE DEFENSE: The defendant's offering of evidence to prove some new fact in order to avoid judgment against him.

CHAPTER XI BANKRUPTCY: A petition to restructure finances so that a debtor can continue to operate while paying his debts.

DEBENTURES: Financial obligations of a corporation bought and sold as investments.

DUE DILIGENCE: One's attention to the matter at hand which is required to prevent liability.

MATERIAL: Important; substantial.